USING TAXES
TO REFORM
HEALTH INSURANCE

USING TAXES TO REFORM HEALTH INSURANCE

Pitfalls and Promises

HENRY J. AARON

LEONARD E. BURMAN

editors

BROOKINGS INSTITUTION PRESS
Washington, D.C.

Library of Congress Cataloging-in-Publication data
Using taxes to reform health insurance : pitfalls and promises / Henry J. Aaron and
Leonard E. Burman, editors.
   p.   cm.
Includes bibliographical references and index.
Summary: "Examines the role that taxes currently play, the likely effects of recently
introduced health savings accounts, the challenges of administering major subsidies for
health insurance through the tax system, and options for using the tax system to expand
health insurance coverage"—Provided by publisher.
ISBN 978-0-8157-0125-5 (pbk. : alk. paper)
1. Insurance, Health—United States. 2. Taxation—United States. I. Aaron, Henry J.
II. Burman, Leonard. III. Urban Institute IV. Brookings Institution.
[DNLM: 1. Insurance, Health—economics—United States. 2. Taxes—economics—
United States. 3. Health Care Reform—economics—United States. W 275 AA1 U933
2008]
HG9383.U85 2008
368.38'200973—dc22   2008038083

9 8 7 6 5 4 3 2 1

The paper used in this publication meets minimum requirements of the
American National Standard for Information Sciences—Permanence of Paper for
Printed Library Materials: ANSI Z39.48-1992.

Typeset in Adobe Garamond

Composition by Peter Lindeman
Arlington, Virginia

Printed by R. R. Donnelley
Harrisonburg, Virginia

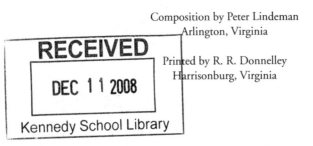

Contents

Acknowledgments

We thank Robert Faherty and the staff of Brookings Institution Press for their efforts in publishing the volume and are grateful to Diane Hammond and Anthony Nathe for expert editing.

Julianna Koch, Renee Hendley, and Kathleen Elliott Yinug attended to the million little and big details that made the conference and book possible.

This project was a collaborative effort with the American Tax Policy Institute, which provided financial support. Additional financial support was provided by the generous contributors to the Tax Policy Center, a joint effort of the Brookings Institution and the Urban Institute. Views expressed here are those of the authors alone.

USING TAXES
TO REFORM
HEALTH INSURANCE

1

Introduction

HENRY J. AARON AND LEONARD E. BURMAN

F ollowing the collapse of President Bill Clinton's health reform proposal in 1994, most elected officials became unwilling to talk about major government action to change private health insurance arrangements. Democrats were shell-shocked by the political fallout from the Clinton debacle, to which some attributed the loss of control of both houses of Congress in 1994. Most Republicans were ideologically unsympathetic to federal tinkering with private health insurance decisions. And so for years both parties shunned the issue. No longer. Health system reform has once again become politically salient, consistently ranking among the top three issues in public opinion polls, along with the Iraq War and the economy.[1] Presidential candidates in both parties have put forward alternative visions of how to reform the delivery of and payment for health care services.

The reasons for renewed interest are straightforward. Health care spending has outpaced income growth for decades and in 2007 absorbed an estimated 16 percent of gross domestic product and approximately 25 percent of total federal outlays. Continuation of this trend would squeeze other government services, force massive tax increases, or balloon the federal debt. Unabated growth of private health care spending would also eventually seriously strain most household budgets. Partly because of rising costs, the number of Americans without health insurance of any kind has grown steadily. By 2006, 46.5 million (or 17.8 percent) of the population under age sixty-five were uninsured. If per capita health care costs keep growing faster than income, as the aging of the population and advances in medical technology make virtually certain, the number of uninsured will also continue to increase. Perhaps most galling, rapidly growing spending has not translated into consistently high quality. In fact, the quality of care even for the well insured is extremely uneven—superb for some but subpar for many.

Although elected officials may have taken a vacation from health system reform, analysts never did. The fledgling subdiscipline of health economics blossomed and matured. Among the shortcomings of the U.S. health payment system, to which these economists point, the current tax treatment is near the top. Under current law, premiums for employer-sponsored insurance (ESI) are excluded from both income and payroll taxes. The self-employed may deduct their premiums from income tax but not payroll taxes. But people who cannot get health insurance at work must pay their premiums out of after-tax income. The ESI exclusion thus favors employer-sponsored health insurance over all other forms of insurance as well as over other types of consumption expenditure.

The value of the ESI exclusion is large. Employers who pay a dollar in employee wages must also pay payroll tax for Social Security and Medicare— 7.65 percent up to the Social Security taxable earnings ceiling, $102,000 in 2008, and 1.45 percent above that amount.[2] The employee must pay the same payroll tax as the employer as well as personal income tax. For a worker subject to the full Social Security and Medicare payroll tax and a 25 percent marginal income tax rate, the combined tax rate is 37.4 percent.[3] That means that added earnings that cost an employer $1 will pay for 62.6 cents worth of goods and services *other than health care* but for $1 of health insurance services. For a family whose insurance costs $10,000 a year, the cost of modest coverage in many communities, the tax subsidy for health insurance relative to other consumption with the same market price is $3,740. The favorable tax treatment is worth less to taxpayers who face lower marginal income or payroll tax rates and more to those who face higher rates.

The exclusion encourages employees to get health insurance at work if they can. And it means that at a given cost many employers can offer workers a more valuable compensation package if it includes health insurance than if it does not. There are exceptions. Some workers place little value on health insurance. And the costs to employers of administering health insurance—particularly those companies with rapid job turnover and that employ few workers—may exceed the value of the tax benefits and any premium discounts the employers might be able to negotiate.

Although employers may write the checks for health coverage, employees ultimately bear the burden in the form of lower wages, at least in theory. The theory is that employers decide how much expense they are willing to incur to hire workers and are largely indifferent to how that cost is divided among cash wages, health insurance, and other fringe benefits. Employers are assumed to be interested in hiring the best workforce that they can at a given cost. If workers want employer-sponsored health insurance because of the discounts available to groups or because of tax advantages, employers will offer it, but they will not increase what they are willing to pay for a given workforce.

Employer sponsorship reduces the cost of health insurance to workers not only because of tax advantages but also because selling costs do not increase proportionately with the size of the group. Thus large employers incur lower average health insurance costs than do small employers. Furthermore, group insurance pools risks by covering the old and the young, the sick and the well, under one plan. That means that people with health problems do not face the very high premiums that they would confront if they had to buy insurance individually. For both reasons, employment is a natural base for insurance coverage.

However, the current system also has serious shortcomings. The tax advantage, for example, is poorly targeted. It is large for high-income filers, who need little help affording health insurance, and small or nonexistent for people with low incomes, for whom health insurance is unaffordable. Companies that employ disproportionate numbers of low-wage workers are therefore less likely to sponsor and pay for health insurance coverage than are companies employing higher-wage workers. The tax advantage for low-income, self-employed workers to buy insurance is similarly small. And the exclusion does not apply to nonworkers, regardless of income.

In addition, the tax advantage is costly. Relative to a system in which the value of employer-sponsored insurance is included in taxable compensation, the exclusion will reduce federal income tax revenues by $169 billion in 2009, more than one-quarter of federal spending on health care services. Other tax advantages accorded health care spending will reduce federal revenues by an additional $12 billion in 2009. There can be little doubt that a targeted system of incentives could promote health insurance coverage better than current tax provisions do.

Furthermore, the tax advantage is unlimited. Health insurance, however costly, is excluded from taxation as long as it is purchased by an employer or by a self-employed worker and as long as it qualifies under the broad definitions set by the Internal Revenue Service.[4] Because of this feature, the tax advantage encourages particularly generous coverage: low or no deductibles, low-cost sharing at the time health care is used, and coverage of services of comparatively low value. This feature weakens the price sensitivity of both health care consumers and health care suppliers and likely results in higher prices and greater use of services than would occur if the tax advantage were limited. In addition, this feature is thought to encourage costly technological changes rather than cost-reducing innovations, thereby fueling the rapid growth of health care spending.

The fact that health insurance is linked to a particular job means that insurance coverage can distort labor market decisions. When, say, a current job provides generous coverage, and the employee or a covered family member has an expensive medical condition, and a prospective job offers inadequate or no health insurance, the employee may be stuck in the job with the better health insurance. A worker who loses a job faces the prospect of also losing tax-free health insurance coverage, which can be especially costly to those with health problems that would make nongroup insurance prohibitively expensive.[5]

Political Initiatives to Fix the Problem

These shortcomings of the current tax treatment of health insurance have generated a range of reform proposals over the past quarter century.

The first plan to receive presidential support was put forward in 1983 during the presidency of Ronald Reagan. That plan would have kept the exclusion but capped it at $175 a month for family coverage and $70 a month for individual coverage. These caps are low by today's standards, but a quarter century ago they exceeded the premiums paid for almost all employees. However, the limit was to be indexed for general inflation, not for the more rapid increase in health care costs, in the correct expectation that the cap would gradually become binding as growth of health insurance spending and insurance premiums outpaced other prices, gradually forcing people to use after-tax, rather than before-tax, dollars to determine whether to buy more or less insurance. In other words, the tax treatment at the margin of income used to pay for health insurance would be the same as that of income used to pay for other consumption. Although congressional hearings were held on this proposal, it drew little support and languished. Had the plan been adopted, it would have ended one flaw of tax exclusion: the fact that it is open ended. But this shift in tax rules would not have dealt with the other problems. Notably, it would have continued to bestow the largest tax incentives on high-income filers and done little to help low- and moderate-income filers, who then as now constitute the bulk of the uninsured.

In 2005 President George W. Bush received recommendations from his Advisory Panel on Federal Tax Reform to renew the call for capping the tax exclusion of employer-financed health insurance. The panel proposed to cap the exclusion of employer-financed premiums at $11,500 a year for family coverage and $5,000 a year for single coverage. In addition, the panel proposed to end the income tax bias (but not the payroll tax bias) that favored group coverage through employers by allowing all filers to deduct from their taxable income the health insurance premiums that they themselves paid. The reason for this new provision was the belief held by some analysts that individuals would do a better job than employers in selecting insurance coverage that satisfied their wants and that insurance companies would offer a variety of plans to compete in this market. Such competition, it was believed, would hold down premiums and, indirectly, the price and use of health care services. Furthermore, the exclusion was to be indexed for general price inflation, not for health care spending. This proposal, like the initiative during the Reagan administration, was controversial—and the Bush administration simply ignored the panel's recommendations.

In 2007 the Bush administration put forward a more imaginative plan. Premiums paid by employers would be imputed to individuals and treated as taxable income for both income and payroll tax purposes. However, taxpayers would be entitled to a deduction—$15,000 for couples filing jointly and $7,500 for individuals—if they were covered by approved health insurance. The deduction would be available whether filers received health insurance as a fringe benefit or bought it themselves, and the deduction would apply to payroll taxes as well as income taxes. Notably, the full deduction would be available even if insurance cost less, a provision that would encourage filers to shop for inexpensive coverage because the tax subsidy would not increase with spending. The objective of this plan was to end the tax bias in favor of employment-based coverage and to remove the incentive for overly generous coverage. Like President Reagan's cap proposal, the new standard deduction would be indexed to general price inflation rather than health inflation, putting downward pressure on health insurance spending over time.

Although the plan embodied a new idea, it suffered a familiar fate: failing to advance to the floor of either house of Congress. Critics assailed the plan because it did little to reverse the skew in favor of high-bracket filers and because it offered little or nothing to filers with too little taxable income computed after personal exemptions and other deductions to take full advantage of the health deduction. In fact, just as under the current system, the largest gains would accrue to those with the highest incomes. In addition, sick or older people faced a serious risk of becoming uninsured if employers dropped coverage because they would confront high premiums in the nongroup market and might be denied coverage altogether. If employers decided to drop coverage because their employees could enjoy the same tax benefits on their own as they derived from coverage through work, the poor health risks might encounter unaffordable premiums when they tried to buy insurance.

Whether and how to modify the tax treatment of health insurance also became a key issue in the 2008 presidential campaign. The Republican nominee, John McCain, proposed to grant tax filers a refundable tax credit of $5,000 for family coverage and $2,500 for single coverage for the purchase of health insurance either at work or in the individual nongroup market. As under the president's proposal, the value of employer-sponsored health insurance would be included in workers' taxable incomes, although it would remain exempt from payroll tax. Unlike the Reagan and Bush plans, which depended on a deduction, Senator McCain's credit proposal would provide equal assistance regardless of income, a significant improvement. As under the president's proposal, some employers would likely stop offering coverage. Others might begin to offer it, as the fringe benefit would be more valuable to lower- and middle-income employees than the current exclusion is. The value of the credit would be indexed to general inflation, which means that it would cover a declining share of health costs over time. Like President Bush, Senator McCain expressed the intent to reform the individual nongroup market to help those with high health costs find affordable insurance, but as of this writing he has not indicated what measures he would support to achieve this objective.

The Democratic candidate, Barack Obama, has called for a system that would provide universal access to health insurance coverage. Income-related subsidies would help people afford health insurance. Insurance, private or public, would be available through a central insurance exchange that would administer subsidies and ensure that no one was denied coverage because of preexisting conditions. Senator Obama would mandate coverage for children but not for adults. Employers above a certain, unspecified size would be subject to a tax if they did not offer coverage. Small employers who offer insurance would quality for subsidies. His campaign literature did not specify the amounts of the subsidies or the penalty tax, nor the precise way in which the mandate for covering children would be enforced.

What Is Viable Policy?

The current tax treatment of health insurance is an accident of history and hard to defend. The practical question is how to change those incentives without jeopardizing coverage for the roughly 177 million Americans who are now covered by employment-based health insurance.

One key to successful health insurance is risk pooling, the combination of people in large groups, so that the potentially ruinous costs from serious illnesses are averaged over healthy and sick people. Roughly two-thirds of the variation in health care spending from year to year is random and unrelated to any identifiable personal characteristics. If the risks associated with such random variations are pooled, where each person pays an equal share of those costs, nearly everyone gains from the reduction in risk. In good years premiums are greater, and in bad years they are less, than the total cost of the health care they use, but these costs are never ruinous. This protection against insupportable financial loss is what insurance is all about. The remaining one-third of the variation in health care use is related to personal characteristics such as age, occupation, and personal medical history. Whether and how predictable risks should be shared is much more complicated and controversial.

Risk pooling can occur by requiring insurers to sell insurance to everyone and to charge everyone in large groups similar premiums. Alternatively, it can be achieved by tax-financed public subsidies that provide assistance to people with varying health insurance risks. In either case, subsidies are necessary to help those with low incomes afford insurance coverage. The current U.S. system encourages pooling at the place of employment for those who work. It pools the elderly and disabled through Medicare and the poor through Medicaid. Maintaining pooling is necessary to prevent very high insurance premiums for some people or the selective denial of access to care.

The current tax exclusion is flawed policy for the reasons already stated: it helps most those who need it least, it is fiscally burdensome, it may contribute to an undesirable increase in health care spending by encouraging some people to buy too much insurance, and it causes job lock. It is a very poor mechanism to help those who are currently uninsured gain coverage.

But simply repealing the current exclusion of employer-financed premiums is not a reasonable option. Many employers would drop coverage. Their workers would have to buy insurance in the nongroup market. Some would face premiums they cannot afford. Others might shortsightedly decide not to buy insurance and find themselves bereft of protection when illness strikes. So the question of what to do about the current tax exclusion has several parts: whether to cap the exclusion or to end it—and what to put in its place.

Capping the exclusion is an unsatisfactory option as it does nothing for low-income families and thus would not directly increase coverage. It would, however, increase revenues, which could be used to subsidize health insurance for those with low incomes. President George W. Bush's 2007 proposal to replace the exclusion with a deduction available to all who are adequately insured contains the kernel of a constructive reform by capping the benefit and delinking the incentive to buy insurance from the place of employment. It would become an attractive option if the deduction were converted to a refundable credit, perhaps related to income, and if it were linked to regulation of the individual health insurance market to ensure that coverage was available to all customers at affordable rates. Analysts debate whether these policies should be supplemented by one or more additional reforms. One reform could be a mandate requiring all people or selected groups to have insurance (to ensure that the healthy do not simply remain uninsured until they think they need coverage). Another could be public coverage of very large outlays (to protect insurance companies from very large losses, the threat of which could encourage them to compete primarily by attracting good risks and repelling bad risks).

History, Analysis, and Solutions

Because tax policy so strongly influences current health insurance arrangements, changes in tax rules are likely to be central to any meaningful health reform. Accordingly, the Urban Institute and the Brookings Institution, with financial support from the American Tax Policy Institute, commissioned the studies that form this volume. These chapters are divided into two sections. The first describes the current system in some detail and indicates why it needs to be reformed. The second part indicates some directions that reform might take.

The Current System and Why It Needs Reform

Robert Helms describes the origins of current tax policy and its influence on health insurance and health care spending. Modern U.S. health insurance originated in the 1930s partly as a response to the personal financial travail and the economic distress of hospitals during the Great Depression. Health insurance spread rapidly during World War II in large measure because wartime wage and price controls banned most increases in wage rates but allowed employers to liberalize fringe benefits such as health insurance. After the war, unions, which covered a much larger proportion of the nation's workforce than they do today, negotiated aggressively and successfully for employer-financed health insurance. Government extended health insurance coverage to the aged, disabled, and poor through Medicare and Medicaid, both enacted in 1965. Nonetheless, the numbers of uninsured began to increase. The rising cost of health care, generated by the proliferation of medical technologies and therapies and by the increase in insurance coverage itself, pushed up total health care spending, which made health insurance unaffordable for a growing number of Americans. Helms emphasizes the cost-increasing incentives of current tax rules and argues that these rules should be modified as part of any comprehensive reform of health insurance arrangements.

Leonard Burman, Bowen Garrett, and Surachai Khitatrakun describe current tax arrangements and the distortions that they generate. Still, they argue, pushing those currently insured through work into the nongroup market could be problematic because the nongroup market for health insurance suffers from a number of shortcomings. The market for health insurance, they argue, will not function adequately without significant government involvement. They provide data on the revenue cost of current health care tax incentives relative to an income tax system in which income devoted to health care was treated the same as income devoted to other (unsubsidized) forms of consumption. They document the regressive character of these incentives measured in absolute terms and in relation to per capita cost of health care spending. They explain some of the problems that afflict the market for health insurance and conclude that the current exclusion of employer-financed health insurance from personal income and payroll taxes is both ill suited to promote insurance coverage and incompatible with a sensible definition of taxable income.

Lisa Clemans-Cope presents information about health savings accounts (HSAs). Up to age sixty-five people may deposit funds in an HSA if they are enrolled in a high-deductible insurance plan. Deposits, investment income, and qualifying withdrawals from an HSA are tax free, making these accounts more tax favored than any other form of saving available to households. Clemans-Cope points out that the combination of HSAs and high-deductible insurance should be particularly attractive to people with low expected health care outlays and comparatively high incomes. Low outlays facilitate the accumulation of large account balances, and high tax rates mean that being shielded from them is particularly valuable. For this reason, she argues, the combination of HSAs and high-deductible insurance may erode the pooling necessary to hold down private group insurance premiums by causing those who expect to spend little on health care to opt out of comprehensive insurance.

Henry Aaron, Patrick Healy, and Surachai Khitatrakun explain that HSAs are best regarded as an incentive for the purchase of high-deductible health insurance and as retirement saving incentives but argue that HSAs are poorly designed for either function. They report the experience of a medium-size company that offered a combination of HSAs and high-deductible insurance, a package that was financially more favorable than other insurance options. Nevertheless, only a minority of eligible employees enrolled. The authors indicate a number of possible reasons for this seemingly irrational decision, suggesting alternative incentives that might be more effective in encouraging the purchase of high-deductible insurance. They note that enrollment in HSAs and high-deductible insurance plans has been rather slow. In addition, HSAs are flawed tax policy, as they provide regressive opportunities to avoid tax, even by those who do no net saving.

Jessica Vistnes, William Jack, and Arik Levinson examine the effects of flexible spending accounts, which permit employees to direct a part of their earnings into a pool that is not subject to income or payroll taxes and from which out-of-pocket health care spending may be paid. These accounts extend the tax advantages of employer-financed premiums to out-of-pocket spending. The only drawback is that unused funds in these accounts are forfeited at year's end. Despite this risk, flexible spending accounts might encourage employees (and their employers acting on their behalf) to select insurance plans that have higher deductibles or larger copayments (fixed charges for health care) and coinsurance (percentage charges for health care) than would otherwise be the case. Data confirm this expectation only in part. Flexible spending accounts seem to boost coinsurance rates slightly, but they are not associated with increases in deductibles or copayments.

Mary Hevener and Charles Kerby, two attorneys who have specialized in the legal and administrative aspects of health plans and compensation tax issues, describe a number of legal and technical problems with the current tax administration. They present a primer on current rules governing flexible spending accounts, group and individual health plans, HSAs, COBRA health benefits (an acronym for the Consolidated Omnibus Budget Reconciliation Act of 1985) for workers who leave employment in which they were insured, and the health coverage tax credit, which is available to some workers judged to have lost employment because of international trade. They recount the IRS's history of administering— or failing to administer—these and other provisions, including notably the requirement that health benefits not discriminate in favor of highly compensated workers. They conclude that if the IRS is given sufficient resources and the public is prepared to accept some amount of administrative failure, the agency could, in principle, manage the various tax-based reforms now under consideration. But they argue that nontax approaches to finance and administer an extension of health insurance coverage might be better.

Directions for Reform

Janet Holtzblatt brings her long experience with the Treasury Department to her consideration of the problems that the Internal Revenue Service will have to solve if it becomes the agency charged with administering laws to reform the financing and delivery of health care insurance. The first problem is how to reach a targeted population with subsidies without very large increases in compliance burdens and administrative costs. The second is how to enforce a mandate and eligibility rules for a subsidy without increasing noncompliance with this provision and with other aspects of the tax system. The third challenge arises from the fact that final income tax returns are not due until well after the end of the year for which they are computed. This delay works acceptably for taxes but would not be tolerable for the enforcement of mandates to carry health insurance or for the delivery of subsidies for health insurance that people must have continuously. She then examines specific plans for using tax policy to reform the tax system from the standpoint of their enforceability.

Jason Furman emphasizes that health system reform should be designed to make at least some progress on each of the three major problems with current health care arrangements: too many people are uninsured, health care is costly but much of it produces negligible benefits, and Medicare and Medicaid threaten to produce insupportable budget deficits. Any proposal that exacerbates any of these problems should be rejected, Furman argues. He especially indicts two proposals: the extension to all health care spending of the current exclusion from income and payroll taxes of health insurance premiums paid by employers; and the extension of deductibility to include all premiums for non-group insurance. Although these proposals would equalize tax treatment of health insurance paid in different ways—a plus in terms of fairness—each moves in the wrong direction with respect to equalizing the taxation of income used for health care versus income used for other purposes, and each would aggravate projected long-term budget deficits. Furman advocates an alternative package of reforms, including income-related, refundable, and advanceable sub-sidies for the purchase of insurance; an individual mandate or automatic enroll-ment; the creation of a new organization, much like one recently created in Massachusetts (the Health Connector), to pool large numbers of people for insurers; and publicly managed reinsurance to guarantee that affordable insur-ance is available to those at high risk while keeping premiums reasonable for those in good health.

Jeffrey Liebman and Richard Zeckhauser apply insights from behavioral eco-nomics, a recently developed field that incorporates findings from social psy-chology and sociology, to modify some of the basic assumptions of traditional economic analysis. People routinely make mistakes in coping with improbable or uncertain events. They tend to overweight current costs and underweight future benefits. They shy away from thinking about bad outcomes. And they are unable to rank in a consistent way objects that embody complex and diverse attributes. They stick with the status quo, even when they would not choose it if they were making the choice anew. Their decisions are heavily influenced by default options, even when the cost of changing them is miniscule. Liebman and Zeckhauser explain why all of these cognitive frailties come into play in making decisions about health insurance and the use of health care services. They argue, for example, that some of these mental traits justify subsidies for health insurance and for insuring inexpensive health care episodes for which people can easily afford to pay without help. The potential importance of these warnings is underscored by recent research that finds that giving care away for free or even paying patients to use the care can reduce the long-run cost of treat-ing some conditions. Examples include screening for blood sugar in diabetics and some drug regimens for chronic illnesses.

The book concludes with comments from Peter Orszag, Congressional Bud-get Office director, on the sources of high per person health care spending in the United States, the means of slowing the growth of this spending, and the rea-sons that such a slowdown need not compromise the quality of health care.

Notes

1. See, for example, the Kaiser Health Tracking Poll, March 2008 (www.kff.org/kaiser-polls/upload/7752.pdf).

2. In addition, employers levy unemployment insurance taxes at rates that vary from state to state. Generally, the cap for such taxes is quite low—under $10,000 in more than half of states—and thus we ignore the effect of such taxes in the rest of the book.

3. The combined tax rate is computed as follows: let s equal the payroll tax rate applied to employers and employees and t equal the marginal income tax rate. The employer's cost of an additional dollar of cash wages is $(1 + s)$, while the employee nets $(1 - s - t)$. The effective tax rate is $1 - [(1 - s - t)/(1 + s)]$, which can be simplified as $(2s + t)/(1 + s)$. For a payroll tax rate of 7.65 percent on both worker and employer and a 25 percent personal income tax rate: $(2*0.0765 + 0.25)/1.0765 = 0.374$.

4. Technically speaking, the exclusion is not unlimited. Although group insurance premiums above $50,000 a year are not excluded from tax, this limit is so high that it has little bearing on the insurance choices under any group plan.

5. The Consolidated Omnibus Budget Reconciliation Act of 1985 allows terminated workers to purchase insurance from their employers for no more than 102 percent of the average premium in the firm. However, this cost, which is not eligible for the tax exclusion, can be a great financial burden for someone who has lost a job. Workers who have had ESI are guaranteed nongroup insurance under the provisions of the Health Insurance Portability and Accountability Act of 1996 (HIPAA), but that insurance is typically much more expensive than insurance that a healthy person could purchase.

2

Tax Policy and the History of the Health Insurance Industry

ROBERT B. HELMS

> Long before the Christian era, it was the custom among the more affluent
> people in [ancient China] to pay the doctor as long as they continued in good
> health. When disability overtook them, the medical man's compensation was
> stopped, and if his ministrations were unavailing in effecting recovery, the
> executioner relieved the doctor of his cares.[1]

For the last six decades, health insurance coverage has been provided primarily through policies offered to workers at their place of employment. In
2006 employer-based insurance covered 161.7 million people, approximately
62.2 percent of the nonelderly population.[2] Individually purchased policies covered an additional 6.8 percent of the nonelderly, while public programs covered
17.5 percent. Approximately 18 percent had no health coverage.[3] By contrast, in
1940 before World War II, only 9 percent (12.3 million) of the population had
any form of coverage for medical expenses.[4] By any definition, the dominance of
employer-based health insurance coverage has strongly influenced the economic
performance of the health care sector, shaping both the demand for and supply
of medical services and products. As a consequence, the role of private health
insurance must be a central part of any serious discussion of health care reform.[5]

This chapter explores the historical development of the private health insurance industry with special emphasis on how tax policy affected the economic
performance of the industry and the health delivery system. While my approach

I would like to thank my research assistant Tal Manor as well as Tom Miller, Ted Frech,
John Sheils, Robert Anderson, and Warren Greenberg for help in tracking down historic references and data. I also thank Len Burman, Henry Aaron, and Alan Viard for helpful comments on an earlier draft. None of these is responsible for any remaining errors nor do they
necessarily agree with my conclusions.

is historical, my main objective is to consider how tax policy might be used to bring about effective and efficient reform. I shall explore the historical development of the health insurance industry, review some of the economic literature explaining this development, and consider the implications of changes in tax policy on the future of the health reform debate.

The Growth of the Health Insurance Industry

Because important changes in national policy and medical technology occurred during World War II, the war is a convenient dividing point for looking at the history of the health insurance industry.[6]

The Prewar Period

Although one can find early examples of accident and marine insurance in ancient China and nineteenth-century America, the modern form of health insurance in the United States dates from the early 1930s.[7] With incomes and employment dropping during the Depression, hospitals were faced with reduced revenue and empty beds. To maintain revenue, several local hospitals began to develop what became known as hospital service plans. These plans entailed the collection of small payments from employees of large firms and school districts in exchange for which contributors were promised hospital care when needed. Twenty-six such plans were in operation by 1933.[8] The growth of these plans prompted the American Hospital Association (AHA) to establish a commission to set standards and approve the plans. Several criteria for approval—for example, the plans had to be nonprofit and provide coverage for all physicians and hospitals in an area—reduced competition among hospitals.[9] The AHA and the hospitals also promoted state laws authorizing these plans to operate as nonprofits, to be tax-exempt, and to be free of much of the state insurance regulation including state premium taxes.[10] The AHA commission adopted the name Blue Cross in 1946.

The early development of health insurance for physician services also started in the 1930s but followed a path somewhat different from that of hospital insurance. Most physicians, represented by the American Medical Association (AMA), strongly opposed any form of health insurance, which they saw as a threat to their income. They developed their own version of prepaid plans for physician services to forestall what they saw as a threat from the growth of hospital insurance and because of the continuing advocacy by some to expand Social Security to provide compulsory health insurance.[11] The AMA also lobbied for legislation in the states that would enable the establishment of prepaid plans but insisted that these plans provide indemnity coverage, which paid physicians a fixed amount for each condition or kind of service. Indemnity coverage allowed the physician to "balance bill" the patient and preserved the physician's ability to charge different prices to different patients.[12] The AMA plans adopted the name Blue Shield in 1946.[13]

Commercial health insurance followed a somewhat different path. As late as the 1920s, hospitals were viewed as dangerous places where people went to die. These perceptions began to change in the 1930s with improvements in hospital management, higher professional standards for physicians, and the development of sulfa drugs to help control infections. Commercial companies that sold other forms of insurance and had previously regarded health insurance as a high-risk venture began to notice the growing success of the Blue Cross and Blue Shield plans. They began in the late 1930s to experiment with their own commercial products.[14] Policy changes and medical advances during the war combined to accelerate the growth of commercial health insurance in the postwar period.

Two Events during World War II

Alexander Fleming first published his discovery of penicillin in 1929, but it was not until 1940 that Howard Florey and Ernst Chain developed a method to manufacture it in a useful form. This advance led to highly successful clinical trials in 1940 and 1941, the provision of penicillin to soldiers during the war, and large-scale production in 1946. This development as well as the development of even more effective antibiotics, such as prontosil in 1939, streptomycin in 1944, chloromycetin in 1947, and terramycin in 1950, allowed for a major improvement in the control of infections and made it possible to greatly expand the use of surgery.[15]

Life expectancy in sixteen developed countries increased from thirty-nine years in 1940 to sixty years by 1970.[16] According to Victor Fuchs and Samuel Preston, "about two-thirds of the increase was attributable to better health technology and similar structural changes and only one-third to a rise in per capita income."[17] These advances and others in medical education and technology helped persuade people that medical care might be worth paying for (see table 2-1). In other words, medical advances beginning in World War II helped increase the demand for medical care and in turn health insurance as a means of paying for medical care.

Another major development during World War II was a somewhat unintended change in tax policy. To prepare to fight a war in Europe and the Pacific, Congress established the War Production Board to coordinate the production of war-related materials. In a massive exercise in government management and control, the agency forbade the production of "nonessential" consumer goods and directed materials and labor to the production of planes, ships, weapons,

Table 2-1. *Major Advances in Medicine*

1928	Alexander Fleming discovers penicillin.
1932	Gerhard Domagk discovers the first sulfa drug, Printosil.
1937	Max Theiler develops vaccine for yellow fever; Daniel Bovet develops first antihistamine.
1940	Howard Florey and Ernst Chain develop penicillin as an antibiotic.
1940–41	Successful clinical trials for penicillin are conducted.
1943	Selman Waksman discovers the antibiotic streptomycin.
1946	First randomized clinical trials of streptomycin for the treatment of tuberculosis are started; large scale production of penicillin begins.
1950	Terramycin is developed.
1952	Open-heart surgery begins with implantation of artificial heart valves.
1954	First successful kidney transplant is conducted; plastic contact lenses are produced.
1957	Albert Sabin develops a live polio vaccine; Clarence Lillehei devises first compact heart pacemaker.
1963	Measles vaccine is licensed for general use in the United States.
1967	Christiaan Barnard performs human heart transplant; Rene Favaloro develops coronary bypass operation.

Source: Susan B. Carter and others, *Historical Statistics of the United States, Millennial Edition*, vol. 2 (Cambridge University Press, 2006), pp. 500–01, table Bd-A; Melissa A. Thomasson, "From Sickness to Health: The Twentieth-Century Development of U.S. Health Insurance," *Explorations in Economic History* 39, no. 3 (2002): 233–53, pp. 236–37.

and other war materials. In the economic sphere, two other agencies sought to control wartime inflation. The Office of Price Administration instituted a system of rationing and price controls. The National War Labor Board instituted wage controls and an elaborate procedure to ensure wartime production by avoiding labor disputes. With a large increase in farm and industrial production and the recruitment of soldiers, the board had its hands full trying to control wages during a period of large labor shortages. The immediate goal of these agencies was to limit wage increases to 15 percent of wages in January 1941.[18] Most unions pledged not to strike. Nonetheless, the effort to keep war production going forced the board into a massive bureaucratic battle to establish rules about almost every aspect of employment, including wage rates, raises, inflation adjustments, overtime pay, vacation pay, and promotions.[19]

One of the issues the board had to deal with was the growing use by employers, who were forbidden to raise wages, of fringe benefits, such as pensions and health insurance, to attract labor. Faced with an almost impossible enforcement task, the board seems to have taken the easy way out by adopting IRS rules that treated fringe benefits differently from cash wages. The board ruled that the pension and health insurance benefits were not subject to wage controls, a pol-

Table 2-2. *Ratio of Health Insurance Premiums to Disposable Personal Income*

Year	Total Premiums[a] (billions of dollars)	Disposable Personal Income (billions of dollars)	Ratio
1940	0.3	75.7	0.40
1945	0.7	150.2	0.47
1950	1.9	206.9	0.92
1955	4.3	275.3	1.56
1960	7.5	350.0	2.14
1961	8.3	364.4	2.28
1962	9.2	385.3	2.39
1963	10	404.6	2.47
1964	11.1	438.1	2.53
1965	12.1	473.2	2.56
1966	12.7	511.9	2.48
1967	13.5	546.5	2.47
1968	15	591.0	2.54
1969	17.3	634.2	2.73
1970	20	687.8	2.91

Source: Health Insurance Institute, *Source Book of Health Insurance Data, 1971–1972* (New York, 1972).

a. Total premiums include insurance company premiums as well as Blue Cross and Blue Shield and other hospital-medical plans.

icy that reinforced the IRS rule that such benefits were not to be treated as taxable income.[20] As one member of the board explained, "The problem though was that we had to keep down inflation. So we agreed to allow increases in various benefits that we felt would not be inflationary—vacations, insurance, and so on."[21] There is no indication that the board debated this policy or anticipated its future consequences. Inattention to distant effects is unsurprising because health insurance was not widespread, it cost only 0.4 percent of disposable income in 1940, and it increased only to 0.47 percent by 1945 (table 2-2).[22]

The policies established by the National War Labor Board for the enforcement of wage controls mimicked IRS rules regarding the taxation of income.[23] In the early war years, the IRS did not consider employer-provided fringe benefits such as pensions, health insurance, and life insurance to be included in taxable income. Similarly, the board also did not consider fringe benefits paid by the employer as a way to control wartime wages, but added the provision that nonwage benefits should be reasonable. They defined *reasonable* as not greater than 5 percent of annual income.[24] Because fringe benefits cost little in these early years of health insurance, the National War Labor Board had few difficul-

Table 2-3. *Population and Economic Growth in the Postwar Period, 1945–75*

Variable	1945	1975	Change (percent)
Population[a] (in millions)	140	216	+ 54.3
Women in the workplace[a] (in millions)	16.7[b]	37.1	+ 122.3
Per capita disposable income[c]	5,285	8,944	+ 69.2

Sources: population—Susan B. Carter and others, *Historical Statistics of the United States, Millennial Edition*, vol. 1 (Cambridge University Press, 2006), table Aa6-8; women—Census Bureau, *Statistical Abstract of the United States, 1968*: table 310, *1977*: table 627; income—*Statistical Abstract of the United States, 1990*: table 695.

a. In millions.

b. In 1947.

c. In constant 1982 dollars.

ties enforcing this standard. A limit on the tax treatment of employer-provided *life* insurance, added to the tax code in 1964, is still in place.[25] The provision of employer-provided health insurance is still open-ended. After several changes in IRS policy regarding the taxation of fringe benefits following the war, Congress clarified the policy in 1954 by passing legislation to exclude the cost of employer-provided benefits from taxable income. The IRS issued new implementing regulations soon after.[26]

The Postwar Period, 1946–75

In retrospect it is easy to see that many of the social and economic upheavals during the war had large effects on the nation following the war. The nation's efforts to fight a global war had expanded industrial capacity. It led to a large increase in the participation of women in the labor force, encouraged large numbers of workers to move from the agricultural Midwest and South to industrial areas, accelerated the introduction of new technologies into the production process, and led to the baby boom. Large increases in employment, income, and economic growth ensued during the three decades following the war (see table 2-3). A growing fraction of workers were employed by large companies in the industrial and services sectors. Demand for health insurance increased because of rising incomes and a growing appreciation for the value of medical care.[27] People with higher incomes to protect were willing to pay for medical care that they expected would allow them to live longer and more productive lives.

Meanwhile, improvements in data collection and analysis allowed insurance companies to evaluate the relative risk and set prices for potential health insurance buyers. Improvements in administrative procedures and record keeping allowed them to expand insurance coverage to larger markets. In addition, sev-

Figure 2-1. *Percentage of Population with Hospital and Surgical Coverage, 1940–75*[a]

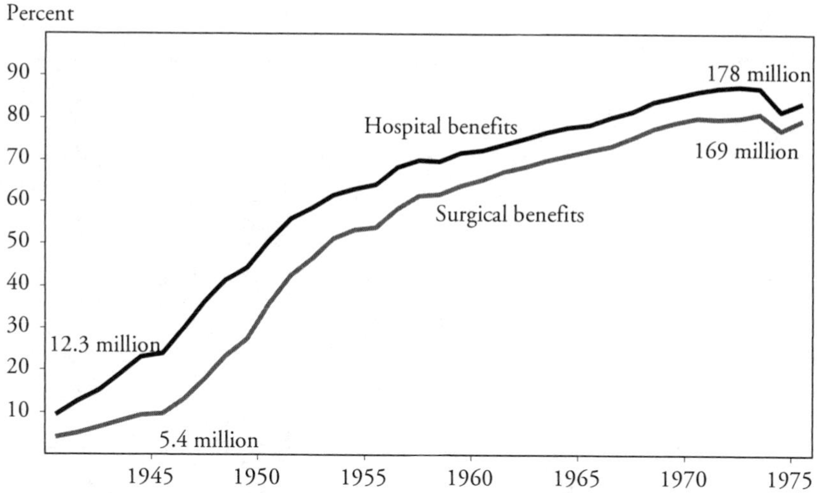

Percent

Source: Susan B. Carter and others, *Historical Statistics of the United States, Millennial Edition*, vol. 2 (Cambridge University Press, 2006), table Bd294-305.

a. This series is based on household interviews and is not the same source as the series in figure 2-2.

eral factors lowered the cost of selling to employer groups relative to selling to individuals. Employees were younger and healthier than nonworking adults, and it cost less to sell and administer insurance through employers or unions than to sell to individuals. Most companies other than those with few workers could avoid adverse selection since employees usually choose where to work for reasons other than to get health insurance. Figure 2-1 illustrates the rapid growth in hospital and surgical insurance coverage in the postwar period. The total number of people covered for hospital care, the earlier and most prominent form of insurance, increased from 12.3 million in 1940 to 178 million in 1975. However, as illustrated in figure 2-2, coverage of people in employer groups expanded relative to coverage of people who bought individual, nongroup policies.[28] The replacement of individual insurance by group insurance was unique to health insurance and did not occur in other lines of insurance such as fire, casualty, and automobile insurance, all of which were also expanding in the postwar period.

No history of health insurance would be complete without some mention of the role of unions. Although the labor movement has a long history of interest in health and safety issues and legislation, its ability to include health insurance benefits was enhanced by a series of policy decisions made by the National War

Figure 2-2. *Private Hospital Insurance Coverage, 1940–75*

Millions

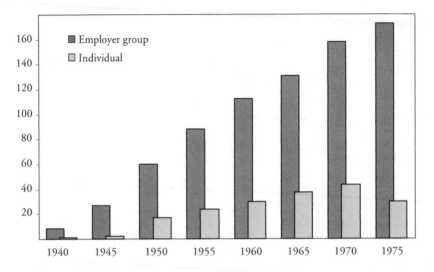

Source: Susan B. Carter and others, *Historical Statistics of the United States, Millennial Edition,* vol. 2 (Cambridge University Press, 2006), table Bd294-305. "Employer group" is the total of persons covered by Blue Cross/Blue Shield plus insurance company group policies. This series is based on health insurance industry data (from the Health Insurance Institute), so it may contain more duplication of coverage than the series used in figure 2-1.

Labor Board (1945), the National Labor Relations Board (1949), and the Supreme Court (1949).[29] These rulings enabled unions to bargain for health benefits as part of wage negotiations under collective bargaining arrangements. The number of workers covered by health insurance negotiated by unions increased from 600,000 in 1946 to 12 million workers and 17 million dependents by 1954, approximately one-quarter of health insurance enrollees in the United States.[30] That unions increased the number of workers covered and the extent of benefits does not refute the importance of tax policy in the development of health insurance.[31]

Health Insurance in the Last Three Decades

Since the mid-1970s, the expansion of public programs accounts for most of the growth of health insurance.[32] Medicare and Medicaid, passed in 1965 as extensions of the Social Security Act, covered three large populations that private health insurance had not reached in large numbers—the aged, the disabled, and the poor.[33] Both programs adopted the fee-for-service payment method used by

Figure 2-3. *Private Group Health Benefits as a Share of Total Compensation, 1960–2006*

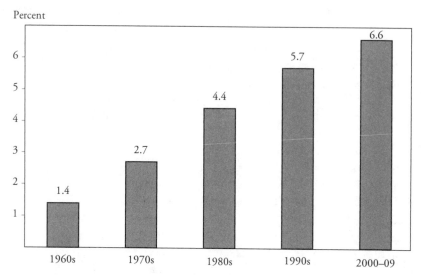

Source: Paul Jacobs, "Wages and Benefits: A Long-Term View," Snapshots: Health Care Costs (Menlo Park, Calif.: Kaiser Family Foundation, February 2008).

the Blues and by most private insurance companies. These payment policies were advantageous to providers in large measure because they perpetuated the weak incentives of consumers and providers to consider the cost of medical care. The result was the continued rapid growth of U.S. health care spending and the onrushing challenges to public and private budgets.

The federal government responded to cost increases by gradually applying administrative cost controls to hospitals and physicians that serve Medicare patients. State Medicaid programs reduced reimbursement rates, restricted benefits and eligibility, and tried, sometimes by quite dubious means, to shift costs to the federal government.[34] These policies had the unintended effect of perpetuating the fee-for-service system of payments and putting more pressure on private insurance plans to control their own costs.

Meanwhile, employer-based health insurance coverage continued to spread, in absolute terms and relative to individual insurance. The costs of these benefits increased faster than cash wages or other fringe benefits. Over the course of nearly five decades from 1960 through 2006 "employer payments for health benefits have increased as a share of total compensation in every decade, reaching 7.2 percent of compensation in 2006."[35] Figure 2-3 shows the average annual shares of private group insurance (benefits as a share of total compensation) over five decades.

Several major changes affecting private health insurance during this period are directly related to tax policy. The first was the spread of self-insurance prompted by federal legislation and court decisions.[36] The Blues lobbied for and obtained exemptions from state premium taxes that were not extended to commercial insurance. Under federal law, companies that self-insured were not subject to state regulation, which meant that self-insuring companies could avoid state premium taxes as well as many other provisions of state regulation. Such exemptions were especially appealing to firms operating in multiple states. Some large firms could take over the entire operation of providing health insurance. Others contracted with an insurance company to administer the health insurance plan while the firms retained the risk of paying the promised benefits. The many variations on this arrangement all fell under the IRS provisions that exclude the employer's cost from the income of the employee.

The second major development was the gradual growth and then apparent decline of managed care. This movement was the result of federal legislation and employers' efforts to control the ever-increasing cost of health insurance.[37] These changes were important because they forced the Blues and the commercial insurance companies to change the way they paid hospitals, physicians, and suppliers of medical products. Insurers and employers were learning that they could not afford to continue paying providers on the basis of costs and charges, an inherently inflationary method of payment. The managed care movement, which peaked in the mid-1990s, allowed health care plans to selectively contract with providers for the provision of care. Instead of paying on the basis of costs or charges, the plans could offer selected hospitals or groups of physicians exclusive access to their insured populations in exchange for discounted rates for medical services. Again, there were many variations in these arrangements, but they helped cut the growth in medical costs from 1988 to 1996.[38] In fact, their very success may have contributed to their decline, commonly called "the managed care backlash," the movement away from the use of selective contracting and other unpopular cost-saving practices adopted by employers. Despite the apparent decline of managed care, managed care and the market competition it promotes continue to influence market performance.[39]

A third major development was the emergence of a new form of health insurance that combined the features of catastrophic coverage and high deductibles with tax-favored savings accounts that could be used to help pay the high deductibles.[40] This new movement resulted from two pieces of legislation that established Medical Savings Accounts (MSAs) in 1996 and Health Savings

Figure 2-4. *Marginal Tax Rates for the Highest Income Tax Bracket, 1940–2002, and for Medium-Income Families, 1955–2002*[a]

Marginal tax rates

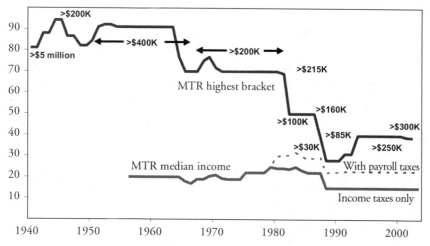

Sources: Internal Revenue Service, "Data Release: Personal Exemptions and Individual Income Tax Rates, 1913–2002" (www.irs.gov/pub/irs-soi/02inpetr.pdf); Elaine M. Maag, "Marginal Tax Rates, 1955–2005," *Tax Notes* (February 13, 2006): 777. The data are available from the Tax Policy Center at "Historical Federal Income Tax Rates for Family of Four" (www.taxpolicycenter.org/ taxfacts/displayafact.cfm?Docid=226) and "Average and Marginal Combined Federal Income and Employee Social Security and Medicare (FICA) Tax Rates" (www.taxpolicycenter.org/taxfacts/Content/PDF/family_inc_hist.pdf).

MTR = marginal tax rate.

a. The highest bracket includes taxable income more than (approximately) indicated amounts.

Accounts (HSAs) in 2003.[41] (See chapters 4 and 5 for more on these new forms of health insurance.)

An additional influence may have worked to decrease the demand for health insurance beginning in the 1980s.[42] As shown in figure 2-4, Congress reduced maximum marginal tax rates from a high of 91 percent in 1963 to approximately 39 percent in 2008.[43] The reduction in marginal tax rates reduced the tax advantage for some employees of employer-financed health insurance. Moreover, employer-financed health insurance is also excluded from payroll taxes, the rates of which were increasing during this period. Figure 2-4 shows that marginal tax rates for families with median income may have increased slightly from the early 1960s until now.[44] In addition, higher-income workers are more likely to have employer-provided private coverage and receive the greatest advantage from the tax exclusion.[45] Any future increase in marginal tax rates would again lower the net price of employer-financed health insurance.

Economic Studies of the Effects of Tax Policy on Health Insurance

Analysts disagree sharply on the role of tax policy in shaping private health insurance.[46] According to one noneconomist: "The tax preference didn't spawn the group health insurance market any more than federal highway construction gave birth to the automobile."[47] This argument rests on the observation that health insurance expanded when employers were not contributing much to the cost of the premiums.[48] Another line of argument rests on the observation that since consumers have responded weakly to tax incentives for saving there is no reason to think that they responded strongly to tax incentives favoring employer-financed health insurance. The counterargument, mostly from economists, denies that the analogy holds. As David Cutler has said, "Changes (in the taxation of fringe benefits) may be among the most important effects of tax reform. For every study showing that saving is unresponsive to taxation, another study shows that the demand for fringe benefits is responsive to taxation."[49]

In contrast, the leading textbooks in health economics, as illustrated in the quotes below, list the exclusion of employer-based health insurance from taxable income as a major cause of the absolute growth in coverage and the diversion of that coverage to group policies offered by employers (see box 2-1).

The channels through which tax policy increases the demand for group health insurance are straightforward.[50] Tax policy subsidizes the purchase of health insurance in two ways. First, a deduction is allowed for medical expenses in excess of 7.5 percent of adjusted gross income. This deduction reduced taxes by an estimated $4.5 billion in 2007. Second, the exclusion of the value of employer-provided insurance from the employee's taxable personal income and from payroll taxes reduced revenues by $133.8 billion in 2007 (see figure 2-5).[51] Because employer-financed health insurance premiums are deductible by employers as a business expense, this form of compensation is not taxed at all.

Tax policy increases the demand for health insurance by providing a government-funded discount for health expenditures and employer-provided health insurance. The higher the filer's marginal tax rate (MTR), the greater is the discount. Because the tax subsidy lowers the net cost of a given level of health insurance, employees typically gain if their employers buy insurance rather than if the employees buy such coverage themselves. The size of the gain has varied over time. In 1969 the effective MTR ranged from 13 percent for incomes under $1,000 to 36 percent for incomes of more than $25,000.[52] The average discount was 15 percent. By 1981 the average discount had risen to 24 percent.[53] A more recent study from 1985 through 1995 finds an average MTR of 35.6 percent.[54] Martin Feldstein and Elisabeth Allison concluded that the subsidy "causes a substantial revenue loss, distributes these tax reductions very

---

Box 2-1. *Tax Incentives and Employment-Based Health Insurance*

Leading texts on health economics all argue for the importance of tax incentives in the spread of employment-based health insurance.

—Phelps: The cumulative effects of the federal income tax subsidy of health insurance could be very large indeed. . . . In the aggregate, it seems possible that the health sector would be at least 10 to 20 percent smaller without the tax subsidy for health insurance. Lest this seem "small," we can translate that difference into something that represents 1.5 to 3.0 percent of the gross national product.[1]

—Morrisey: The tax treatment of employer-sponsored health insurance is a key factor in the structure of U.S. health insurance markets.[2]

—Feldstein: The favorable tax treatment of employer-paid health insurance lowers the price of insurance and leads to a much greater demand for insurance than would have otherwise occurred. . . . Government tax policy has stimulated the demand for health insurance and has increased its comprehensiveness.[3]

—Folland, Goodman, and Stano: One of the most important factors in the increased demand for health insurance in the post–World War II era has been the tax treatment of health insurance.[4]

1. Charles E. Phelps, *Health Economics* (Reading, Mass.: Addison-Wesley, 1997), pp. 356–57.
2. Michael A. Morrisey, *Health Insurance* (Washington: Health Administration Press, 2008), p. 203; see also his chapter summary, p. 214.
3. Paul J. Feldstein, *Health Care Economics*, 6th ed. (Clifton Park, N.Y.: Delmar Learning, 2005), pp. 121, 122.
4. Sherman Folland, Allen Goodman, Miron Stano, *The Economics of Health and Health Care*, 5th ed. (Upper Saddle River, N.J.: Pearson Education, 2007), p. 221.

---

regressively, encourages an excessive purchase of insurance, distorts the demand for health services, and thus inflates the prices of these services."[55]

Melissa Thomasson conducted an empirical study that examined the effects of tax policy on health insurance following a change in IRS rules in 1954 regarding what could be excluded from employee income.[56] Using two household surveys by the National Opinion Research Center, one conducted before the change (1953) and another four years after the change (1958), combined with premium information from a large health insurance company and esti-

Figure 2-5. *Health-Related Tax Expenditures, 1968–2009*

Billions of dollars

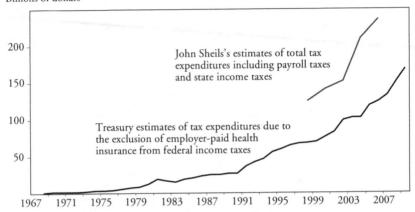

Sources: Data displayed are from several sources. The estimates of tax expenditures due to the exclusion of employer-based health insurance from federal income taxes are from the period 1968–79 from Eugene Steuerle and Ronald Hoffman, "Tax Expenditures for Health Care," *National Tax Journal* 32, no. 2 (June 1979), p. 101; for 1980–88 from Special Analyses G of the federal budgets; for 1989–94 from Robert Anderson, Office of Management and Budget (OMB); for 1995–2009, see OMB, *Analytical Perspectives Budget of the United States Government, Fiscal Year 1997* (www.gpoaccess.gov/usbudget/fy97/pdf/spec.pdf) through *Analytical Perspectives Budget of the United States Government, Fiscal Year 2009*. The Lewin Group estimates are as follows: 1998 is from John Sheils and Paul Hogan, "Cost of Tax-Exempt Health Benefits in 1998," *Health Affairs* 18, no. 2 (March–April 1999), pp. 176–81; 2000 and 2006 estimates are from personal communications from John Sheils. Data for 2004 are from John Sheils and Randy Haught, "The Cost of Tax-Exempt Health Benefits in 2004," *Health Affairs*, web exclusive, W4-109.

mates of each household's marginal tax rate, Thomasson measured the effect of the tax change on the probability that each household would have health insurance.[57] On the basis of her analysis, she concluded that the tax treatment of health insurance had major effects on the demand for health insurance and the growth of employer-based coverage:

—The demand for group health insurance increased;

—The tax subsidy increased the amount of coverage purchased by 9.5 percent;

—There was a shift from individual insurance to group insurance;

—Households with group policies bought larger amounts of coverage after the tax subsidy was enacted in 1954;

—Households with higher marginal tax rates were more likely to have group coverage and to have purchased larger amounts of coverage than they did before 1954.[58]

It is also worth noting that Thomasson did another empirical study of the increased demand for and growth of health insurance using state data from

1931 to 1955. This study led her to conclude that the growth of the health insurance market between 1930 and 1950 was due to a variety of forces: improvements in medical technology stimulated the demand for health insurance; insurance companies began offering insurance to employee groups; and government policy in the 1940s and 1950s reinforced this trend and cemented today's employer-based system of private health insurance.[59]

Figure 2-5 combines data from several sources to show total tax expenditures for health insurance from 1968 through 2009.[60] These measures are controversial and do not measure the welfare loss from excess insurance. I include them here because they are the only available historical series indicating the size and rate of growth of the tax subsidy to employer-based health insurance coverage. Figure 2-6 shows that tax expenditures have increased over the long term relative to gross domestic product, current mandatory expenditures by the federal government, and national health expenditures.[61]

There are two important points to notice about tax expenditures. First, the largest and most rapidly growing component is the exclusion from federal income taxes of employer-paid premiums and payroll taxes. In nominal dollars, tax expenditures from federal income and payroll taxes grew from $1.1 billion in 1968 to $133.8 billion in 2007.[62] Second, since 2000, total tax expenditures (including the effect of payroll taxes and state income taxes) have been increasing on average about $16 billion each year compared with average annual increases in Medicare spending of $29.5 billion and in Medicaid of $9.5 billion.[63] If more people continue to move into higher tax brackets there is every reason to believe that the tax advantage for employer-based health insurance will continue to increase in both absolute and relative terms.[64]

The Inefficiency of the Tax Treatment of Health Insurance

Students of health policy have pointed out that the tax treatment of health insurance creates winners and losers. The winners include providers who earn extra income and employees and their dependents who are insured but who otherwise would not be covered.[65] The losers include all consumers who have to buy health insurance and medical care in markets that are less competitive than they would have been without the tax subsidy.[66] This group includes all those with nongroup health insurance, those with no health insurance, and all taxpayers who bear a larger tax burden to pay for the higher costs of public health programs. Taking examples from economists, legal scholars, and physicians, the health policy literature has described this inefficiency in the health sector in at least the following four ways:

Figure 2-6. *Federal Tax Expenditures for Health Insurance as a Percentage of GDP, Federal Mandatory Spending, and National Health Expenditures, 1968–2007*

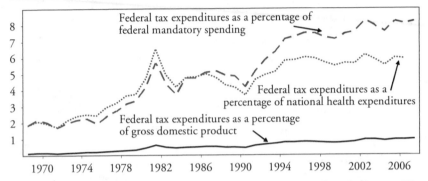

Percent

Sources: For the estimates for tax expenditures, see figure 2-5; GDP is from the Bureau of Economic Analysis, *National Income and Product Accounts* (www.bea.gov/national/nipaweb/Select-Table.asp?Popular=Y); federal mandatory spending is from Congressional Budget Office, *The Budget and Economic Outlook: Fiscal Years 2008 to 2018* (January 2008), table F-5; national health expenditures are from the Centers for Medicaid and Medicare Services (www.cms.hhs.gov/NationalHealthExpendData/02_NationalHealthAccountsHistorical.asp).

—*The deadweight loss from the tax subsidy.* This measure shows the net loss to society from higher prices and increased output induced by the subsidy, 1.5 to 3.0 percent of gross national product according to one estimate.[67]

—*The benefit-cost no-man's-land.* This is the term Clark Havighurst and James Blumstein apply to care that provides positive benefits that are not worth as much as they cost. The term *flat-of-the-curve medicine* has a similar meaning. Havighurst and Blumstein argue that the tax subsidy of employer-based insurance has pushed us into the area of no additional benefits.[68] As Havighurst says, "With unwise, unlimited tax subsidies distorting the design of private health insurance in cost-increasing ways, a great deal of preventable overspending on health care does indeed occur in the United States."[69]

—*Geographical variations in medical spending and outcomes.* John Wennberg and his colleagues at Dartmouth have shown that there is little correlation between medical expenditures and medical outcomes in large and small geographical areas. They have argued that medical practice, dominated by local custom and incentives to overspend, has resulted in enormous waste and inefficiency.[70]

—*Labor market distortions.* The tax treatment of health insurance distorts labor markets in two ways. First, the availability of health insurance on a current job may discourage labor mobility that is otherwise economically optimal. A worker with insurance coverage in one job may be reluctant to become self-employed or take the chance on a period without coverage. Workers covered by plans that use restricted networks of providers may mean that they must change providers if they switch jobs, even if the new plan includes health insurance. Second, because larger firms face lower administrative costs and can spread risk of health expenditures more efficiently than small companies can, the tax subsidy to the purchase of employer-based coverage gives more advantages to larger firms than to smaller firms. This tends to raise wages in larger firms relative to smaller firms, creating an artificial inducement to change employment patterns in ways that may not be based on the relative productivity of labor.[71]

The Case for Tax Reform

My broad conclusion from this summary is that tax policy change is a necessary (but not sufficient) condition to bring about effective reform of our health care system. By effective reform, I do not mean some overly theoretical textbook version of an economic result but a real-world movement toward a system that gives more rewards for medical care that provides more value and improved medical outcomes to consumers. There are lots of good ideas for improving the performance of health markets through such things as the adoption of electronic medical records, more use of comparative effectiveness information, and the design of health plan benefits that promote cost-effective prevention. But first, employees and employers have to have a reason to invest more in these strategies. Trying to reform the behavior of consumers, providers, and employers through regulations, mandates, and controls, while leaving the distorting effects of tax policy in place, will prove to be a long and frustrating exercise. If there is no change in tax policy, an increasing proportion of the relatively wealthy and healthy of the population will have more reason to take advantage of the discount for the purchase of group insurance provided by the tax exclusion. This will perpetuate the inefficient incentives that are behind the continuing increases in medical costs. Legislative language requiring all players in health markets to change their behavior will have little chance of success unless those players have strong incentives to change in the first place.

While tax policy reform may be a necessary condition for efficient reform, I take strong exception to those who say that any change will destroy our employment-based system of health insurance.[72] Our current system is the result of almost a century of gradual developments from forces affecting the demand and supply of medical care and health insurance. Tax policy was not the only force affecting this system, but it exerted a strong influence on the development of labor markets and the health insurance industry. A change in tax policy, especially one that changes the open-ended nature of the tax exclusion, will be required to give everyone a reason to redesign health insurance in a more cost-effective way.[73] A return to the ancient Chinese model of health insurance might work, but it is even less likely that Congress would be able to execute that policy than reform the present tax system.

Notes

1. Edwin J. Faulkner, *Health Insurance* (New York: McGraw-Hill, 1960), pp. 510–11.

2. Paul Fronstin, "Sources of Health Insurance and Characteristics of the Uninsured: Analysis of the March 2007 Current Population Survey," *EBRI Issue Brief* 310 (Employee Benefit Research Institute, October 2007), figure 1.

3. As explained by Fronstin, details may not add to totals because individuals may receive coverage from more than one source.

4. Melissa A. Thomasson, "The Importance of Group Coverage: How Tax Policy Shaped U.S. Health Insurance," *American Economic Review* 93, no. 4 (September 2003): 1373–84, p. 1374. Thomasson's source is the *Source Book of Health Insurance Data* (New York: Health Insurance Institute, 1960).

5. A recent Commonwealth Fund survey found that 86 percent of those polled indicated that a candidate's views on health care reform would be very important or somewhat important in deciding on whom to vote for president in 2008. See Sara A. Collins and Jennifer L. Kriss, "The Public's Views on Health Care Reform in the 2008 Presidential Election," Issue Brief (New York: Commonwealth Fund, January 15, 2008), figure 1.

6. This section relies on an earlier article of mine and several books and articles that explore in more detail the historical development of the industry. See Robert B. Helms, "The Tax Treatment of Health Insurance: Early History and Evidence, 1940-1970," in *Empowering Health Care Consumers through Tax Reform*, edited by Grace-Marie Arnett (University of Michigan Press, 1999), pp. 1–25; Faulkner, *Health Insurance*; Thomasson, "The Importance of Group Coverage"; Thomasson, "From Sickness to Health: The Twentieth-Century Development of U.S. Health Insurance," *Explorations in Economic History* 39, no. 3 (2002): 233–53; Thomasson, "Health Insurance in the United States," EH.NET Encyclopedia, edited by Robert Whaples (April 18, 2003) (http://eh.net/encyclopedia/article/thomasson.insurance. health.us [March 6, 2006]); Rosemary A. Stevens, "Health Reform in 2007: What Can We Learn from History? (www.ehcca.com/presentations/uninscong1/stevens_h1.doc [January 30, 2008]).

7. Rosemary A. Stevens, "Health Reform in 2007," p. 3; Faulkner, *Health Insurance*, pp. 510–40.

8. Michael A. Morrisey, *Health Insurance* (Washington: Health Administration Press, 2008), p. 5.

9. H. E. Frech III, *Competition & Monopoly in Medical Care* (Washington: AEI Press, 1996), pp. 102–30.

10. Thomasson, "Health Insurance in the United States," p. 4.

11. Thomasson, "From Sickness to Health," p. 239.

12. Ibid. Charging different prices based on one's ability to pay goes by several names: *price discrimination, multipart pricing,* and *Ramsey pricing.* The practice can increase the revenue of the seller (physician) as long as reselling can be prevented. Most physician services are not physical products, so they are almost impossible to resell. For an explanation of price discrimination in medicine, see Rubin A. Kessel, "Price Discrimination in Medicine," *Journal of Law and Economics* 1 (1959): 20–53.

13. Blue Cross and Blue Shield operated as separate organizations until their merger into the Blue Cross and Blue Shield Association in 1977. See Morrisey, *Health Insurance,* p. 11.

14. Thomasson, "From Sickness to Health," p. 236.

15. Susan B. Carter and others, eds., *Historical Statistics of the United States, Millennial Edition,* vol. 2 (Cambridge University Press, 2006), pp. 500–01, table Bd-A.

16. Victor R. Fuchs, *The Health Economy* (Harvard University Press, 1986).

17. Ibid., p. 280.

18. Beth Stevens, "Blurring the Boundaries: How the Federal Government Has Influenced Welfare Benefits in the Private Sector," in *The Politics of Social Policy in the United States,* edited by Margaret Weir and others (Princeton University Press, 1988), pp. 132–33.

19. Examples of these rules and proceedings can be found in National War Labor Reports, *Reports and Decisions of the National War Labor Board* (Washington: Bureau of National Affairs, 1943), pp. 4, LXIV.

20. Ibid., Section 1002.8: "To the extent that an insurance and pension benefit inuring to an employee is reasonable in amount, such benefit is not considered as salary as defined in Section 1002.6."

21. E. Robert Livernash, as quoted by Beth Stevens, "Blurring the Boundaries," p. 133.

22. *Source Book of Health Insurance Data, 1971–1972* (New York: Health Insurance Institute).

23. Treasury Department, *Regulations of Commissioner of Internal Revenue—Part 1002—relating to Stabilization of Salaries,* issued December 2, 1942, in National War Labor Reports, *Reports and Decisions of the National War Labor Board,* pp. 4, LXIV–LXIX.

24. In response to a question about premiums paid by the employer for "group life, health, and or accident insurance," the National War Labor Board said, "Under Section 4000.1 . . . of the regulations issued by the Director of Economic Stabilization, such premiums do not constitute wages or salaries if they are deductible under Section 23(a) of the Internal Revenue Code and do not exceed five per cent of the employee's annual salary or wages." See *Interpretative Bulletins of the National War Labor Board,* issued April 5, 1943, General Order 14, Miscellaneous, Question 9, in National War Labor Reports, *Reports and Decisions of the National War Labor Board,* pp. 7, XXI–XXII. See also Paul Starr, *The Social Transformation of American Medicine* (New York: Basic Books, 1982), p. 311.

25. Joseph A. Pechman, "Individual Income Tax Provisions of the Revenue Act of 1964," *Journal of Finance* 2, no. 2 (May 1965): 255.

26. Public Law (P.L.) 83-591, 83 Cong., 2 sess. (August 16, 1954); Internal Revenue Code of 1954, Section 106. For more information on the 1954 tax code, see Selma Mushkin, "The Internal Revenue Code of 1954 and Health Programs," *Public Health Reports* 70, no. 8 (August 1955): 791–800.

27. There was a 31 percent increase in real wages in manufacturing, not including fringe benefits, in the decade after 1945. See Starr, *The Social Transformation of American Medicine,* p. 313. See also this chapter's table 2-2 on the gradual increase in premiums relative to disposable income.

28. Carter and others, *Historical Statistics of the United States, Millennial Edition*, table Bd294-305. Group coverage is the total of Blue Cross/Blue Shield coverage. This series is based on health insurance industry data (Health Insurance Institute), so it may contain more duplication of coverage than the series used in figure 2-1.

29. Concerning the labor movement's interest in health and safety issues, see Herman M. Somers and Anne R. Somers, *Doctors, Patients, and Health Insurance* (Brookings, 1961), pp. 232–46; Morrisey, *Health Insurance*, pp. 3–10; Stevens, "Health Reform in 2007." Regarding the policy decisions that enabled health insurance benefits, see Thomasson, "Health Insurance in the United States," p. 8.

30. Starr, *The Social Transformation of American Medicine*, pp. 312–13.

31. For a historical account placing major emphasis on the role of unions, see Somers and Somers, *Doctors, Patients, and Health Insurance*, p. 237. It is interesting to note that Somers and Somers never mention the possibility that tax policy affected the development of health insurance.

32. For more complete descriptions of this history, see Starr, *The Social Transformation of American Medicine*, especially chapters 3–5; Frech, *Competition & Monopoly in Medical Care*, pp. 102–46; Morrisey, *Health Insurance*, chapters 9–11.

33. Medicare, Title XVIII of the Social Security Act, Health Insurance for the Aged and Disabled, U.S. Code §§1395-1395ccc, subchapter XVIII, chapter 7, Title 42 (www.ssa.gov/OP_Home/ssact/title18/1800.htm).

Medicaid, Title XIX of the Social Security Act, Grants to States for Medical Assistance Programs, U.S. Code §§1396-1396v, subchapter XIX, chapter 7, Title 42 (www.ssa.gov/OP_Home/ssact/title19/1900.htm). For an overview of these programs, see Morrisey, *Health Insurance*, pp. 315–32, 349–65.

34. For a description of Medicaid financing, see Robert B. Helms, "The Medicaid Commission Report: A Dissent," *Health Policy Outlook* no. 2 (Washington: American Enterprise Institute for Public Policy Research, January 11, 2007) (www.aei.org/publication25434).

35. Paul Jacobs, "Wages and Benefits: A Long-Term View," Snapshots: Health Care Costs, (Menlo Park, Calif.: Henry J. Kaiser Family Foundation, February 2008) (www.kff.org/insurance/snapshot/chcm012808oth.cfm).

36. The Employee Retirement Income Security Act of 1974 (ERISA), P.L. 93-406, 88, 93 Cong., 2 sess., U.S. Statutes 829 (September 2, 1974). See also Jon R. Gabel, Gail A. Jensen, and Samantha Hawkins, "Self-Insurance in Times of Growing and Retreating Managed Care," *Health Affairs* 22, no. 2 (March–April 2003): 202–10.

37. HMO Act of 1973, 42 U.S.C. § 300e.

38. Morrisey, *Health Insurance*, p. 158.

39. Ibid., pp. 172–73.

40. Such plans are often called consumer-driven health plans (CDHP).

41. Health Insurance Portability and Accountability Act of 1996, P.L. 104-191, 104 Cong.; Medicare Prescription Drug, Improvement, and Modernization Act of 2003, P.L. 108-173, 108 Cong.

42. Paul J. Feldstein, *Health Care Economics*, 6th ed. (Clifton Park, N.J.: Thomson Delmar Learning, 2005), pp. 122, 480.

43. Marginal tax rates for the highest bracket were 91 percent from 1954 through 1963. They exceeded this amount briefly during WWII (94 percent in 1944 and 1945) and in 1952 and 1953 (92 percent). See Internal Revenue Service, "Data Release: Personal Exemptions and Individual Income Tax Rates, 1913–2002," table 1 (www.irs.gov/pub/irs-soi/

02inpetr.pdf [March 17, 2008]). Because deductions and exemptions are phased out over certain income ranges, effective tax rates may exceed 39 percent. In addition, low-income filers may experience implicit tax rates greater than 39 percent because of reductions in the earned income tax credit.

44. Elaine M. Maag, "Marginal Tax Rates, 1955–2005," *Tax Notes* (February 13, 2006): 777 (www.taxpolicycenter.org/ UploadedPDF/1000875_Tax_Fact_02-13-06.pdf).

45. See chapter 3 of this volume, Leonard Burman, Bowen Garrett, and Surachai Khitatrakum, "The Tax Code, Employer-Sponsored Insurance, and the Distribution of Tax Subsidies."

46. For a more complete discussion of the effects of tax policy on health and labor markets, see Congressional Budget Office, *The Tax Treatment of Employment-Based Health Insurance* (Washington, 1994), pp. 17–32. For a summary of more recent studies, see Morrisey, *Health Insurance*, pp. 209–13.

47. Robert Cunningham, "Joint Custody: Bipartisan Interest Expands Scope of Tax-Credit Proposals," *Health Affairs*, Market Watch: Health Tracking web exclusive (September 18, 2002): W290–W298, p. W297. See also Paul Fronstin, "The Tax Treatment of Health Insurance and Employment-Based Health Benefits," *EBRI Issue Brief* 294 (Employee Benefit Research Institute, June 2006).

48. For a counterargument by a noneconomist, see Beth Stevens, "Blurring the Boundaries," pp. 132–34. See also the direct response to Cunningham, "Joint Custody," by Tom Miller, *Health Affairs*, web exclusive (October 8, 2002).

49. David Cutler, "Comment by David Cutler," in *Economic Effects of Fundamental Tax Reform*, edited by Henry J. Aaron and William G. Gale (Brookings, 1996), p. 162.

50. The following relies heavily on my article "The Tax Treatment of Health Insurance," pp. 9–15.

51. Office of Management and Budget, *Analytical Perspectives Budget of the United States Government, Fiscal Year 2009*, section Federal Receipts and Collections (www.whitehouse.gov/omb/budget/FY2009/apers.html).

52. Martin Feldstein and Elisabeth Allison, "Tax Subsidies of Private Health Insurance," in *Hospital Costs and Health Insurance*, edited by Martin Feldstein (Harvard University Press, 1981), p. 208, table 7.2.

53. Ibid., p. 174.

54. As reported by Morrisey, *Health Insurance*, p. 211.

55. Feldstein and Allison, "Tax Subsidies of Private Health Insurance," p. 216.

56. Thomasson, "The Importance of Group Coverage," p. 1374, referring to P.L. 83-591, 83 Cong. 2 sess. (August 16, 1954); Internal Revenue Code of 1954, Section 106. An earlier working paper version of this study is available through the National Bureau of Economic Research (www.nber.org/papers/w7543).

57. Each survey asked about the family's prior year's experience.

58. Thomasson, "The Importance of Group Coverage," p. 1382.

59. Thomasson, "From Sickness to Health," p. 251.

60. Data displayed in figure 2-5 are from several sources. The estimates of tax expenditures due to the exclusion of employer-based health insurance from federal income taxes are from the period 1968–79 from Eugene Steuerle and Ronald Hoffman, "Tax Expenditures for Health Care," *National Tax Journal* 32, no. 2 (June 1979): 101; for 1980–88 from Special Analyses G of the federal budgets; for 1989–94 from Robert Anderson, Office of Management and Budget; for 1995–2009, see *Analytical Perspectives Budget of the United States Gov-*

ernment, Fiscal Year 1997 (www.gpoaccess.gov/usbudget/fy97/pdf/spec.pdf) through *Analytical Perspectives Budget of the United States Government, Fiscal Year 2009.* The Lewin Group estimates are as follows: 1998 is from John Sheils and Paul Hogan, "Cost of Tax-Exempt Health Benefits in 1998," *Health Affairs* 18, no. 2 (March–April 1999): 176–81; 2000 and 2006 are from personal communications from John Sheils. Data for 2004 are from John Sheils and Randy Haught, "The Cost of Tax-Exempt Health Benefits in 2004," *Health Affairs*, web exclusive, W4-109.

61. Mandatory or direct spending is defined by the Congressional Budget Office as "the budget authority provided by laws other than appropriation acts and the outlays that result from that budget authority." See *The Tax Treatment of Employment-Based Health Insurance*, p. 170. This spending is often referred to as *entitlement spending.*

62. Tax expenditures for out-of-pocket medical expenses and health insurance premiums (not shown) increased from $1.5 billion in 1968 to only $4.8 billion in 2007.

63. The estimate of the increase in average total tax expenditures of about $16 billion per year is from a personal communications from John Sheils. See also the Centers for Medicare and Medicaid Services, "National Health Expenditure Accounts" (Baltimore, Md.) (www.cms.hhs.gov/NationalHealthExpendData/02_NationalHealthAccountsHistorical.asp #TopOfPage).

64. In a separate estimate, Sheils has estimated total tax expenditures to grow to $294 billion by 2009. Personal communication from John Sheils based on estimates contained in John Sheils and Randy Haught, *President Bush's Health Care Tax Deduction Proposal: Coverage, Cost and Distributional Impacts* (Falls Church, Va.: The Lewin Group, January 2007) (www.lewin.com/NR/rdonlyres/B45E2670-8A65-4817-B68B-83B818616DDF/0/Bush HealthCarePlanAnalysisRev.pdf).

65. Some have even credited this tax policy with keeping health insurance predominately in the private sector, a path not followed by most other developed countries. See Starr, *The Social Transformation of American Medicine*, p. 334.

66. "The effect of this artificially expanded use of insurance is an increase in the demand for health care and a resulting rise in its price." See Feldstein and Allison, "Tax Subsidies of Private Health Insurance," p. 215. Feldstein and Allison's statement is in the context of comparing the results of having the tax subsidy relative to what would have happened without the subsidy. Later research has raised questions about researchers' ability to measure price increases in medical markets where there is substantial change in technology. For a discussion of these issues, see Jack E. Triplett, ed., *Measuring the Prices of Medical Treatments* (Brookings, 1999).

67. Charles E. Phelps, *Health Economics* (Reading, Mass.: Addison-Wesley, 1997), p. 357.

68. Clark C. Havighurst, *Health Care Choices* (Washington: AEI Press, 1995), pp. 93–103.

69. Ibid., p. 101.

70. For information on the Dartmouth Atlas Project and their many publications, see their website at www.dartmouthatlas.org.

71. For a more detailed explanation of labor market distortions with number examples, see Congressional Budget Office, *The Tax Treatment of Employment-Based Health Insurance*, pp. 20–23.

72. See, for example, the title to a Tax Analysts (publisher of *Tax Notes*) conference, "Tax-Free Healthcare: Build it Up, or Blow it Up?" in *Tax Notes* 111, no. 11 (June 12, 2006):

1255. My response is Robert B. Helms, "Mission Improbable: No One Is Going to Blow Up Health Insurance," *Tax Notes* 111, no. 11 (June 12, 2006): 1262–264.

73. In previous work using 1994 data, Jonathan Gruber and James Poterba estimated that the use of an upper limit on the tax exclusion (a tax cap), "would achieve two-thirds or more of the reduction in insurance spending that obtains with the elimination of the tax subsidy, but it would have a much smaller effect on the insurance coverage decision." See Jonathan Gruber and James Poterba, "Fundamental Tax Reform and Employer-Provided Health Insurance," in *Economic Effects of Fundamental Tax Reform*, edited by Aaron and Gale, p. 154.

3

The Tax Code, Employer-Sponsored Insurance, and the Distribution of Tax Subsidies

LEONARD E. BURMAN, BOWEN GARRETT,

AND SURACHAI KHITATRAKUN

About 46 million Americans under age sixty-five, including 9 million children, lack health insurance. They receive less preventive care when healthy and poorer care when sick than do the insured. Furthermore, the public ultimately shoulders much of the burden of paying for the medical treatment of the uninsured, either through higher taxes or higher health care costs.

The fact that many people cannot afford or choose not to obtain health insurance is not necessarily a cause for public intervention in the health insurance market. Poor people cannot afford many things. The best solution to the problems of poverty may be measures to increase incomes, not measures to subsidize particular types of spending.

On the other hand, subsidies for health care may be justified on other grounds. Health insurance costs more than it would in a perfect market for several reasons. First, insurance means that patients do not directly bear the full cost of the care they use. As a result, they consume some care that may be of relatively little value. This phenomenon, known as moral hazard, means that insurance is more expensive than it would be if people used only care that is worth its full cost. Second, people who expect to use health care heavily—such as those with chronic conditions and people who plan to have children—are more likely to want insurance (other things held the same) than are people who do not

We are grateful to Henry Aaron, Linda Blumberg, Dan Halperin, and Anup Malani for helpful comments, and to Greg Leiserson and Carol Rosenberg for excellent research assistance. The views expressed are those of the authors and should not be attributed to the Urban Institute, its trustees, or its funders.

expect to use much health care. Since insurers can only imperfectly match premiums to expected use, they have to assume that purchasers have higher costs than average. (This feature of insurance is called adverse selection.) As a result, only those who are sicker than average get a good deal from insurance. Everyone else gets a bad deal, unless they can align themselves with a large group with heterogeneous health status. The existence of free (even if inadequate) emergency health care for those with low incomes deters them from buying health insurance, because free care provides a safety net and because uncompensated care tends to raise the cost of care for those with insurance. Finally, healthy people—especially in the nongroup market—can only imperfectly insure against the costs of developing chronic illnesses, because premiums for nongroup health insurance tend to increase more over time for sick people.

The government does, in fact, intervene heavily in the market for health insurance. Low-income households—and especially low-income children, those deemed medically needy, military families and veterans, and the elderly—benefit from publicly provided insurance. Many other working-age individuals and families receive sizable tax subsidies. Health insurance paid for by employers is a tax-free fringe benefit—exempt from both income and payroll taxes. This subsidy is the single largest government intervention in the health insurance market for workers. In addition, the self-employed can deduct health insurance premiums from their taxable income.

Health insurance tax breaks for workers have worked in one sense: employer-sponsored insurance (ESI) covers more than two-thirds of workers and their families. Encouraging people to get insurance at work reduces the problem of adverse selection. It also offers those who work continuously for companies that sponsor health insurance plans a kind of renewable insurance. However, the subsidy is poorly targeted. The value of the tax exclusion grows with income. It is worth little or nothing to those with low incomes, even though they are the ones most likely to be deterred by cost from getting insurance.

The tax subsidies also exacerbate the moral hazard problem. Generous tax benefits, especially for those with high incomes, encourage people to choose more generous coverage. To address this problem, Congress enacted a provision in 2003 aimed at encouraging employees to purchase high-deductible health insurance, either directly or through their employers. High-deductible health insurance reduces moral hazard by increasing the price of health care at the time of use for expenditures up to the level of the deductible.

In this chapter, we summarize the tax advantages of employer-sponsored health insurance, examine the arguments for government intervention in the health insurance market, and review the arguments for and against providing health insurance through the workplace. We analyze how the tax subsidies for employer-sponsored insurance are distributed and evaluate evidence on how the ESI exclusion affects health insurance coverage.

Tax Subsidies for Employer-Sponsored Health Insurance

Employer contributions to employee health insurance are nontaxable fringe benefits, excluded from total compensation for income or payroll tax purposes. On average, employers pay nearly 82 percent of ESI premium costs for single coverage and 76 percent for family coverage.[1]

Section 125 of the Internal Revenue Code allows employers to set up so-called cafeteria plans for administering certain employee benefits. A cafeteria plan allows employees to choose to receive part of their compensation either in cash or as one or more nontaxable fringe benefits, including health insurance. Flexible spending accounts (FSAs) are similar to cafeteria plans. They allow employees to set aside a portion of annual compensation through regular salary reductions to pay for out-of-pocket expenses for medical and dental services, prescription drugs and eyeglasses, and the employee's share of the cost of employer-sponsored health insurance. FSA balances unspent at the end of the year are forfeited to the employer.[2] Employees pay no income or payroll tax on the medical expenses paid through a cafeteria plan or FSA. As a result, employees with access to a section 125 plan or an FSA may pay for all or most of their medical costs with pretax dollars. Most other consumption must be paid with after-tax dollars. This differential constitutes the tax subsidy to health insurance. Most workers can use pretax dollars to pay for their share of ESI premiums, though small employers offer these plans at lower rates than large employers do.[3]

Employers may purchase insurance for their employees or provide insurance themselves—that is, self-insure. Most self-insured plans are managed by a third-party administrator. Section 105 of the Internal Revenue Code sets out nondiscrimination rules for benefits provided by self-insured plans. These rules aim to prevent highly compensated managers from providing generous tax-free benefits for themselves that are not available to rank-and-file workers.[4] The Employee Retirement Income Security Act of 1974 (ERISA) exempts self-insured plans from state mandates and health insurance premium taxes that apply to third-party insurers.

The Consolidated Omnibus Budget Reconciliation Act of 1985 (COBRA) amended ERISA to require employers with twenty or more employees who provide health insurance (whether self-insured or not) to allow participants and other beneficiaries (that is, family members) to buy continuing coverage for eighteen months after it would otherwise cease for any reason, including termination, death, or divorce. Employers can charge covered employees their premium cost plus 2 percent for continuation of coverage. Workers who become disabled may retain coverage beyond the eighteen-month period by paying a premium up to 150 percent of the employer's average cost.

Other tax provisions that relate to health insurance coverage are summarized in the introductory chapter to this volume. Chapter 4, by Lisa Clemans-Cope, and chapter 5, by Henry Aaron, Parick Healy, and Surachai Khitatrakun, describe health savings accounts.

Government Intervention in Health Insurance Markets

Most markets work well without much government interference. But sometimes the logic of the marketplace breaks down. The market for health care and health insurance fails in many ways, as a result of which an unregulated insurance market would provide insurance inefficiently or fail entirely for millions of Americans, including those who are most vulnerable.

Adverse Selection

The Achilles' heel of the health insurance market is adverse selection. Sellers know how much it will cost to supply most goods. The seller sets a price to cover production cost plus a modest profit. Consumers buy the good if the value to them exceeds the price.

In the case of health insurance, the relationship breaks down. Most people want insurance if they can get it at a reasonable price because insurance protects them from financial risk. But adverse selection causes insurance to be more expensive than it would otherwise be because those who buy insurance tend to be sicker than average, which is reflected in premiums. So insurance, especially in the nongroup market, is often a bad deal for healthy consumers.

Insurers have imperfect information about the health of their customers. Because the purchase of health insurance is voluntary, those who expect to have the highest health care costs are most likely to buy it. An insurer that offered insurance to all comers (something that most states do not require insurers to do) would have to charge premiums that are higher than they would have to be if everyone enrolled, because high-cost users would be most likely to enroll. The high premiums would further dissuade healthy people from buying insurance. As the health status of the pool of covered people eroded, premiums would get higher and higher, making it even less attractive to relatively healthy people. In the extreme, this so-called "death spiral" could cause the insurance market to self-destruct altogether.[5]

The fact that it does not work out this way is because insurers are not passive in this process. They profit most if they can attract a healthier-than-average customer base. Insurers exclude preexisting conditions and use other methods to attract the healthiest individuals.[6] The consequence is that the nongroup health insurance market works best for healthy people. If you are sick and need health insurance and you do not get it at work or through a public program, you will face high and possibly unaffordable premiums or be excluded from coverage altogether.

One might think that buying insurance when healthy and maintaining continuous coverage would guarantee that the insured has access to affordable insurance when ill, but it does not work that way in practice. The problem is the way insurers set premiums in the nongroup market. Those who buy a nongroup policy are included in a pool with other policyholders who purchase the same product at the same time. The original premium is low because underwriting guarantees that the original pool is healthier than average. Future premiums depend on the experience of people in the group. Eventually, some people in the group become ill and the premiums start to rise. Healthy people in the group discover that they can pay a lower premium if they buy into a new, healthier group. (Sometimes their own insurer will offer them a new policy with a lower premium.) As healthy people drop out of the group, premiums start to rise very fast for a person—a diabetic for example—who has no alternative. The consequence is that those who get sick either end up paying very high premiums or find insurance unaffordable and drop coverage altogether.[7]

Evidence shows that Californians who enroll in nongroup health insurance when healthy and who later contract a chronic illness pay significantly higher premiums than do new subscribers who are healthy but less than new enrollees with chronic conditions.[8] Even those who remain healthy pay more than new subscribers, although the additional premium is smaller than it is if they become ill, demonstrating that there is more pooling of risks in the nongroup market than is commonly thought.

Moral Hazard

Insurance gives individuals an incentive to consume health care because they pay only a fraction of the cost. For example, if insurance pays 90 percent of the cost of a drug, for example, an insured person would be willing to try a $100 prescription even if the expected value was only $11. Without insurance, the drug would not be purchased. Insurers try to counteract this tendency by managing care—that is, not covering procedures and therapies of low value—but managed care has met with resistance in many markets.

However, Jeffrey Liebman and Richard Zeckhauser (chapter 10) argue that the way individuals evaluate health risks and make economic decisions creates a counteracting bias, so that without moral hazard people would consume too little care. Thus moral hazard might be a virtue in this market.[9] Further, the lion's share of growth of health expenditures has been attributed to advances in medical technology, not to moral hazard.[10] Efforts to limit moral hazard, then, could do more harm than good if they reduce the incentive for medical innovation.

Free Riders

Because hospitals generally do not turn away very sick people who need care, the incentive to purchase insurance is diminished, especially for people who have little wealth to protect. The incentive to forgo insurance because someone else will pay for it in the case of emergency or serious illness is called the free-rider problem, another classic market failure. As a result of free riders, some of the cost of health insurance goes to provide care for people who do not have their own insurance—that is, people who choose to ride free.[11]

Incomplete Markets

Finally, a necessary condition for economic efficiency is the existence of markets that allow people to insure against future as well as current risks. But as noted, it is virtually impossible in the nongroup market for people to insure fully against future illness. Inability to renew policies on favorable terms may also arise in the group market because the premiums of employer-sponsored plans are underwritten. A large employee group partially solves this problem by continually refreshing the pool with healthy members who participate in the group for reasons largely unrelated to health status. Small employers or large employers in declining industries, however, may be even more vulnerable to poor health outcomes than individuals in the nongroup market.

It is unclear what policy would balance these competing market failures to maximize social welfare. For example, mandating health insurance coverage would eliminate adverse selection (although not the incentive for insurers to try to attract the healthiest people), but without other restrictions, it would maximize moral hazard. There may also be other objectives, such as offsetting income disparities or helping those with poor health status, that further complicate the problem. In this section, we explore how well the current approach of using tax subsidies to promote the purchase of health insurance through employment relationships balances the competing sources of market failure. We also describe the distributional effects of the tax exclusion for ESI.

Advantages and Disadvantages of ESI

The main advantage of subsidizing ESI is that employment may effectively pool health insurance risks because people choose employment for many reasons other than their expected use of health care. Workplace pooling works best for large companies. Small groups experience large year-to-year variation in average health expenditures.[12] This instability creates a substantial risk that small companies will face large year-to-year premium increases.[13]

Pooling through large groups has another advantage: administrative and marketing costs are lower for large than for small groups.[14] Collecting premiums as a part of payroll processing is less expensive than direct billing and may also be an effective way to encourage participation, because individuals like to break up large expenses into small, automatically collected pieces.[15] Also, participation rates are higher if the choice workers face is framed in terms of opting out of, rather than opting into, an insurance plan.[16] Large groups also have bargaining power to lower costs when dealing with insurers and providers. And to the extent that workers can count on long-term employment with an established company, ESI may provide more protection against premium increases than an individual plan might.

But ESI has drawbacks as well. It is an imperfect pooling mechanism. In a small firm, if one person gets sick, average costs can jump. Also, ESI provides limited renewability at best. People can lose their jobs or employers can decide to curtail or drop coverage because of, for example, unacceptably large premium increases. Although no better mechanism for pooling or renewability currently exists in the market for individual insurance plans, such a mechanism might have arisen were it not for the large tax subsidy for ESI. For example, if professional associations, unions, or religious institutions were subsidized, they might also offer group health insurance policies to their members, much as they do with life insurance.[17]

The tax advantages of ESI amplify the advantage of large firms over small ones as payers for health insurance. To see why, imagine a world without a tax exclusion for ESI. Many large companies might still offer health insurance because of their advantages in pooling and administrative costs. Few small firms would. Now introduce a tax exclusion: taxes fall for employees of all companies that offer health insurance but not for employees of companies that do not. Since large firms have reason to offer health insurance even without a subsidy, the subsidy favors large offering firms over small ones that don't offer. With a subsidy for ESI, some small firms respond to pressure from their employees to offer this valuable tax-free fringe benefit, but their compensation costs would increase relative to large firms because, for a given package or benefits, health insurance is more expensive for small firms. The higher benefit costs place smaller firms at a competitive disadvantage in hiring (whether they offer insurance or not). Effectively, the tax exclusion for ESI is a differential labor subsidy; it is most valuable to large companies, which are most likely to sponsor insurance and pay part of the premiums. Thus the tax code distorts allocation of labor in favor of large firms. It thereby reduces production efficiency because it induces some workers who might be more productive at small firms to shift to or remain in large firms.

The subsidy for ESI also creates other inefficiencies. It gives employers an incentive to contract with outside companies that do not offer health insurance appropriate to low-income and younger workers who tend to value insurance less than older and higher-income workers do. It also distorts decisions about work and retirement.[18]

For all its imperfections, however, ESI covered almost 70 percent of American workers in 2006 (table 3-1). Not surprisingly, higher-income workers were much more likely to be covered by ESI than those with lower incomes. About 45 percent of workers with incomes under $20,000 were covered by ESI, compared with 86 percent of workers with incomes over $40,000. Full-time, full-year workers were much more likely to get ESI than part-time or part-year workers. And workers at large firms were much more likely to be covered by ESI than those working for small firms. Nonetheless, more than half of employees at small firms (fewer than twenty-five employees) were covered by their own or their spouse's ESI. More than 30 percent were covered by their own employer (not shown in table).

Beneficiaries of the ESI Tax Exclusion

The subsidy for ESI is worth more to those with high incomes than to those with low incomes for several reasons. First, because the subsidy is provided in the form of an exclusion from income, it is most valuable to those who face high marginal tax rates. Second, those with low incomes are much less likely to be in jobs that offer health insurance than people with higher incomes.[19] Third, those with low incomes who have ESI offers are less likely to participate.[20]

Compensation in the form of health insurance rather than wages typically reduces both income tax and payroll tax liability. For example, people in the 10 percent federal income tax bracket save $100 in income taxes and another $76.50 in Social Security and Medicare payroll taxes for every $1,000 of wages that is converted to employer contributions toward health insurance premiums. Their employers also save payroll taxes on the excluded wages, and the tax savings are likely passed on to workers for reasons presented below. In most states, workers with ESI also pay less state income tax. Thus the combined value of income and payroll tax exclusions can reduce the overall cost of health insurance by 25 percent or more for middle-income families.

Table 3-1. *Primary Source of Health Insurance for Workers Aged 18 to 64, by Demographic Category, 2006*

Workers and demographic characteristics	Workers (millions)	Percent distribution by coverage type				Uninsured
		Private		Public		
		Employer	Individual	Medicaid	Other	
Total number of workers	147.1	69.8	5.7	4.6	1.1	18.8
Age						
18–34	53.7	59.0	6.7	7.0	1.0	26.3
35–54	71.7	75.4	4.7	3.5	0.9	15.5
55–64	21.7	77.6	6.4	2.6	2.3	11.1
Worker's annual income						
Less than $20,000	41.3	45.2	8.1	19.4	1.7	34.6
$20,000–$39,999	46.7	70.5	4.9	3.8	1.1	19.7
$40,000 or more	59.1	86.3	4.6	1.3	0.8	7.0
Family poverty level						
Less than 100 percent	12.8	20.8	9.4	18.5	1.4	49.8
100–199 percent	23.3	41.6	7.0	9.7	1.5	40.2
200–299 percent	24.3	66.2	5.9	3.9	1.5	22.5
300–399 percent	20.5	79.0	5.4	2.1	1.0	12.5
400 percent or more	66.2	87.6	4.5	1.2	0.9	5.8
Work status						
Full-time/full-year	104.0	76.1	4.3	2.8	0.8	16.0
Full-time/part-year	18.6	55.0	6.2	8.7	1.5	28.7
Part-time/full-year	12.9	57.2	11.2	7.4	1.5	22.3
Part-time/part-year	11.6	50.5	10.9	12.0	2.9	23.6
Business size (number of workers)						
Self-employed	13.5	47.9	18.9	4.1	1.5	27.6
Fewer than 25	29.6	51.8	7.8	6.3	1.2	33.0
25–99	17.8	68.3	4.7	4.9	1.1	21.1
100–499	17.3	75.0	3.3	4.4	0.7	16.6
500–999	6.6	79.2	2.7	4.8	0.6	12.7
1,000 or more	41.0	78.1	3.3	4.5	1.0	13.0
Public sector	21.0	86.9	2.5	2.9	1.6	6.2

Source: Kaiser Commission on Medicaid and the Uninsured, *Health Coverage in America: 2006 Data Update*, October 2007 (www.kff.org/uninsured/7451.cfm).

The value of the tax exclusion increases sharply with income because income tax rates rise with income. About 31 percent of households were in the zero income tax bracket in 2007.[21] They did not save any federal income taxes from reducing their taxable wages.[22] Another 45 percent were in the 10 or 15 percent brackets. The income tax exclusion is worth 15 cents on the dollar or less to those households. Fewer than one-quarter of households faced marginal tax rates of 25 percent or higher.

Thus the lowest-income taxpayers receive no direct benefit from the income tax exclusion. Indeed, the exclusion might even harm some very low-income workers by reducing their earned income tax credit, as explained below. Low-income workers do receive a benefit from the exclusion of payroll taxes. The exact amount depends on whether workers or employers ultimately pay the employer's portion of payroll taxes. Most economists believe that workers pay the tax in the form of lower wages. To see why, suppose that an employer is willing to pay $20,000 to a particular worker before considering taxes. If the employer has to pay payroll taxes at a rate of 7.65 percent, the employee now costs more than he or she is worth to the employer. Either the employee will not be hired, or compensation would have to decline to $18,579 or less to make the employee attractive to the employer. (Payroll tax on $18,579 is $1,421, so the total after-tax cost of the employee is $20,000.) Thus, at least in the long run, employees are likely to pay the cost of the employer portion of payroll taxes in the form of lower wages. The exception to this rule would be situations in which compensation is not set freely in a competitive labor market. For example, employers of workers earning the minimum wage cannot lower wages. There may also be an indirect benefit to low-wage workers whose employers offer insurance because high-wage workers value it highly enough that they are willing to implicitly subsidize low-wage workers.

There are several complicating factors. First, the Social Security tax is not a pure tax. More taxes paid translate into future benefits, especially for lower-income workers. One estimate is that the lifetime effective Social Security tax rate (including both payroll taxes and benefits) for employees with low covered earnings was negative in 1990.[23] That is, the present value of Social Security benefits exceeds the value of tax paid for people with very low earnings. If employees understand that their current taxes will produce a valuable future benefit, then it may be inappropriate to treat Social Security payroll contributions as a tax for lower-income people.[24] Thus workers with low lifetime incomes may view the tax savings from health insurance as conveying no benefit at all, since they sacrifice more than a dollar of retirement benefits for every tax dollar saved now. For higher-income workers, however, future benefits are only a fraction of taxes paid on the last dollar of covered earnings. In addition, the

Medicare portion of the payroll tax—1.45 percent of earnings—is a pure tax since benefits are not tied to contributions.

Another complication is that workers with very low incomes may be indirectly hurt by the ESI exclusion because of its interaction with the refundable earned income tax credit. The credit phases in as earnings increase; so a reduction in earnings can actually *increase* taxes (reduce refunds). A family with two children and earnings below about $12,000 would lose $40 of earned income credits for every $100 of lost salary. So their marginal tax price of employer contributions to health insurance that is offset by lower cash wages than would otherwise be paid is $1.40, which may more than offset any price advantage of "subsidized" group insurance over "unsubsidized" nongroup insurance. This situation is uncommon because of the recently increased federal minimum wage and the rare occurrence of ESI among those with very low wages. But it does illustrate how mismatched the tax exclusion is to the needs of low-income workers.

All in all, the health insurance tax incentive provides little benefit to low-income workers. Considering income taxes and the Medicare payroll tax (but not the Social Security tax), the after-tax "price" of the portion of health insurance provided by employers was 97.1 percent of the pretax price for the 20.9 percent of employees in the zero income tax bracket in 2004 (see figure 3-1). That is, the subsidy created by the exclusion from income and Medicare payroll taxes was worth $0.029 on each $1.00 excluded. Employees in the 10 percent bracket pay a tax price of 87.3 percent, while those in the 15 percent bracket pay a tax price of 82.4 percent and those in the 25 percent tax bracket face a tax price of 72.5 percent. The 0.5 percent of taxpayers in the highest 35 percent tax bracket face a tax price of 62.6 percent. Put differently, the subsidy rate is almost thirteen times bigger for the richest 0.5 percent of taxpayers than it is for the poorest 21 percent.

If one also counts the reduction in Social Security taxes as a tax subsidy, then tax prices decrease. The tax price faced by low-income workers falls from 97.1 percent to 85.8 percent of premiums. Someone in the 15 percent federal income tax bracket faces a tax price for health insurance of as little as 72 percent of premiums. In the 25 percent tax bracket, the price is under 63 percent. For very high-income taxpayers, the price can fall to about 53 percent, but most people in the 35 percent tax bracket are not subject to Social Security taxes on the margin, so the 63 percent tax price is more accurate.[25]

As noted, all of these estimates assume that the full benefit of the ESI exclusion accrues to the individual receiving insurance. If higher-income employees implicitly cross-subsidize lower-income employees (who are not willing or able to pay the full cost of health insurance premiums), then these simple calculations understate the benefits to low-income workers and overstate the benefits to those with high incomes.[26]

Figure 3-1. *Tax Price of Health Insurance by Income Tax Bracket for the Nonelderly Employed, 2007*[a]

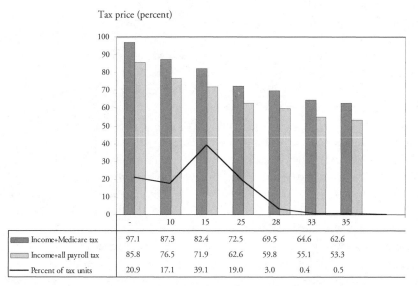

Tax price (percent)

	-	10	15	25	28	33	35
Income+Medicare tax	97.1	87.3	82.4	72.5	69.5	64.6	62.6
Income+all payroll tax	85.8	76.5	71.9	62.6	59.8	55.1	53.3
Percent of tax units	20.9	17.1	39.1	19.0	3.0	0.4	0.5

Income tax bracket (percent)

a. The assumption is that the entire premium is paid out of before-tax income. The first bar includes the effect of income and Medicare payroll tax. The second includes the effect of Social Security (OASDI) payroll taxes.

For the formula for tax price, see note 3 of chapter 1. The tax price does not include the effect of implicit taxes and subsidies caused by income-related phase-outs or phase-ins. For number of tax units by bracket, see T07-0086 (www.taxpolicycenter.org/t07-0086).

Effective Tax Subsidy Rates

The tax exclusion for ESI provides a subsidy for health insurance that varies among both individuals and companies. Individuals get no benefit from the tax exclusion if their employer does not offer health insurance or if they are not eligible for it, as is often the case with part-time workers. The subsidy rate generally depends on the percentage of the health insurance premium paid by the employer. However, most employers offer employees section 125 plans, which allow employees to pay for their own share of premiums with pretax income. Thus the subsidy usually applies to the entire premium. For employees with access to ESI, the overall size of subsidies is governed by the amount of the premiums, and the subsidy rate depends on their income and payroll tax rates.

Nearly all factors that lead to high subsidy rates on health insurance increase with income. The likelihood that an employee has employer-sponsored insurance coverage increases dramatically with income (table 3-2). Only 22 percent of families with a working-age employee with incomes below $10,000 have health insurance through an employer, compared with over 80 percent of families with incomes above $50,000. Lower-income families are less likely to work in jobs that offer health insurance coverage. Even if employers offer insurance to full-time employees, low-income people are more likely to work either part time or part year and therefore would be ineligible for health coverage.

Like the subsidy rate, the value of the tax exclusion also increases dramatically with income. Among families with employer-sponsored health insurance, the premiums for those with incomes below $30,000 average less than $5,500, whereas premiums for families with incomes above $75,000 average more than $7,200. Higher-income families tend to have higher premiums because they are more likely to be covered by multiple policies or have family rather than self-only coverage.[27] The upward trend in premiums is less pronounced when married and single tax filers are examined separately. Premiums range from $6,800 to $8,100 for joint filers and show no discernible trend for singles and heads of household (probably because higher-income singles are less likely to have children). In addition, lower-income families are more likely to have coverage for less than a full year, due to part-year employment. Finally, as explained above, the benefit of any tax exclusion is greatest for high-income families because the income tax is progressive.

Putting all these factors together, the picture is of a tax subsidy that overwhelmingly favors middle- and upper-income households. Families in the lowest income group receive average tax savings (including both income and payroll taxes) worth 12 percent of their premiums, compared with a savings worth 31 percent or more of premiums for the highest income groups.[28] Consequently, the highest-income families pay much lower after-tax premiums than those with low incomes.

The bottom line is that the subsidy is not focused on those who most need help paying for health insurance. Assuming that health insurance premiums are paid instead of wages (so both the employer share and the employee share of premiums are ultimately paid by workers), the after-tax cost of employment-based health insurance is a much larger share of income for low-income workers than for high-income workers. Figure 3-2 plots the after-tax premium cost as a percent of income and the tax subsidy rate as a percent of the premium for each income group. Health insurance premiums after tax are 72 percent of income for the poorest households, but their subsidy rate is less than 10 percent. Those with incomes of $100,000 to $200,000 receive subsidies equal to almost 35 percent of premiums, even though premiums would amount to less than 10 percent of their income without a subsidy.

In total, we estimate that the tax expenditure for ESI coverage was $147 billion in 2004. Of the tax breaks associated with ESI, 16 percent goes to the nearly 44 million families earning less than $30,000, while 30 percent goes to the 15 million families earning more than $100,000 a year. Clearly, tax subsidies for ESI are not flowing to the workers and families who would benefit from them the most.

Overall Effects of ESI Tax Exclusion

Although far from ideal, the ESI exclusion allows many millions of Americans to get health insurance at work. Several studies estimate the elasticity of employers' offering insurance with respect to the price of coverage. Three studies examine the elasticity of offer with respect to the tax price of coverage in particular. Jonathan Gruber and Michael Lettau estimate an overall elasticity of employers' offering insurance with respect to the tax price of the median worker of –0.25—and twice that for small firms.[29] Mark Stabile also finds small firms to be more sensitive to tax price changes than large firms are.[30] An elasticity of –0.25 means that a 20 percent increase in the tax price would reduce the number of employees offered insurance by 5 percent. For Gruber and Lettau's sample, eliminating the exclusion from income and payroll taxes would increase the tax price of the median worker by 58 percent—from 0.63 to 1.0—implying a 15.5 percent reduction in offering, concentrated in small and medium-size firms. Elasticity of spending is even larger, at –0.7, implying a 45 percent overall decline in spending on ESI if the tax benefits were eliminated.

Critics of the current system point out that, in addition to its other flaws, it discourages innovation in the insurance market, a criticism that is almost surely valid. If tens of millions of employees lost insurance at work (an implication of Gruber and Lettau's estimates), there would be a much larger potential market for nongroup insurance. Insurers would likely invent inexpensive products that were attractive to healthy enrollees. And as noted earlier, alternative pooling mechanisms might arise to limit the ravages of adverse selection. The net effect, as Gruber and Lettau acknowledge, is that the overall change in health insurance coverage from such a massive change might well be smaller than they estimate.

But the change could also be substantially larger. Anne Royalty estimates an overall tax price elasticity of offer of –0.6, more than twice the elasticity of –0.25 estimated by Gruber and Lettau.[31] Further, as Gruber and Lettau note, virtually all large employers in their sample offered insurance. So their model

Table 3-2. *ESI Tax Subsidies for Tax Units with a Working-Age Employee, 2004*

Cash income class (thousands of dollars)	Tax units with worker					Tax units with ESI				
	Number (millions)	Percentage offered ESI	Percentage covered by ESI	Average premium (dollars)	Average subsidy (dollars)	Subsidy as percentage of premium	Subsidy as percentage of after-tax income	After-tax premium as percentage of after-tax income	Income tax rate on exclusion (percent)	Percentage of tax subsidy
A. All tax units[a]										
Less than 10	12.5	56.9	21.7	4,895	580	11.9	9.7	72.2	-2.1	1.1
10–20	16.6	66.0	40.0	5,313	1,168	22.0	8.4	29.7	8.8	5.4
20–30	14.9	78.2	58.7	5,443	1,622	29.8	7.6	17.9	17.4	9.8
30–40	11.9	84.9	70.9	5,638	1,621	28.8	5.8	14.3	16.1	9.7
40–50	9.3	88.0	76.2	5,874	1,733	29.5	5.0	11.9	16.5	8.8
50–75	16.5	90.1	80.9	6,595	1,960	29.7	4.4	10.4	16.8	19.7
75–100	10.1	92.1	85.1	7,286	2,298	31.5	3.9	8.5	19.2	15.8
100–200	11.8	91.5	85.9	7,686	2,690	35.0	3.2	5.9	25.8	22.6
200 and over	3.5	86.7	81.2	7,706	2,943	38.2	1.0	1.6	31.2	7.0
All	107.5	80.2	63.9	6,422	1,945	30.3	3.5	8.1	18.6	100.0
B. Married										
Less than 10	1.3	60.9	40.8	6,845	433	6.3	7.7	114.1	-7.9	0.2
10–20	3.1	63.7	43.3	7,309	1,458	19.9	10.3	41.2	6.6	2.1
20–30	3.2	77.0	57.8	7,297	1,998	27.4	9.3	24.6	14.8	4.1
30–40	3.2	85.0	70.1	7,690	2,084	27.1	7.5	20.0	14.3	5.3
40–50	3.5	87.0	74.6	7,706	2,072	26.9	6.1	16.5	13.8	6.2
50–75	9.2	91.3	82.2	7,777	2,162	27.8	4.9	12.8	14.7	19.7
75–100	7.7	93.4	86.7	7,942	2,450	30.8	4.3	9.6	18.4	20.3

100–200	10.0	93.1	88.1	8,051	2,829	35.1	3.4	6.2	25.8	31.9
200 and over	3.1	88.7	83.6	8,013	3,071	38.3	1.0	1.7	31.3	10.0
All	44.4	87.1	77.1	7,839	2,401	30.6	3.3	7.5	19.2	100.0
C. Single and heads of household										
Less than 10	11.1	56.3	19.3	4,368	607	13.9	9.9	61.6	0.1	2.9
10–20	13.2	66.3	38.7	4,709	1,070	22.7	7.6	26.0	9.6	12.0
20–30	11.3	78.3	58.5	4,844	1,504	31.1	7.1	15.7	18.8	22.0
30–40	8.3	84.7	70.9	4,709	1,410	29.9	5.0	11.7	17.3	18.4
40–50	5.6	88.8	77.4	4,592	1,480	32.2	4.2	8.8	19.4	14.2
50–75	6.9	88.4	79.0	4,651	1,595	34.3	3.4	6.6	21.8	19.2
75–100	2.3	87.8	79.7	4,453	1,625	36.5	2.5	4.4	25.0	6.6
100–200	1.7	82.0	72.5	4,441	1,432	32.2	1.5	3.1	26.3	3.8
200 and over	0.4	72.3	64.2	4,293	1,502	35.0	0.4	0.7	29.5	0.9
All	61.0	75.0	54.0	4,661	1,377	29.5	4.0	9.5	17.3	100.0

Source: Tax Policy Center calculations based on the HIPSM database.

a. Tax units with negative incomes are not shown but included in the totals.

Figure 3-2. *ESI Subsidy Rate and Premium Burden, by Income, 2004*[a]

Percent

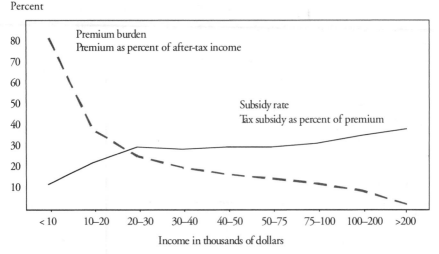

a. Subsidy includes income tax and Social Security and Medicare payroll tax savings.

cannot predict a change in offering rates among that group because there is no variation in the dependent variable. But such an unprecedented change might cause some large employers to stop offering ESI—for example, employers with workforces in which many young, lower-paid workers are unwilling to sacrifice wages for health insurance. With a large tax subsidy, highly compensated employees are willing to subsidize lower-compensated employees because they gain enough from the tax exclusion and the other advantages of the employer group to make it worth paying a disproportionate share of premiums. Without the large tax subsidy, the balance would change dramatically. If some large employers dropped coverage, the overall market response could be much larger.

Moreover, while the reduction in insurance spending might portend more effective cost containment, which would have a salutary effect on prices for health care and insurance (and help those who get little or no subsidy under the current system), some cost containment strategies could reduce coverage, especially among vulnerable groups. Most notably, if the predominant form of cost containment turned out to be high-deductible health insurance plans or less subsidization of low-income employees by those with higher incomes in the firm, workers with low incomes or low expected health costs might opt out. Using a simulation model of the value of coverage expansions to different populations, Sherry Glied concludes that high-deductible health insurance plans may make some of the low-income uninsured worse off.[32]

Based on everything economists now know, eliminating the ESI exclusion would likely significantly increase the number of uninsured. It is possible that an invigorated free market could solve all the problems that would arise if the tax breaks associated with ESI were simply ended, but the long list of market failures associated with health insurance means that belief in such a benign outcome would rest more on blind faith than on economic evidence.

Conclusion

Although many markets would work best without direct government involvement, the market for health insurance is not one of them. The market for health insurance is affected by almost every market failure imaginable. The main government intervention for working-age Americans and their families is the exclusion from income and payroll taxes of employer contributions for ESI, which reduced revenues by $147 billion in 2004.

In one sense, the tax exclusion has succeeded. More than two-thirds of Americans under age sixty-five get their insurance at work. Large employers can offer insurance at relatively low cost, and almost all do. However, the employer group works less well for small firms. And the tax exclusion is poorly targeted. Low-income workers can face health insurance premiums equal to 72 percent of their incomes, but the income tax subsidy is worth little or nothing to them, and they are disproportionately likely to lack insurance. High-income people, for whom insurance would be affordable and desirable even without tax breaks, receive the largest share of the tax benefits. Also, the open-ended subsidy provides an incentive to get overly generous insurance with few controls on spending.

Eliminating the subsidy without providing a better-targeted alternative would surely reduce the number of people with health insurance. Estimates suggest that the number of firms offering insurance would decline by more than 15 percent, and these would be mostly small and medium-size firms. The people most likely to lack insurance would be those with poor health status—for whom nongroup insurance is unavailable or unaffordable—and those with low incomes. It is possible that the health insurance market would find new ways to pool insurance among those who no longer get it at work. It is also possible that more large firms would drop coverage if the after-tax cost of insurance increased dramatically than current empirical estimates indicate.

There are many reasons to think that we could do better than the current system, but we could also make the situation worse. The following chapters in this volume consider various options to improve upon the current system.

Notes

1. John P. Sommers, "Offer Rates, Take-Up Rates, Premiums, and Employee Contributions for Employer-Sponsored Health Insurance in the Private Sector for the 10 Largest Metropolitan Areas, 2004," Statistical Brief 150 (Rockville, Md.: Agency for Healthcare Research and Quality, 2006).

2. Treasury Notice 2005-86 allows employees a grace period of two and a half months beyond the end of the calendar year to submit charges for reimbursement under a health FSA if the employer permits.

3. Twenty percent of small firms (3 to 199 workers) and 73 percent of large firms (200 or more workers) that offer health benefits offer flexible savings accounts. Sixty percent of small firms and 92 percent of large firms allow employees to make pretax premium payments through section 125 plans. Kaiser Family Foundation and Health Research Educational Trust, "Employer Health Benefits: 2007 Summary of Findings" (Chicago: 2007).

4. In contrast, no nondiscrimination rules apply to the provisions of commercially purchased health insurance. The Tax Reform Act of 1986 included a new section 89, which established nondiscrimination rules for employee health and welfare benefits, but the new restrictions raised a firestorm of protest among business interests and others and were repealed in 1989.

5. Michael Rothschild and Joseph Stiglitz, "Equilibrium in Competitive Insurance Markets: An Essay on the Economics of Imperfect Information," *Quarterly Journal of Economics* 90, no. 4 (1976): 629–50.

6. Joseph P. Newhouse, "Reimbursing Health Plans and Health Providers: Efficiency in Production versus Selection," *Journal of Economic Literature* 34 (1996): 1236–63.

7. Mark A. Hall, "The Structure and Enforcement of Health Insurance Rating Reforms," *Inquiry* 37 (Winter 2000): 376–88.

8. M. Susan Marquis and Melinda B. Buntin, "How Much Risk Pooling Is There in the Individual Insurance Market?" *Health Services Research* 41, no. 5 (2006): 1782–800.

9. Moral hazard is an endemic problem in insurance and not unique to health care. It initially referred to the increased likelihood that homes would catch fire once covered by insurance, due both to laxity in avoiding fire risks and to arson. The latter interpretation is the "immoral" aspect of moral hazard (which clearly does not apply in the health insurance case). For an early and cogent explanation of moral hazard and its implications in the context of health care, see Mark V. Pauly, "The Economics of Moral Hazard: Comment," *American Economic Review* 58, no. 3, part 1 (June 1968): 531–37.

10. Joseph P. Newhouse, "Medical Care Costs: How Much Welfare Loss?" *Journal of Economic Perspectives* 6, no. 3 (1992): 3–21.

11. Mancur Olson, *A New Approach to the Economics of Health Care* (Washington: American Enterprise Institute, 1982).

12. David Cutler, "Market Failure in Small Group Health Insurance," Working Paper 4879 (Cambridge, Mass.: National Bureau of Economic Research, 1994).

13. However, some research suggests that small groups may pool risks better than thought. See Mark Pauly and Bradley Herring, *Pooling Health Insurance Risks* (Washington: American Enterprise Institute, 1999).

14. Alan C. Monheit, Len M. Nichols, and Thomas M. Selden, "How Are Net Health Insurance Benefits Distributed in the Employment-Related Market?" *Inquiry* 32 (Winter 1995): 379–91.

15. Richard Thaler, "Saving and Mental Accounting," in *Choices over Time*, edited by George Loewenstein and Jon Elster (New York: Russell Sage Foundation, 1992).

16. Ibid.

17. Mark Pauly and Bradley Herring, "Expanding Coverage via Tax Credits: Trade-Offs and Outcomes," *Health Affairs* 20, no. 1 (2001): 9–26.

18. Congressional Budget Office, *The Tax Treatment of Employment-Based Health Insurance* (Government Printing Office, 1994).

19. Philip F. Cooper and Barbara Steinberg Schone, "More Offers, Fewer Takers for Employment-Based Health Insurance: 1987 and 1996," *Health Affairs* 16, no. 6 (1997): 142–49.

20. Lisa Clemans-Cope and Bowen Garrett, "Changes in Employer-Sponsored Health Insurance Sponsorship, Eligibility, and Participation: 2001 to 2005" (Washington: Kaiser Commission on Medicaid and the Uninsured, 2007).

21. See www.taxpolicycenter.org/t07-0086.

22. Some people in the zero bracket who receive ESI may benefit from the exclusion of employer-sponsored health insurance from taxable income. Some people's incomes are below the filing threshold simply *because* their health insurance premiums are excluded from income. For example, an individual earning $8,950 in 2008 had no taxable income (www.taxpolicycenter.org/taxfacts/displayafact.cfm?docid=474). However, if the employer had stopped contributing $2,000 toward health insurance and instead increased the worker's wages by that amount, the worker would have positive taxable income and owe $200 in tax on it. Note, though, that few people at this income level receive ESI (see table 3-2). There are also families in the 10 percent tax bracket who would receive no benefit from the tax exclusion because nonrefundable tax credits such as the dependent care tax credit, education credits, and the nonrefundable portion of the child tax credit offset all of their income tax liability.

23. Martin Feldstein and Andrew Samwick, "Social Security Rules and Marginal Tax Rates," *National Tax Journal* 45, no. 1 (1992): 1–22.

24. Feldstein and Samwick (ibid.) point out that many individuals with low covered earnings were not in fact poor but earned most of their income working for state and local governments that were exempt from the Social Security payroll tax.

25. On the other hand, phantom taxes caused by the phase-out of the AMT exemption, itemized deductions, and other provisions can add as much as 7 percentage points to the effective tax rate for upper-middle- and upper-income taxpayers. However, since these taxes are obscured by the complexity of the tax law, it is unclear that they would affect most taxpayers' decisions. See Greg Leiserson, "Income Taxes and Tax Rates for Sample Families, 2006" (www.taxpolicycenter.org/uploadedpdf411402_sample_families.pdf).

26. None of the calculations that follow includes the effect of such cross-subsidization.

27. The premium data we use are firm-size group averages for single and family coverage. Therefore the premium variation by income group in table 3-2 is driven mostly by the mix of single versus family coverage.

28. The tax subsidy discussed herein reflects both the federal income tax and the payroll tax. It considers both the employer's share of premiums and the worker's share when workers are able pay their share with pretax dollars under section 125 plans.

29. Jonathan Gruber and Michael Lettau, "How Elastic Is the Firm's Demand for Health Insurance?" *Journal of Public Economics* 88, nos. 7–8 (2004): 1273–93.

30. Mark Stabile, "The Role of Tax Subsidies in the Market for Health Insurance," *International Tax and Public Finance* 9, no. 1 (2002): 33–50.

31. Anne B. Royalty, "Tax Preferences for Fringe Benefits and Workers' Eligibility for Employer Health Insurance," *Journal of Public Economics* 75, no. 2 (2000): 209–27.

32. Sherry Glied, "Is Something Better than Nothing? Health Insurance Expansions and the Content of Coverage," in *Frontiers in Health Policy Research,* vol. 6, edited by D. Cutler and A. Garber (MIT Press, 2003).

Comment by Daniel Halperin

M y comments apply to the whole book and attempt to apply my expertise in tax policy. First, I was surprised by references to the nondiscrimination test applicable to self-insured medical plans.[1] Under this test if a self-insured plan discriminates in favor of high-income employees, benefits payable to such employees may be taxable.

I knew the test was there. I think I was in the Department of Treasury when it was enacted. But I have read a number of articles detailing how state regulation of medical insurance plans can be avoided by self-insuring; and not one of the authors of those articles mentions the potential downside of the nondiscrimination test. Since I assume that a significant number of lower-income employees decline coverage, it seemed likely that the IRS is not enforcing this test. A reading of all the chapters reveals two things. First, a larger percentage of employees accept coverage than I had thought, so perhaps discrimination is not a major problem.[2] Second, my assumption that the IRS is not enforcing the test is probably true.[3]

The purpose of the nondiscrimination test was to prevent small businesses from covering generally uninsured medical expenses only for the highest paid people by paying out cash only to them. It was not focused on discrimination in insurance-type arrangements, where it was assumed that such discrimination was not a problem. Thus it is not surprising that the IRS is not interested in applying the test in this situation.

It is interesting that many of the tax rules relating to health are not based on health policy considerations. The original exclusion for health insurance was adopted by the IRS because the IRS felt that it was difficult to allocate the costs of health insurance to individual employees and also, since amounts were small, it was not that important.[4] Of course, now it is important.

Similarly, there is some discussion in these chapters about flexible spending accounts. The legislative approval of these arrangements in 1978 was a by-product of legislation establishing what are now 401(k) savings plans. One assumption was that allowing employees an exclusion for the purchase of health insurance, even if by way of a salary reduction, would make it easier for employers to offer health insurance because they would not have to worry about shortchanging employees who were not interested in such insurance. They could have cash, while those who wanted health insurance would retain the tax exemption. Therefore, presumably we would have more insurance. The authors seem to think that this result is not necessarily good and may well even be bad. It seems that we have two problems. One is that 47 million people do not have health insurance. The other is that the rest of us do. So it is hard to know exactly what to worry about.

Soon after the idea of salary reduction was approved, employers or their advisers figured out that salary reduction rules could be applied not only to insurance premiums, which is what people were talking about as the legislation was enacted, but also to out-of-pocket medical expenses. My immediate reaction was that that interpretation amounted to an end run around the requirement that deductions for medical expenses must exceed 7.5 percent of adjusted gross income. I believed that creating a way around that floor was clearly not intended by the 1978 legislation and that the Treasury should do something about it as fast as possible. Neither Treasury nor Congress halted flexible spending accounts, however. I now learn that maybe it is a good thing, because FSAs might reduce the moral hazard of insurance because the ability to pay out-of-pocket medical expenses with before-tax income reduces people's desire for high-cost policies.[5]

So it is complicated, and I think it certainly does suggest that having Treasury be one of the lead agencies in determining health policy does not work very well. I certainly learned that when I was at Treasury. The IRS has no interest in improving the health system. That is not part of its mission. Given the many social objectives Congress insists on trying to achieve with tax measures, I became convinced after seven years at Treasury that the IRS needs its own health office, its own housing office, and its own energy office. Maybe things are better now, but I think that such offices within Treasury may still be a good idea.

Treasury officials decided in 1943 to exempt health insurance premiums because it was too difficult to allocate the cost among employees. I would assume that problem would remain should we decide to repeal the exclusion. Harvard does print the value of the health insurance they pay for on my monthly pay stub. But I assume that that is the pro rata allocation of what it costs for family coverage and has nothing to do with my age, which presumably makes me a lot more expensive. If we eliminated the tax exemption and simply allocated employers' costs on a pro rata basis, the young would be overtaxed and the old would be undertaxed. To avoid that problem we have to make premium allocations a lot more sophisticated than they are today.

Allocation difficulties also complicate the question of who benefits from the tax subsidy (a point touched upon in a number of chapters though it is not central to any of them). It is suggested that after-tax wages adjust so that the tax exemption lowers employment costs and prices (assuming that the tax benefits are a subsidy to companies offering health insurance).[6] On this reasoning, employees do not benefit at all; customers do.

If provision of health insurance results in a wage cut by either the pretax cost of health insurance or the cost plus the tax savings, it is not clear whose wages are cut.[7] Sometimes we assume that each employee gets a pay cut equal to the pro rata cost of health insurance. If that is true, then the young are paying too much—unless there are salary adjustments elsewhere. Or are wages cut by an equal percentage? Then high-paid employees actually pay more for health insurance. Some employers pay health insurance centrally. That is what my university employer does. It imposes a fringe benefit charge on each academic unit as a percentage of payroll. That means that the high-salary faculty of business, law, and medicine pay a lot more for health insurance than does the faculty of arts and sciences. It is not clear how that is reflected in setting individual salaries.

So it may be that the highly paid actually gain enough from the tax exclusion and the other benefits of health insurance that they are willing to subsidize the less compensated. In other words, their wages are cut by more than their share of the premiums. We often assume that this occurs with retirement benefits. A lot of the writing on ERISA suggests that since the nondiscrimination test requires that the low income participate and since the low income will not accept sufficient pay cuts, the highly paid have to allocate part of their tax savings to encourage the low paid to be part of the plan. If there are reasons even in the absence of a nondiscrimination test that employers must provide health insurance to the low paid, it may be that high earners help pay for it by splitting their tax savings with the low paid. If that is true then that would be lost if we no longer had employment-based insurance. If we had individual policies or even if everything were paid out of salary reduction, then it would be the individual paying for himself—and that would of course make the tax exclusion even more absurd.

I do a lot of work in retirement income and pension benefits and I have been asking this question of people for about forty-five years: Who pays for health insurance? I do not get any clear answers. Manufacturers tell you that they pay for health insurance, that it does not come out of wages, and that is why American cars are too expensive. Others say that the costs of health insurance and pensions reduce wages. If wages are reduced across the board or by some percentage of pay, it is hard to tell who benefits from the tax exclusion. Of course, you can respond that in a perfect labor market individual wages must adjust. So I give up.

Notes

1. See especially Leonard Burman, Bowen Garrett, and Surachai Khitatrakun, chapter 3, this volume. Also see Jason Furman, chapter 9.

2. Furman claims that 82 percent accept coverage.

3. See Mary Hevener and Charles Kerby, chapter 7.

4. See Robert Helms, chapter 2.

5. See Jessica Vistnes, William Jack, and Arik Levinson, chapter 6, who suggest that the evidence is not strong. See also Furman.

6. See Furman.

7. See Jeffrey Liebman and Richard Zeckhauser, chapter 10.

COMMENT BY ANUP MALANI

Chapter 3, by Leonard Burman, Bowen Garrett, and Surachai Khitatrakun, has three basic themes. First, there are significant imperfections and thus inefficiencies in health care markets. Insurance markets, in particular, are subject to problems of adverse selection and moral hazard. Second, the tax code permits employees to deduct the cost of employer-paid health insurance from their income before calculating income taxes. Because income tax rates are progressive, the deductions are regressive. That is, higher-income individuals face higher tax rates, so deductions afford them greater discounts. Third, eliminating tax breaks for employer-sponsored health insurance (ESI) would increase the ranks of the uninsured. Eliminating the tax code–based discount would increase the price of health insurance and decrease consumption of health insurance. I do not disagree with these points, but I want to note some important caveats to the authors' claims.

Consider first the claim that health care markets are imperfect and thus inefficient. Because the remainder of the chapter focuses on health insurance, the authors do not have to make the claim that these markets are imperfect. It is sufficient for them to note—as many others have—that health insurance markets are subject to adverse selection and generate moral hazard. The adverse selection problem is that healthy people do not want to participate in the same risk pool as sick people. Whenever another company—or even the same company—offers a lower-coverage, thus lower-cost, plan, many of the healthy depart the pool. This segmentation of risk undermines insurance for the sick.[1] The moral hazard is that health insurance lowers the out-of-pocket marginal cost of care after sickness or injury below the actual marginal cost, which causes excessive consumption of care.

The authors discuss other imperfections in health care markets, such as information asymmetries between doctors and patients and free riding on publicly provided emergency care. But these are largely orthogonal to their primary concern: the tax subsidy for purchase of health insurance. In any case, the list of inefficiencies omits other important imperfections. The most important is, perhaps, a preference for the welfare of others, or altruism. Any theory of health care markets must explain why the government spends roughly $300 billion on Medicaid and conditions Medicare participation on the provision of limited emergency room care.[2] One reasonable theory is that people have a preference for helping the poor or the sick in need of urgent care. The problem with relying on altruism to solve social problems—especially what is called pure altruism—is free riding. Why should I help the poor if you will do it? Mandatory contributions (better known as taxes) are a common response. This may explain Medicaid and public subsidies for obligations created by the Emergency Medical Treatment and Active Labor Act (EMTALA).

Of course, government transfers of this sort cause their own imperfections. A good example is the free riding that the authors discuss: some people do not buy health insurance because they can go to the emergency room free of charge. But the bigger implication is that if I agree to pay for the care of a poor person, the conduct of that poor person affects the amount I have to pay. If he smokes, I pay more. If he does not work, I pay more. In other words, while the public program corrects the externality due to altruism, the program creates second-order externalities to my wallet that flow from the poor person's behavior. My aim here is not to suggest that altruism is central to the authors' discussion of tax breaks for health insurance but that sometimes the solutions to one market imperfection create another.

The central question for the authors is, What is the appropriate baseline? A world without the problem that insurance corrects? Or a world with insurance but not its side effects? Let me be more concrete. The reason people buy health insurance is that they want to avoid the financial risk of costly medical episodes. By paying a premium, with certainty they reduce or avoid random wealth shocks due to illness. Insurance does suffer from adverse selection, which reduces the degree of insurance to the extent that one is in a risk group populated by few other people, and from moral hazard, which increases the cost of care. But people may prefer limited health insurance with higher health costs to no insurance. So is it appropriate to focus solely on the side effects of health insurance? To put it another way, knowing the costs of insurance is only part of the question. How should one value the reduction of risk that health insurance provides?

A second benefit of health insurance, and one that is often overlooked, flows from its impact on innovation. Improvements in health care depend on innovation, much of it in the form of drugs or devices. Because innovation is typically a public good, there is insufficient incentive to supply it. The solution we have chosen is patents. Innovators are given a fixed period of time (twenty years) during which they alone are allowed to sell their innovations. This monopoly allows them to extract a monopoly profit, or at least a supracompetitive return, which serves as an inducement to innovate. The problem is that the solution creates a secondary problem: monopoly pricing generates deadweight loss. The monopolist prices above marginal cost; individuals who value the product more than marginal cost but less than the monopoly price cannot purchase the product. This lost opportunity is inefficient. There is quite a large literature on this problem; the problem accounts for proposals to award monetary prizes rather than patents to spur innovation.

As it happens, health insurance provides the health sector some protection from this problem. To some significant degree, moral hazard from health insurance solves the problem of deadweight loss from patents.[3] The logic is that health insurance lowers the out-of-pocket price of drugs and devices to something near their marginal cost. Hence patents on these products do not raise their price above competitive levels from the perspective of end users. Nor is there any loss of incentive to innovate, because the insurance company pays the full monopoly price of the patented product. This extra payment generates a positive externality of health insurance that reduces and may negate the problem of moral hazard for drugs and devices. In the overall balance, it reduces the cost of the tax break for employer-purchased health insurance.

Let me now turn to the second theme of the chapter: that the tax deduction for ESI favors the rich. I have four concerns about this claim. The first concern, I admit, may not be not very constructive. But it is politically salient, at least among some voters, so it cannot be ignored. The concern is that the reason the ESI favors the rich is not because of the ESI per se but because we have a progressive tax code. The rich pay a higher income tax rate, so an income tax deduction will afford them a greater benefit. If the code were not progressive, the rich would gain no more than the poor. There are two possible solutions to this problem (other than to adopt a nonprogressive income tax, which may be worse than the problem itself). One approach is to eliminate the ESI deduction and subsidize health insurance through some other means. The hurdle facing this strategy is that eliminating the deduction substantially increases administrative costs. Under current arrangements, the employer does not have to report anything to the Internal Revenue Service (IRS), and the IRS does not need any information about health insurance to implement the deduction. If we got rid of the ESI deduction, the employer would have to impute health insurance costs for each worker, and the IRS would have to verify those costs.

The other way to address the regressivity of the deduction is to supplement it with some subsidy that disproportionately favors the poor. This leads to my second concern with the authors' claim. Should the regressivity of the ESI deduction be judged on its own? Or in combination with government policies that are progressive? Again, I am thinking of Medicaid. Only individuals with incomes below certain ceilings (which range from 11 percent of the federal poverty line for nonworking parents in Alabama to 409 percent of the poverty line for working parents in New Mexico) and with minimum assets are eligible for Medicaid.[4] Medicaid is funded out of general revenues, which are largely generated from high-income individuals. For example, the Congressional Budget Office projects that, in 2008, the top 20 percent of income earners will account for 79.1 percent of all individual income taxes paid and 63.8 percent of all federal taxes paid.[5] These high-income individuals are unlikely to ever be eligible for Medicaid, let alone in the year in which they pay taxes. Thus it is likely that more than half of Medicaid—or roughly $150 billion, including state moneys—is a transfer from the top 20 percent of earners to the bottom 5 percent of earners. This amount is larger than the Office of Management and Budget's $133 billion estimate of the total value of the ESI subsidy to all taxpayers in 2007.[6] If my back-of-the-envelope calculations are roughly correct, the package of Medicaid plus ESI deduction may not be regressive.

My third concern with the claim that the ESI subsidy is regressive is whether the authors are judging the subsidy against the proper counterfactual.[7] If the government were to eliminate the ESI subsidy, perhaps the rich would respond by seeking tax benefits elsewhere in the tax code. For example, they might seek a more generous mortgage interest deduction. The authors are correct to claim that the ESI subsidy is ceteris paribus regressive: that is, it is regressive if we ignore the fact that eliminating it might trigger other changes in the tax code that are ceteris paribus regressive. But just as the proper counterfactual for eliminating the ESI would not ignore the policy's effect on health insurance demand in the health insurance market, it should not ignore the policy's effect on the demand for other tax breaks in the political market. If the political market's reflex to the elimination of the ESI is a more ceteris paribus regressive scheme, then the ESI subsidy might actually be effectively progressive. Even if the reflex is a less regressive scheme, the effective regressivity of the ESI subsidy may be less than what the authors contend.

My fourth concern with the authors' regressivity claim is that regressivity of the financial costs of a benefit, as borne by the government, is not the appropriate measure of an in-kind benefit. The appropriate measure is the regressivity of the utility derived from a benefit by the beneficiaries. The ESI deduction is only helpful if you buy health insurance, hence it is a subsidy for health insurance. A major goal of health insurance, in turn, is to provide health care, which in turn is intended to provide health. It is that health that ultimately provides utility to beneficiaries. So to calculate how regressive the ESI deduction is, one would want to know whether health insurance is more productive in terms of health for the rich than for the poor. The authors note that the tax price elasticity of employer spending on health insurance is –0.7.[8] Moreover, a review of the literature demonstrates that insurance is associated with better health, though the relationship is far from perfect.[9] But this literature does not tell us whether the poor benefit more or less than the rich. There are reasons to suspect that the rich benefit more than the poor: they are more educated and are thus more likely to use health insurance or to comply with treatment regimens. But there are also reasons to suspect that the poor have a higher return to health expenditure than the rich because the poor are sicker than the rich to begin with. If the rich benefit more than the poor, the ESI deduction increases the health gap between the rich and the poor even more than the authors suggest. But if it is the other way around, the health gap between the two may be smaller than the tax price discount suggests.[10]

My final concern with the regressivity claim is a bit of nitpick: degree of regressivity strongly depends on which tax schemes you consider. For example, when Social Security taxes are included, the disparity between the tax prices for the rich and the poor fall from 44 percentage points (53 to 97) to 22 percentage points (63 to 85). It is still a gap, but a much smaller one.

The authors conclude with a cautionary note: even if there are inefficiencies from health insurance and the ESI deduction is regressive, eliminating it may increase the number of the uninsured. One can quibble with their estimate of how much the consumption of insurance will fall. Perhaps the authors' preferred estimate of tax price elasticity cannot be extrapolated to the case where the tax price rises to one (or no) discount.[11] Moreover, rich employees may have inelastic demand for health insurance that offsets the elasticity of demand for health insurance by businesses. (This possibility would also imply that eliminating the deduction would not end regressivity as measured by health outcomes.) Finally, there may be other safety nets (such as EMTALA) that would limit the impact of eliminating the deduction.

But these objections are minor. It would be hard to dispute that the elimination of ESI would not have a significant effect on insurance consumption and health care. The bigger problem with the authors' caution is that no one seriously proposes simply to eliminate the ESI deduction. For example, the Democrats propose elimination of the ESI deduction only as a way to raise revenue to fund an expansion in government spending on health care. Perhaps the authors intend their caution to encourage the bundling of other health insurance proposals with tax reform. In that case, it is well taken. But if that is not the intent, then I respond to their caution with one of my own: be careful about the proper counterfactual. Just eliminating the ESI deduction may appear worse for the uninsured than the usual package of reforms that includes an ESI deduction.

Notes

1. Because health insurance contracts are short-term contracts, it also undermines insurance for the healthy before they learn whether they will remain healthy or become sick in the future.

2. Federal and state Medicaid spending was $303.882 billion in 2006, according to the Kaiser Family Foundation (www.statehealthfacts.org/comparemaptable.jsp?ind=177&cat=4 [April 2008]). Regarding Medicare, the Emergency Medical Treatment and Active Labor Act requires those hospitals that participate in Medicare to maintain an emergency room to screen patients that present themselves for an emergency condition and, if the patient has an emergency condition, to stabilize the patient before transfer or to treat the patient.

3. Darius Lakdawalla and Neeraj Sood, "The Welfare Effects of Public Drug Insurance," Working Paper 13501 (Cambridge, Mass: National Bureau of Economic Research, 2007).

4. Figures are from Kaiser Family Foundation (www.statehealthfacts.org/comparetable.jsp?ind=205&cat=4&sub=54&yr=63&typ=2&o=a [May 2008]).

5. Congressional Budget Office, "Effective Federal Tax Rates under Current Law, 2001 to 2014" (www.cbo.gov/ftpdocs/57xx/doc5746/08-13-effectivefedtaxrates.pdf [August 2004).

6. Office of Management and Budget, "Analytic Perspectives, Budget of the United States Government, Fiscal Year 2009" (www.whitehouse.gov/omb/budget/fy2009/pdf/spec.pdf).

7. This criticism was originally made by Clark Havighurst and Barak Richman, "Distributive Injustice(s) in American Health Care," *Law and Contemporary Problems* 69 (2006): 7–82.

8. They cite Jonathan Gruber and Michael Lettau, "How Elastic Is the Firm's Demand for Health Insurance?" *Journal of Public Economics* 88, nos. 7–8 (2004): 1273–93.

9. See, for example, Helen Levy and David Meltzer, "What Do We Really Know about Whether Health Insurance Affects Health?" in *Health Policy and the Uninsured,* edited by Catherine McLaughlin (Washington: Urban Institute, 2004). A recent and interesting contribution is Joseph Doyle, "Health Insurance, Treatment, and Outcomes: Using Automobile Accidents as Health Shocks," *Review of Economics and Statistics* 87 (2005): 256–70, which uses health shocks to travelers to address the problem that people self-select into insurance.

10. Of course, the same logic that suggests that progressive taxation causes the ESI deduction to be regressive also suggests that if the rich benefit from health insurance more than the poor, eliminating the ESI deduction will not benefit the poor all that much. It will mainly hurt the rich.

11. The authors cite Gruber and Lettau, "How Elastic Is the Firm's Demand for Health Insurance?"

4

Health Savings Accounts: Recent Trends and Potential Effects on Coverage and Health Insurance Markets

LISA CLEMANS-COPE

I n 2003 the Medicare Prescription Drug, Improvement, and Modernization Act (also called the Medicare Modernization Act or MMA) established health savings accounts (HSAs), which allow tax benefits for out-of-pocket health spending when paired with a high-deductible health insurance plan (HDHP).[1] This may be the most significant tax law change affecting health insurance coverage since the exclusion of employer-sponsored insurance (ESI) was codified in 1954. HSA advocates argue that the high deductibles will encourage health consumers to pay more attention to the costs and benefits of health care options, putting downward pressure on health spending. Critics worry that the combination of HSAs and HDHPs (henceforth referred to as HDHP–HSAs) will be most attractive to healthy people with enough income to afford the risk associated with high deductibles, and their exit from traditional insurance pools will make such insurance unaffordable to those with chronic health problems and low incomes.

This chapter surveys early data on the availability of and enrollment in HDHP–HSAs and discusses their effects on insurance coverage and health spending. The chapter first provides an overview of HSAs and the context in which they arose. The chapter then presents information on offer rates of these types of plans in the group market, enrollment in the group and nongroup markets, and an overview of the basic features of HDHP–HSAs in the marketplace. Next is a discussion of how HDHP–HSAs may affect health care costs and ser-

I am grateful for helpful comments and suggestions from Len Burman, Linda Blumberg, Henry Aaron, and Edwin Park.

vice use. Data are presented regarding the health care expenses of individuals in relation to the features of a typical HDHP–HSA. The next section addresses effects of HDHP–HSAs on coverage and the group and nongroup health insurance markets. Potential tax advantages of HDHP–HSAs for the currently uninsured are discussed. The chapter concludes with suggestions for future HDHP–HSA-related policies and presents some unanswered questions relevant to future research on this subject.

Background

In 1996 Congress made tax-favored medical savings accounts (MSAs)—a precursor to today's HSAs—available to the self-employed and workers of employers with 50 or fewer employees.[2] Like HSAs, MSAs had to be used in conjunction with an HDHP. MSAs were much more limited than HSAs. There were eligibility restrictions, and contributions could be made by either the employee or the employer, but not by both. Initially, insurers had little interest in these new plans. However, with the return of double-digit increases in private insurance premiums in 2001, policies with higher deductibles, greater cost sharing, and lower premiums began to attract attention from employers seeking to limit their spending on health benefits.[3]

As discussed by Jessica Vistnes, William Jack, and Arik Levinson in chapter 6, employers have also used flexible spending accounts (FSAs) to reduce employee's after-tax health care costs and soften the impact of benefit reductions.[4] FSAs can allow employees to use pretax dollars to pay for qualified health care services not covered by health insurance or health insurance premiums. FSAs need not be combined with an HDHP or, indeed, with any other health plan. Nonmedical withdrawals are not allowed, and any dollars remaining in the FSA at the end of the plan year are forfeited to the employer. Therefore, unlike HSAs, FSAs cannot be used as a savings vehicle.

Health reimbursement arrangements (HRAs), authorized by the IRS in 2002, provide another vehicle for employers to provide tax-free contributions for employees' health care expenses.[5] HRAs need not be accompanied by an HDHP and only can be funded by employer contributions. Withdrawals may be only for qualified medical expenses as defined by the employer. The employer owns the HRA account, and any unexpended funds remain with the employer when an employee leaves the job. Most HRAs do not generate investment income, since employers typically reimburse claims directly as a business expense.[6] Thus, in contrast to HSAs, HRAs do not allow the account holder to trade off health care spending against other forms of consumption. Participation in an HRA or FSA generally disqualifies an individual from contributing toward an HSA.

Individuals may contribute to an HSA only when covered by a qualifying HDHP, and they may not have any other health insurance coverage.[7] Contributions to HSAs made by individuals are deductible from their income for federal income tax purposes, but the contributions are generally not deductible from payroll taxes. In contrast, employer contributions to HSAs are excluded from the employee's income for federal income tax and employment tax (that is, Social Security, Medicare, and Federal Unemployment Tax Act) purposes. Unused funds in the HSA may accumulate and earn interest, dividends, or capital gains free of tax. Funds may be withdrawn tax free for qualified medical expenses of the individual who owns the HSA or of the spouse or dependent. Health insurance premiums may not be paid out of an HSA except in special circumstances.[8] Funds may be withdrawn from HSAs for nonqualified medical expenses, but such withdrawals are included in taxable income. Withdrawals before the age of 65 are also subject to a penalty unless the account holder is disabled. Unlike HRAs and FSAs, HSA withdrawals do not have to be substantiated to be recognized as qualified medical expenses.[9] Like IRAs, HSAs are owned by the individual and completely portable. However, unlike IRAs, the tax advantages of contributions to HSAs do not phase out as income increases. In addition, contributions, earnings, and medical withdrawals to HSAs may all occur without tax, unlike any other tax-preferred savings vehicle. (See chapter 5 by Henry Aaron, Patrick Healy, and Surachai Khitatrakun.)

The cost sharing features of HDHPs are intended to make individuals more sensitive to health care costs. Health insurance plans with higher deductibles have long been offered in the nongroup and small group health insurance markets.[10] However, HSAs introduced new tax advantages affecting the out-of-pocket expenditures related to these HDHPs. In 2008 individuals who own an HSA must be covered by a health plan with an annual deductible of at least $1,100 for single coverage and $2,500 for family coverage.[11] As discussed below, average deductibles among those holding HDHP–HSAs are substantially higher than those minimums. Proponents of HDHP–HSAs argue that providing individuals enrolled in these plans with information on health care costs and quality along with appropriate financial incentives will result in more efficient health care purchases relative to care purchased under plans with less cost sharing.[12]

The lower premiums of HDHPs relative to health insurance plans with lower cost sharing are also cited as an attractive feature of HDHP–HSAs.[13] HDHPs tend to have lower premiums than more comprehensive insurance plans because they cover a smaller share of health care expenditures than traditional insurance. However, the premium savings might be limited for two reasons. First, while claims processing is reduced for HDHPs because a larger proportion of insured do not reach the deductible, administrative "loading" costs, which include the costs of administering and marketing health insurance plans, will not fall proportionately with benefits.[14] Second, some plans cover routine preventive services for enrollees before their spending reaches the deductible, so the expected cost of these services will be included in premiums. However, two other factors would tend to result in larger premium reductions. First, by increasing the out-of-pocket price paid by many patients, medical spending may fall. A second and less obvious reason that HDHPs tend to have lower premiums is that they tend to attract healthy people who expect to have low medical expenses. Because health insurance premiums are based on enrollees' underlying expected health care costs, a plan that attracts a lower-cost population would generally have lower premiums than one that attracts a higher-cost population, even if the cost sharing and covered benefits were identical.[15]

The tax law limits several other features of HDHP–HSAs. In 2008 annual out-of-pocket liability for deductibles and other health care expenses in HDHP–HSAs were limited to $5,600 for single coverage and $11,200 for family coverage. These annual out-of-pocket maximums apply only to health spending on covered benefits (that is, health expenses deemed to be reimbursable based on a plan's benefit design) that are received from a provider (for example, a physician or a hospital) within the plan's provider network.[16] The maximum annual HSA contribution is limited to $2,900 for single coverage and $5,800 for family coverage in 2008. Before 2007, IRS regulations stipulated that contributions to HSAs could not exceed the HDHP deductible. But under current law, an individual enrolling in an HSA-qualified HDHP has no tax incentive to choose a higher deductible than the minimum required. To encourage savings for health expenses after retirement, individuals who are aged 55 and older are allowed to make additional "catch-up" contributions. As noted, certain preventive medical benefits may be covered before the deductible is met. Those benefits include periodic health evaluations, routine prenatal and well-child care, immunizations, tobacco cessation programs, obesity weight loss programs, and certain screening services.[17]

HSA advocates have proposed numerous other changes to make HDHP–HSAs more attractive.[18] Proposals include providing an income tax deduction for premiums paid for HDHPs purchased in the nongroup market, expanding the definition of HSA-qualifying HDHPs to include plans with a 50 percent or more coinsurance requirement, and allowing larger employer contributions to HSAs of employees who are chronically ill or who have a spouse or dependent who is chronically ill.

Description and Trends of HDHP–HSAs

Although HSAs have been available since 2004, there are no nationally representative data on who is offered an HDHP–HSA, who is enrolled, and what the features of the plans and accounts are. Nevertheless, the available data suggest that HDHP–HSAs constitute a small share of the health insurance market. For some groups, the offer of and enrollment in HDHP–HSAs may have increased slightly between 2006 and 2007, but overall, firms' offers and enrollments in HDHP–HSAs appear to be stable. This section of the paper reviews recent data reflecting offer of, enrollment in, and features of HDHP–HSA plans.

Offer in the Group Market

In 2006 surveys suggested that the percentage of employers offering HSA-qualified HDHPs would increase significantly in the coming year, particularly among large employers. In 2006, 4 percent of firms not offering an HDHP–HSA reported that they were "very likely" to offer an HDHP–HSA the next year. An additional 19 percent reported that they were "somewhat likely" to offer an HDHP–HSA. Eleven percent of firms with 5,000 or more workers that did not offer an HDHP–HSA reported that they were "very likely" to offer an HDHP–HSA the next year.[19]

However, those intentions appear to have been unrealized. Among all firms offering health insurance, 7 percent offered an HDHP–HSA in 2007, which was not statistically different from the previous year's rate of 6 percent (table 4-1).[20] At the same time, there was a statistically significant increase in the rate of medium-size firms (those with 200 to 999 employees) offering an HDHP with either an HSA or an HRA, from 5 percent in 2006 to 13 percent.[21] In 2007 less than one-fifth of employees enrolled in their employer's offer of ESI worked in firms that offered an HDHP with either an HSA or an HRA, but this statistic varies by firm size.[22] Among firms with 5,000 or more employees, 25 percent of covered employees worked in firms that offered an HDHP with either an HSA or an HRA compared with 12 percent of covered employees in firms with 3 to 99 employees offering similar plans.[23]

Enrollment in the Group and Nongroup Markets

Overall, enrollment in group HDHP–HSAs appears to be relatively flat between 2006 and 2007.[24] In 2007, 5 percent of covered employees were enrolled in HDHPs with either an HSA or an HRA, which was not statistically different from the previous year (table 4-1).[25] Small firms are less likely to offer these types of plans than are large firms; however, employees in small firms are more likely to opt for an HDHP–HSA if offered that option. Eight percent of covered workers

Table 4-1. *Summary of Offers of an HDHP–HSA and Enrollment Data, 2007*
Among offering firms[a]

Percentage of firms offering HSA-qualified HDHP	
All firm sizes	7
Percentage of firms offering an HDHP with an HSA or HRA[b]	
3–199 workers	10
200–999 workers	13*
1,000 or more workers[c]	18
Percentage of covered workers in firms that offer an HDHP with an HSA or HRA[d]	
All firm sizes	18
3–199 workers	12
200–999 workers	13
1,000–4,999 workers	20
5,000 or more workers	20

Enrollment[a]

Percentage of workers enrolling in an HDHP with an HSA or HRA, among covered workers[a]	
All firm sizes	5
Small firms: 3–199 workers	8[d]
Large firms: 200 or more workers	4[d]
Number of covered workers enrolled in an HSA-qualified HDHP[a]	
Covered workers	1.9 million
Number of enrollees (including family members) in an HSA-qualified HDHP[e]	
Group enrollees	3.4 million
Nongroup enrollees	1.1 million

*Estimate is statistically different from estimate for previous year shown ($p < .05$).

a. Henry J. Kaiser Family Foundation and Health Research and Educational Trust (Kaiser–HRET), *Employer Health Benefits, 2007 Annual Survey* (Menlo Park, Calif., and Chicago, 2007), exhibits 4.3, 4.4, 5.1, 5.2, and 8.3.

b. These data must be interpreted with caution as the characteristics of HSAs and HRAs differ substantially, as noted in the chapter. Among offering firms in 2007, 3 percent offer an HPHP–HRA.

c. Additional statistics are available for firms within this size. The percentage of firms offering an HDHP with an HSA or HRA, among offering firms in 2007, was 17 percent among firms with 1,000–4,999 workers and 22 percent among firms with 5,000 or more workers. Tests for statistical significance of differences from the estimate for the previous year were not shown for these firm size categories.

d. Test of statistical difference from estimate for previous year is not available.

e. America's Health Insurance Plans (AHIP), "January 2007 Census Shows 4.5 Million People Covered by HSA/High-Deductible Health Plans" (Washington: AHIP, Center for Policy and Research, April 2007) (www.ahipresearch.org/PDFs/FINAL%20AHIP_HSAReport.pdf).

in small firms (those with 3 to 199 employees) enrolled in an HDHP with either an HSA or an HRA, while only 4 percent of covered employees at large firms (those with 200 or more employees) did so.[26] This may be in part because small firms are much more likely than large firms to offer just one plan type. Thus, when a small firm offers an HDHP with either an HSA or an HRA, it is often the only option.

In 2007 approximately 1.9 million covered workers were enrolled in an HDHP–HSA.[27] Including dependents, the group market had approximately 3.4 million people enrolled.[28] Among all enrollees in HDHP–HSAs in the group and nongroup markets, those in firms of more than 50 employees may account for nearly half (49 percent) of all enrollees.[29] Empirical evidence regarding the characteristics of those enrolling in HDHP–HSAs is scant.[30] However, several studies show that enrollees in HDHPs (with or without a savings option) are healthier and have higher incomes on average than those enrolling in more comprehensive plans.[31] In 2007 approximately 1.1 million people were enrolled in HDHP–HSAs in the nongroup market.[32] Available evidence suggests that most early purchasers of HDHP–HSAs in the nongroup market had moderate to high incomes.[33] In 2005 tax filers who reported having an HSA or who were enrolled in certain HSA-eligible plans had an average adjusted gross income of $139,000 compared with $57,000 for enrollees in traditional insurance plans.[34]

HDHP–HSA Benefit Packages in the Group and Nongroup Markets

In the group market, average premium levels and cost sharing features of HDHP–HSA plans differ from those of a more traditional health insurance plan, as shown in table 4-2. Average annual premiums (including employee and employer shares) for single and family coverage in HDHP–HSAs are lower than premiums of those enrolled in Preferred Provider Organization (PPO) plans, the leading plan type, which covers approximately 57 percent of insured workers.[35] Average plan deductibles for employees enrolled in HDHP–HSAs are substantially above the statutory minimum for HSA-qualifying HDHPs.[36] In fact, 33 percent of employees enrolled in family coverage HDHP–HSA plans had a deductible of more than $5,000.[37] The annual plan averages for maximum out-of-pocket liability were substantially lower than the allowed maximums. For prescription drug benefits, workers enrolled in an HDHP with an HSA or HRA are more likely than those enrolled in other plans to face the same cost sharing expenses for all drugs regardless of the type, whereas other plans are more likely to tier cost sharing according to whether the drug is classified as a generic or a preferred drug.[38] Fourteen percent of employees enrolled in an HSA-qualified HDHP do not receive coverage for preventive health care benefits before their out-of-pocket health expenditures exceed the deductible.[39]

In the nongroup market, the extent to which average premium levels reflect the types of risks enrolled as opposed to the cost sharing features of the plan is unclear. In the nongroup market, premiums are based mostly upon premium rating regulations, guaranteed issue rules, and benefit packages. These factors vary across states and determine the risk characteristics of those enrolling in each nongroup market. Because of these complexities, average premiums among those enrolled in HDHP–HSAs in the nongroup market belie the tremendous premium variation faced by individuals and families. Compared with HDHP–HSAs in the group market, HDHP–HSAs in the nongroup market may have similar out-of-pocket maximum liability but higher deductibles.[40] In addition, a larger share (41 percent) of nongroup enrollees in an HSA-qualified HDHP do not receive coverage for preventive health care benefits before their out-of-pocket health expenditures exceed the deductible compared with 14 percent or less of those enrolled in HSA-qualified HDHPs through the group market.[41]

Contributions to HSAs

Despite the tax subsidies, many enrollees in HSA-qualified HDHPs do not have HSAs. Between 2005 and 2007, 40 to 50 percent of participants did not open an HSA account.[42] In 2007, 66 percent of employers offering single coverage and 47 percent offering family coverage through an HDHP–HSA did not contribute to the HSA account.[43] Among those employers who did contribute, employer contributions to HSAs averaged $806 for single coverage and $1,294 for family coverage (see table 4-2).

An analysis of tax return data reflecting the average deductions for HSA contributions in 2004 shows that when HDHP–HSAs were purchased primarily through the nongroup market, about 45 percent of tax filers reported no HSA contributions. Those filers that did report an HSA contribution reported an average contribution of $2,100.[44] Higher-income taxpayers contributed more than those with lower incomes. Another survey reported that 69 percent of those holding an HSA in 2006 had account balances of less than $1,000, while 12 percent had account balances of more than $2,500.[45]

Effect of HDHP–HSAs on Costs and Service Use

Historically, health care expenditures have grown faster than GDP—a trend that is expected to continue.[46] Although technological advances in diagnosis and treatment of medical conditions are generally acknowledged to be the main drivers of increased growth in health expenditures, the structure of cost sharing in health insurance plans can affect the amount of health services used.[47] Com-

Table 4-2. *Summary of Average HDHP–HSA Benefit Package in the Group Market Compared with 2007 Statute Limitations and PPOs, 2007*[a]

2007 dollars

Plan type	Total annual premium		In-network deductible		Maximum annual out-of-pocket liability		Firm contribution to HSA when more than $0	
	Single	Family	Single	Family	Single	Family	Single	Family
2007 limits for HSA-qualifying HDHP	...	...	> 1,100	> 2,200	< 5,500	< 11,000	...	...
HDHP–HSA	3,826	9,666	1,923	3,883	3,090	6,505	806	1,294
Preferred Provider Organization (PPO)								
Small firms (3–199 workers)	4,881	12,219	667	1,419	n.a.	n.a.	...	...
Large firms (200 or more workers)	4,546	12,525	382	899	n.a.	n.a.	...	...

Sources: Henry J. Kaiser Family Foundation and Health Research and Educational Trust (Kaiser–HRET), *Employer Health Benefits, 2007 Annual Survey* (Menlo Park, Calif. and Chicago, 2007); Department of the Treasury, "General Explanations of the Administration's Fiscal Year 2008 Revenue Proposals."

n.a. Not available.

... Not applicable.

a. PPOs cover about 57 percent of covered workers. Nongroup HDHP–HSAs may have similar maximum out-of-pocket expenses but higher deductibles.

prehensive health insurance plans make most care appear very inexpensive or even free to participants. Thus people may consume health services even if their benefit is far less than the actual cost.[48] Proponents of HDHP–HSAs argue that expanding enrollment in high-deductible plans would provide individuals a greater incentive to be prudent purchasers of health care, which would reduce medical spending.[49] Since out-of-pocket medical spending paid out of an HSA receives the same tax subsidy as contributions to health insurance, high-deductible plans are no longer tax penalized relative to more comprehensive health insurance policies.

This section of the paper reviews existing literature and presents descriptive statistics to describe the potential effects of HDHP–HSAs on health care spending and use of health care services.

Effects of HDHPs and HDHP–HSAs on Health Care Spending

Theory and evidence suggest that health insurance plans with higher deductibles should lower health spending in relation to spending under plans with lower deductibles. The RAND Health Insurance Experiment (HIE), conducted between 1974 and 1982, showed that spending was lower when consumers faced higher cost sharing.[50] Families with a deductible of up to approximately $6,000 (in 2004 dollars) used 25 to 30 percent fewer services than those in the free-care plan.[51] On the basis of the HIE and other studies, some researchers suggest that HDHP–HSAs could produce cost savings of between 2 and 7 percent compared with spending under traditional insurance.[52] In addition, recent empirical evidence indicates that people enrolled in an HDHP with a health spending account may have lower total health spending than those in traditional PPOs, but they may spend more than those enrolled in Health Maintenance Organizations (HMOs), after controlling for a variety of characteristics including illness burden and income.[53]

Cost savings due to high-deductible plans studied in the RAND HIE study came through two different routes: a reduction in services used per episode of care and a reduction in the number of episodes of care.[54] The reduction in services used in an episode of care came primarily from an increase in the marginal price of care, while the reduction in the number of episodes came primarily from an increase in the average price of care.

Potential reductions in total health care spending from switching coverage from a traditional plan to a high-deductible plan depend on the distribution of an individual's health care expenses relative to each plan's deductible and out-of-pocket liability. For people spending less than traditional low deductibles, there is little incentive to reduce spending. For those whose expenses fall between traditional low deductibles and a high deductible, the increase in the marginal cost of out-of-pocket spending under the high-deductible plan may provide incentives to curtail unnecessary use of services and to seek out lower-cost care.

For seriously ill individuals with medical costs that exceed the high deductible, out-of-pocket financial burdens may increase or decrease under the high-deductible plan relative to the traditional plan, depending on the maximum out-of-pocket liabilities in the traditional and high-deductible plans. If maximum out-of-pocket liabilities are substantially higher under the high-deductible plan, financial burdens may be larger, particularly for chronically ill individuals who repeatedly reach the maximum out-of-pocket financial liability. Moreover, for people with high medical costs, the lower premiums associated with less generous plans such as HDHPs may not offset the increased out-of-pocket liability. This is particularly true if premiums vary with an individual's characteristics, such as health and age, as is common in the nongroup market.

Seriously ill individuals enrolled in a high-deductible plan may reduce their health care spending somewhat in relation to a seriously ill person's spending under a more comprehensive plan. But these savings may come with adverse health outcomes; the RAND HIE found that people who were in worse health cut spending in ways that harmed their health. Spending reductions came from a reduction in the number of episodes of their care (for example, fewer doctor visits) rather than a cost savings through curtailing unnecessary services. For these individuals, managed care techniques may be more effective in constraining costs without causing adverse health effects.

Since very ill patients account for most health care spending, large systemwide cost savings will require curtailing their spending, an area in which HDHP–HSAs fall short. Table 4-3 shows total health care expenses for nonelderly, single individuals (adults aged 19 to 64 with no other family member) under the assumption that they have health insurance through a simulated single policy HDHP.[55] This simulated health insurance is a single coverage plan with a "high" deductible of $2,500, coinsurance of 20 percent, and a maximum annual out-of-pocket liability of $3,500. Total health care expenses include out-of-pocket and insured costs. While 78.7 percent of individuals have total health care expenditures below the high deductible of $2,500, their expenditures accounted for just 12.3 percent of total expenditures for this group. Those individuals whose total spending exceeded the high deductible accounted for 87.7 percent of total expenditures.[56] Since the vast majority of health care costs are associated with spending that exceeds the average high deductibles associated with HSA-qualified HDHPs, increasing the marginal price of care through a higher deductible is likely to have a modest effect on total health spending. Significantly reining in spending through cost sharing would require increasing the average cost among the high spending enrollees who incur the majority of costs.

Table 4-3. *Total Health Care Expenses, in Relation to the Deductible, for Insured Nonelderly Individuals*[a]

HDHP: typical "high" deductible (dollars)[b]	2,500
HDHP: typical coinsurance (percent)	20
HDHP: typical maximum out-of-pocket liability (dollars)	3,500
Number of individuals deemed to be candidates for a single policy (millions)	61.1
Total health care expenditures if insured through the typical single HDHP (billions of dollars)	186.5
Single policy candidates with total health care expenditures less than the deductible	
Share of single policy candidates (percent)	78.7
Average health care expenditures (dollars)	477
Percentage of total health care expenditures	12.3
Single policy candidates with total health care expenditures more than the deductible	
Share of single policy candidates (percent)	21.3
Average health care expenditures (dollars)	12,592
Percentage of total health care expenditures	87.7

Source: Estimates are based on Lisa Clemans-Cope and others, "The Health Insurance Policy Simulation Model (HIPSM, Version 1): Overview and Technical Documentation" (Washington: Urban Institute, 2008).

a. Individuals are deemed candidates for single coverage in an HDHP plan in this table if they are a nonelderly adult (aged 19–64) with no other family member. Health care expenses include out-of-pocket and insured costs, assuming enrollment in a simulated typical HDHP single policy (as outlined in the table). All dollars are in 2008 values.

b. The HDHP–HSA policy deductibles are slightly higher than those reported in the Kaiser–HRET for group policies. They are intended to reflect average annual deductibles in the nongroup market, as reported in America's Health Insurance Plans (AHIP), "January 2007 Census Shows 4.5 Million People Covered by HSA/High-Deductible Health Plans" (Washington: AHIP, Center for Policy and Research, April 2007).

Effects of HSAs on Health Care Spending

HSAs might have different effects on health care spending in the short run than over the long run. In the shorter term, David Richardson and Jason Seligman argued that health care spending could increase, since the after-tax cost of certain expenditures below the deductible of HDHP–HSA plans could be significantly reduced compared with these costs under traditional plans.[57] In addition, some health expenses qualify for tax-free HSA withdrawals that are not covered under most traditional health insurance plans, such as eyeglasses, acupuncture, and some nonprescription medicine.[58] However, Richardson and Seligman do not consider that HDHP–HSA enrollees often have an incentive to allow some or all HSA balances to accumulate as a tax-sheltered savings vehicle.[59]

If enrollees simply use their HSA accounts as a savings vehicle over the longer term, HSA-related incentives may not affect the distribution of costs between premium and out-of-pocket components relative to costs in an HDHP without an HSA. Some data support this view; in 2005 average contributions to HSAs were more than twice as much as average withdrawals, and 41 percent of those contributing to an HSA did not withdraw any funds over the course of a year.[60] Still, for some, the presence of a savings account combined with a high-deductible plan may mitigate reductions in health care spending that would have been achieved under an HDHP without an HSA, because some individuals may consider funds in an HSA account as allocated for current health spending as opposed to potential long-term savings or savings for future health spending.

Potential for HDHP–HSA Enrollees to Shop Around for Services

To some extent, the potential for HDHP–HSAs to affect total health costs also relies on whether patients can shop around or bargain with providers over prices for health care services, but opportunities are limited. The Center for Studying Health System Change investigated experiences regarding consumer shopping for health services, including the market for LASIK eye surgery, and found that unless the service is nonurgent, is relatively uniform in quality across providers, and involves relatively little medical judgment as to diagnosis, consumer shopping showed little potential to reduce costs.[61] Adding to the difficulty, some providers report that when patients request prices for health services, confidentiality agreements with payers prevent providers from supplying actual prices, and the price ranges that they give may be wide.[62]

Effects of HDHP–HSAs on Service Use

As described above, a particular concern is whether spending reductions in responses to a high deductible come from eliminating excessive and unwarranted care or from eliminating health-enhancing care. Although Paul Fronstin and Sara Collins reported that people enrolled in an HDHP with or without a health spending account used health services at a similar rate as people enrolled in more comprehensive plans, they as well as Karen Davis, Michelle Doty, and Alice Ho found that HDHP enrollees were much more likely to report that they missed or delayed health care or did not fill a prescription because of costs and that these problems were exacerbated for people with lower incomes or those in worse health.[63] More recently, John Rowe and others found that people enrolled in a high-deductible health insurance plan with a health spending account use preventive services at approximately the same rates as those enrolled in PPOs.[64]

Effects of HDHP–HSAs on Coverage in the Group and Nongroup Health Insurance Markets

Enrollment in group or nongroup HDHP–HSAs and the resulting effects on the markets and coverages depends on the extent to which potential enrollees value the tax advantages of HSAs in relation to alternative health insurance options or being uninsured. This section will begin with a discussion of these trade-offs for individuals and families with different characteristics such as differing tax rates, current health insurance coverage, and expected costs of health insurance under alternative plans. Next, this section discusses the potential effects of increased employer offers of high-deductible plans such as HDHP–HSAs and the effects of HDHP–HSAs in the nongroup market, including the potential for adverse selection in the group market and issues that affect coverage through the nongroup market.

Potential Tax Advantages of HDHP–HSAs for the Currently Uninsured

Total enrollment in HDHP–HSAs—estimated to be about 4.5 million in 2007, which includes the group and nongroup markets—is small, particularly when compared with the number of uninsured, estimated to be approximately ten times larger. Thus the impact of HDHP–HSAs on the number of uninsured has been relatively small so far. This may be due in part to the fact that the currently uninsured are disproportionately low income and benefit relatively little from the tax benefits available through HSAs. Table 4-4 shows that 69.8 percent of uninsured children and 70.0 percent of uninsured nonelderly adults—about 30.4 million people in all—have family incomes below 200 percent of the federal poverty level (FPL).[65] Table 4-4 also shows the distribution of the nonelderly population by the effective marginal tax rate (EMTR).[66] The uninsured are the most likely to have a zero or negative tax liability compared with those with private health insurance through ESI or nongroup policies. Fully 29.2 percent of uninsured children and 38.9 percent of uninsured adults have an EMTR of zero or less. Thus most of the currently uninsured would obtain little tax benefit from contributing to an HSA. Moreover, a recent study by Paul Jacobs and Gary Claxton found that currently uninsured households have far fewer financial assets with which to absorb the potential out-of-pocket costs of an HSA-qualifying HDHP.[67] The authors found that only about half of the households with an uninsured family member had enough financial assets to afford a health insurance deductible of $1,000, which is less than the statutory minimum deductible for an HSA-qualifying HDHP covering a single individual.

Table 4-4. *Effective Marginal Income Tax Rates and Family Income as a Percentage of the Federal Poverty Level, by Health Insurance Status for Children and Nonelderly Adults*[a]

	All[b]		ESI		Uninsured	
	Millions	Percent	Millions	Percent	Millions	Percent
Effective marginal income tax rate (percent)						
Children						
Zero or less	15.56	19.6	3.49	8.1	2.24	29.2
> 0–10	9.37	11.8	2.62	6.1	1.21	15.7
> 10–20	28.64	36.2	19.63	45.7	2.18	28.4
More than 20	25.62	32.4	17.18	40.0	2.06	26.8
All children	79.19	100.0	42.92	100.0	7.69	100.0
Adults						
Zero or less	39.61	21.8	11.18	9.8	13.93	38.9
> 0–10	10.69	5.9	4.41	3.8	3.73	10.4
> 10–20	74.70	41.0	53.43	46.7	12.42	34.7
More than 20	57.04	31.3	45.43	39.7	5.70	15.9
All adults	182.04	100.0	114.44	100.0	35.79	100.0
Family Income by percentage of federal poverty level (FPL)						
Children						
Less than 200 percent of FPL	37.06	46.8	10.64	24.8	5.37	69.8
200 percent of FPL or higher	42.13	53.2	32.28	75.2	2.32	30.2
All children	79.19	100.0	42.92	100.0	7.69	100.0
Adults						
Less than 200 percent of FPL	68.09	37.4	22.92	20.0	25.05	70.0
200 percent of FPL or higher	113.95	62.6	91.52	80.0	10.73	30.0
All adults	182.04	100.0	114.45	100.0	35.79	100.0

Source: Estimates are based on Lisa Clemans-Cope and others, "The Health Insurance Policy Simulation Model (HIPSM, Version 1): Overview and Technical Documentation" (Washington: Urban Institute, 2008).

ESI = employer-sponsored insurance; SCHIP = State Children's Healt Insurance Program.

a. These estimates are based on microdata that are a matched version of the March 2005 Current Population Survey (CPS) Annual Social and Economic Supplement (ASEC), the February 2005 CPS Contingent Work and Alternative Employment Supplement, and the 2004 Statistics of Income (SOI) public use tax file. The data have been weighted to reflect national rates of insurance in the most recent March CPS ASEC, data-year 2006, and have been adjusted to account for the undercount of Medicaid enrollees in the CPS. Income tax rates and family income by FPL are based on income as reported in the SOI.

b. "All" includes children and adults who are insured through ESI, the nongroup market, Medicaid and SCHIP, or other public insurance or who are uninsured.

Potential Effects of Increased Employer Offers of HDHP–HSAs

When employers offer a high-deductible plan in addition to a more comprehensive plan, employees sort themselves into the available plans on the basis of many criteria. Some employees who were previously uninsured because of high premium rates in comprehensive plans may now choose to purchase the HDHP or HDHP–HSA coverage. However, employees who currently decline an employer offer of ESI are more likely to have lower incomes and be less able to afford the cost sharing imposed by the high deductible. They also get little or no benefit from the tax advantages of an HSA.[68] Those employees who do enroll in the high-deductible option may include many with relatively low expected health expenditures. Retaining enrollment of price-sensitive individuals or healthy ones or both in the high-deductible option may depend in part on successfully attracting other primarily healthy individuals to the plan and leaving less healthy individuals in a separate, more comprehensive health plan.

The rationale for combining healthy and less healthy people into the same health insurance risk pool is that it allows health care spending burdens to be spread more evenly across the population and over time. Most enrollees in a given health insurance plan are in good health and use fewer covered benefits in a given year than the population average uses. This allows the premium payments from those in better health to subsidize health care for those enrollees who have higher expenditures in that year.[69]

Among large employers who offer multiple plans, less healthy individuals tend to choose the more comprehensive plan and healthier individuals choose the less comprehensive plan—a phenomenon known as *adverse selection*. This sorting could cause premiums to escalate in the more comprehensive plan because its participants have higher health costs than average. This type of selection has been observed in several contexts. David Cutler and Sarah Reber described adverse selection at Harvard University when a less generous HMO health insurance plan option was added as an alternative to a more generous PPO health insurance plan.[70] While the less healthy university enrollees stayed in the more generous option, the healthier enrollees switched to the less generous option because of the lower premiums available in the HMO option. Eventually, because of the resulting health risk selection into the PPO or the HMO, the PPO premiums increased so much that the university dropped the more generous option. In another example of adverse selection, Len Burman reported that the Federal Employees Health Benefits Plan (FEHBP) dropped a slightly more generous low-deductible health insurance option after experiencing significant risk selection of healthier employees into the slightly less generous high-deductible option.[71] More recently, evidence arose suggesting adverse risk selection in enrollment for Medicare prescription drug plans.[72]

Some analysts forecast a slow erosion of employer-sponsored coverage due to adverse selection, which suggests that the introduction of high-deductible plans as a choice for employees may precipitate "the disappearance of generous plans, even if these plans had been operating efficiently."[73] Thus some individuals with insurance coverage may find that they are underinsured and have to bear a greater burden for their own health expenses, becoming vulnerable to a potentially large financial risk year after year.

Potential Effects of HDHP–HSAs in the Nongroup Market

Health insurance purchased directly from a health insurance carrier in the nongroup market can be an alternative to group insurance. Although the nongroup market has high administrative loads as opposed to the group market, the nongroup market has become a focus of attention among those studying mechanisms for expanding coverage, since the uninsured are primarily low-income individuals who do not have access to employer-sponsored health insurance. In 2005 approximately 70 percent of uninsured employees did not have access to an offer of insurance from their own or a family member's employer.[74] However, the nongroup market currently covers a small share of the population, and there is little evidence to suggest that the introduction of HSAs has substantially expanded this market.[75] Rates of enrollment in nongroup health insurance have been fairly flat between 2003 and 2006.[76] Furthermore, the low-income, currently uninsured population will continue to face financial barriers to enrollment because of the difficulty of paying for premiums for even the high-deductible plans and may also have difficulty meeting the cost sharing requirements, regardless of whether or not the plan has an HSA.

Moreover, some currently uninsured low-income individuals and families may have difficulty gaining offers in the nongroup market because of preexisting health problems, which are more prevalent among those with low incomes.[77] Nongroup health insurance markets in most states allow insurers to charge individually risk-adjusted premiums, which are based on an individual's characteristics such as medical history, age, gender, and credit score.[78] Premiums can often vary significantly on the basis of these factors.

Policies offering expanded tax preference to HDHP–HSAs purchased through the nongroup market may erode employer-based coverage, particularly among small firms who have individuals in poor health. Healthy workers in small firms with less healthy individuals may decline an offer of group coverage and instead obtain their coverage through an HDHP–HSA in the nongroup market. Group premiums for individuals left in the small group coverage—

some of whom cannot obtain offers in the nongroup market because of illness or other personal characteristics—may then increase dramatically, leading to decreases in offer and take-up rates in smaller firms.[79] Thus, while healthier small group employees may gain coverage, those who are less healthy may be uninsured at higher rates, particularly in the absence of nongroup reforms, such as regulations limiting medical underwriting.

Conclusion

There are numerous proposals that aim to expand enrollment in high-deductible health insurance plans with health savings accounts.[80] In the long term, the effect of HDHP–HSA plans on coverage and the character of health insurance plans depends on the features of the new policies implemented and on how employers and individuals respond. Previous research by Jonathan Gruber has found that proposals are more likely to reduce uninsurance when they are structured such that those who are currently least likely to purchase coverage (such as lower-income individuals) receive the greatest tax benefit, while those who are likely to purchase coverage even in the absence of a subsidy (the high-income individuals) receive little or no subsidy.[81] The tax advantages associated with current HDHP–HSAs, as well as many new proposals regarding the expansion of HDHP–HSAs, generally confer greater benefits to those who are higher income and thus likely to purchase health insurance even without HSA tax incentives.

The extent to which new policies to expand enrollment in HDHP–HSAs will cause adverse selection in the group market is related to how many employers offer a choice of health insurance plans and patterns of enrollment. In the long run, coverage expansions gained through increased enrollment in HDHP–HSAs must be weighed against the problems of adverse selection and adverse health outcomes from inappropriate health service use in response to increased cost sharing, both of which may have a relatively larger impact on low-income and less healthy individuals.

In addition, policymakers should consider options for policies concerning HDHP–HSAs that may be useful in addressing adverse consequences for low-income or less healthy individuals. One issue is that HSA-qualifying HDHPs leave low-income and less healthy individuals liable for potentially large financial burdens. Developing alternative policies that allow income-related cost sharing (for example, lower deductibles for those with lower incomes) would help address this issue. Another issue is the recent change toward a fixed statutory limit for the maximum annual HSA contribution, rather than a maximum contribution based on the deductible amount. This has undermined cost containment incentives by eliminating the incentive of enrollees to choose a higher deductible than the minimum required.[82] In addition, the change to a fixed maximum contribution is most beneficial to higher-income enrollees, who would be most likely to contribute the maximum contribution to their HSA, and these individuals are unlikely to require extra inducements to gain health insurance.

Most important, before policies that include expanded tax preferences for HDHP–HSAs are undertaken, policymakers need a clearer understanding of the trade-offs. How large are the tax savings relative to the premium and out-of-pocket expenditures under alternative health insurance plans, and how much do they vary by income and health status? To what extent are these tax savings a cost to the government? To what extent are these tax savings similar to what an individual would have received through a traditional plan in the group market? Are there better options for pooling risk and increasing cost containment? Answering these questions will be a focus for policy-related research in the future.

Notes

1. Elizabeth Purcell and Shosanna Tanner, "Health Savings Accounts," Notice 2004-2 (Department of the Treasury, Internal Revenue Service, Office of Division Counsel/Associate Chief Counsel (Tax Exempt and Government Entities), January 12, 2004). "Section 1201 of the Medicare Prescription Drug, Improvement, and Modernization Act of 2003, Pub. L. No. 108-173, added section 223 to the Internal Revenue Code to permit eligible individuals to establish Health Savings Accounts (HSAs) for taxable years beginning after December 31, 2003" (www.irs.gov/irb/2004-02_IRB/ar09.html).

2. The Health Insurance Portability and Accountability Act of 1996 added Internal Revenue Code, Section 220, which permitted eligible individuals to establish Archer MSAs.

3. V. Goff, "Consumer Cost Sharing in Private Health Insurance: On the Threshold of Change," NHPF Issue Brief 798 (George Washington University, 2004).

4. Paul Fronstin, "Health Savings Accounts and Other Account-Based Health Plans," Issue Brief 273 (Washington: Employment Benefit Research Institute, 2004).

5. IRS Revenue Ruling 2002-41 and Notice 2002-45, Health Reimbursement Arrangements, *Internal Revenue Bulletin* 2002-28 (IRS, July 15, 2002).

6. Scott Weltz and Shelley Brandel, "Alphabet Soup: HSAs, HRAs, and MSAs," client *notes* 1 (2004) (Seattle, Wash.: Milliman USA, Inc.) (www.milliman.com/expertise/healthcare/publications/cc/index.php). However, an HRA may generate investment income if funded through a voluntary employee's beneficiary association (VEBA) trust, under Internal Revenue Code section 501(c)(9).

7. The Internal Revenue Service (IRS) allows some additional employer health benefits such as discount cards for certain prescription drugs. See Diane Weber, "Getting around the Limits of an HSA," Money Management Q&As (Medical Economics, August 18, 2006) (http://medicaleconomics.modernmedicine.com/).

8. IRS guidelines state that HSA funds may be used to pay health insurance premiums when an individual is collecting federal or state unemployment benefits or has health insur-

ance coverage through COBRA with a former employer. HSA funds may be used also to pay for premiums related to long-term care insurance. For individuals aged 65 and over, HSA funds can be used toward Medicare premiums or an individual's share of the premium related to employer-sponsored insurance coverage or both. See Department of the Treasury, "HSA Frequently Asked Questions" (Office of Public Affairs, March 14, 2006) (www.treas.gov/offices/public-affairs/hsa/faq_using.shtml#hsa8).

9. Legislation requiring substantiation of qualified HSA withdrawals was proposed by the House Committee on Ways and Means on April 9, 2008. See GovTrack.us, "H.R. 5719: Taxpayer Assistance and Simplification Act of 2008" (www.govtrack.us/congress/bill.xpd?bill=h110-5719).

10. J. Gabel and others, "Individual Insurance: How Much Financial Protection Does It Provide?" *Health Affairs* web exclusive (April 17, 2002): W172–W181 (http://content.healthaffairs.org/cgi/reprint/hlthaff.w2.172v1.pdf); Henry J. Kaiser Family Foundation and Health Research and Educational Trust (Kaiser–HRET), Employer Health Benefits Annual Survey, 2003–07 (www.kff.org/insurance/ehbs-archives.cfm). This is an annual national survey of private and public employers with three or more employees.

11. Department of the Treasury, *General Explanations of the Administration's Fiscal Year 2009 Revenue Proposals* (February 2008) (www.treas.gov/offices/tax-policy/library/bluebk08.pdf).

12. K. Baicker, W. H. Dow, and J. Wolfson, "Lowering the Barriers to Consumer-Directed Health Care: Responding to Concerns," *Health Affairs* 26, no. 5 (September–October 2007): 1328–332 (http://content.healthaffairs.org/cgi/reprint/26/5/1328.pdf).

13. Ibid.

14. M. V. Pauly and L. Nichols reported that marketing expenses account for the largest share of nongroup loading costs. See M. V. Pauly and L. Nichols, "The Nongroup Health Insurance Market: Short on Facts, Long on Opinions and Policy Disputes," *Health Affairs* web exclusive (October 23, 2002).

15. In addition, B. Fuchs and J. James pointed out that marketing may influence premium rates for new enrollees in HDHP–HSAs: Insurers may offer discounted premium rates to first-time customers to increase enrollment in new HDHP–HSA plans; however, these discounts may not persist. See B. Fuchs and J. James, "Health Savings Accounts: The Fundamentals," NHPF Background Paper (George Washington University, April 2005) (www.nhpf.org/pdfs_bp/BP_HSAs_04-11-05.pdf).

16. Services that count toward meeting the deductible may only include services that would otherwise be covered once the deductible has been met. Therefore, many HSA-qualified medical expenses may not count toward the deductible. For example, if a family purchases an HDHP–HSA policy in the nongroup market and chooses not to pay the extra premium costs for routine maternity care (also known as a maternity rider), health expenditures for maternity care may not count toward the deductible. In addition, under current law, the minimum deductible level and maximum out-of-pocket liability apply only to in-network health expenditures. As observed by E. Park, there is no statutory limit regarding maximum out-of-pocket liability for out-of-network health care expenditures. See E. Park, "Informing the Debate about Health Savings Accounts: An Examination of Some Misunderstood Issues" (Washington: Center on Budget and Policy Priorities, June 13, 2006) (http://www.cbpp.org/6-13-06health2.pdf).

17. Fuchs and James, "Health Savings Accounts: The Fundamentals"; IRS, "Health Savings Accounts and Other Tax-Favored Health Plans," Publication 969 (Department of the Treasury, 2005).

18. J. Rovner, "Bush Makes Push for Health Care Savings Plans," National Public Radio Online (February 8, 2006) (www.npr.org/templates/story/story.php?storyId=5179309); Fuchs and James, "Health Savings Accounts: The Fundamentals"; M. Feldstein, "Health and Taxes," *Wall Street Journal* Commentary (January 19, 2004).

19. Kaiser–HRET, Employer Health Benefits Annual Survey, 2006, exhibit 8.13 (www.kff.org/insurance/7527/upload/7527.pdf).

20. Kaiser–HRET, Employer Health Benefits Annual Survey, 2007 (http://www.kff.org/insurance/7672/upload/76723.pdf). In 2007 the Kaiser–HRET survey included responses from 3,078 firms, with 1,997 firms responding to the full survey. The survey had an overall response rate of 49 percent in 2007 and included a relatively small number of firms that offered HSAs. Thus the generalizability of their findings is limited. In addition, offer rates must be interpreted with caution, as survey authors report that "some employers report offering single but not family coverage." (See footnote 5, page 121.)

21. As discussed above, the characteristics of HSAs and HRAs differ substantially. In short, the HRA does not allow the account holder to trade off health care spending against other forms of consumption, which is a key advantage claimed for HSAs. Data reflecting HDHP with either an HSA or HRA (collected by the Kaiser–HRET Employer Health Benefits Annual Survey) defines a plan as having a *high* deductible when the deductible is $1,000 or more for single coverage and $2,000 or more for family coverage in 2007.

22. Kaiser–HRET, Employer Health Benefits Annual Survey, 2007.

23. Ibid.

24. Ibid.

25. Ibid.

26. Ibid.

27. Ibid.

28. America's Health Insurance Plans (AHIP), "January 2007 Census Shows 4.5 Million People Covered by HSA/High-Deductible Health Plans" (Washington: AHIP, Center for Policy and Research, April 2007) (www.ahipresearch.org/PDFs/FINAL%20AHIP_HSAReport.pdf). AHIP claims that "virtually all" companies that offer HDHP–HSAs participated in the survey. Although AHIP also conducted this survey in 2006, no definitive comparisons can be assessed between the two years since the January 2006 survey could not distinguish between nongroup, small group, and large group for approximately 1 million enrollees.

29. This statistic should be interpreted with caution. The authors of the AHIP study note that the survey that produced this statistic categorizes enrollees by firm size according to each insurer's own definition of small or large firms, where *large firms* were generally those with more than 50 employees. In addition, some insurers did not report enrollment separately by firm size.

30. E. Park and R. Greenstein, "Latest Enrollment Data Still Fail to Dispel Concerns about Health Savings Accounts," revised (Washington: Center on Budget and Policy Priorities, January 30, 2006) (www.cbpp.org/10-26-05health2.pdf).

31. Paul Fronstin and Sara R. Collins, "Early Experience with High-Deductible and Consumer-Driven Health Plans: Findings from the EBRI/Commonwealth Fund Consumerism in Health Care Survey" (Washington: Employee Benefit Research Institute and New York: Commonwealth Fund, December 2005); D. Plocher, C. Lai, and N. Garrett,

"Options Blue: Population Profile Analysis Working Paper" (Blue Cross and Blue Shield of Minnesota, November 30, 2005); Government Accountability Office (GAO), *Federal Employees Health Benefit Program: Early Experience with a Consumer-Directed Health Plan*, GAO-06-143 (November 2005).

32. AHIP, "January 2006 Census Shows 3.2 Million People Covered by HSA Plans" (Washington, March 9, 2006) (www.ahipresearch.org/pdfs/HSAHDHPReportJanuary2006.pdf); AHIP, "January 2007 Census Shows 4.5 Million People Covered by HSA/High-Deductible Health Plans." Because of inconsistencies between the 2006 and 2007 AHIP surveys, it is not possible to assess whether this constitutes an increase or a decrease over the 2006 number of nongroup enrollees.

33. eHealthInsurance, "Health Savings Accounts: The First Six Months of 2005" (July 25, 2005); Assurant Health, "Quick Facts: Health Savings Accounts" (Milwaukee, Wis.: September 16, 2005).

34. GAO, *Health Savings Accounts: Participation Increased and Was More Common among Individuals with Higher Incomes*, GAO-08-474R (April 1, 2008).

35. Kaiser–HRET, Employer Health Benefits Annual Survey, 2007.

36. IRS-defined minimum deductibles were unchanged between 2007 and 2008; similarly, plan averages for deductibles were virtually unchanged between the 2006 and 2007 Kaiser–HRET surveys. See also (www.treasury.gov/offices/tax-policy/library/bluebk07.pdf).

37. Kaiser–HRET, Employer Health Benefits Annual Survey, 2007.

38. Ibid.

39. Ibid.

40. AHIP, "January 2007 Census Shows 4.5 Million People Covered by HSA/High-Deductible Health Plans."

41. AHIP, "A Survey of Preventive Benefits in Health Savings Account (HSA) Plans, July 2007" (Washington, November 2007) (www.ahipresearch.org/pdfs/HSA_Preventive_Survey_Final.pdf); Kaiser–HRET, Employer Health Benefits Annual Survey, 2007.

42. GAO, *Health Savings Accounts: Participation Increased and Was More Common among Individuals with Higher Incomes.*

43. Kaiser–HRET, Employer Health Benefits Annual Survey, 2007.

44. GAO, *Consumer-Directed Health Plans* GAO-06-798 (August 2006) (www.gao.gov/new.items/d06798.pdf).

45. AHIP, "January 2007 Census Shows 4.5 Million People Covered by HSA/High-Deductible Health Plans." These figures were based on a relatively small sample of HDHP–HSAs enrollees.

46. J. A. Poisal and others, "Health Spending Projections through 2016: Modest Changes Obscure Part D's Impact," *Health Affairs* 26, no. 2 (2007): w242–w253.

47. T. Bodenheimer, "High and Rising Health Care Costs. Part 2: Technologic Innovation," *Annals of Internal Medicine* 142, no. 11 (2005): 932–37 (www.annals.org/cgi/reprint/142/11/932.pdf).

48. M. V. Pauly, "The Economics of Moral Hazard," *American Economic Review* 58, no. 3 (1968): 531–37; Richard J. Zeckhauser, "Medical Insurance: A Case Study of the Tradeoff between Risk Spreading and Appropriate Incentives," *Journal of Economic Theory* 2, no. 1 (1970): 10-26.

49. Baicker, Dow, and Wolfson, "Lowering the Barriers to Consumer-Directed Health Care: Responding to Concerns"; P. D. Mango and V. E. Riefberg, "Health Savings Accounts: Making Patients Better Consumers," *McKinsey Quarterly* (January 2005).

50. Joseph P. Newhouse and the Insurance Experiment Group, *Free for All? Lessons from the Rand Health Insurance Experiment* (Harvard University Press, 1993); Joseph P. Newhouse, "Consumer-Directed Health Plans and the RAND Health Insurance Experiment," *Health Affairs* 23, no. 6 (2004): 107–13.

51. Newhouse, "Consumer-Directed Health Plans and the RAND Health Insurance Experiment."

52. M. B. Buntin and others, "Consumer-Directed Health Plans: Implications for Health Care Quality and Cost," report prepared for the California HealthCare Foundation (Menlo Park, Calif.: RAND, June 2005). An important difference between the health plans offered in the RAND HIE and the current structure of HDHP–HSAs is that deductibles in the experiment were related to income: families were randomly assigned to have a maximum out-of-pocket liability of 5, 10, or 15 percent of income or of $1000, whichever was lower. Moreover, the HIE found that for people who were poor and less healthy, the reductions in use of health services had adverse effects on health, despite the income-related liability maximums. See also Newhouse, "Consumer-Directed Health Plans and the RAND Health Insurance Experiment."

53. S. T. Parente, R. Feldman, and J. B. Christianson, "Evaluation of the Effect of a Consumer-Driven Health Plan on Medical Care Expenditures and Utilization," *Health Services Research* 39, no. 4, part II (2004): 1189–210.

54. Newhouse, "Consumer-Directed Health Plans and the RAND Health Insurance Experiment."

55. Data are estimates based on Lisa Clemans-Cope and others, "The Health Insurance Policy Simulation Model (HIPSM, Version 1): Overview and Technical Documentation" (Washington: Urban Institute, 2008). The analysis presented here does not include simulated premiums.

56. In a similar analysis, Linda Blumberg and Len Burman (2004) estimated that 79 percent of all spending occurs above the minimum HSA-qualified HDHP deductible, and those whose spending exceeded these minimum deductibles incurred more than 95 percent of all spending (including spending above and below the deductible). See Linda Blumberg and Len Burman, "Most Households' Medical Expenses Exceed HSA Deductibles" (Washington: Urban Institute, August 16, 2004) (www.urban.org/url.cfm?ID=1000678).

57. David P. Richardson and Jason S. Seligman, "Health Savings Accounts: Will They Impact Markets?" *National Tax Journal* 60, no. 3 (September 2007): 455–67.

58. For tax filers who itemize deductions, health expenses in excess of 7.5 percent of adjusted gross income may be deducted from taxable income.

59. See chapter 5 by Henry J. Aaron, Patrick Healy, and Surachai Khitatrakun; S. T. Parente and R. Feldman, "Do HSA Choices Interact with Retirement Savings Decisions?" in *Tax Policy and the Economy*, edited by James M. Poterba, vol. 22 (MIT Press, 2008), pp. 81–108.

60. GAO, *Health Savings Accounts: Participation Increased and Was More Common among Individuals with Higher Incomes.*

61. P. Ginsburg, "Consumer Price Shopping in Health Care" (Washington: Center for Studying Health System Change, March 15, 2006). (Cited in E. Park, "Informing the Debate about Health Savings Accounts: An Examination of Some Misunderstood Issues.")

62. Healthcare Financial Management Association (HFMA) Executive Roundtable, "Health Savings Accounts: Are You Prepared?" (Westchester, Ill., December 2006). In addition, professional fees for certain medical staff may be an extra cost in addition to the proce-

dure price, such as fees for an anesthesiologist. These fees can be substantial and may vary according to the staff available at the time of the service.

63. Fronstin and Collins, "Early Experience with High-Deductible and Consumer-Driven Health Plans: Findings from the EBRI/Commonwealth Fund Consumerism in Health Care Survey"; Karen Davis, Michelle M. Doty, and Alice Ho, "How High Is Too High? Implications of High-Deductible Health Plans" (New York: Commonwealth Fund, April 2005).

64. John W. Rowe and others, "The Effect of Consumer-Directed Health Plans on the Use of Preventive and Chronic Illness Services," *Health Affairs* 27, no. 1 (January–February 2008): 113–20.

65. See notes to table 4-4. Estimates are based on Lisa Clemans-Cope and others, "The Health Insurance Policy Simulation Model (HIPSM, Version 1): Overview and Technical Documentation."

66. *Effective marginal tax rates* are defined as the additional federal income tax liability incurred if an individual's income were to increase by $1. Effective marginal tax rates differ from statutory marginal tax rates because of phase-ins and phase-outs of a variety of credits (such as the Earned Income Tax Credit) and deductions and because of the alternative minimum tax. See G. Leiserson, "Income Taxes and Tax Rates for Sample Families, 2006" (Washington: Urban Institute and Brookings, Tax Policy Center, December 2006) (www.taxpolicy-center.org/publications/url.cfm?ID=411402).

67. Paul D. Jacobs and Gary Claxton, "Comparing the Assets of Uninsured Households to Cost Sharing under High-Deductible Health Plans," *Health Affairs* web exclusive (April 15, 2008) (http://content.healthaffairs.org/cgi/reprint/hlthaff.27.3.w214v2 [April 15, 2008]).

68. Lisa Clemans-Cope and B. Garrett, "Changes in Employer-Sponsored Health Insurance Sponsorship, Eligibility, and Participation: 2001 to 2005" (Menlo Park, Calif.: Henry J. Kaiser Family Foundation, Kaiser Commission on Medicaid and the Uninsured, December 2006) (www.kff.org/uninsured/7599.cfm).

69. J. C. Robinson, "Reinvention of Health Insurance in the Consumer Era," *Journal of the American Medical Association* 291, no. 15 (2004): 1880–886.

70. David M. Cutler, and Sarah J. Reber, "Paying for Health Insurance: The Trade-Off between Competition and Adverse Selection," *Quarterly Journal of Economics* 113, no. 2 (May 1998): 433–66.

71. Len Burman, "Medical Savings Accounts and Adverse Selection" (Washington: Urban Institute, 1997).

72. S. Rubenstein, "Humana Cuts Forecast, Shares Tumble," *Wall Street Journal*, March 13, 2008 (http://s.wsj.net/article/SB120532620556430155.html).

73. Sherry A. Glied and D. K. Remler, "The Effect of Health Savings Accounts on Health Insurance Coverage" (New York: Commonwealth Fund, April 2005) (http://www.common-wealthfund.org/publications/publications_show.htm?doc_id=274002).

74. Lisa Clemans-Cope and B. Garrett (Urban Institute, 2006). Unpublished estimates are based on the February 2005 Contingent Work Supplement of the Current Population Survey (CPS) and the March 2005 Annual Social and Economic (ASEC) Supplement of the CPS.

75. Some had suggested that HDHP–HSAs in the nongroup market likely would be attractive to unhealthy individuals who usually reach or exceed out-of-pocket maximums. However, this phenomenon likely was limited sharply by two features of the nongroup market. First, in the nongroup markets, higher premiums can generally be charged for a given

plan to unhealthy individuals. Therefore, these nongroup carriers can segment unhealthy enrollees and avoid pooling their health expenses with healthier enrollees. Second, tight medical underwriting practices are nearly ubiquitous in the nongroup market, except in a small number of states. Research has shown that underwriting practices limit the availability of nongroup coverage offers for those with chronic conditions and that offers of coverage are affected by even mild medical conditions. See Pauly and Nichols, "The Nongroup Health Insurance Market: Short on Facts, Long on Opinions and Policy Disputes"; K. Pollitz, R. Sorian, and K. Thomas, "How Accessible is Individual Health Insurance for Consumers in Less-than-Perfect Health?" (Menlo Park, Calif.: Henry J Kaiser Family Foundation, June 2001) (www.kff.org/content/2001/20010620a/report.pdf). Since few states have guaranteed issue laws that would allow those in poor health to have open access to the nongroup market, it is likely that HSA-qualifying plans in the nongroup market will be limited to healthy individuals.

76. U.S. Census Bureau, Current Population Survey, Annual Social and Economic Supplements (2000–07) (www.census.gov/hhes/www/hlthins/historic/hihistt4.html).

77. Pollitz, Sorian, and Thomas, "How Accessible Is Individual Health Insurance for Consumers in Less-than-Perfect Health?" For a discussion of the relationship between income and health status, see, for example, J. Currie and W. Lin, "Chipping Away at Health: More on the Relationship between Income and Child Health," *Health Affairs* 26, no. 2 (March–April 2007): 331–44.

78. *Block underwriting*, used to produce rated premiums for selected groups of individuals in the nongroup market, is also used in the nongroup market to assess profit and to "evaluate the financial impact and risk characteristics of retained versus cancelled groups." Presentation from J. Gallasso of Actuarial Modeling, January 30, 2008 (jgalasso@actuarialmodeling.com).

79. Linda J. Blumberg, "Health Savings Accounts and Tax Preferences for High Deductible Policies Purchased in the Non-Group Market: Potential Impacts on Employer-Based Coverage in the Small Group Market," testimony before the House Small Business Committee, Subcommittee on Workforce, Empowerment and Government Programs, 108 Cong., 2 sess. (Washington: Urban Institute, March 18, 2004) (http://www.urban.org/url.cfm?ID=900696); Glied and Remler, "The Effect of Health Savings Accounts on Health Insurance Coverage."

80. For example, as of June 25, 2008, the 110th Congress had introduced seventy-six bills related to health savings accounts (thomas.loc.gov).

81. Jonathan Gruber, "Covering the Uninsured in the U.S.," Working Paper W13758 (Cambridge, Mass.: National Bureau of Economic Research, January 2008) (http://www.nber.org/papers/w13758.pdf).

82. In 2006 the maximum annual HSA contribution limit was changed to a fixed statutory limit for single and family coverage, with maximum annual contributions to HSAs in 2008 of $2,900 for single coverage and $5,800 for family coverage.

5

What's in a Name?
Are Health Savings Accounts Really
Health *Savings Accounts?*

HENRY J. AARON, PATRICK HEALY, AND SURACHAI KHITATRAKUN

ealth savings accounts (HSAs) are tax-sheltered savings instruments available to people under the age of 65 who buy high-deductible (HD) health insurance. Chapter 4, by Lisa Clemans-Cope, describes the origin of and rules governing HSAs. Together with high-deductible health insurance, HSAs compose *consumer-directed health care,* a strategy for revamping payment for financing medical services. The principal purpose of HSAs is to encourage and enable people to switch from low-deductible health insurance to plans that cover only large or catastrophic expenditures. Advocates also hope that reduced premiums as well as the tax advantages of HSAs will encourage the previously uninsured to buy coverage.

We do not evaluate whether encouraging people to shift to high-deductible insurance is a good or a bad idea. Rather, we focus on whether HSAs are well designed to encourage that shift. Our conclusion is that they are not. We begin by recounting the experience of one medium-size company that added to its menu of health insurance options a combination of high-deductible health insurance and HSAs. Although this new offering dominated the option most employees had previously used, fewer than half of those eligible actually took it. We then turn to an exposition of how a fully rational person behaving in an economically optimal manner should respond to HSAs. We conclude that in most circumstances such a rational economic decisionmaker should regard HSAs not as *health* savings accounts but as *super-retirement* savings accounts.[1] We show that HSAs have the greatest appeal to those in relatively high tax brackets, and

We thank Len Burman for extensive comments, analytical assistance, and corrections.

we compute the magnitude of those incentives. We return then to speculate on why the employees in the company described earlier did not enroll in what appeared to be a superior health insurance option. We conclude by sketching alternative incentives that we believe would be fairer and more effective than HSAs in encouraging enrollment in high-deductible plans.

Leaving Money on the Table

In 2007, four years after federal legislation authorized HSAs, coverage of HSA-eligible, high-deductible health insurance plans reached 4.5 million, just 2.6 percent of those with employment-based health insurance.[2] Of this total, 1.1 million enrolled as individuals, the remainder through group plans.[3] Roughly half of those eligible to open HSAs did not do so.[4] Owners of an HSA had incomes averaging more than twice that of the average tax filer. For somewhat more than half of all employees eligible for HSAs, employers contribute part of the allowed HSA deposit on behalf of the employee. The average employer contribution in 2007 was $428 for single coverage and $714 for those with family coverage.[5] Available data do not indicate what share of the difference between premiums for regular health insurance and high-deductible insurance these contributions represent.[6] What is clear, however, is that in nearly half of plans employers contribute nothing to their employees' HSAs.[7]

Will High-Deductible Health Plans with Health Savings Accounts Reduce Total Health Care Spending?

Previous research has shown that high-deductible insurance may or may not reduce total health care spending.[8] Taken in isolation, added cost sharing through the increased deductible tends to lower spending. But most HD plans have an out-of-pocket threshold after which insurance is nearly complete. Many low-deductible plans include significant cost sharing—copayments or coinsurance—above the deductible. The small fraction of catastrophic cases that breach the threshold dominate medical spending—approximately 5 percent of the population accounts for half of total health care spending.[9] Moreover, evidence suggests that this group may face *lower* average cost sharing under high-deductible plans than under ordinary health insurance.[10] Consequently, the prospect of a significant reduction in medical expenditures remains cloudy unless elected officials tolerate exposing patients to an increased share of current health outlays and patients are willing to accept that risk. The overall effect on spending of a shift from ordinary to high-deductible health insurance, therefore, depends on the composition of coverage and the pattern of health care spending in the covered population. Thus in some cases a shift from conventional to high-deductible insurance may not generate any savings for employers to share with employees.

In one class of cases, however, the shift to high-deductible coverage is certain to generate reduced premiums. This situation occurs when the employer raises the deductible but keeps coverage otherwise unchanged. In this case, premiums fall (at least in the short run) for two reasons: the number of claims by those with total spending below the increased deductible will fall, reducing both benefit payments and administrative costs, and the amount patients must pay for care will rise for at least some employees, leading to reduced use. Whether these near-term savings can be sustained is unclear. If employees forgo low-benefit care, savings are likely to endure. If they forgo high-benefit care, such as drug therapy to control blood sugar among diabetics, future medical expenditures may rise. Most high-deductible plans offer first-dollar coverage of preventive services with little or no cost sharing, and more than half offer those services without any maximum.[11] In these situations, overall health insurance costs may fall, permitting employers to deposit funds in their employees' HSAs and still save money. Depending on the design of the insurance plan, the amount deposited, and the pattern of health expenditures of the employee group, the employer's HSA deposit may more than offset the added out-of-pocket cost exposure of the employee. In such cases, both the employer and the employee may come out ahead financially.[12] The employer saves more in premiums than it contributes to the employee's HSA. And employees come out ahead financially because their out-of-pocket spending rises less than the amount that the employer deposits in their HSAs.

A Case Study—and a Puzzle

The experience of one mid-size company illustrates this possibility. It also indicates that most employees may choose to stay in conventional insurance even when it is not in their financial interest to do so.

The company had 666 employees eligible for health insurance benefits under a company plan in 2007 (see table 5-1). Most employees worked in either Washington, D.C., or Massachusetts. Employees in both sites could enroll in an HMO—Harvard Pilgrim Health Care in Massachusetts or Kaiser Permanente in Washington, D.C. Alternatively, employees in either site could enroll in a preferred provider plan (PPO) managed by Harvard Pilgrim under one of two cost sharing regimes. Under one PPO option, enrollees paid no deductible and modest copayments if they stayed within the PPO network and a modest deductible if they went out of network (see table 5-2). Under the other option they faced a deductible of $1,500 for single coverage and $3,000 for coverage of families or for single persons with one dependent. If employees chose the high-

Table 5-1. *Company Profile*

Employees eligible for health insurance				
Total	666			

Gender				
Male	428			
Female	238			

Location and plan enrollment	Massachusetts	Washington, D.C., area	Other	Plan total
Harvard/Pilgrim HMO	211	...	...	211
Harvard/Pilgrim PPO	47	56	16	119
Harvard/Pilgrim HSA/ HD PPO	47	53	12	112
Kaiser HMO	...	68	...	68
Aetna HMO	...	...	4	4
Total insured	305	177	32	514
Waived coverage	78	58	16	152
Location total	383	235	48	666

Compensation levels of plan enrollees				
Less than $50,000	135			
$50,000–99,999	246			
$100,000 or more	133			

... Not applicable.

deductible plan, the company deposited two-thirds of the deductible amount—$1,000 for single enrollees and $2,000 for families or single persons with one dependent—in an HSA. The two PPO plans covered the same services and the same network of providers. The premiums for both employees and the employer are shown in table 5-3. Table 5-1 shows the plans selected by the employees. No information is available on the use of health care services by enrollees or on saving behavior before the high-deductible HSA option became available at the start of 2005.

Employees had three choices to make.

—Should they waive coverage?

—If they accepted coverage, should they enroll in an HMO?

—If they chose not to enroll in the HMO, should they take conventional PPO coverage or high-deductible coverage?

Did employees answer these three questions sensibly? On the first two questions, we have too little information to judge. Under company policy, employees have to enroll in the company plan if they are not covered in some other way, for example, through the plan of a spouse or other relative. We have no data on the

Table 5-2. *Benefits under Conventional PPO and PPO HSA*

	Best Buy HSA PPO		PPO		HMO
	In-network	Out-of-network	In-network	Out-of-network	
Annual deductible	\$1,500 individual \$3,000 family		none	\$250 individual \$500 family	no
HSA contributions to offset deductible	individual: up to \$1,000 family: up to \$2,000 plus optional employee contributions (see HSA booklet for details)		none	none	none
Office visit copay	\$20[a] (for services that require a copay)	covered at 80 percent after deductible	\$20	deductible applies, then covered at 80 percent	\$15
Emergency room	covered at 100 percent after deductible	covered at 100 percent after deductible	\$50	\$50	\$50
Inpatient admission (IP)[b]	covered at 100 percent after deductible	covered at 80 percent after deductible	\$250	deductible applies, then covered at 80 percent subject to IP copayment	\$250
Outpatient surgery (OP)	covered at 100 percent after deductible	covered at 80 percent after deductible	\$250	deductible applies, then covered at 80 percent subject to OP copayment	\$250
Chiropractic coverage	yes, up to \$500 per year after deductible	yes, up to \$500 per year after deductible	yes, up to \$500 per year	yes, deductible applies, then covered	yes, up to \$500 per year

Benefit	Best Buy HSA PPO	($20 copay per visit)	at 80 percent, up to $500 per year	($15 copay per visit)
Outpatient mental health coverage[c]	covered at 100 percent after deductible. Best Buy HSA PPO members receive up to 24 visits per year, individual or group therapy	covered at 80 percent after deductible. individual therapy[d] up to 24 visits per year, $20 per visit; group therapy[d] up to 25 visits per year, $10 per visit	individual therapy[d] up to 24 visits per calendar year; deductible applies, then covered at 80 percent; group therapy[d] up to 25 visits per calendar year; deductible applies, then covered at 80 percent	individual therapy[d] up to 24 visits per year, $15 per visit; group therapy[d] up to 25 visits per year, $10 per visit
Prescription drugs (30-day retail)	Covered after deductible with these copayments: Retail — Tier 1 $10, Tier 2 $25, Tier 3 $40 Mail — Tier 1 $20, Tier 2 $50, Tier 3 $80	Retail — Tier 1 $10, Tier 2 $25, Tier 3 $40 Mail — Tier 1 $20, Tier 2 $50, Tier 3 $80	Retail — Tier 1 $10, Tier 2 $25, Tier 3 $40 Mail — Tier 1 $20, Tier 2 $50, Tier 3 $80	Retail — Tier 1 $10, Tier 2 $25, Tier 3 $40 Mail — Tier 1 $20, Tier 2 $50, Tier 3 $80
Annual out-of-pocket maximum	$3,000 individual $6,000 family	none	$2,000 individual $4,000 family	$2,000 individual $4,000 family

Source: Harvard Pilgrim HealthCare brochure (2007).

a. Some services are covered with a $20 copayment, such as routine physical exams, routine eye exams, and annual GYN exams. You may also receive some tests that are subject to the deductible during a preventive exam. Certain preventive services are covered in full, such as mammograms, pap smears, prostate screenings, and immunizations. Most services are subject to the deductible.

b. Please contact Harvard Pilgrim Member Services for information about inpatient care for Mental Health and Substance Abuse. Call 1-800-874-0817 (TTY: 1-800-637-8257).

c. No visit limits apply to outpatient mental health treatment for biologically based mental disorders, rape-related mental or emotional disorders, and nonbiologically based mental, behavioral, or emotional disorders for children and adolescents.

d. Combined maximum of individual and group therapy visits not to exceed 25 per calendar year.

Table 5-3. *Premiums: Individual and Company Shares*[a]
Dollars

Plan and family size	Biweekly rates based on salaries of								
	Less than $50,000			$50,000 to $99,999			More than $100,000		
	E	C	Total	E	C	Total	E	C	Total
Harvard Pilgrim PPO									
Individual	54.24	204.03	258.27	80.06	178.20	258.27	105.89	152.38	258.27
Family	146.35	550.54	696.89	216.03	480.85	696.89	285.72	411.16	696.89
Harvard Pilgrim HMO									
Individual	36.55	137.48	174.03	53.95	120.08	174.03	71.35	102.68	174.03
Family	98.67	371.17	469.84	145.65	324.19	469.84	192.64	277.21	469.84
Harvard Pilgrim Best Buy HSA PPO									
Individual	33.29	125.23	158.52	49.14	109.38	158.52	64.99	93.52	158.52
Individual + 1	66.58	250.45	317.03	98.28	218.75	317.03	129.98	187.05	317.03
Family	99.86	375.68	475.55	147.42	328.13	475.55	194.97	280.57	475.55
Kaiser									
Individual	29.43	110.73	140.16	43.45	96.71	140.16	57.47	82.69	140.16
Family	79.47	298.98	378.45	117.32	261.13	378.45	155.17	223.29	378.45
Aetna									
Individual	37.13	139.66	176.79	54.80	121.98	176.79	72.48	104.30	176.79
Family	100.89	379.56	480.45	148.94	331.51	480.45	196.99	283.47	480.45
Share	21	79		31	69		41	59	

E = employee cost; C = company cost.
a. Medical rates effective January 1, 2007.

nature of coverage of the 23 percent of employees who waived enrollment under this company's plan and, hence, whether it was a sensible choice. Nor do we have data on what considerations entered into the decision on whether or not to enroll in the HMO. Premiums for HMO enrollment in Massachusetts were lower than premiums for any other form of coverage and were only slightly higher than PPO coverage in the Washington area. But HMO and PPO coverage differs in many ways. What is clear is that far more employees in Massachusetts than in Washington, D.C.—55 percent compared with 29 percent—selected HMO coverage. The fact that the Harvard Pilgrim HMO was ranked as the top HMO in the nation, while the Washington Metropolitan Area Kaiser plan was ranked 93rd out of 250 rated plans, may explain this difference.[13]

On the third question, however, it is clear that slightly more than half of those who elected PPO coverage chose the conventional plan rather than the high-deductible HSA plan and that they made a costly, if not an irrational, decision. Regardless of total spending on health care, the out-of-pocket cost to patients was lower if they elected the high-deductible HSA option than if they took conventional coverage (see appendix tables 5A-1 and 5A-2). The amount the company deposited in employees' HSA accounts more than compensated each enrollee for the added out-of-pocket spending resulting from the higher front-end cost under the high-deductible plan. We return presently to consider why employees "left money on the table," something that wholly rational and fully informed people would not have done.

Homo Economicus Meets Health Savings Accounts

The term *health savings account* comprises a particular set of tax rules that apply to special savings accounts available only to those who buy high-deductible insurance. HSAs are triply tax exempt if withdrawals are used to pay for health care. First, HSA deposits are not subject to personal income tax (and, if funded through a cafeteria plan, to payroll tax). Second, investment earnings on these deposits are exempt from tax when earned. Third, withdrawals used for health care are untaxed.[14] Withdrawals used for nonhealth purposes are subject to ordinary income tax and a penalty tax, the same rules that apply to 401(k) plans or ordinary IRAs.[15] In 2008 those enrolled in high-deductible plans with single (or family) coverage are allowed to make contributions of up to $2,900 ($5,800 for family coverage) a year.[16]

The Certainty Case

What role should HSAs play in the saving and health expenditure plans of an "economically rational" household? We begin with the unrealistic assumptions

Table 5-4. *Tax Rate on Out-of-Pocket Health Care Spending Financed by $1 of Pretax Earnings Saved in Alternative Accounts and then Withdrawn*

Saving account	Current year health care spending	Health care spending in n years
Ordinary taxable savings	$1 - (t + t_w)$	$[1 - (t + t_w)][1 + r(1 - t)^n]$
		$[1 - (t + t_w)](1 + r)^n$ [if withdrawn after age 59½]
Tax-sheltered savings[a]	$1 - (t + t_w + t_p)$	$(1 - (t + t_w + t_p)(1 + r)^n$ [if withdrawn before age 59½]
		$(1 + r)^n$ [if withdrawn for health care at any age]
Health savings accounts	1	$(1 - t)(1 + r)^n$ [if withdrawn for nonhealth outlays after 65th birthday]
		$(1 - (t + t_p)(1 + r)^n$ [if withdrawn for nonhealth outlays before 65th birthday]

a. Ignores possible employer match to 401(k) deposits, which are not subject to payroll tax.

that a household is entirely certain about future income, health care spending, expenditures after retirement and after the age of 65, as well as the rate of return on savings, that tax rates remain constant, and that the saver is not subject to annual limits on an HSA and tax-sheltered saving. Such a household may save in any one of three ways: in ordinary taxable accounts in which deposits are made from after-tax income and investment earnings are subject to tax in the current year; tax-sheltered savings accounts (such as IRAs or 401(k)s) in which investment earnings are not taxed currently and either deposits or withdrawals are taxed; or HSAs in which deposits, investment earnings, and withdrawals for health purposes are all tax free.

Suppose that the household allocates $1 of pretax earnings to current or future health care spending through one of the three saving vehicles. Table 5-4 shows how much health care (or other expenditures) that $1 of pretax earnings will buy in the current year or *n* years in the future, where *r* is the rate of return on savings, and t, t_p, and t_w are the income tax rate, the penalty tax rate for early withdrawal from tax-sheltered accounts and HSAs, and the payroll tax rate, respectively. We ignore the important fact that many employers match employee contributions to 401(k)s. These matches take a wide variety of forms. If sufficiently generous, these employer-matched contributions can make 401(k)s more attractive than unmatched HSAs. Whether employers offer 401(k)s and on what terms depends in part on what employers think that their employees will find most attractive and in part on paternalistic motivations. In either case, the advent of HSAs should influence the 401(k) terms that an employer chooses to offer.[17] For example, an employer might drop a 401(k) plan and replace it with high-deductible insurance and an HSA to which it makes a matching contribution. This example illustrates that HSAs have created an inextricable linkage between pension and health care policies.

All out-of-pocket spending on health care should be financed through the HSA, because $1 of earnings buys more health care if it comes from an HSA than if it comes from any other source. The household should continue to save exclusively through HSA deposits as long as HSA balances are less than the discounted present value of current-year and future-year health care spending (up to the statutory limit on annual deposits). This policy is optimal because the tax treatment of out-of-pocket health care spending is more favorable if it is financed by withdrawals from an HSA than if it is financed in any other way. It is also more favorable than the tax treatment of earnings used for nonhealth consumption at any time, however financed. Paying for health care from an HSA avoids all tax, but paying for nonhealth care consumption from an HSA at any time does not avoid all tax.

If HSA balances exceed the discounted present value of current plus anticipated future health care spending, then additional saving should normally be done through tax-sheltered accounts. Tax on investment earnings is deferred in both cases, but withdrawals between the ages of 59 and a half and 65 for purposes other than health care spending are subject to a penalty tax of 10 percent, in addition to ordinary income tax, if drawn from HSAs but not if taken from tax-sheltered accounts. In fact, this penalty tax is one reason why it would make sense in some cases to save or to keep balances in ordinary taxable saving accounts, particularly if a person is near the age of 59 and a half and withdrawals from savings are considered likely. Other than situations where the present value of the penalty tax exceeds the present value of deferral, all saving beyond that permitted in an HSA should be done through tax-sheltered accounts, and any funds in taxable accounts should be moved to tax-sheltered accounts. Annual ceilings on deposits in tax-sheltered accounts and HSAs may prevent full use of this option. If the household can borrow at rates not greater than the investment yield on savings plus penalty tax on early withdrawals, it would be rational to borrow to avoid premature withdrawals altogether.

These observations lead to a number of simple saving rules. First, savings should in general be made through HSAs up to the allowable annual limit and next in tax-sheltered accounts up to the annual limit. Only if savings exceed the sum of these annual limits, or if the present value of penalty tax on early withdrawals is high enough, should savings be made in ordinary taxable savings accounts. Second, up to the point where the present expected value of penalty taxes on possible withdrawals becomes large enough, assets should be shifted from taxable savings accounts to HSAs or to sheltered accounts as expeditiously as possible. Third, withdrawals to pay for health care should be made from HSAs.

Qualifications because of Risk

Contrary to the assumptions in the preceding section, key elements in saving decisions are uncertain. These include uncertainties regarding future income and consumption requirements and, therefore, about the need to make premature withdrawals; the rate of return on saving; future tax rates; future out-of-pocket medical outlays; and retirement income requirements because of uncertain longevity. These factors create offsetting risks. For example, higher- or lower-than-anticipated out-of-pocket medical outlays during retirement would mean that HSA balances would be too small or too large to cover all such outlays. This risk may create the possibility of a welfare gain from saving more than expected future health outlays in HSAs and less in tax-sheltered accounts. The reasoning is that if health care expenses are larger than anticipated, having oversaved in HSAs will result in a tax saving. But if health care expenses are less than anticipated, HSA balances can be used for other consumption on the same terms as funds in tax-sheltered accounts. This creates the possibility of a welfare gain from saving in HSAs more than the discounted present value of expected future out-of-pocket medical expenses.[18] The possibility of an earlier-than-expected death means that funds already deposited in HSAs may end up not being used for health care outlays, leaving potential tax savings unrealized. This risk creates an incentive to pay for all out-of-pocket health care spending from HSAs as soon as possible. Thus it is rational to pay all out-of-pocket spending from HSAs but to maximize saving through HSAs and to build up balances larger than the present expected value of future out-of-pocket health care spending if it is possible to do so.

Limits on Tax-Sheltered Saving

Congress has set maximums on annual deposits to tax-sheltered accounts and HSAs. Few households save more than the sum of these limits in any year. For the small proportion that do, it is rational to divert spending from other consumption to pay for out-of-pocket health costs, rather than to use HSA balances. The reason is that the marginal value of consumption would be equated

Table 5-5. *Tax Credit on Taxable Savings Account*[a]

Deposit made to taxable savings account at n years before withdrawal	Tax rate		
	0 percent	*15 percent*	*30 percent*
40	7.65	41.93	64.93
30	7.65	38.05	60.09
20	7.65	33.46	53.91
10	7.65	28.52	46.78
1	7.65	23.2	38.54

a. Tax credit in the year of deposit to a taxable savings account that is necessary to produce an accumulation in year forty that is equal to that under a health savings account. Interest rate is 5 percent.

with marginal returns on *taxable* saving, $(1 - t - t_w)[1 + r(1 - t)]^n$, which is below the marginal return on balances in HSA accounts, $(1 + r)^n$ if used for health care or $(1 + r)^n(1 - t)$ if used for nonhealth consumption.

How Big is the HSA Advantage?

The value of tax deferral or tax exemption obviously increases with the tax burden one would otherwise face (see table 5-5). For filers who face a zero marginal tax rate after the age of 65, HSAs are on a par with 401(k)s or ordinary IRAs in financing spending during old age.[19] Contributions to both by individuals may avoid the individual, but not the employer, part of the payroll tax.[20] But HSAs are superior to 401(k)s (ignoring matching contributions by employers) and ordinary IRAs for health care spending. Funds can be withdrawn from HSAs tax free to pay for health care at any age. Withdrawals from 401(k)s or ordinary IRAs are subject to income tax (except to the extent that health care outlays exceed 7.5 percent of adjusted gross income) and to penalty tax if withdrawn before the age of 59 and a half (unless withdrawals are for certain narrowly defined hardship situations).[21] For people in higher tax brackets, the relative advantage of HSAs over tax-sheltered and taxable saving is much larger.

Because out-of-pocket health care spending tends to rise with age, planning on how to pay for health care after retirement is a necessary component of financial planning for retirement. The larger the proportion of a given amount of wealth that one holds in an HSA at the age of 65, the greater is the expected value of potential retirement consumption. The reason is that out-of-pocket health care spending during retirement is uncertain, which means that there is a chance that any accumulated HSA balance will be used up for health care spending, avoiding tax that would have to be paid if funds were drawn from ordinary tax-sheltered saving.

Why Don't People Enroll in Health Savings Accounts?

For purposes of this paper, this question takes two forms. Why didn't the employees of the company described above take advantage of a plan that would have made every one of them financially better off? And why would anyone enroll in high-deductible insurance and not automatically take advantage of the "sweetest deal" around for savers?

With respect to the company described above, there are at least four possible explanations for why employees did not enroll in the high-deductible plan. First, the literature distributed by Harvard Pilgrim misleadingly attributes to the high-deductible HSA variant of its PPO offering a "greater potential for out-of-pocket costs" than that presented by the conventional PPO (table 5-6). This statement does not take into account the company's contribution to the HSA of each employee who selects the high-deductible option. As the calculations reported in appendix tables 5A-1 and 5A-2 show, once one allows for these contributions, this statement is false. Still, employees may have been deterred from enrolling by this "authoritative" appraisal of risks. A second possible reason is status quo bias. As Jeffrey Liebman and Richard Zeckhauser point out (in chapter 10), people tend to keep on doing what they have been doing unless there is a salient reason to change. Even if it is virtually costless to change from current practice or from a default option, people are reluctant to switch. Third, some high-deductible plans may require enrollees to keep track of medical outlays and submit documentation that the deductible has been met. Under conventional PPOs, the insurer normally receives all bills, providing reimbursement to the patient or to physicians only after the deductible has been met.[22] Finally, some people may see health savings accounts and high-deductible insurance as an element of a conservative agenda for health care reform and resist adopting a plan at odds with their political preferences.[23]

Two other possible explanations for why people "left money on the table" can be set aside. One might be that the financial advantages of the high-deductible HSA option may be transitory because the company might stop making HSA deposits or relative premiums might shift, and people would worry that they might have to leave their customary physicians. This concern is not well founded as both PPO options use the same network. If the terms of the HD HSA option become unattractive, enrollees can shift plans without changing their source of care. A second possible explanation might be that the high-deductible HSA option is new and unfamiliar and that people simply do not understand it. Health insurance is complicated, and comparing complicated plans is a challenge even to the well educated. It is worth noting, however, that the educational level of this group is unusually high. Of 666 employees eligible

Table 5-6. Consumer Information Supplied by Harvard Pilgrim Health Care

Options	Best Buy HSA PPO	PPO	HMO	Comments
Potential for out-of-pocket costs	high	mid-range	low	Best Buy HSA PPO members have an annual $1,500 individual and $3,000 family in-network deductible and a $1,500 individual and $3,000 family out-of-network deductible. However, routine physical exams and other preventive care visits require a $20 copayment (in network). Deductible costs can be offset with your Health Savings Account (HSA). Company contributes $1,000 per individual and $2,000 per family to this account as your employer. PPO members have out-of-network deductibles, then coinsurance. In-network doctor's visits are covered with copayments.
Bills and paperwork	high	high	low	Best Buy HSA PPO and PPO members will get bills for the deductible, then coinsurance, when using certain services.
Referrals required	no	no	yes	Members in the HMO choose a PCP from Harvard Pilgrim's extensive provider network. HMO members need PCP referrals for most specialist visits (referrals are not required for some services, such as annual eye exam and an annual GYN exam). Best Buy HSA PPO and PPO members do not need to choose a PCP and referrals are not required.
Coverage for seeing doctors who do not participate with Harvard Pilgrim	yes	yes	yes—medical emergencies only	With few exceptions, care is not covered for HMO members if they visit non-participating providers. Best Buy HSA PPO and PPO members have the added choice of seeing providers who do not participate with Harvard Pilgrim. Such out-of-network coverage is at 80 percent after their deductible is met for Best Buy HSA PPO members, and 80 percent after deductible for PPO members.

Source: Harvard Pilgrim HealthCare brochure (2007).

Table 5-7. *Company Cost of Coverage: Conventional PPO Compared with High-Deductible HSA PPO*

Compensation levels of plan enrollees (dollars)	Company Premium Plus HSA Deposit		
	Conventional PPO	High-deductible HSA	Difference
Individual			
< 50,000	5,305	4,256	1,049
50,000–99,999	4,633	3,844	789
≥ 100,000	3,962	3,432	530
Individual + 1			
< 50,000	14,314	8,512	5,802
50,000–99,999	12,502	7,688	4,814
≥ 100,000	10,690	6,863	3,827
Family			
< 50,000	14,314	11,768	2,546
50,000–99,999	12,502	10,531	1,971
≥ 100,000	10,690	9,295	1,395

for company health insurance coverage, all but 92 have at least a college degree and 376 have advanced degrees (M.A., Ph.D., or professional degrees). Furthermore, this challenge would not deter *homo economicus*.

Not only do employees stand to benefit financially from enrolling in the HD HSA option rather than in conventional PPO coverage, the company appears to save money each time an employee elects HD HSA rather than conventional PPO coverage—several thousand dollars in some cases (see table 5-7). Unfortunately, available data do not permit us to determine whether these apparent savings are real or illusory. The two PPO plans are experience-rated separately. Favorable selection of low-cost enrollees into the HD HSA option could explain much or all of the apparent difference in premiums. As we have no data on use of health care services before the HD HSA option was available and no information on health status of enrollees in each option, we cannot determine whether the HD HSA option simply reduces claims and administrative costs or actually lowers use of services. Whether or not the HD HSA option reduces total costs for the company, there is no doubt that it saves the employees money.

Not all HD HSA plans are so attractive. Nearly half of sponsoring companies do not contribute to their employees' HSAs. The average contribution among those companies that do contribute is lower than that of the company examined here. In most cases, at least some employees are exposed to more financial risk than those employees under consideration here. Furthermore, Liebman and Zeckhauser show a number of reasons in addition to those we have considered why people, rationally or irrationally, may decline the combined offer of high-deductible insurance and HSAs. Many of the cognitive frailties that they list are likely to affect individual decisions on whether health savings accounts justify abandoning the seeming security of low-deductible health insurance, particularly when the switch entails an increase in financial risk.

Perhaps the most important element of health savings accounts is that they are complex. Most health economists have erroneously regarded HSAs simply as instruments for financing the increased deductibles that workers who enroll in HD plans face during their working years. It would be unsurprising if enrollees were similarly confused. Furthermore, HD HSA plans elevate the salience of financial considerations at the time people are ill. Health economists have long speculated that the avoidance of the need to think about financial matters when one is ill is an important motivation for health insurance.[24] The benefits of HSAs are long deferred and call upon enrollees to appreciate the slow accretion of gains from tax exemption. The correct perception of such deferred gains also depends on the accurate appraisal of distant events, some of which are of low probability. Liebman and Zeckhauser note the evidence that people are not able, in general, to calculate correctly the value of such gains.

Are Health Savings Accounts the Best Way to Sell High-Deductible Insurance?

If the objective of authorizing HSAs is to encourage people to shift from low- to high-deductible insurance, are HSAs the most effective way of encouraging this shift? And are HSAs good policy on other grounds? We believe that the answer to both questions is no and that advocates of high-deductible insurance should consider other incentives to promote it. We suggest some candidates.

Health Savings Accounts—Flawed Tax Policy, Flawed Health Policy

Many health policy analysts view HSAs simply as an inducement to buy high-deductible health insurance. The shortcomings of HSAs as tax policy are well understood by tax experts. The tax-policy indictment is simple. HSAs have two purposes: to encourage the purchase of high-deductible insurance and to boost saving so that enrollees in high-deductible plans will have enough money to meet current out-of-pocket medical expenses. On the first score, the problem with HSAs is that depositors can reduce their tax liability even if they save nothing. To the extent that taxpayers pay for HSA deposits by moving other saving to HSAs, they do not increase their own capacity to pay medical bills (other than by cutting their own taxes). Their tax cuts lower national saving because private saving is unchanged but government revenues drop, thereby increasing budget deficits. On the second score, as we noted earlier, the tax incentives rise with the taxpayer's marginal tax rate, but it is not clear why the benefits of high-deductible insurance increase with one's marginal tax rate. As both wealth and income are closely, and positively, correlated with marginal tax rates, those with low income who typically have low net worth have little incentive to create HSAs and, therefore, are given weak incentives, at best, to choose high-deductible insurance. Furthermore, the proportion of those without health insurance is higher among those with low incomes who are likely to face low or even zero income tax rates than it is among those with high incomes who are likely to face higher tax rates.

The first shortcoming is virtually inescapable whenever a saving incentive applies selectively to certain classes of assets. As a practical matter, it is probably impossible to stop those who save nothing from capturing the benefits of saving incentives as long as tax rules for all saving are not uniform. A large and conflicting literature has grown up on whether and how much tax-sheltered savings accounts may have boosted saving. As of now, this literature is largely irrelevant to the question of whether HSAs would boost saving, as few households deposit as much as they are allowed in existing tax-sheltered accounts.

The second shortcoming could be avoided if the incentive to buy high-deductible insurance were changed from a deduction or exclusion to a matching grant or refundable credit. Grants and credits can easily be made the same for everyone regardless of income. Alternatively, they can be graduated with more paid to those with low incomes rather than to those with high incomes or wealth. The cost of the grant or credit per dollar of HSA deposit could be set to approximate average generosity of current HSA rules—that is, to the excess cost of HSA deposits beyond those of equal deposits in other tax-sheltered saving. The present value of that cost is approximately equal to the average marginal tax rate on deposits. This method of computing costs follows from the fact that HSA treatment of investment earnings and of withdrawals closely resembles that of Roth IRAs and Roth 401(k)s; the difference is that HSA deposits are also tax exempt (see table 5-4).

The credit or grant approach would not correct the problem that people can take advantage of the HSA tax incentives without actually adding to their savings. But the incentive to buy high-deductible insurance would be shifted in some measure from upper-income to lower- and middle-income groups. The advantages of the grant or credit approach over HSAs resemble those of proposals for matching grants or refundable tax credits calibrated to saving over conventional IRA and 401(k) rules.

Incentives could take other forms. For example, the government could selectively offer people who buy high-deductible insurance a lump sum bonus or percentage match to 401(k) or IRA deposits. It could directly subsidize premiums of high-deductible insurance. It could offer immediate tax cuts selectively to people who buy high-deductible insurance. The cost of such incentives would be recorded in current budgets and recognized immediately. In contrast, much of the added cost of HSAs is incurred decades into the future well outside the budget windows now in use. Thus, although HSAs have so far been ineffectual in encouraging high-deductible insurance, they appear inexpensive because they generate costs that are unrecognized under current budget accounting rules. Full recognition of the costs of a program, it should be acknowledged, is often an obstacle to its acceptance. If concealment of the full budget costs of the incentive to buy high-deductible insurance is considered necessary for its adoption, one could offer enrollees in such plans a write-up of earnings used in computing future Social Security benefits conditioned on deposit in an ordinary savings account of some fraction of the deductible amounts of the high-deductible insurance plan. An increase in average earnings under Social Security would raise benefits most for those with low average earnings.

Finally, there is basis for concern about the impact of HSAs on pooling that is necessary for effective insurance. If the use of HSAs was confined to group coverage and employers shared any savings from reduced premiums with employees, then the example of the company described earlier illustrates that workers and employers both might save money. Even then it is important that insurance plans be designed carefully so that cost-sensitive enrollees be shielded from increased cost sharing on high-benefit services. But the larger risk is that employers, perturbed by large and unpredictable increases in insurance premiums, may use the availability of HSAs as a justification for dropping group coverage, thereby pushing their employees into the currently dysfunctional individual health insurance market.

Conclusion

Health savings accounts are an important policy innovation. Well-designed high-deductible group insurance can promote increased cost sensitivity while preserving the pooling necessary for effective insurance. HSAs serve as a carrot to induce people to switch from traditional to high-deductible insurance, but they are poorly designed to achieve this goal. Although promoting well-designed high-deductible group insurance may be good policy, policymakers should consider other incentives to promote its adoption.

Table 5A-1. Net Cost of Health Coverage for Various Levels of In-Network Health Care Use, by Plan[a]
Dollars

Earnings and family size	Total health care spending															
	$0		$250		$500		$1,000		$2,000		$5,000		$10,000		$50,000	
	PPO	PPO/HSA	PPO	PPO/HSA	PPO	PPO/HSA	PPO	PPO/HSA	PPO	PPO/HSA	PPO	PPO/HSA	PPO	PPO/HSA	PPO	PPO/HSA
Less than $50,000																
Single	1,410	−135	1,440	115	1,560	365	1,750	865	1,870	1,505	1,990	1,545	2,110	1,565	2,255	1,960
Single + 1 dependent	3,805	−269	3,835	−19	3,955	231	4,145	731	4,265	1,731	4,385	2,911	4,505	2,931	4,650	3,326
Family	3,805	596	3,835	846	3,955	1,096	4,145	1,596	4,265	2,596	4,385	3,776	4,505	3,796	4,650	4,191
$50,000 to less than $100,000																
Single	2,082	278	2,112	528	2,232	778	2,422	1,278	2,542	1,918	2,662	1,958	2,782	1,978	2,927	2,373
Single + 1 dependent	5,617	555	5,647	805	5,767	1,055	5,957	1,555	6,077	2,555	6,197	3,735	6,317	3,755	6,462	4,150
Family	5,617	1,833	5,647	2,083	5,767	2,333	5,957	2,833	6,077	3,833	6,197	5,013	6,317	5,033	6,462	5,428
$100,000 or more																
Single	2,753	690	2,783	940	2,903	1,190	3,093	1,690	3,213	2,330	3,333	2,370	3,453	2,390	3,598	2,785
Single + 1 dependent	7,429	1,380	7,459	1,630	7,579	1,880	7,769	2,380	7,889	3,380	8,009	4,560	8,129	4,580	8,274	4,957
Family	7,429	3,069	7,459	3,319	7,579	3,569	7,769	4,069	7,889	5,069	8,009	6,249	8,129	6,269	8,274	6,664

PPO = preferred provider organization.

a. Net out-of-pocket cost = premium + cost sharing − HSA deposit.

Table 5A-2. *Net Cost of Health Coverage for Various Levels of Out-of-Network Health Care Use, by Plan*[a]
Dollars

									Total health care spending							
	$0		$250		$500		$1,000		$2,000		$5,000		$10,000		$50,000	
Earnings and family size	PPO	PPO/HSA	PPO	PPO/HSA	PPO	PPO/HSA	PPO	PPO/HSA	PPO	PPO/HSA	PPO	PPO/HSA	PPO	PPO/HSA	PPO	PPO/HSA
Less than $50,000																
Single	1,410	−135	1,660	115	1,740	365	1,920	865	2,005	1,435	2,960	2,065	3,972	3,077	11,505	10,860
Single + 1 dependent	3,805	−269	4,055	−19	4,305	231	4,470	731	4,595	1,731	5,555	3,131	6,617	4,143	14,150	11,926
Family	3,805	596	4,055	846	4,305	1,096	4,470	1,596	4,595	2,596	5,555	3,996	6,617	5,008	14,150	12,791
$50,000 to less than $100,000																
Single	2,082	278	2,112	528	2,232	778	2,422	1,278	2,542	1,918	2,662	1,958	2,782	1,978	2,927	2,373
Single + 1 dependent	5,617	555	5,647	805	5,767	1,055	5,957	1,555	6,077	2,555	6,197	3,735	6,317	3,755	6,462	4,150
Family	5,617	1,833	5,647	2,083	5,767	2,333	5,957	2,833	6,077	3,833	6,197	5,013	6,317	5,033	6,462	5,428
$100,000 or more																
Single	2,753	690	2,783	940	2,903	1,190	3,093	1,690	3,213	2,330	3,333	2,370	3,453	2,390	3,598	2,785
Single + 1 dependent	7,429	1,380	7,459	1,630	7,579	1,880	7,769	2,380	7,889	3,380	8,009	4,560	8,129	4,580	8,274	4,957
Family	7,429	3,069	7,459	3,319	7,579	3,569	7,769	4,069	7,889	5,069	8,009	6,249	8,129	6,269	8,274	6,664

PPO = preferred provider organization.

a. Net out-of-pocket cost = premium + cost sharing − HSA deposit.

Notes

1. Stephen T. Parente and Roger Feldman test for an interaction between health saving accounts and retirement saving in "Do HSA Choices Interact with Retirement Saving Decisions?" in *Tax Policy and the Economy*, vol. 22, edited by James M. Poterba (University of Chicago Press, 2008, forthcoming). Their data set from a particular company found very low take-up rates of HSAs. Perhaps for that reason, they were unable to reject the null hypothesis that saving through HSAs does not affect other retirement saving.

2. America's Health Insurance Plans (AHIP), "January 2007 Census Shows 4.5 Million People Covered by HSA/High-Deductible Health Plans" (Washington: AHIP, Center for Policy and Research, April 2007) (www.ahipresearch.org). Nearly 180 million people are insured by employer-sponsored plans. Employment-based health insurance estimate is from U.S. Census Bureau, *Current Population Survey, 2007 Annual Social and Economic (ASEC) Supplement* (Washington, 2008), table HI01: "Health Insurance Coverage Status and Type of Coverage by Selected Characteristics: 2006: All Races."

3. Twenty-seven percent of those who enrolled as individuals were previously uninsured. See AHIP, "January 2007 Census Shows," p. 5. Data on the proportion of those covered in groups who were previously uninsured are not reported.

4. Government Accountability Office, "Health Savings Accounts: Participation Increased and Was More Common among Individuals with Higher Incomes," letter to Rep. Henry A. Waxman and Rep. Pete Stark, GAO-08-474R (Washington, April 1, 2008).

5. Henry J. Kaiser Family Foundation and Health Research and Educational Trust, *Employer Health Benefits: 2007 Annual Survey* (Menlo Park, Calif. and Chicago 2007), p. 125, exhibit 8.5.

6. The Kaiser and HRET survey reports average premiums for HSA-qualified high-deductible plans and for insurance that does not qualify for savings options (including health reimbursement accounts). But there is no information on the nature of coverage or the age and location—and therefore the relative premiums—of enrollees in these two types of plans.

7. Whether employees benefit directly from premium savings in this case depends on whether employers pay for all premiums, pay for a proportion of premiums, or pay a flat amount toward premiums. Employees save nothing on premiums in the first case, save part of the premium reduction in the second case, and save all or part of the premium reduction in the third case (depending on whether the employer's initial payment was less than or greater than the high-deductible premium). However, employees may still benefit indirectly if employers distribute back premium savings to their employees.

8. Estimates of the change in health care expenditures after the introduction of HSAs range from a 1 percent increase to an 8 percent decrease. See Jürgen Jung and Chung Tran, "The Macroeconomics of Health Savings Accounts," Working Paper 2007-023 (Indiana University–Bloomington, Center for Applied Economics and Policy Research, March 27, 2008); Congressional Budget Office, *Consumer-Directed Health Plans: Potential Effects on Health Care Spending and Outcomes* (Washington: December 2006); Emmett B. Keeler and others, "Can Medical Savings Accounts for the Nonelderly Reduce Health Care Costs?" *Journal of the American Medical Association* 275, no. 21 (June 1996): 1666–71; Dahlia K. Remler and Sherry A. Glied, "How Much More Cost Sharing Will Health Savings Accounts Bring?" *Health Affairs* 25, no. 4 (July–August 2006): 1070–78.

9. Steven B. Cohen and William Yu, "The Persistence in the Level of Health Expenditures over Time: Estimates for the U.S. Population, 2004–2005," Statistical Brief 191 (Rockville,

Md.: Agency for Healthcare Research and Quality, Medical Expenditure Panel Study, November 2007) (http://www.meps.ahrq.gov/papers/st191/stat191).

10. Remler and Glied, "How Much More Cost Sharing Will Health Savings Accounts Bring?"

11. AHIP, *A Survey of Preventive Benefits in Health Savings Account (HSA) Plans, July 2007* (Washington: AHIP, Center for Policy and Research, November 2007).

12. Whether the insured person's welfare will increase under high-deductible insurance is less clear. Switching from low- to high-deductible insurance will cause the insured person who correctly weighs benefits and costs of care to forgo services that yield benefits greater than their share of outlays under low-deductible plans but less than their share under high-deductible plans. Whether the financial gain of the shift compensates for this loss is not at all clear. If the insured irrationally forgo high-benefit care because of increased charges under high-deductible plans, they are likely to suffer losses in excess of any financial gain.

13. U.S. News and World Report, "2007 Commercial Health Plan Rankings" (www.usnews.com/directories/health-plans/index_html/plan_cat+commercial/).

14. If health care spending exceeds of 7.5 percent of adjusted gross income, the excess over 7.5 percent of income is actually subsidized. This excess is deductible from personal income tax and, therefore, reduces tax liability. The subsidy equals the taxpayer's marginal tax rate multiplied by the excess of spending over 7.5 percent of adjusted gross income.

15. One difference between rules for 401(k) plans and ordinary IRAs and HSA rules is that the penalty tax for premature withdrawals stops at age 59 and a half for 401(k)s and IRAs but continues to age 65 for HSAs.

16. Enrolles aged 55 and older can make "catch-up" contributions of an additional $900 in 2008. All amounts are adjusted for inflation. Qualifying plans must have a deductible of at least $1,100 for single ($2,200 for family) coverage and stop-loss caps of $5,600 ($11,200 for family). See U.S. Department of the Treasury website "2008 HSA Indexed Amounts" (www.ustreas.gov/offices/public-affairs/hsa/pdf/rp-2007-36.pdf).

17. As indicated below, savings in amounts below the HSA limits should in general be made through HSAs, if available. Because workers most likely to save such modest amounts are likely to be those with low or moderate wages, they will have reduced incentives to join 401(k) plans. Such selective movement from 401(k)s to HSAs could cause the 401(k) plan to fail to qualify under nondiscrimination rules that require widespread employee participation.

18. The welfare gain is not ensured, however. With a concave utility function and uncertain future health care spending, oversaving may not be optimal, as the welfare gain from additional income in the future may not offset the welfare loss from reduced current-period consumption. The welfare gain is ensured if the saver uses current-period borrowing on which interest payments are deductible to fund HSA deposits in excess of anticipated health care spending.

19. The text statement ignores the fact that capital gains that are earned in tax-sheltered accounts are taxed as ordinary income when they are withdrawn, but gains earned in taxable accounts bear lower capital gains rates that are levied only when the gains are realized. Capital gains are also sheltered from taxes until realized. Deferral of tax on accrued gains means that if investors follow a buy-and-hold policy, even these reduced taxes are deferred until they are realized. Favorable treatment of capital gains reduces, and may reverse, the relative advantage of ordinary tax-sheltered accounts over taxable accounts, but this does not apply to HSAs, which are exempt from all tax.

20. Contributions by employers avoid both. But most contributions are made by individuals.

21. The hardship situations are as follows: if the account holder becomes totally disabled; to comply with a court order to give the money to a divorced spouse, a child, or a dependent; when one is separated from service, through permanent layoff, termination, quitting, or taking early retirement after the age of 54; if one loses one's job in the year one turns age 55, or later; and if one loses one's job and sets up a payment schedule to withdraw money in substantially equal amounts over the course of one's life expectancy.

As far as income taxes are concerned, HSAs are on a par with Roth IRAs for filers facing zero marginal personal income tax rates at the time funds are deposited. Tax rates at the time of withdrawal are irrelevant in both cases, just reversing the comparison of HSAs with 401(k)s and ordinary IRAs.

22. According to an official with the company, "The health plan, Harvard Pilgrim, keeps track of all the medical expenses because the employee still shows their HPHC health card at the time of service, and the employees still get the group health plan negotiated rates from providers (vs. retail rates.) However, because record keeping is not always accurate, etc., employees do have to pay more attention to their medical bills and should keep records themselves on eligible expenses that meet the deductible."

23. Lois A. Vitt and Ray Werntz examine the resistance of employees to switching to high-deductible insurance in "Listening to Consumers: Value-Focused Health Benefits and Education," *EBRI Issue Brief* 313 (Washington: Employee Benefit Research Institute, January 2008).

24. Victor Fuchs, "From Bismarck to Woodcock: The 'Irrational' Pursuit of National Health Insurance," *Journal of Law and Economics* 19, no. 2 (August 1976): 347–59.

Case Study of a Successful HSA

DOUGLAS P. STIVES

My CPA firm, the Curchin Group, saved tens of thousands of dollars when we established high-deductible health insurance plans with health savings accounts (HDHP–HSAs). My firm's clients report similar savings and note that their employees are very pleased to have the option of participating in an HDHP–HSA.

Table A compares the costs of an HDHP offered by the firm in 2002, before HSAs existed. Considerable money was saved. For family coverage, the cost of a $1,000 deductible health insurance policy was about $10,000 per year. Under this policy a family would spend $1,000 out of pocket, mostly with after-tax money, and the employer and employee together spent $10,000 in pretax dollars for insurance. Total annual exposure was $11,000.

By selecting the $3,000 deductible policy, the total cost rose to a maximum of $11,200. The employee would save money if he or she did not spend more than $2,800 on medical care. The potential savings, especially for healthy employees, were significant.

Only three employees at the Curchin Group chose the $3,000 deductible policy. Since all three participants involved families who were healthy and filed no claims during 2002, their premiums dropped $400 to $7,800 for 2003. Right on schedule, the $1,000 deductible coverage cost went up 20 percent.

In 2004 the gap increased. If an employee resisted the $3,000 deductible option and stayed at a $1,000 deductible, his or her exposure in 2004 was $14,000 ($13,000 for insurance plus the $1,000 deductible). Meanwhile the $3,000 deductible group could not spend more than $11,000 even if they were unlucky enough to incur $3,000 in medical costs.

Table A. *Curchin Group Annual Cost of Health Insurance for Family Coverage*[a]
Dollars

	Deductible		
Year	1,000	3,000	5,000
2002	10,000	8,200	—
2003	12,000	7,800	—
2004	13,000	8,000	—
2005[b]	14,532	10,296	6,432
2006	15,480	11,028	7,116
2007	15,708	11,376	7,428

Source:
—Not applicable.
a. Single and husband and wife coverages cost proportionately less.
b. HSA first established.

An HSA Offered in 2005

The firm set up an HSA in 2005, the first year that HSAs were available. A $5,000 deductible was chosen to provide even greater savings. In 2007 the potential saving of at least $4,280 was available: $16,708 ($15,708 for insurance with a $1,000 deductible) compared with $12,428 ($7,428 for insurance plus $5,000 in deductible).

For a healthy family spending only $1,000 on medical costs, the savings were $8,280. It is difficult to understand why anyone would elect to stay with a staggering cost of over $15,000 for health insurance when a minimum saving of $4,280 is available. The answers seem to be fear, lack of understanding, or most likely, the failure of an employer to make the switch to a HDHP attractive to employees.

One employee at the Curchin Group commented: "If I go into the high deductible plan, I will save some money for my portion of the insurance cost, but it looks like the firm is saving money too." He was right because the firm pays 40 percent of insurance costs and the employees pick up 60 percent pre tax. To save itself and its employees money, the firm agreed to contribute its savings to the participating employees' health savings accounts. The law permits employers to do this with pretax money. Smart employees voluntarily contribute the balance of the annual limit, which is $5,850 for family coverage in 2008. The employee also gets a "before AGI" deduction for his or her HSA contribution. This provides a "no losers" solution to reducing the cost of health coverage.

The numbers in table B illustrate the cost sharing arrangement Curchin offers to its employees.

Table B. *Cost Savings with an HDHP–HSA for the Curchin Group*

Employee cost for family coverage[a]	
$1,000 deductible: 60 percent of $15,708	$9,425
$5,000 deductible: 60 percent of $ 7,428	$4,457
Annual savings to employee with an HDHP	$4,968
Employer also saves 40 percent of $8,280	
($15,708 – $7,428)	$3,312[b]

a. Company pays 40 percent of health insurance.
b. Employer contributes $3,312 to an HSA for the employee.

Net cost to employee to maintain quality HDHP coverage with company contribution to HSA	
Employee's cost for insurance with $5,000 deductible	$4,457
Employer's contribution to HSA	$3,312
Net cost to employee	$1,145

There are also considerable nonfinancial benefits to participating in a high-deductible health insurance plan with a health savings account, including less contact with insurance companies, fewer rules regarding coverage and reimbursement, faster payments to providers, more control by participants, and fewer unnecessary medical procedures and drugs.

Both papers expressed concern about this last point, but those concerns may be misplaced. Wisely, most HDHP arrangements exempt annual physical examinations and other well care services from deductibles. It also seems relevant to suggest that adults should be mature enough to decide on which medical care costs, medicines, and other costs they need to spend money. In my experience, it is unlikely that taxpayers will take better care of themselves and get better care if they have a lower deductible health insurance plan. Indeed, too many participants in a low-deductible plan consult doctors, admit themselves to hospitals, and take medications for no justifiable reason.

One employee at Curchin was notorious for making appointments with several doctors in December of each year after exceeding the $1,000 deductible. This employee would take many hours off from work for doctor's appointments and return with bags full of prescription drugs. Typically the employee would end up sick from a disease picked up sitting in a doctor's office. When asked why this annual practice was attractive, the employee said, "I'm entitled to medical care, and since it's covered by insurance, why shouldn't I take advantage of it?" This attitude is all too prevalent in the United States and is partly responsible for high insurance costs and the outrageous overuse of prescription drugs. Stand in line at any drug store and marvel at the quantities of drugs people take at little or no cost to them, or at least that is what they believe.

Finally Curchin convinced the employee to join the firm's HDHP–HSA. Since joining the $5,000 deductible plan, the year-end doctor's visits stopped, and the employee's general health improved.

Conclusion

Health savings accounts are far from perfect and will not work for all companies, but readers are encouraged to challenge insurance advisors and employee groups who discard or discredit HSAs. Healthy and generally young groups will definitely benefit, and for less selective groups, savings are more than likely to be significant over time. Some adjustment of the tax laws to provide more tax benefits for lower-income taxpayers and perhaps less benefits for higher-income individuals might make the rules fairer.

6

Tax Subsidies for Out-of-Pocket Health Care Costs

JESSICA VISTNES, WILLIAM JACK, AND ARIK LEVINSON

Each year, around the time employers have open enrollment for their benefits plans, newspapers publish stories headlining that employer-provided health insurance is becoming less generous. A 2003 *New York Times* story observed that "employers are shifting a growing share (of costs) onto people who make the heaviest use of medical services." A 2005 story in the same paper said companies are "shifting more costs to consumers, in the form of much higher deductibles, co-payments, or premiums." And last year the *Los Angeles Times* wrote that "95 percent of covered workers are now responsible for copayments and shared costs."[1]

These trends have not gone unnoticed by academic economists, who offer a number of explanations for them. Some point to falling marginal tax rates, which reduce the implicit subsidy to employer-provided health insurance, and increasing Medicaid eligibility, which gives low-wage employees an insurance option outside their employer.[2] Others attribute the decreasing generosity of employer-provided insurance to the increase in female labor force participation.[3] With more two-career couples, employers may have an incentive to induce their

The research mentioned in this chapter was conducted while Jessica Vistnes was also a Census Bureau research associate at the Center for Economic Studies. The authors would like to thank Jonathan Gruber, Henry Aaron, and Leonard Burman for their helpful comments on an earlier version; Andrew Mosso for his help with the MEPS-IC data; and Roland McDevitt, Laura Gandolfo, Jon Gabel, and Cheryl Fahlman for sharing the actuarial values they constructed from the MEPS-IC. The views expressed are those of the authors, and no official endorsement by the Bureau of the Census, the Department of Health and Human Services, or the Agency for Healthcare Research and Quality is intended or should be inferred. This essay has been screened to ensure that no confidential data are revealed.

119

employees to choose the health insurance benefit offered by their spouse's employer, creating a race to the bottom in insurance generosity.

We examine a different explanation for the declining generosity of employer-provided health insurance: federal tax policy. The past three decades have seen an increasing number of mechanisms by which employees can arrange to pay their out-of-pocket health care costs (those costs not covered by their insurance plans) with pretax dollars, effectively subsidizing out-of-pocket costs at a rate equal to the employees' marginal tax rates. The first such mechanism is a flexible spending account (FSA). FSAs were enabled by section 125 of the Internal Revenue Service Code, enacted in 1978. FSAs allow employees to set aside pretax earnings each year (during open enrollment) and to spend the money from that account on out-of-pocket health care costs without ever paying taxes on the income. FSAs are only available through employers, but account holders are not required to have any particular type of health insurance—or even to have insurance at all. One curious feature of an FSA is that account funds not spent on health care by year's end are forfeited.[4] The number of employers offering their workers FSAs has been growing since 1978. By subsidizing out-of-pocket costs, FSAs may be inducing employers to offer, and employees to choose, less generous, less costly health insurance.

In addition to the growth of FSAs, since the late 1990s other federal tax policies have been introduced that subsidize out-of-pocket costs. Health reimbursement accounts (HRAs) work like FSAs except that the accounts must be funded by employers and cannot be drawn from employees' deferred salaries; and medical savings accounts (MSAs) enable self-employed individuals to obtain the same type of subsidy. Finally, in 2003 Congress added a fourth program, health savings accounts (HSAs). HSAs, like FSAs, are accounts into which people can deposit pretax earnings to be spent on health care costs not covered by their insurance policies. HSAs are not tied to employment, and unused funds are not forfeited at year's end; indeed, retained funds accumulate earnings on a tax-free basis.[5] However, to qualify for an HSA, participants must be covered by a high-deductible health plan, exposing them to high out-of-pocket costs.[6] The availability of all of these types of subsidies means that health care costs not covered by insurance impose less of a burden on health care consumers, and as a consequence people may be willing to opt for less generous insurance.

In this chapter we ask whether, empirically, the availability of FSAs increases the market-provided level of cost sharing. We have a number of motivations. First, we want to document whether the increasing cost-sharing trends noted by the media are associated with the presence or absence of FSAs. If we find that cost sharing has increased more rapidly for employers that offer an FSA, that would suggest that the growth in FSA availability has played a role in the observed cost-sharing increases. Second, the newest of the subsidy programs, HSAs, *requires* increased cost sharing. If, given the subsidy, employers would have offered (and consumers would have chosen) high-deductible health insurance anyway, then this requirement may not have a significant negative effect on HSA take-up rates. However, if the subsidy does not lead people voluntarily to choose high-deductible plans, then the requirement that they do so may slow the spread of HSA accounts.

These subsidies also have consequences for social welfare that are worth noting here, although we do not directly address them empirically. If coinsurance rates, copayments, and deductibles increase sufficiently as a result of FSAs, then net-of-tax cost-sharing rates could also rise, resulting in a more efficient level of health care use.[7] However, any efficiency gains would have to be weighed against any distributional concerns (such as subsidies concentrated among high-income taxpayers) and the economic cost of collecting revenue to finance the subsidy. In addition, we would need to account for behavioral concerns that individuals may overreact to copays and deductibles and therefore get too little health care.[8] However, we only measure whether the subsidies cause gross-of-tax cost-sharing rates to rise.

Finally, we are interested in this issue because of our previous finding that establishments whose employees have access to FSAs offer health insurance plans with higher cost sharing, controlling for the endogenous decision by employers to offer FSAs.[9] That earlier work uses data from the Robert Wood Johnson Employer Health Insurance Survey (EHIS), a cross-sectional survey of insurance plans offered by employers in ten states in 1993. But much about health insurance has changed since 1993, such as increased availability of FSAs, additional mechanisms for subsidizing out-of-pocket costs, and working spouses' access to these subsidies. If workers' out-of-pocket costs can be subsidized via other sources, there may be less of a difference today than in 1993 between the health insurance offered by employers with FSAs and that offered by those without FSAs.

In fact, some work using more recent data does suggest that consumers respond to tax subsidies for out-of-pocket expenses by purchasing less generous insurance. One study examined FSA participation by employees of a large public university.[10] Thirteen percent of eligible employees participated in 2003, contributing an average of $1,257 to their accounts. The employees who chose to participate in the FSA tended to choose the university's insurance plans with relatively high expected out-of-pocket costs. In the words of the authors, "these employees are creating their own 'consumer-driven' plan." Our analysis differs in that we examine data from many employers across the nation, while they focus on the employees of one large employer.

In this chapter we update and extend our earlier analysis in several ways. First, we use the 2005 Medical Expenditure Panel Survey–Insurance Component (MEPS-IC), allowing us to get a more recent view of whether FSAs increase cost sharing. Second, we extend the applicability of the results to a wider geographic area, from the ten states in the EHIS data to the nationally representative MEPS survey. Third, we examine a wider range of cost-sharing outcomes, such as the physician copayment rate, the physician coinsurance rate, and the overall deductible level. In addition, we attempt to account for the overall generosity of a health plan by examining the actuarial value of the plan, a measure that uses all available information in the MEPS-IC to calculate the proportion of total medical expenditures paid by insurance. Finally, we attempt to differentiate, through the use of survey weights, between employers' decisions about which plans to offer and employees' decisions about which plan to enroll in.

In the end, we partially replicate the fundamental result of earlier work, finding some evidence that employers that offered their employees access to FSAs in 2005 had health insurance plans with higher coinsurance rates. However, that result does not appear for alternative measures of cost sharing, such as physician copayment rates, deductibles, and the actuarial value of insurance plans. This outcome may hinge partly on the way we identify the effect of FSAs. Because employers' decisions to offer FSAs cannot be considered exogenous with respect to their insurance plans' level of cost sharing, the earlier work uses instruments for FSA provision in a two-stage least-squares framework. The same approach is adopted here, but as we show below, the instruments work less well with the 2005 MEPS data than they did with the 1993 EHIS data. Perhaps by 2005 enough employers had adopted FSAs that adopters and nonadopters have become more dissimilar in unobservable ways, making it more difficult to find instruments to predict FSA adoption but not to predict cost-sharing rates. Or perhaps by 2005 enough households had access to these types of subsidies through alternative mechanisms that the effect of FSAs on cost sharing cannot be discerned by comparing employers with such accounts to employers without them.

Some Intuitive Theory

We hypothesize that the tax subsidy for out-of-pocket health care expenditures alters the optimal (or market-provided) health insurance contract, leading to less generous policies with lower premiums. The intuition is simple.[11] People buy insurance because they are risk averse. Fully insured people who face zero marginal costs for health care, however, will use too much health care because they perceive it as free. To ameliorate this moral hazard, insurance contracts limit coverage, possibly by requiring consumers to pay some of the ex post costs. While higher cost sharing reduces moral hazard, it also increases the risk faced by patients. The optimal insurance contract trades off these two concerns, equating the marginal disutility of increased risk exposure with the marginal efficiency gains from decreased moral hazard.

Some authors suggest that cost sharing can induce inefficiently low consumption of services if, for example, higher out-of-pocket costs deter compliance with treatment regimens.[12] These behavioral concerns would be crucial to any normative welfare implications of the effect of FSAs. Without taking a position on these alternative models, we attempt to measure how tax subsidies alter the choices people make between risk and moral hazard. This is an important question, regardless of whether one believes that without the subsidies people would choose too much or too little health care.

How do taxes affect the trade-off between risk exposure and moral hazard? Since 1954 the U.S. Internal Revenue Service (IRS) has explicitly exempted from payroll and income taxes the health insurance premiums paid by employers on behalf of their employees. This exemption subsidizes the purchase of health insurance by employees at a rate equal to their marginal tax rate. Because only the premiums are subsidized, and not the out-of-pocket costs, the trade-off between risk reduction and moral hazard is tilted towards risk reduction. Employees would, in this case, choose the more generous employer-sponsored insurance; and because this more generous insurance has lower cost sharing, it exacerbates moral hazard and induces inefficient excess use of health care services.[13]

Various public policies now offset the distortion caused by the 1954 exemption of employer-paid premiums. FSAs, MSAs, HRAs, and HSAs all subsidize out-of-pocket expenditures, meaning that both ex ante premiums and ex post cost sharing can be paid with pretax dollars. These subsidies to out-of-pocket cost sharing have two effects. First, for a given cost-sharing arrangement, the ex post price of health care services faced by consumers is lower, increasing their use and increasing the efficiency cost from the initial subsidy on premiums. But second, by reducing employees' out-of-pocket health care costs, the subsidies increase employees' willingness to accept higher cost sharing in exchange for lower premiums. This second effect, by putting more responsibility for costs in the hands of patients, decreases the moral hazard inefficiency associated with policies with subsidized premiums.

Because these two effects of subsidizing out-of-pocket costs work in opposite directions, the welfare consequences are uncertain.[14] Given the subsidy, employees opt for less expensive health insurance that covers fewer expenses. However, the equilibrium insurance arrangement may have lower net-of-tax cost sharing than without the out-of-pocket subsidy, in which case FSAs exacerbate the deadweight loss associated with the premium subsidy. If the net-of-tax cost sharing is higher, FSAs mitigate the deadweight loss from the premium subsidy. Of course, these efficiency gains may be mitigated by concerns about distributional effects, the deadweight loss of collecting revenue to finance the subsidy, and behavioral concerns if people react to cost sharing by purchasing too little health care.

Using data from 1993, our earlier work found that the coinsurance rates for firms with FSAs were 7 percentage points higher than for firms without FSAs, relative to a sample average of 17 percent.[15] This finding suggests that increasing out-of-pocket costs may be caused in part by government subsidies such as FSAs. It also suggests that one market consequence of the FSA subsidy is that employees choose higher cost sharing. Whether this remains true today or is applicable to other cost-sharing requirements, such as copayments or deductible levels, is the subject of this analysis.

Testing the Theory

We want to know the causal effect of tax subsidies on the cost-sharing elements of health insurance contracts, where the presence of a tax subsidy is measured by access to an FSA. The obvious problem in measuring such an effect is that firms choose whether or not to offer their employees access to FSAs at the same time that they decide on the menu of their health insurance plans. In addition, employees choose to enroll in a plan and an FSA at the same time.

This simultaneity bias may work in either direction. FSAs might tend to be a feature of generous employee benefit plans, including retirement plans, child care programs, and comprehensive health insurance with low cost sharing. In this case, FSAs will be associated with low cost sharing. Or it may be that cost sharing increases for some other reason and that employers respond to this increase by offering their employees access to FSAs. If employers respond to increased cost sharing by offering their employees access to FSAs, we could have the causality exactly backward: we want to measure the degree to which FSAs increase cost sharing when in fact cost-sharing increases encourage the spread of FSAs. Similarly, there may be ambiguous enrollment decisions. For example, employees who participate in FSAs may opt for high-deductible insurance, or employees with high-deductible insurance may opt to participate in FSAs.

To account for the endogeneity of decisions, we follow prior work and estimate versions of

$$(6\text{-}1) \qquad\qquad \kappa_i = X_i\beta + \gamma F_i + \varepsilon_i,$$

where k is a measure of the cost sharing (the actuarial value of a plan, physician coinsurance rates or copayments, and overall deductible levels) of insurance plan i; F_i is an indicator for whether or not the employer offering plan i also offers access to an FSA; and X_i is a vector of other plan and employer characteristics.[16] Because F is endogenous, we do not estimate equation 6-1 directly. Instead, we first predict F using a probit as a function of variables Z, not included in X, and then use the predicted probabilities as instruments for F in the equation.

For instruments, Z, we consider three employer characteristics, all in the spirit of the earlier work. The first is the firm's age. Our theory is that older firms are more likely to have FSAs, ceteris paribus, probably because these complex employee benefits are not a top priority for the human resources departments at new businesses. Moreover, a firm's age seems unlikely to be related to cost sharing, after controlling for other observable employer characteristics.

As a second instrument in Z, we use a dummy for whether or not the firm has multiple establishments, to capture economies of scale in administering FSAs. The idea here is that there are almost certainly economies of scale in both FSA administration and health insurance provision, but the health insurance economies may not spread across different establishments of the same firm in different jurisdictions, where doctors belong to different hospitals and networks. Firm size variables capture both types of efficiencies, but the multiestablishment firm dummy captures only—or at least mostly—the scale economies of FSA administration. Finally, as a third instrument we use the fraction of the establishment's workforce that is eligible for health insurance, to capture the benefits to the employer and its employees of establishing an FSA. We also try using subsets of these three instruments, where for each subset we include the omitted instrument as a covariate in the equation. As we show, though these instruments worked well with the 1993 data, they do not with these 2005 MEPS-IC data.

Data and Descriptive Statistics

To test whether subsidizing out-of-pocket health care costs encourages increased cost sharing, we turn to the MEPS-IC, a large, annual, nationally representative survey of establishments in the United States.[17] The MEPS-IC contains information on whether an establishment offers health insurance, the number and type of plans it offers, and the characteristics of those plans, including total premiums for single and family coverage, employee and employer contributions toward premiums, and specific benefit provisions. These detailed data are collected for as many as four offered plans per establishment.

From 2001 to 2005 the percentage of establishments offering an FSA rose from 14 percent to 20 percent (figure 6-1). Because the growth and prevalence

Figure 6-1. *Private Sector Establishments with FSAs, 2001–05*

Percent

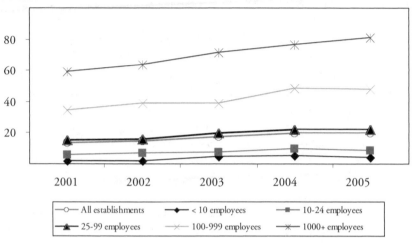

Source: MEPS-IC.

of FSAs has been mostly a large-firm phenomenon, the proportion of employees with access to an FSA is larger—rising from 50 percent in 2001 to 61 percent in 2005 (figure 6-2). In 2005 only 4 percent of the smallest firms (with fewer than 10 employees) offered an FSA, compared with 81 percent of the largest firms (those with 1,000 or more employees). Two surprising facts emerge from figures 6-1 and 6-2. First, almost thirty years after the legislation enabling the creation of FSAs, use of the accounts is still growing. Second, by 2005 the accounts were still not universal even among the largest employers.

Is a relationship between FSA availability and cost sharing apparent in simple descriptive comparisons? Table 6-1 reports estimates of physician coinsurance and copayment rates and deductible levels for active employees enrolled in health insurance plans at employers with and without FSAs. From 2001 to 2005, only about 18 percent of enrollees had plans with physician cost sharing in the form of coinsurance rates. In comparison, about three quarters of enrollees had copayments for physician visits, and the levels of those copayments increased from $15 to $19 (2005 dollars). At the same time, rising numbers of enrollees faced positive deductibles (44 to 62 percent), and the average size of those deductibles increased from $431 to $614.

Our main interest, however, is whether these trends differ for plans with and without FSAs. Coinsurance rates declined for enrollees with access to an FSA but remained stable for those without such access (figure 6-3). Coinsurance rates fell from 18.97 to 17.61 percent for enrollees at establishments with FSAs

Figure 6-2. *Private Sector Employees with FSAs, 2001–05*

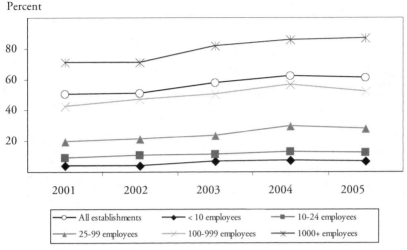

Percent

Source: MEPS-IC.

and remained close to 19 percent for enrollees at establishments without FSAs. This is exactly opposite to what our theory would predict: that FSAs increase coinsurance rates.

A similar trend is evident for copayments and deductibles. Copayments increased from $14.97 to $18.10 (up 21 percent) for enrollees with FSAs and from $15.66 to $19.71 (up 26 percent) for enrollees without FSAs (figure 6-4). Deductibles rose from $376 to $528 (an increase of 41 percent) for enrollees at establishments with FSAs, while deductibles rose from $486 to $764 (57 percent) for enrollees without FSAs (figure 6-5). Again, we would have expected the biggest increase in cost sharing to have occurred where cost sharing was subsidized, that is, where employees have access to FSAs.

Of course, these descriptive comparisons may reflect confounding factors and therefore do not rule out the possibility that the rise in the prevalence of FSAs has been associated with increased cost sharing over time. In order to move beyond the descriptive statistics and try to address the causal effect of FSAs on cost sharing, we turn to a multivariate analysis based on equation 6-1.

Results

To examine the effect of FSAs on cost sharing, we estimate versions of equation 6-1 in which the cost-sharing measure (κ) is an estimate of the proportion of

Table 6-1. *Cost sharing requirements for Private Sector Health Insurance Enrollees, 2001–05*[a]

Year	Number of active employee enrollees (thousands)	Physician visit cost sharing				Physician visit cost sharing	
		Percentage with positive coinsurance rate	Coinsurance rate (percent)	Percentage with positive copayment rate	Copayment rate (2005 dollars)[a]	Percentage with positive individual deductible	Individual deductible (2005 dollars)
All enrollees							
2001	63,020	18	18.94	76	15.30	44	431
2002	61,173	16	17.90	76	16.65	46	453
2003	60,348	18	18.05	74	17.43	50	511
2004	60,632	18	18.69	73	18.53	57	542
2005	60,648	18	18.16	74	18.68	62	614
Enrollees with FSA access							
2001	32,699	19	18.97	77	14.97	42	376
2002	32,717	17	17.52	76	16.25	44	375
2003	35,967	20	17.84	73	16.76	47	448
2004	38,719	18	18.36	74	18.07	55	453
2005	38,598	20	17.61	74	18.10	62	528
Enrollees without FSA access							
2001	30,321	17	18.90	75	15.66	46	486
2002	28,456	15	18.42	76	17.10	48	537
2003	24,381	16	18.43	75	18.40	56	588
2004	21,913	17	19.30	73	19.35	60	684
2005	22,050	16	19.37	74	19.71	62	764

Source: 2001-2005 MEPS-IC, private sector establishments.

a. The sample includes all establishments that offer insurance and all comprehensive health insurance plans from the 2001–05 survey years. Included are cases in which cost-sharing measures or the presence of a FSA are imputed to ensure that the descriptive statistics are nationally representative. In addition, all cost variables were inflation adjusted (using the CPI, all items) to constant 2005 dollars. The estimates for physician coinsurance rates and copayment rates exclude plans that have both a coinsurance rate and a copayment rate for physician visits.

Figure 6-3. *Private Sector Coinsurance Rates, with and without FSAs, 2001–05*

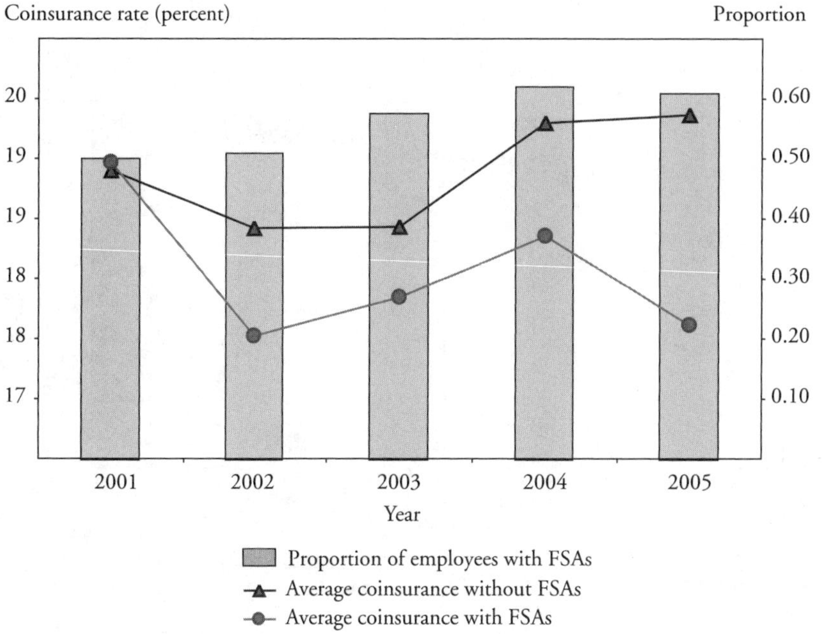

Coinsurance rate (percent)   Proportion

Source: MEPS-IC.

total health care costs paid by the insurance plan.[18] This actuarial value combines information on physician and hospital coinsurance/copayment rates, deductibles, out-of-pocket maximum levels, and covered services into one estimate, which represents the proportion of a given population's medical expenditures that would be paid by the insurance plan. These actuarial values were calculated for the overall population with employment-related insurance and for the population at different levels of the distribution of medical expenditures (that is, high users and low users). Since the values were calculated using the 2002 MEPS-IC, to apply them to our 2005 data we regressed the 2002 values on cost-sharing measures available in both the 2002 and 2005 data sets and used the 2002 model to predict actuarial values for 2005.[19] Estimates from one version of these models is presented in table 6A-2.

In some respects, estimating models of actuarial values is advantageous in that the entire spectrum of cost sharing can be accounted for in one equation. However, if the effects of FSAs operate in different directions on different cost-sharing requirements, these effects can be obscured. Therefore, in addition to the regressions using actuarial values, we estimated separate versions of the mod-

Figure 6-4. *Private Sector Copayment Rates, with and without FSAs, 2001–05*

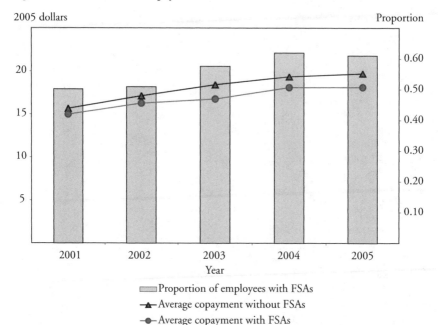

2005 dollars   Proportion

Year

☐ Proportion of employees with FSAs
▲ Average copayment without FSAs
● Average copayment with FSAs

Source: MEPS-IC.

els for deductible levels and plans that have physician cost sharing in the form of coinsurance and copayment rates.

Note that one disadvantage in estimating the physician copayment and coinsurance rates separately is that it may introduce some selection bias into the estimates if FSAs are associated with different plan types. We had considered combining the two physician cost-sharing measures into one variable—for example, by dividing the copayment rate by the average cost of a physician visit. However, the resulting percentage is highly dependent on the estimate for the cost of the physician visit, which can vary widely depending on the type of physician and also whether we use mean or median values. Another concern is that plans that are structured with physician copayments typically do not have deductibles that apply to physician visits.[20] Therefore, our physician cost-sharing equations embody some information on deductibles as well. To address this issue, we performed sensitivity tests in which we estimated equations for plans with only positive values of coinsurance and copayment rates.

We used survey weights to estimate two versions of our model, one that reflects plans that were offered to eligible employees and the other that reflects plans selected by enrollees.[21] It is possible that the results from the latter model

Figure 6-5. *Private Sector Deductible Levels, with and without FSAs, 2001–05*

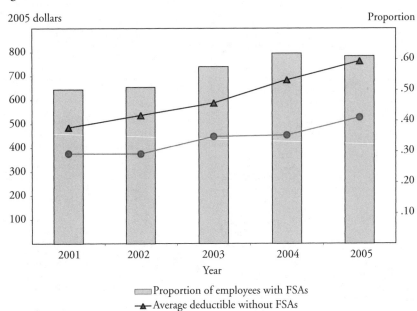

Source: MEPS-IC.

might be smaller in magnitude than the eligibility-weighted results. This might occur, for example, if employers believe that access to an FSA is all that is important when considering which plans to offer employees, but enrollees take into account whether or not they will participate in the FSA. For example, one study finds that FSA participation in the firm they analyzed was quite low.[22] If enrollees do not expect to enroll in an FSA, then their choice of insurance plan would be unlikely to reflect availability of an FSA. In addition, if employees have not accurately predicted medical expenditures in the past and put too little money in their FSAs, they would have had a share of their out-of-pocket costs that were not tax subsidized and might take this experience into account when selecting their level of cost sharing.

To control for worker characteristics we included measures of the proportion of employees who are female, the proportion age fifty or older, the proportion who belong to a union, and the proportion in three wage categories. Establishment characteristics include establishment size and firm size (as categorical variables), the establishment's industry, and a categorical set of measures for the firm's age, whether it is part of a multiunit firm, and its organization form. In

Table 6-2. *First-Stage Probit of Whether or Not a Private Sector Employer Offers an FSA*[a]

	Copayment	Coinsurance	Deductible	Actuarial value
Instruments				
Firm age 3–4	−.907*	−.032	−.783*	−.840*
	(.440)	(.632)	(.399)	(.427)
Firm age 5–9	−.312	.328	−.330	−.359
	(.369)	(.508)	(.335)	(.352)
Firm age 10–19	−.484	.052	−.530	−.546
	(.364)	(.495)	(.331)	(.347)
Firm age ≥20	−.407	.317	−.437	−.438
	(.360)	(.483)	(.328)	(.344)
Multiplant firm	.311**	.615**	.339**	.341**
	(.084)	(.136)	(.076)	(.079)
Proportion employees eligible	.403**	.040	.323*	.294*
	(.145)	(.234)	(.126)	(.133)
Exogenous regressors				
Proportion of workers earning <$10/hr	−1.652**	−1.791**	−1.728**	−1.769**
	(.174)	(.323)	(.167)	(.174)
Proportion of workers earning $10 to $23/hr	−.942**	−1.167**	−.992**	−1.003**
	(.133)	(.266)	(.126)	(.133)
Proportion of workers unionized	−.220	−.376*	−.239*	−.227*
	(.127)	(.175)	(.108)	(.111)
Proportion of female workers	.252	-.276	.127	.190
	(.135)	(.220)	(.120)	(.126)
Proportion of workers >50 yrs old	.236	-.286	.179	.207
	(.184)	(.324)	(.160)	(.168)
Top state marginal income tax rate	.007	.015	.010	.009
	(.010)	(.015)	(.009)	(.009)
Firm size: 10–24 employees	.135	-.046	.165	.055
	(.137)	(.247)	(.124)	(.131)

addition, we included the top income tax rate for the state in which the establishment is located and categorical variables for the nine census divisions.

Table 6-2 presents probit estimates of the likelihood of having an FSA, given establishment and region characteristics. These estimates were used to generate predicted probabilities of having an FSA, which were in turn used as instruments in equation 6-1. The estimates in each of the four columns were constructed using separate samples of plans for the coinsurance, copayment, deductible, and actuarial value analyses.

The first set of regressors are intended as instruments—predictors of FSA availability that are uncorrelated with the error term in equation 6-1. The age dummies are for the most part not statistically significant, even collectively.

Table 6-2. *First-Stage Probit of Whether or Not a Private Sector Employer Offers an FSA*[a] (continued)

	Copayment	Coinsurance	Deductible	Actuarial value
Firm size:	.863**	.613**	.825**	.813**
25–99 employees	(.136)	(.227)	(.123)	(.130)
Firm size:	1.364**	1.233**	1.375**	1.337**
100–999 employees	(.147)	(.233)	(.135)	(.142)
Firm size:	2.224**	1.493**	2.073**	2.024**
1,000+ employees	(0.163)	(.256)	(.145)	(.151)
Establishment size:	.288**	.375*	.283**	.339**
10–24 employees	(.089)	(.177)	(.082)	(.086)
Establishment size:	.181*	.215	.201*	.237**
25–99 employees	(.089)	(.160)	(.082)	(.085)
Establishment size:	.044	.239	.048	.088
100–249 employees	(.101)	(.169)	(.098)	(.100)
Establishment size:	.406**	.300	.358**	.371**
250+ employees	(.105)	(.160)	(.101)	(.104)
N	16,559	4,937	21,540	19,766
Joint test of instruments $F(7)$	4.24**	3.75**	5.10**	4.63**
Joint test of age of firm variables $F(5)$	1.47	.87	1.44	1.39
Joint test of proportion eligible and multiplant $F(2)$	11.41**	10.46**	14.26**	12.68**

Source: 2005 MEPS-IC, private sector establishments. See note with table 6-3 for a description of the sample.

a. Independent variables also include ownership type, industry, census division, and demographic data availability dummies and a measure for whether firm age is missing.

*Significant at 5% level

**Significant at 1% level

Employers in multiestablishment firms are more likely to offer FSAs, even controlling for firm and establishment size. And in all samples except coinsurance, establishments with a higher proportion of employees eligible for health insurance are more likely to offer FSAs.

Among other establishment characteristics, employers with more highly paid employees are more likely to offer FSAs, and those with a higher proportion of unionized workers are less likely to do so. Large establishments and those belonging to large firms are more likely to offer FSAs. The state's top marginal income tax rate is not statistically significant, perhaps because differences in this variable are mostly absorbed by the census division fixed effects—or perhaps

Table 6-3. *Cost-Sharing Equations, Eligibility Weighted*[a]

Independent variable	Copayment		Coinsurance		Deductible		Actuarial value	
	OLS	2SLS	OLS	2SLS	OLS	2SLS	OLS	2SLS
FSA	.712*	−2.002	.295	6.864**	−34.997*	−222.874*	.004	.017
	(.319)	(1.862)	(.606)	(2.434)	(15.385)	(90.935)	(.002)	(.011)
Proportion workers earning less than $10/hr	3.046**	1.869	1.374	4.693*	82.494	−6.492	−.010	−.004
	(.751)	(1.045)	(1.610)	(2.089)	(43.903)	(53.828)	(.005)	(.007)
Proportion workers earning $10–$23/hr	1.244*	.667	−.950	1.089	41.665	−3.317	.0007	.004
	(.598)	(.738)	(1.425)	(1.639)	(30.902)	(37.404)	(.004)	(.005)
Proportion workers unionized	−3.783**	−3.902**	−.2897**	−2.251*	−44.794	−54.599*	.006	.007*
	(.541)	(.566)	(1.085)	(1.124)	(26.650)	(27.226)	(.003)	(.003)
Proportion female workers	−.470	−.249	1.380	1.857	13.934	23.325	−.009*	−.010*
	(.580)	(.568)	(1.250)	(1.278)	(31.049)	(32.488)	(.004)	(.004)
Proportion workers age 50 or older	−1.139	−.957	1.004	1.188	98.312*	108.885**	−.013	−.014*
	(.797)	(.828)	(1.650)	(1.637)	(42.093)	(41.816)	(.005)	(.006)
Top state marginal income tax rate	.036	.039	.156	.132	.075	.507	.0001	.00009
	(.056)	(.057)	(.103)	(.107)	(2.113)	(2.162)	(.0003)	(.0003)
Firm size: 10–24 employees	1.007	1.003	1.334	1.722	12.351	12.907	−.001	−.001
	(.592)	(.594)	(1.469)	(1.570)	(32.078)	(32.219)	(.005)	(.004)
Firm size: 25–99 employees	.283	.797	−1.876	−2.872*	−103.364**	−68.840*	.014**	.012**
	(.554)	(.673)	(1.303)	(1.416)	(29.440)	(33.428)	(.004)	(.005)
Firm size: 100–999 employees	−.453	.663	−.112	−3.019	−136.159**	−56.752	.010*	.004
	(.529)	(.885)	(1.140)	(1.679)	(26.828)	(47.400)	(.004)	(.006)
Firm size: 1,000+ employees	−.858	.986	1.378	−2.333	−210.768**	−88.299	.008*	−.0002
	(.569)	(.141)	(1.169)	(1.872)	(28.111)	(62.268)	(.004)	(.008)
Estab. size: 10–24 employees	−.468	−.289	.324	−.446	−13.468	−.332	.007*	.005
	(.440)	(.454)	(1.052)	(1.197)	(18.783)	(19.907)	(.003)	(.003)

Estab. size: 25–99 employees	-.439	-.367	1.318	.988	22.417	29.300	-.002	-.003
	(.414)	(.422)	(.912)	(.999)	(18.206)	(18.682)	(.003)	(.003)
Estab. size: 100–249 employees	.052	-.040	1.826*	1.732	-7.169	-12.513	.003	.003
	(.450)	(.463)	(.918)	(1.035)	(20.575)	(21.070)	(.003)	(.003)
Estab. size: 250+ employees	-.981*	-.833	-.110	-.300	-32.972	-24.201	.009**	.008**
	(.419)	(.428)	(.887)	(1.056)	(18.811)	(20.309)	(.003)	(.003)
N	16,559	16,559	4,937	4,937	21,540	21,540	19,766	19,766
R^2	.08	.06	.11	.04	.10	.08	.09	.08

Source: 2005 MEPS-IC, private sector establishments.

a. Independent variables also include ownership type, industry, census division, and demographic data availability dummies. The copayment sample includes those plans that have no cost sharing for physician visits or in which cost sharing is expressed as a copayment for each visit. The coinsurance sample is similar except that in addition to including those cases with no physician visit cost sharing it includes those with a positive coinsurance rate. Both of these samples exclude the small percentage of plans in which there is both coinsurance and a copayment for a physician visit. However, they also overlap in that both include plans with zero values for cost sharing for physician visits, since zeroes could either be considered as copayment or coinsurance rates. The deductible sample includes those cases with either a zero or a positive deductible. The actuarial value sample includes all plans except those with imputed values for coinsurance, copayment, and deductible variables.

* significant at 5% level;

** significant at 1% level.

because the relevant tax variation is across wage categories, rather than states, and is explained by the categorical wage variables.

Table 6-3 presents our basic estimates of equation 6-1 for each measure of cost sharing. In each case, we report both an OLS version as a benchmark and a 2SLS version using the predicted values of F. Each pair (OLS and 2SLS) was run separately for the four measures of cost sharing: copayment, coinsurance, deductible, and actuarial value.

While the OLS result for copayment rates points to a positive effect of FSAs on these levels, this result disappears in the 2SLS model. In contrast, the results for coinsurance rates indicate that, in the OLS regression, the coefficient on the FSA dummy is small in magnitude and statistically insignificant. However, once we instrument for the FSA dummy, we find a large and statistically significant coefficient, which suggests that the presence of an FSA increases coinsurance rates by close to 7 percentage points, a large jump given that the average coinsurance rate for enrollees is 18.19 percent (table 6-1).[23] While the coefficient in the deductible model is statistically significant, it is in the wrong direction, suggesting that the tax subsidy for out-of-pocket expenses *decreases* cost sharing. We do not find a statistically significant FSA coefficient in the actuarial value model.

Our results for coinsurance rates (eligible employee weighted) are similar to those in the earlier work, which finds a coefficient of 1.4 in the OLS regression for coinsurance rates and a coefficient of 6.8 in the instrumental variables regression.[24] In fact, the 2SLS coefficients are almost identical. However, while these results replicate those in the earlier work, they are less convincing in this current context due to problems with the instrumental variables. For example, in the first-stage probit for the coinsurance model, firm age and eligible worker variables are not good predictors of whether an employer offers an FSA. Of the three instruments we include in the model, only the multiplant variable serves as a good predictor. Unfortunately, this variable is also a good predictor in the coinsurance rate equation, casting doubt on its validity as a good instrument (table 6-4). The coinsurance results are also somewhat sensitive to specification tests.

As indicated in tables 6-2 and 6-4, we encountered similar difficulties with our instruments in the copayment, deductible, and actuarial value models. For example, firm age does not perform well in predicting FSA availability in any of these three models. In addition, while the multiplant and eligible worker variables do predict FSA availability in these models, the eligible worker variable also predicts copayment levels. It is encouraging that neither the multiplant variable nor the eligible worker variable predicts deductible or actuarial values. However, a concern with using these variables as instruments is that a priori we would not have expected the instruments to perform differently in the different models since all estimate various forms of the same general concept—generosity of coverage.

Table 6-4 presents FSA coefficients for various specification tests as well as enrollment-weighted results. The first set of specification tests drops an individual instrument from the first-stage model and includes it in the second-stage model. The next set of tests includes all three variables in the first-stage models but excludes the multiplant and eligible worker variables from the second stage in various combinations (as indicated).

As seen in table 6-4, the FSA coefficients in the actuarial value models are statistically insignificant across all specifications. Similarly, the negative coefficient in the deductible equation is consistent across all specifications, achieving statistical significance in many eligibility-weighted, but not enrollment-weighted, models. The negative coefficient in the coinsurance rate equation is, in all but one case, statistically insignificant.

In addition to the sensitivity of the results to different instruments, another area of importance is the interrelationship between coinsurance/copayment rates and deductibles. As mentioned above, one complication with looking at physician copayment and coinsurance rates separately is that each equation embodies some information on deductible levels as well. Plans that are expressed as copayments for physician visits do not require satisfying a deductible for physician visits, whereas plans with coinsurance rates may or may not also have deductibles for physician visits. This aspect of plan design may, in fact, explain some of the unexpected results for copayments. While most of the negative coefficients in table 6-4 in the copayment model are statistically insignificant, one specification did yield a negative and statistically significant coefficient. This unexpected result could be due to movement from zero values to positive values in the data, which may also reflect eliminating deductibles for physician visits. To test this, we estimated models restricted to plans with positive copayments. Since in a number of cases this test also yields negative and, in many cases, statistically significant coefficients, these findings suggest that the negative results are driven by something other than the copayment/deductible relationship.

Similarly, it is possible that the positive coefficient in the coinsurance rate equation reflects the movement from zero to positive values and an implicit movement, due to plan design, to a positive deductible that applies to physician visits. In this model, unlike the copayment model, these two confounding factors move in the same direction. In models subset to positive values of the coinsurance rate we do not find an effect of FSAs on coinsurance rates.

Conclusions

Tax subsidies for out-of-pocket health care expenses (those not covered by health insurance) have existed in various forms for almost three decades. Given a

Table 6-4. *FSA Coefficient in Models with Alternative Specifications from Instrumental Variables Regression Models*

FSA coefficient	Copayment	Coinsurance	Deductible	Actuarial value
Baseline (table 6-3)	−2.002	6.864**	−222.874*	.017
	(1.862)	(2.434)	(90.935)	(.011)
Enrollment weighted, IV:	−1.582	4.432	−151.246*	.010
original specification	(1.967)	(2.374)	(77.225)	(.011)
Eligibility weighted specifications				
Drop age of firm	−2.723	4.962*	−210.383*	.019
	(1.600)	(2.461)	(93.120)	(.012)
Significant in 2nd stage	No	Yes	No	No
Drop multiplant firm	−2.524	3.615	−176.057	.017
	(1.961)	(2.747)	(92.295)	(.013)
Significant in 2nd stage	No	Yes	No	No
Drop proportion eligible	−1.183	7.004**	-203.167*	.014
	(1.927)	(2.407)	(96.608)	(.012)
Significant in 2nd stage	Yes	No	No	No
Include as instrument				
Just multiplant	−1.603	4.939*	−197.990*	.016
	(1.596)	(2.342)	(95.843)	(.012)
Just proportion eligible	−2.799	−1.372	−162.526	.022
	(1.695)	(2.460)	(97.125)	(.014)
Both multiplant and	−2.460	4.742*	−211.163*	.019
proportion eligible	(1.562)	(2.366)	(90.959)	(.012)
Enrollment weighted specifications				
Drop age of firm	−2.877	3.574	−152.307	.012
	(1.608)	(2.332)	(86.149)	(.012)
Significant in 2nd stage	No	Yes	No	No
Drop multiplant firm	−2.165	.248	−110.402	.008
	(2.066)	(2.578)	(90.012)	(.14)
Significant in 2nd stage	No	Yes	No	No
Drop proportion eligible	−.213	4.571	−129.941	.004
	(2.095)	(2.349)	(80.132)	(.012)
Significant in 2nd stage	Yes	No	No	No
Include as instruments:				
Just multiplant	−.957	3.705	−123.671	.004
	(1.622)	(2.285)	(85.894)	(.012)
Just proportion eligible	−3.470*	−2.037	−98.974	.009
	(1.724)	(2.426)	(93.547)	(.014)
Both multiplant and	−2.543	3.506	−146.077	.010
proportion eligible	(1.556)	(2.308)	(82.218)	(.012)

Source: 2005 MEPS-IC, private sector establishments.
*Significant at 5% level
**Significant at 1% level

subsidy for out-of-pocket costs, insurance purchasers may opt for less expensive insurance, with lower premiums and higher deductibles, knowing that uncovered expenses are subsidized. In this chapter we analyze data from a nationally representative survey of employers, the MEPS-IC, to examine whether employees with access to FSAs choose health insurance with greater cost sharing or are offered such insurance by their employers.

We examine a number of dimensions of cost sharing, including physician copayment and coinsurance rates, overall deductible levels, and actuarial values, which represent summary measures of the generosity of a health plan. We find mixed evidence that FSAs change the cost sharing of insurance plans. On average, coinsurance rates for employer-sponsored health insurance have been falling for those plans whose enrollees have access to FSAs but not for those plans whose enrollees do not have access; copayments and deductibles have been rising more slowly, exactly opposite to the theoretical prediction. When we control for other plan and establishment characteristics and attempt to control for the endogenous decision by firms to offer FSAs, we do find some evidence that coinsurance rates are higher than they otherwise would be in establishments with FSAs. However, these results are not robust. We find no evidence that FSAs increase copayments, deductibles, or the actuarial value of the health plan.

The sensitivity of our results to various specifications may arise from the challenges we encountered addressing the endogenous nature of the decision to offer an FSA. Instruments that worked well in an earlier study using 1993 data perform poorly using the 2005 MEPS-IC data. This difficulty may have arisen from the growth in the availability of FSAs. As more employers offer FSAs, those employers that do not offer them may differ from those that do in unobservable ways, making it more difficult to find instruments predicting FSA adoption but not cost-sharing rates. Alternatively, it may be that by 2005 employees had access to alternative mechanisms for subsidizing out-of-pocket costs (HRAs, MSAs, HSAs, or their spouses' tax-subsidized accounts), and as a consequence the effect of FSAs alone cannot be identified by comparing employers with and without the accounts.

Finally, our analysis so far focuses on the financial measures of plans, such as the actuarial value of the plan, the physician coinsurance or copayment rate, and deductibles. These measures all ignore the nonmonetary value to consumers of other aspects of plans, such as restricting the type of providers available and imposing other nonprice controls. One area for future research is the relationship between FSAs and employers' and employees' decisions with respect to health maintenance and preferred provider organizations in addition to other plan types.

Table 6A-1. *Means and Standard Deviations of Independent Variables*[a]

	Copayment sample	Coinsurance sample	Deductible sample	Actuarial value sample
Firm age 3–4	.018	.012	.016	.015
Firm age 5–9	.049	.028	.046	.045
Firm age 10–19	.125	.095	.114	.112
Firm age 20 or older	.564	.639	.587	.587
Firm age: missing	.233	.219	.228	.231
Multiplant firm	.661	.735	.683	.689
Proportion employees eligible	.875	.873	.874	.875
	(.179)	(.180)	(.181)	(.179)
Proportion workers earning less than $10/hr	.122	.137	.125	.126
	(.227)	(.239)	(.231)	(.230)
Proportion workers earning $10–$23/hr	.351	.348	.343	.346
	(.336)	(.333)	(.333)	(.333)
Wage data available (1 = yes)	.659	.662	.654	.657
Proportion unionized workers	.089	.110	.090	.091
	(.225)	(.256)	(.227)	(.228)
Union data available (1 = yes)	.922	.911	.911	.918
Proportion female workers	.332	.345	.331	.334
	(.311)	(.310)	(.311)	(.309)
Female data available (1 = yes)	.718	.732	.714	.719
Proportion workers age 50 or older	.159	.168	.159	.160
	(.176)	(.180)	(.176)	(.174)
Age 50 or older data available (1 = yes)	.684	.674	.676	.679
Top state marginal income tax rate	5.576	5.550	5.571	5.56
	(3.217)	(3.023)	(3.201)	(3.19)
Firm size: 10–24 employees	.076	.058	.072	.069
Firm size: 25–99 employees	.149	.108	.139	.137
Firm size: 100–999 employees	.233	.215	.226	.231
Firm size: 1,000+ employees	.486	.567	.509	.512
Establishment size: 10–24 employees	.132	.099	.126	.123
Establishment size: 25–99 employees	.247	.242	.242	.241
Establishment size: 100–249 employees	.182	.198	.187	.189
Establishment size: 250+ employees	.352	.374	.360	.365
N	16,559	4,937	21,540	19,766

Source: 2005 MEPS-IC, private sector establishments. See note with table 6-3 for a description of the sample.

a. When data were unavailable, the values for those observations were set to 0. Omitted category for establishment size and for firm size is <10 employees, for firm age is <3 years, and for the wage distribution is proportion earning >$23/hr. Standard deviations are shown only for continuous variables.

Table 6A-2. *Actuarial Value Model, Using Eligible Employee Weights*[a]

Independent variable	Coefficient (standard error)
Individual overall deductible	−.0000627**
	(1.71e-06)
Hospital deductible	−.0000133**
	(2.73e-06)
Physician deductible	−.000031**
	(8.68e-06)
Hospital copay	−.000022 **
	(1.55e-06)
Hospital coinsurance rate	−.0013454**
	(.0000394)
Physician copay	−9.00e-06
	(.0000446)
Physician coinsurance rate	−.0031331**
	(.0000649)
Out-of-pocket maximum level	−4.41e-06**
	(2.55e-07)
Indicator for no out-of-pocket maximum	−.0130254**
	(.000829)
Dental coverage	−.002546
	(.0005579)
Drug coverage	.1138775**
	(.0012534)
HMO plan	.0600126**
	(.0006725)
Point-of-service plan	.0174495**
	(.0006539)
Fee-for-service plan	−.0356156**
	(.0015263)
Constant	.7534314**
	(.0014464)
N	29,366
R^2	.885

Source: 2002 MEPS-IC, private sector establishments.

a. The omitted category for plan type is preferred provider organization.

*Significant at 5% level

**Significant at 1% level

Notes

1. "Workers Feel Pinch of Rising Health Costs," *New York Times,* October 22, 2003, p. C1; "When Health Insurance Is Not a Safeguard," *New York Times,* October 23, 2005, p. 1.1; and "Workers Paying More for Coverage; Employees Are Taking on More of the Rising Cost of Job-Sponsored Healthcare Plans," *Los Angeles Times,* September 12, 2007, p. C1.

2. Jonathan Gruber and Robin McKnight, "Why Did Employee Health Insurance Contributions Rise?" *Journal of Health Economics* 22, no. 5 (2003): 1085–104. For a cross-sectional study of the effect of public insurance options on employer decisions, see Thomas Buchmueller and others, "The Effect of SCHIP Expansions on Health Insurance Decisions by Employers," *Inquiry* 42, no. 3 (2005): 218–31.

3. David Dranove, Kathryn Spier, and Laurence Baker, "Competition among Employers Offering Health Insurance," *Journal of Health Economics* 19 (2000): 121–40. For a cross-sectional study of this issue, see Jessica Vistnes, Michael Morrissey, and Gail Jensen, "Employer Choices of Family Premium Sharing," *International Journal of Healthcare Finance and Economics* (2006): 25–47.

4. Since unused funds are forfeited, individuals need to predict their medical expenditures for the year in order to make FSA allocations. If they use more medical care than expected, then those additional out-of-pocket costs would not be subsidized through the FSA. If they use less, then they face incentives to accelerate expenditures near the end of the year. (Recent changes allow unused FSA contributions to be rolled over for a two-and-a-half-month grace period in the following year.) In this chapter we do not address these nonlinearities and treat the deduction of out-of-pocket expenses as open-ended.

5. As Henry Aaron, Patrick Healy, and Surachai Khitatrakun (chapter 5) note, because of the tax-free accumulation inside HSAs, account owners may have little incentive to spend the funds, even on qualified health care expenses.

6. The pairing of an HSA with a high-deductible plan is sometimes referred to as a consumer-driven health plan (CDHP).

7. William Jack and Louise Sheiner, "Welfare-Improving Health Expenditure Subsidies," *American Economic Review* 87, no. 1 (1997): 206–21.

8. See Jeffrey Liebman and Richard Zeckhauser (chapter 10); and Joseph P. Newhouse, "Reconsidering the Moral Hazard–Risk Avoidance Tradeoff," *Journal of Health Economics* 25 (2006): 1005–14.

9. William Jack, Arik Levinson, and Sjamsu Rahardja, "Employee Cost-Sharing and the Welfare Effects of Flexible Spending Accounts," *Journal of Public Economics* 90 (2006): 2285–301.

10. Barton H. Hamilton and James Marton, "Employee Choice of Flexible Spending Account Participation and Health Plan," *Health Economics* 17, no. 7 (2008): 793–813.

11. The formal theory is in Jack and Sheiner "Welfare-Improving Health Expenditure Subsidies"; and Jack, Levinson, and Rahardja, "Employee Cost-Sharing." Here we simply describe the intuition.

12. Newhouse, "Reconsidering the Moral Hazard–Risk Avoidance Tradeoff," and Liebman and Zeckhauser (chapter 10) discuss these types of behavioral considerations. If patients do not heed their own long-term interests and fail to adhere to costly treatment regimes, they may be made better off by being offered tax subsidies for those costs.

13. Mark Pauly, "The Economics of Moral Hazard: Comment," *American Economic Review* 58 (1968): 531–37; and Martin S. Feldstein, "The Welfare Loss of Excess Health Insurance," *Journal of Political Economy* 81, no. 2 (1973): 251–80.

14. Under certain conditions it can be shown that the increase in nominal cost sharing more than offsets the price-reducing effect of the subsidy; see Jack and Sheiner, "Welfare-Improving Health Expenditure Subsidies."

15. Jack, Levinson, and Rahardja, "Employee Cost-Sharing," show that the net of tax coinsurance rate was the same for firms with and without FSAs, meaning that for the average worker the FSA tax subsidy was entirely offset by an increase in cost sharing. They conclude that FSAs are effectively a "subsidy to health care for high-income workers that is partly offset by efficiency gains at the expense of low-income workers" (p. 2299).

16. James J. Heckman and Richard Robb, "Alternative Methods for Estimating the Impact of Interventions," in *Longitudinal Analysis of Labor Market Data,* edited by James J. Heckman and Burton Singer (Cambridge University Press, 1985).

17. The MEPS-IC is sponsored by the Agency for Healthcare Research and Quality (AHRQ) and conducted by the U.S. Bureau of the Census. Even though the MEPS-IC is called a panel, the data are really a series of independent cross sections of establishments.

18. We constructed a separate set of samples from the MEPS-IC data for these analyses. These samples exclude observations with imputed values for flexible spending accounts and cost-sharing measures and for plans identified by respondents in the MEPS-IC as having an HSA or an HRA. We also restricted attention to 2005, because a change in survey procedures yielded better data for the coinsurance and copayment variables in that year. However, since we also excluded plans with imputed data, we cannot claim that our results are nationally representative.

19. For a detailed description of the 2002 actuarial values used in our analysis, see Jon Gabel and others, "Generosity and Adjusted Premiums in Job-Based Insurance: Hawaii Is Up, Wyoming Is Down," *Health Affairs* 25, no. 3 (2006): 832–43. To give some idea of the range of values, these authors note that the average actuarial value was 83.2 percent in 2002; it was 86 percent for the highest 10 percent of health care users and 72 percent for the lowest 50 percent of users.

20. See Gabel and others, "Generosity and Adjusted Premiums," for a discussion of this issue.

21. Both weights start with the MEPS-IC base plan weight used to produce national estimates of the number of plans and plan characteristics. We modified this weight to create the first weight, which is the plan weight multiplied by the number of eligible employees in the establishment. The second weight is the plan weight multiplied by the number of active employees enrolled in the plan.

22. James Cardon and Mark Showalter, "An Examination of Flexible Spending Accounts," *Journal of Health Economics* 20 (2001): 935–54.

23. The FSA coefficient in the coinsurance model is statistically significant at the 10 percent level.

24. Jack, Levinson, and Rahardja, "Employee Cost-Sharing."

Comment by Jonathan Gruber

Jessica Vistnes, William Jack, and Arik Levinson have written a very timely essay on a critically important topic. There is enormous interest in current policy debates in offering the same kind of tax subsidies to spending outside of employer-sponsored insurance (ESI) as is given to employer-sponsored insurance. There are a variety of ways to accomplish this goal; chapter 6 focuses on one particular approach: flexible spending accounts (FSAs), whereby employees can use a wage deduction to save for their out-of-pocket health care spending.

The central economic question the chapter addresses is whether the existence of an FSA plan at a firm leads that firm to raise the cost sharing of employees enrolled in the firm's health insurance plans. The logic is the following. Health insurance premiums are subsidized, but absent an FSA, out-of-pocket spending is not. As a result, firms distort their compensation toward first-dollar health insurance coverage, since they can deduct the resulting higher premiums. But if both ESI premiums and out-of-pocket spending were deductible, then employees would demand more efficient cost sharing policies.

The empirical analysis models firm cost sharing as a function of FSA availability and demonstrates that having an FSA is associated with higher employee cost sharing (although the findings are fairly sensitive to variations in the empirical specification). In this discussion, I first review some issues with the authors' data and empirical analysis. I then turn to the larger policy issues raised by their discussion.

Data and Empirical Strategy

The MEPS-IC is the best source of information available on the details of health insurance plans for a very large set of employers. Its value is heightened by the fact that only select researchers have access to the data. But there is one data issue on which the authors could have been clearer, and that is the definition of

144

an FSA. Some employers offer section 125 accounts that only allow for pretax premiums. Are those captured as well? Or does the employer need to allow for pretax treatment of all health costs to qualify as an FSA in their sample?

The larger problem is the authors' empirical strategy. The age-old simultaneity problem complicates this strategy: employers choose simultaneously whether to have an FSA and how much the coinsurance rate will be, confounding cause and effect. The authors attempt to solve this problem by using three instruments: the age of the firm, whether this is a multiplant firm, and the percent of workforce eligible for health insurance. But as the authors note, only one instrument matters: the age of the firm. The others are only weakly correlated with FSA availability.

An appropriate instrument is one highly correlated with the endogenous regressor (in this case, FSA availability) and otherwise not correlated with the dependent variable (in this case, coinsurance rates). Unfortunately, none of these instruments seems to me more naturally associated with an FSA offering than coinsurance rates: it seems they would be equally likely to affect both. For example, why should the age of the firm matter for FSA availability but not, independently, for coinsurance rate in the firm's health insurance plan? So while the authors have an excellent data source here, I would challenge them to think harder about how it might be used to devise a more convincing empirical strategy.

Policy Issues

An important accomplishment of this chapter is to raise several timely policy questions. One question is, Should we try to level the playing field for out-of-pocket costs? As noted earlier, there is a clear bias here in favor of employer insurance spending from the ESI tax subsidy. And the policy prescription recommended by many is to subsidize equally out-of-pocket spending

But this seems to me to violate a rule I have been teaching my children since they were very small: two wrongs do not make a right. Rather, they make a wrong-wrong! I see two major problems with this solution. The first problem is that subsidized out-of-pocket spending has two competing effects: reduction in spending through a more rational plan design (the "indirect" effect studied by the authors), and more spending through subsidies to out-of-pocket expenditures (the "direct" effect of these new tax subsidies). In fact, there is still enormous uncertainty about the indirect channel proposed by the authors; despite their valiant efforts, I would still argue we know very little about this key elasticity. But we do have solid evidence on the more direct effect from the RAND health insurance experiment (HIE) and other studies that subsidizing out-of-pocket costs will lead to higher spending. The HIE suggests fairly modest elasticities of out-of-pocket spending in their randomized trial, but recent work by Amy Finkelstein on the introduction of Medicare suggests that these effects can be ten times as large in general equilibrium. Given that we know that out-of-pocket spending will rise, and we do not know whether plan design will improve, this seems a pretty weak case for adding more tax breaks.

But the hurdle for adopting this policy is even higher, because the tax break has a social cost: net government resources pay for the subsidy. The deadweight loss could well offset any gain to health spending efficiency. Moreover, this is a highly regressive policy, since the value of the tax break rises with income. So it is hard to make the case based on existing evidence that social efficiency will rise with a tax break for out-of-pocket health care spending.

Another policy question is, How does a tax deduction for out-of-pocket costs (such as with an FSA) compare with tax subsidies tied to high-deductible health insurance plans (such as with health savings accounts, or HSAs)? There is an interesting trade-off in evaluating these alternatives. On the one hand, since the tax break to HSAs is conditioned on buying a high-deductible plan, these tax breaks are more likely to induce workers to buy a plan with more out-of-pocket spending; that is, the indirect effect studied in this chapter is more likely with an HSA.

On the other hand, HSAs are even more expensive—and even more regressive—than are FSAs (see chapter 4, by Lisa Clemans-Cope). And for many high-income individuals they are just a tax shelter (see chapter 5, by Henry Aaron, Patrick Healy, and Surachai Khitatrakun). So in the end, HSAs amount to an expensive and regressive bribe to hold a particularly cost-efficient type of insurance. An important issue is the welfare implications of using that mechanism rather than just allowing health cost deductibility.

The final policy question relates to another old adage: two wrongs do not make a right, but three lefts do! In this case the three lefts that may be in place in 2009 are the Senate, the House, and the presidency. And the right turn that they may take is transforming the ESI tax break into something more productive. As I have shown in my work for the Hamilton project, we could move to universal health insurance coverage using the type of plan in effect in Massachusetts or the type proposed by John Edwards and Hillary Clinton. And such a plan could be easily financed by getting rid of the ESI exclusion. Indeed, by my estimates, we could have universal health care coverage *and* about $70 billion a year left over for other priorities. In this way we would move to a much more progressive system and also get rid of the incentives for excessive insurance coverage. Can these three lefts make this right?

7

Administrative Issues: Challenges of the Current System

MARY B. H. HEVENER AND CHARLES K. "CHIP" KERBY III

Many of the major health care reform proposals would assign a key administrative role to the IRS. To those who would rely heavily on IRS involvement, we say: Beware! The IRS's track record in administering the existing, relatively simple tax rules governing health care is not heartening.

Much of the challenge in reforming America's health care delivery system relates to the difficulty of administering the tax rules regarding employer-provided and individually purchased health care. The current rules are, for the most part, comparatively simple. However, they permit employer-provided coverage to be denied to part-time employees, who in turn are ineligible for the tax deduction offered for independent contractors' purchases of health insurance. The deduction for individually purchased health care itself offers only limited tax benefits for lower-income workers. If strictly enforced, even the current tax rules might be used to expand health care coverage for lower-paid workers, but the IRS has not done a very good job of administering these rules. For example, the IRS has not finalized cafeteria plan regulations that permit employees to purchase health coverage on a pretax basis, even though the statutory provisions were enacted thirty years ago. In addition, the IRS has paid little or no attention to auditing employer health plans for compliance with nondiscrimination rules and continuation coverage rules. The IRS has found it hard even to administer the very limited tax credit designed to expand health insurance coverage for displaced workers (to say nothing of the Earned Income Tax Credit, a much simpler tax credit designed to transfer funds to low-income workers). None of this should come as a surprise—the principal mission of the IRS is to process tax returns and collect revenue for the federal government, not to ensure the broad availability of employer-provided or individually purchased health care coverage.

147

Before Congress requires the IRS to be heavily involved in the administration of complex schemes to expand health care coverage, an honest and realistic assessment of the administrative challenges that must be met is essential. Any attempt to expand health care coverage through employer and or individual mandates will create powerful incentives for avoidance, evasion, and possibly even outright fraud, either through undervaluation of health benefits that might be subject to income tax or discrimination rules or through claims of excessive individual income tax deductions and credits. It is not our contention that the IRS could not address these challenges. With sufficient resources and public acceptance of some level of administrative failure, the IRS may be able to manage the reforms. The key question that policymakers must consider is whether the IRS is the best agency to address these challenges and if so, whether the IRS will be provided with a sufficient budget and enough staff to administer successfully these proposed fundamental reforms.

Tax Primer

The tax law includes several provisions regarding the tax treatment of health coverage and benefits.[1] Under these provisions, tax treatment differs depending on whether the coverage is provided under a regular accident or health plan, a flexible spending arrangement, or a health savings account; whether the coverage and benefits are provided by an employer or purchased by an individual; and whether the individual purchases coverage on an after-tax basis or on a pre-tax basis under a cafeteria plan—so-called because of the wide range of health and dependent care choices available for individual selection. Other provisions make health coverage tax deductions or tax credits available to certain eligible individuals and require employers to offer continuation coverage to employees and dependents who lose coverage in certain circumstances. Finally, an excise tax equal to 25 percent of an employer's group health plan expenses is triggered if the group health plan makes Medicare the primary payer for any active employees or their beneficiaries, which is in violation of the Medicare Secondary Payer provisions of the Social Security Act. The basic attributes of these various provisions are summarized below.

Accident or Health Plans

An *accident* or *health plan* is defined in IRS regulations as any arrangement that pays amounts in the event of injury or illness; it includes plans providing either medical or disability coverage.[2] A plan may cover one or more employees, and the plan may be insured or self-insured. The IRS regulations defining an accident or health plan have remained substantially unchanged since 1956. The tax treatment of accident or health plan coverage and benefits may be summarized as follows:

Tax treatment of employer-provided coverage. The value of accident or health plan coverage paid for or provided by an employer is excluded from an employee's income and from an employee's wages for employment tax purposes. The exclusion applies whether the employer provides the coverage directly or indirectly. Thus the exclusion applies to coverage provided under a health plan sponsored by the employee's employer or, in the case of the employee's acquiring coverage from a different source, when the employer pays or reimburses the employee's premiums for that coverage. The exclusion is available only for "common law employees"—that is, persons who are correctly classified as "employees" under a complicated set of tests explained in hundreds of court cases and IRS guidelines—but it does not apply to self-employed individuals.

Tax treatment of individually purchased coverage. The cost of accident or health plan coverage purchased by an individual is deductible only if, and to the extent that, the cost of that coverage (combined with other unreimbursed medical expenses) exceeds 7.5 percent of the individual's adjusted gross income.[3] However, the cost of accident or health plan coverage purchased by an employee on a pretax basis under a cafeteria plan is excluded from income as if it were employer-provided coverage. The deduction for individually purchased coverage applies not only to the employee but also to the employee's spouse and dependents, and if the coverage is purchased on a posttax basis, it can cover nondependents, including domestic partners. The cost of accident or health plan coverage bought by a self-employed individual (including sole proprietors, partners, and more-than-2 percent shareholders in an S corporation) who is not eligible to participate in an employer-sponsored plan may be deducted in full.[4] If any company for which such a self-employed individual is performing services either reimburses the self-employed individual for this coverage or provides health insurance coverage directly, that coverage is excludable as a *working condition fringe* (which provides a tax exclusion for any benefits deductible as an ordinary and necessary business expense).[5]

Tax treatment of benefits from employer-provided coverage. If an employer pays for accident or health plan coverage, benefits received by an employee from the plan that are used to pay or reimburse medical expenses of an employee, spouse, or dependent are excluded from the employee's income and from wages for employment tax purposes.[6] Benefits are excludable even if paid merely upon the occurrence of a specific accident, injury, illness, or diagnosis and regardless of whether they are paid in a lump sum or as claims are incurred. Under IRS regulations, this exclusion does not apply to amounts that employees are entitled to receive even if they do not incur expenses for medical care. Amounts paid in excess of actual medical expenses must be included in income.[7] The exclusion for benefits also does not apply in the case of a self-insured accident or health plan that fails to satisfy the nondiscrimination rules applicable to self-insured accident or health plans.[8]

Tax treatment of benefits from individually purchased coverage. If people pay for accident or health plan coverage on an after-tax basis, benefits received by them from the plan are excluded from their income, even if not used to pay for or reimburse medical expenses.[9]

Nondiscrimination Rules

The nondiscrimination rules applicable to self-insured health plans and to cafeteria plans have not been the subject of significant IRS enforcement activity.[10] Consequently, employers that sponsor these plans do not typically incur administrative costs associated with performing nondiscrimination tests or conducting other compliance activities. More important, as a practical matter, it has been extremely difficult for taxpayers even to understand how these discrimination rules are expected to apply. Even though the rules have been in effect since 1978, there is only a limited amount of IRS guidance describing how the rules should be applied.[11] Moreover, because the rules very rarely have been cited in IRS rulings, private rulings, or guidance to the field, there is a lot of confusion about how exactly they should be interpreted. The basic rules are shown in box 7-1.

An employer can elect to test separate plans together or separately for purposes of meeting these nondiscrimination rules. Thus, if one plan fails the nondiscrimination tests, it will not taint others that meet these tests.

Flexible Spending Arrangements

A flexible spending arrangement (FSA) is a special type of accident or health plan, typically established by an employer to reimburse medical expenses up to defined coverage limits (for example, $5,000 per year). Under proposed IRS regulations, an accident or health plan is treated as an FSA if the maximum amount of coverage is less than 500 percent of the total contributions or premiums paid for the coverage.[12] For example, if an accident or health plan limits the maximum reimbursement amount to the amounts contributed by employers and employees, it will be treated as an FSA. If an employer-provided accident or health plan is treated as an FSA, benefits are excluded from an employee's income only if the FSA satisfies certain additional rules. An FSA must provide coverage effective for a defined twelve-month period, provide uniform coverage throughout that period, require the employee to forfeit any unused amounts at the end of the period (the use-it-or-lose-it rule), reimburse only medical expenses that are substantiated, and not reimburse insurance premiums.

Box 7-1. *Nondiscrimination Rules Applicable to Self-Insured Health Plans and to Cafeteria Plans*

1. Under the "nondiscrimination as to eligibility" test, the plan either must be offered to 70 percent of employees (excluding employees with fewer than three years of service and who are under the age of 25, part-time, collectively bargained, and nonresident aliens), 80 percent of whom must participate, or must be offered to a "fair cross-section" of employees, under the same type of rules applicable to qualified retirement plans. The permitted exclusion of younger and part-time workers in particular has contributed to the enormous health coverage gap for these workers.

2. Under the "nondiscrimination as to benefits" test, *all* of the benefits provided to "highly compensated individuals" (HCIs), defined as the top 25 percent of the workforce, (excluding employees with fewer than three years of service and who are under the age of 25, part-time, collectively bargained, and nonresident aliens) must be provided to all other employees.[1] (More important, these exclusion rules are so broad as to permit many employers to design plans that would be blatantly discriminatory were these excluded classes of employees included in the tests.)

3. This "nondiscrimination as to benefits" test applies to the "type of benefit subject to reimbursement" and to the "amount of the benefit subject to reimbursement."

4. There are no examples given in the regulations of discrimination as to a period of coverage, except in the case of a terminated plan, in which case the regulations provide that discrimination exists "if the duration of the plan (or benefit) has the effect of discriminating in favor of [HCIs]."

5. Retiree health plans are automatically deemed to be nondiscriminatory, but only provided that "the type, and the dollar limitations, of benefits provided to retired employees who were [HCIs] are the same for all other retired participants."[2]

6. Two penalties apply to discriminatory plans, depending upon how the rules are violated. If a particular benefit is provided only to HCIs or otherwise discriminates in favor of HCIs, then that benefit is fully taxable to *all* HCIs. If a plan provides the same benefits to all participants, but discriminates as to coverage, then all HCIs under the plan must be taxable on a fraction of their benefits. The fraction equals the total amount reimbursed during the year to HCIs, divided by the total amount reimbursed under the plan to all participants. Obviously, if the plan at issue covers only HCIs, the result is the same under both penalties.

1. Treas. Reg. §1.105-11(c)(2)(iii).

2. As noted in endnote 8, it is not clear that this rule effectively limits the length of time that benefits are provided, and accordingly, it is relatively common for executives to receive posttermination health coverage for many years after termination of service, for which they pay only minimal taxes. The IRS is obviously aware of this practice, because it provided in the golden parachute regulations that any posttermination health benefits that were part of an "excess parachute" were required to be subjected to excise taxes in each year that they are provided, even if the employer otherwise elects to pay in a lump sum the rest of the parachute excise taxes due on future streams of payments. See Treas. Reg. §1.280G-1, Q&A 11(c). Similarly, the IRS provided in the rules under Code § 3121(v)(2) governing the application of FICA taxes to deferred compensation (which generally permit FICA taxes to be applied at the time of vesting) that health benefits cannot be treated as eligible for these special FICA tax timing rules and thus that future streams of taxable heath benefits paid as part of a severance arrangement, as well as disability benefits, are required to be subjected annually to FICA taxes. See Treas. Reg. §§31.3121(v)(2)-1(b)(4)(iv)(B), §§31.3121(v)(2)-1(b)(4)(iv)(C), and §§31.3121(v)(2)-1(b)(4)(v)(A).

In most cases, an FSA is not a funded arrangement. More commonly, an FSA is an unfunded account that is credited with employer and employee contributions. Because of the use-it-or-lose-it requirement, amounts credited or contributed to an FSA in one year cannot be carried over to future years. Typically, FSAs are offered as an option under a cafeteria plan and are financed with employee pretax contributions. But according to IRS proposed regulations, an accident or health plan may be treated as an FSA even if it is not part of a cafeteria plan (for example, a situation in which the FSA is not funded with any employee pretax contributions).

Health Savings Accounts

A health savings account (HSA) is another type of accident or health plan subject to special tax rules.[13] An HSA is a trust or custodial account created or organized in the United States to pay exclusively for qualified medical expenses of the account holder (and the account holder's spouse and dependents, if any). Favorable tax treatment for HSAs is available only for *eligible individuals*. These are people who are covered by a high-deductible health plan and do not have other health insurance coverage other than certain permitted coverages. If statutory requirements are satisfied, an HSA provides favorable tax treatment for contributions, earnings, and distributions (see Lisa Clemans-Cope, chapter 4, for a description of HSAs).

Health Coverage Tax Credit

Some people are entitled to receive a Health Coverage Tax Credit (HCTC).[14] The HCTC pays 65 percent of the cost of qualified health coverage for two principal groups—laid-off workers certified by the Department of Labor as having been displaced by the impact of international trade and people aged 55 to 64 who are receiving pension benefits paid by the Pension Benefit Guaranty Corporation. The HCTC is available only for eligible people who have qualified health coverage—either continuation coverage provided by their former employer (described in more detail below) or coverage provided by state-qualified plans that satisfy certain consumer protection requirements. The HCTC is a refundable tax credit that is available to eligible individuals regardless of whether they have paid federal income tax and is available on a refund (end of year) or advance basis. Individuals are not eligible for the HCTC if they have certain types of other health coverage, including subsidized employer-provided coverage (coverage in which at least 50 percent of the cost is paid by an employer or former employer of the taxpayer or spouse, including pretax contributions under a cafeteria plan) or coverage provided under various federal programs, including Medicare, Medicaid, the State Children's Health Insurance

Program, the Federal Employees Health Benefits Program, and TRICARE (the Department of Defense program for military personnel and retirees and their dependents). The HCTC enrollment processes are exceedingly complex.

COBRA Continuation Coverage

Employer-sponsored group health plans are required to offer COBRA continuation coverage.[15] Continuation coverage rights must be extended to qualified beneficiaries who typically are covered employees and their dependents who lose health plan coverage because of a qualifying event, including the employee's death, termination of employment, reduction in hours, divorce, or a dependent child ceasing to be a dependent. Employers and plan administrators must notify qualified beneficiaries of their COBRA continuation coverage rights, which last eighteen months for employees who have lost coverage because they have lost their jobs or their hours have been reduced and thirty-six months for certain other events.[16] Qualified beneficiaries who elect COBRA continuation coverage may be required to pay 102 percent of the premium cost.

Employers as Primary Payers (Medicare Secondary Payer Rules)

Employers are prohibited from operating or contributing to any group health plan that makes Medicare the primary payer of health benefits for any active employee (or that employee's spouse or dependents).[17] If these rules are violated in any way and to any degree, an excise tax is imposed on the employer equal to 25 percent of the employer's contribution to the group health plan. Although the Social Security Administration has prosecuted vigorously those employers who violated these Medicare Secondary Payer (MSP) rules, the IRS has never issued regulations and apparently has not instituted any provisions for being notified of violations so that it can impose this excise tax.

Administrative Issues and Problems Associated with Current Law

The current tax rules governing health plan coverage and benefits do not impose significant administrative burdens on individuals, employees, employers, health care providers, or the federal government.

Minimal Administrative Burdens
(or IRS Information Reporting Requirements)

For traditional defined benefit health plans, the tax exclusions for coverage and benefits are open-ended, so there is no need for employers to determine and report or for regulators to audit the value of employer-provided health plan coverage or the amount of benefits received. Employers are not required to provide the IRS with information about the existence of a health plan, the specific benefits offered under a health plan, whether employees are covered by a health plan or a cafeteria plan, and whether employees are paying their share of health plan contributions or making FSA contributions on a pretax basis under a cafeteria plan.[18] Similarly, individuals are not required to notify the IRS whether they and their dependents are covered by a health plan or whether they and their dependents are covered by an employer-sponsored health plan. Health care providers are not required to provide the IRS with information about whether their patients are covered under a health plan or whether a patient is covered under an employer-sponsored health plan. Individuals who wish to deduct medical expenses must maintain records sufficient to substantiate those expenses, but they need not submit that information when filing tax returns. HSAs are subject to various reporting requirements imposed on HSA account holders, HSA trustees and custodians, and employers making HSA contributions. However, even though the IRS has statutory authority to impose reporting requirements on employers who sponsor HSA-compatible high-deductible health plans, it has not yet done so.

Vague and Minimally Enforced Nondiscrimination Rules

Although nondiscrimination rules have been part of the law since 1978, there are many reasons for widespread confusion about their application to employer health plans that provide executive-only health coverage. First, there is no clear rule about discrimination concerning "benefit duration" in nonterminated plans. There are no specific examples explaining how duration of benefits is necessarily discriminatory, except for terminated plans, and therefore, some companies argue that offering lifetime benefits to certain executives is not covered under the discrimination rules. However, the regulations also explain that discrimination will be identified, "based on all the facts and circumstances."

Second, there is no clear rule about "free" coverage versus "pay-for" coverage. Because nondiscrimination rules were created before COBRA was enacted, there are no specific examples explaining whether executives can be offered free or discounted health coverage in lieu of COBRA coverage without violating the nondiscrimination rules.

Third, the definition of "self-insurance" is unclear. Some companies have argued that if their health plan includes any element of "risk-shifting," then the entire plan should be exempted from these nondiscrimination rules. This analysis is not supported by the legislative history, but the rules on how to separate the "insured" from the "non-insured" plans have never been explained.

Fourth, no clear rules on testing of "separate plans" exist. It appears that an employer can avoid having all of its HCIs taxed (as a result of discriminating in favor of a few HCIs) simply by separating its potentially discriminatory benefits into a separate plan.

Fifth, there are no examples of whether taxing HCIs on their health coverage is equivalent to charging the COBRA cost. Some employers have argued that so long as they tax HCIs on their health coverage, this is a nondiscriminatory benefit that is not subject to any other penalties.

Finally, and perhaps most startlingly, to the best of our knowledge, no company has ever been audited for discrimination in health benefits. From 1986 through 1989, when employers were dealing with more onerous nondiscrimination rules, it was apparent that virtually no employer's plan could satisfy those onerous rules.[19] But since 1989 the IRS has been curiously uninterested in issuing new guidance or in auditing plans for compliance. Without significant IRS enforcement, it is natural that many employers simply fail to pay attention to potential violations of the nondiscrimination rules.

In 2007 the IRS reproposed its cafeteria plan regulations, many provisions of which had been around since 1984, and provided significantly more detailed nondiscrimination testing requirements for cafeteria plans as well as clarified limitations on the types of benefits that can and cannot be offered under such plans and the conditions under which they can be offered to former employees. Employers expect IRS enforcement activity in this area to increase dramatically, once these rules are finalized. However, surprisingly few public comments have been filed on the reproposed regulations, perhaps because taxpayers have been lulled by years of IRS non-enforcement of discrimination rules into believing that their plans either meet these rules or will never be audited.

Ability to Exclude Many Leased Employees and Other "Contingent Workers"

If employers do, in fact, run nondiscrimination tests, they must take into consideration all full-time employees (including certain "leased employees") in determining whether a qualified retirement plan and certain welfare benefit plans are nondiscriminatory.[20] However, as a technical matter, the IRS revoked its "leased employee" regulations years ago and has been generally inactive in performing any audits of these companies.[21] Meanwhile, the number and types of leased employees have proliferated. They include not only standard part-time and temporary employees but also other employees who may work full-time and long term for a particular service recipient, through one of many types of designated "employers," which may or may not provide any benefits to their workers. These employment companies go by a variety of names, ranging from *leasing organization, PC, loan-out organization,* to *professional employer organization.* None of these terms is defined in the Internal Revenue Code. These three-party arrangements have proliferated in recent years to meet changing demands for products and services, to the point that millions of employees are deemed to be "employed" by these organizations, even though they may perform all their services for separate, single companies that exclude these workers from their benefit plans. However, the IRS has been very slow in issuing guidance on the subject. Instead, in recent years, enforcement of the discrimination rules and other labor law rules mandating the provision of employee benefits has been led more by workers than by the IRS. In most cases the courts have supported employers' ability to exclude these workers from their benefit plans.[22]

Ability to Exclude Independent Contractors

The IRS, for its part, has been surprisingly inactive in challenging worker classifications in recent years. The IRS has issued revenue rulings and developed training materials to train agents in the identification of workers misclassified as independent contractors rather than as employees.[23] However, after the establishment of the Classification Settlement Program in 1996, businesses have been able to settle *all* back years' liabilities for misclassified workers by merely paying underpaid taxes for *one calendar quarter* (or, in some cases, one year), with the liability calculated under extremely generous rules, provided that the businesses reclassify the workers prospectively.[24] This amnesty program provides such tiny potential payroll tax collections that many IRS employment auditors have simply moved on to more fertile grounds.

COBRA

The COBRA requirements impose more significant administrative burdens on employer-sponsored health plans. Employers are required to provide general notices to new plan participants describing their COBRA rights, to provide election notices when a COBRA qualifying event occurs, and to bill and collect COBRA premium payments from qualified beneficiaries who elect COBRA coverage. While some employers perform all of these required COBRA administrative tasks, many employers hire third-party administrators to assist in this process. Most employer efforts to comply with COBRA are prompted by Department of Labor enforcement activities and by the risk of participant lawsuits under ERISA.[25] Although the IRS has the authority to impose excise taxes to enforce compliance with the COBRA requirements, it is not known to have exercised that authority.

Health Coverage Tax Credit Requirements

The HCTC requirements impose complex administrative burdens on eligible individuals, health plan administrators, and related stakeholders such as labor unions and state workforce agencies. A detailed IRS website provides relevant information about the HCTC and the mechanics associated with applying for and receiving the credit, but this information does not alleviate the fundamental complexity of the statutory provision. State workforce agencies and the Pension Benefit Guaranty Corporation (PBGC) must provide eligibility lists to the HCTC program. The HCTC program must then send HCTC program kits to the potentially eligible individuals. People must determine whether they are eligible (the kit consists of a twenty-four-page brochure and enrollment form), enroll in qualified health coverage, and pay the full premium amount for the coverage. For people whose HCTC eligibility is confirmed, premiums are reduced, and the HCTC program then bills them for 35 percent of their premiums, collects the other 65 percent from the IRS, and forwards the total premium to their health plans. People may have to contact several federal and state agencies to confirm their eligibility for the HCTC, and the IRS is not able to share confidential information concerning the eligibility process with state agencies without specific taxpayer authorization. A separate forty-nine-page brochure describes the administrative requirements applicable to health plan administrators who offer qualified health coverage.[26] The complexity of these processes is confirmed by the Government Accountability Office and private research reports that indicate very low participation rates by otherwise eligible individuals.[27]

IRS Attempts to Control Compensation through Codified Tax Penalties

Over the last fifty years, Congress has attempted on several occasions to regulate employer behavior through tax law. In considering whether the IRS is equipped to enforce and administer comprehensive health care reform, any analyst should review how the IRS has handled each of these earlier attempts to accomplish societal goals through tax law.

Nondiscrimination Rules

In 1986 Congress enacted exceedingly complex nondiscrimination requirements that allowed only limited exclusions for part-time and newly hired employees. These rules, as well as rules mandating that these plans be memorialized in writing and communicated regularly to all employees, applied to all health and cafeteria plans with an effective date of January 1, 1989. With surprising speed, the IRS issued several hundred pages of guidance, and Congress enacted numerous technical corrections to the statute. However, taxpayers remained violently opposed to these rules, which likely would have disqualified thousands of health plans across the country. Responding to taxpayer complaints, Congress repealed the entire provision in 1988, before the rules ever took effect, thereby reinstating the very limited nondiscrimination rules applicable to self-insured health plans prior to 1986.

Although no one has proposed to restore the nondiscrimination rules as part of a plan to enforce mandatory health coverage, the experience from 1986 to 1989 teaches two important lessons that would apply to many of the current potential proposals to expand health coverage. First, the valuation of health benefits, a critical component of these nondiscrimination rules, would also be central to any proposal to tax all or any part of health benefits, which is one way to offset the cost of an income tax credit to help cover all taxpayers' purchases of health insurance. Yet, from 1986 until 1989, the IRS struggled unsuccessfully to provide valuation rules. The limited guidance that was ultimately provided, which took years to develop, was universally criticized. It is likely that any revived proposal to tax health benefits would meet with similar strident taxpayer opposition, as the cost of coverage varies with age, geography, family size, and medical history. Second, the mere tracking and identification of health benefit plans and participants proved to be enormously difficult during this period, when it became apparent that many health care plans had never even been "placed in writing" and therefore violated not only the Internal Revenue Code's discrimination rules but also a separate requirement that all health plans should be placed in writing. It is no more likely that health care plans are "in writing" today than then they were twenty years ago. For that reason, it likely will prove staggeringly difficult to track the myriad benefits provided to participants in these unwritten plans.

Golden Parachute Payments

In 1984, in an effort to discourage corporate officials and other key business executives from paying themselves large settlements following a corporate takeover, Congress enacted certain tax penalties on so-called golden parachute payments. These tax penalties are triggered when total compensation, excluding certain exempted payments, are made to or for the benefit of a "disqualified individual." This group includes certain highly compensated employees, certain officers, and major shareholders, as counted during a specific period of time before the change in control. Payments are subject to this penalty if they are made expressly or implicitly contingent on a change in control of a corporation or in the ownership of one-third or more of a corporation's assets and if the aggregate present value of all such contingent payments is 300 percent or more of the recipient individual's historic average compensation (called the "base amount") from the corporation for the five years preceding the change in control.[28] If a payment is a "parachute payment," three tax penalties apply to the payments to the extent that they exceed the portion of the base amount allocated to that payment or (if greater) "reasonable compensation" for services performed after the change in control. These tax penalties include loss of the corporation's deduction, a 20 percent nondeductible excise tax on the individual, and FICA taxation of the payment.

These tax penalties were intended to curb excessive golden parachute contracts. They had the opposite effect, however. As of 1984, approximately 30 to 40 percent of the Fortune 1000 companies provided their senior executives with employment contracts containing change-in-control clauses. By 2001 this percentage had risen to 90 percent. Even more remarkable has been the increase in the size of these parachute contracts. Many include the promise of lifetime posttermination health benefits.[29] Furthermore, the contracts often include "gross-up" agreements, under which the executives are reimbursed for any excise taxes triggered by their contracts.[30] On the basis of this "backfire" effect, critics of both the statute and the regulations have argued that the statute should simply be repealed, as yet another failed attempt to further social policy through the tax law.[31]

Any lessons for health care reform that may be derived from this experience or others described below would depend upon whether the proposed taxation of health benefits is intended to limit discrimination in the provision of benefits (for example, by enacting a "tax disincentive" to maintain policies much more elaborate than the basic policies that would be covered and fostered by a tax credit) or merely intended to fund the enactment of the tax credit (designed to promote universal coverage). If the former, the experience with golden parachute provisions has demonstrated that executives will simply demand tax gross-ups to fund their increasingly elaborate packages of benefits, which would ultimately lead to even more discriminatory health benefit plans than those that currently exist.

Deduction Limit for Executive Compensation

In reaction to what was perceived to be generally excessive salaries of top corporate executives, Congress in 1993 enacted a provision that disallows a corporate income tax deduction for remuneration to certain top company executives in excess of $1 million. This limit is subject to an exception for shareholder-approved "performance-based compensation."[32] Shareholders are allowed to approve the total amount of such compensation under votes taken every five years. Many of the regulatory guidelines applicable to this compensation are relatively simple to meet. Furthermore, any compensation paid *outside* the shareholder-approved performance compensation limits can still be deducted if it is deferred until the year when the executive's service as either an employee or an officer ends or until after the executive's company is acquired.[33] By exempting postretirement payments, the deduction limit simply encouraged companies to pay deferred compensation.[34]

Nonqualified Deferred Compensation Plans

In 2004 Congress enacted new rules for executives' nonqualified deferred compensation plans,[35] because of perceived abuses of such plans and a sudden recognition that there were no IRS guidelines governing these plans.[36] The rules for nonqualified deferred compensation plans provide guidelines governing the timing of deferral elections, certain types of plan investments, and rules under which the deferred compensation can ultimately be distributed. The IRS spent three years developing 800 pages of guidance, but it also announced that it will not issue any private letter rulings or develop any "model plan" to assist taxpayers in dealing with these rules. Accordingly, it remains to be seen what companies will do in amending and operating plans and what IRS agents and courts will do in future years in determining whether companies' plans are in compliance with these enormously complex IRS guidelines.

Deduction Limit for Meals, Entertainment, Travel, Gifts

In 1962 Congress enacted extremely complex limits on deductions for certain types of entertainment, meals, travel, and gifts, as well as "lavish" expenditures in general.[37] In some instances these limits were enacted to discourage the expenditures themselves; in nearly all cases Congress was also trying to raise revenues through these deduction limits. These limits are certainly applicable to many of the listed expenditures. But, as with limits on executive compensation, the IRS took many years to develop guidelines, which in many instances contain amazingly generous exceptions, and has conducted few audits of taxpayers' compliance with these rules. Nor is there any indication that these limits reduced taxpayer expenditures on items covered by this statute.

Administrative Issues Associated with Reform Proposals

Most reform proposals intended to achieve universal coverage, which included some combination of mandates, incentives, insurance market reforms, and changes to the current tax rules. Mandates might require employers to provide, and individuals to have, health plan coverage that satisfies certain requirements. Incentives might be offered to expand access to, or subsidize the cost of, health plan coverage satisfying certain requirements. Insurance market reforms may reduce, eliminate, or standardize state regulation of insurance products. These market reforms also might establish incentives for nonemployer sources of health plan coverage, and expand the types of health plan coverage available. Tax reforms might limit the current exclusion, replace the current exclusion with a tax credit, eliminate the disparities between employer-provided and individually purchased health coverage, tighten nondiscrimination requirements, mandate that part-time employees receive coverage proportional to the hours that they work, and include reporting changes designed to complement other reforms.

Employer Mandates

Employer mandates proposals would require employers to offer health plan coverage satisfying certain requirements or pay a fixed cost per employee or a percentage of payroll to a governmental unit. The expected result is that employees would have a source of coverage either through their employer or through the governmental unit. To administer this requirement, employers would be required to provide detailed information to a regulatory body identifying whether they offer health plan coverage, the type of coverage offered, the number and identity of employees covered or not covered, and a determination by each employer of the payments necessary if it had not offered coverage. Although these reporting requirements could be imposed outside of the tax system, the payment option would almost certainly need to be enforced by the IRS. Thus it is likely that the current employment tax reporting and payment mechanisms would need to be expanded to facilitate the enforcement of an employer mandate.

Considerable IRS oversight would be necessary to discourage employers from trying to avoid an employer mandate by classifying employees as leased employees (hired through another entity), as part-time employees (a loophole that is continually available unless the new legislation prohibits the exclusion of part-time employees), or as independent contractors. Admittedly, the hiring of leased employees would not avoid the requirement that the employee have employer-mandated insurance, but it would simply shift the problem to another employer. However, there are two historic problems that have existed with certain leasing companies' benefits. First, the type of health coverage provided is often less generous than the coverage provided by the employer entity that is receiving the employees' services (although the coverage would have to meet the minimum mandated levels if the leasing company is to operate legally). Second, the IRS has faced problems in recent years with leasing companies that operate in violation of tax and labor laws by underpaying workers, by failing to deposit withholding taxes that have been collected from the employees' wages, and also by failing to deposit the employer share of FICA and unemployment taxes. If such illegally operated companies are already violating payroll tax and labor laws, it is not likely that they would be compliant with rules mandating the provision of health coverage. Accordingly, the new rules implementing any employer-mandated health coverage would have to include penalties imposable not only upon the company (for the disregard of any rules mandating employer health coverage) but also upon the responsible officers of any company that has failed to provide the required coverage and has subsequently gone bankrupt or been liquidated (similar to the enforcement rules currently applicable to payroll tax withholding).[38] As a practical matter, neither of these penalties would be applicable if the hiring company simply classifies the workers as independent contractors who are not hired through any employer company at all. An employer mandate may simply heighten incentives to hire workers as independent contractors, which will further increase the burdens on the IRS to police whether the workers have been correctly characterized as independent contractors as opposed to employees.[39] Indeed, the difficulty of enforcing an employer mandate may drive policymakers to consider an individual mandate.

Individual Mandates

Proposals for individual mandates would require individuals to purchase health plan coverage satisfying certain requirements or face penalties for failure to do so. To enforce an individual mandate, the government would need reliable information confirming that a person had coverage and on the source, type, and duration of coverage. Such information would come from employers, insurers, and individuals. In addition, there is an automatic time lag each year for reporting the lack of coverage as tax returns are not filed until months after year end. In addition, processing of returns would typically take a year or two more before the IRS could identify and take steps to correct failures to obtain coverage. Because so few tax returns are routinely identified for audit—currently less than 1 percent—it would take far longer to identify those who may have provided incorrect information on their filed returns, indicating (whether intentionally or unintentionally) that they had obtained the required levels of coverage. Finally, the enforcement tools available to the IRS are quite limited, even after the IRS may have identified the workers who have inadequate coverage. The agency could not impose coverage on noncompliant filers but would have to assess penalties through such unpopular means as direct assessments, wage garnishments, tax liens, or offsets against tax refunds. Any of these approaches could contribute, quite negatively, to the agency's perceived role as a bully.

Incentives

Incentive proposals would subsidize the purchase of health plan coverage by low- and middle-income families through payments to employers and health insurance plans from whom families would purchase coverage. Alternatively, the government could make payments directly to families. Although there is no particular reason to design these payments in the form of tax credits, the IRS has significant expertise with credits for eligible low-income or economically distressed groups, including the HCTC and the Earned Income Tax Credit. Nevertheless, as noted above, IRS administration of the HCTC has not produced the optimal results anticipated by policymakers.

Insurance Reforms

Insurance reforms would expand access to coverage by eliminating or reducing state regulatory hurdles such as mandated benefits, by creating purchasing pools such as association plans as an alternative to employer-provided coverage, and by encouraging the development of other types of health insurance products such as "bare-bones" or catastrophic policies. Because insurance is currently regulated by the states, it is unlikely that the IRS would need to administer these changes. However, tax changes may be necessary to provide uniform tax treatment for employer-provided coverage and other types of health plan coverage.

Tax Reforms

The universe of tax reform options discussed in connection with health reform proposals includes the following options.

Modify or eliminate the tax exclusion. Some reform proposals would limit the tax exclusion to a specified value either for high-income employees or for all employees. Other reform proposals would eliminate the exclusion entirely. Under either of these proposals, employers would have to value their health plan coverage and then report the taxable portion of the value on appropriate income and employment tax reports, such as the forms W-2 and 941. The IRS would need to develop valuation methods for insured and self-insured plans, respond to requests for information from employers, and audit the health plan valuations reported by employers.

Replace the tax exclusion with a tax credit. Most reform proposals calling for the elimination of the tax exclusion would replace the exclusion with a tax credit. Credits might be available to all or only low- and moderate-income taxpayers. If the exclusion is eliminated, all of the administrative responsibilities described above would also come into play. In addition, the IRS would have to prepare new communication materials for taxpayers and develop reporting requirements to ensure that taxpayers purchased appropriate health plan coverage and an audit program to ensure compliance. These reporting requirements would most likely require employers and health insurance carriers to report the necessary information, as well as the taxpayers seeking the new credit.

Eliminate disparities. Another set of possible reforms would eliminate disparities between employer-provided and individually purchased health plan coverage. For example, the U.S. Internal Revenue Code could be revised to permit individuals to claim an above-the-line deduction for individually purchased health plan coverage. Although this requirement could be enforced solely on audit, the IRS may be more comfortable receiving contemporaneous information about individually purchased coverage from a health insurance carrier.

Tighten nondiscrimination requirements. Another possible reform would be to impose nondiscrimination rules for all health plans. As noted previously, only self-insured health plans are currently subject to nondiscrimination rules. Nondiscrimination rules ensure that tax benefits associated with employer-provided plans are not used solely by highly compensated employees. Admittedly, if the health care system is so radically reformed as to eliminate any tax exclusion for health benefits, then nondiscrimination rules would be needed only to prevent excessive benefits for higher-paid workers. However, limits on golden parachute payments and penalties on companies paying their top executives compensation of more than $1 million per year have completely failed to achieve their stated goals, although the companies that have continued these excessive benefits have paid large tax penalties. It seems likely that if similar tax penalties were imposed on discriminatory health benefits, then discriminatory practices would continue together with increased tax penalties. The second historical lesson to remember, or course, is that Congress's most recent attempt to expand the health benefit nondiscrimination rules led to the enactment, and rapid repeal, of those rules.[40] The expanded nondiscrimination rules and the threatened enforcement of those rules imposed significant administrative and compliance burdens on small employers, their health insurance providers, and the IRS. Any new attempt to expand the nondiscrimination rules would need to take on these challenges. However, to work efficiently, any expansion of the nondiscrimination rules should include elimination of the existing exclusions for workers under the age of 25 and part-time employees.

Initiate new reporting requirements. Many of the reform proposals we have reviewed, especially the employer and individual mandates and tax changes, would impose additional data collection and information-reporting responsibilities on employers, individuals, and health insurance providers. The IRS often has been extremely slow in implementing information-reporting statutes.[41] And even after the IRS has issued implementing regulations and added new boxes to information returns, those returns are not completed for an additional year and not processed or audited for at least a year after that.

Ensure that penalties on individuals are not collected through withholding and are not duplicated at the state level. Care must be taken in designing any penalties for noncompliance with the requirements to purchase health insurance, so as to ensure that any penalties are effectively borne by the individual taxpayers who violate the new requirements (as opposed to their employers), and to avoid designing a federal add-on tax that could be interpreted to apply also for state income tax purposes. History is not a good guide here, since previous tax penalties to encourage certain types of social behavior have been poorly designed.

For example, when Congress designed the federal excise tax on excessive golden parachute payments in 1984, it required the tax to be collected by the employer through income tax withholding, even though the tax is technically imposed only on the executive. If the correct amount of tax is not withheld, under the federal income tax withholding rules, the IRS can choose to impose the taxes either upon the employer (for failure to withhold) or upon the employee (who actually owes the taxes). In practice, the IRS has limited nearly all audits to corporate employers and has never addressed or imposed penalties on individuals. By contrast, the tax penalty for noncompliant, nonqualified deferred compensation plans is imposed on the individuals who defer compensation, presumably to ensure that they do in fact realize the tax consequences of violating these new deferred compensation rules.

Unfortunately, while this tax penalty for violating the new nonqualified deferred compensation plan rules is imposed only on individuals, not employers, it suffers from the second potential pitfall of creating a penalty that is effectively duplicated at the state level. This problem was created because the federal penalty was included not as part of the federal income tax rate structure, but instead is imposed simply as part of the Code, in a provision instructing taxpayers to add 20 percent to their taxes. Accordingly, any states that simply follow the federal tax rules in determining state taxable income are permitted to assume that this increase in federal tax operates as an increase in state tax as well.[42] In adopting penalties to encourage people to buy health insurance, Congress should take care to ensure *both* that these penalties do effectively fall on individuals and further that the penalties are not duplicated at the state level.

Conclusion

Any attempt to mandate universal heath insurance faces the challenge of how to deal with the myriad current tax rules favoring health care coverage and medical expense deductions, which were shown to be replete with coverage exemptions and benefit discrimination under the rules in effect from 1986 through 1989. Although nondiscrimination rules may become less relevant in a system that includes an employer or individual mandate, the existing system's lack of effective limitations on misclassifying workers as "nonemployees" or as "employees of some other employer" (such as a leasing company) will make it extremely difficult to implement any tax penalties or incentives merely by focusing on employer-provided coverage. It is obvious that some radical reform is necessary, but the past thirty years of experience have shown that the IRS has been extremely slow in developing implementing regulations or in enforcing tax penalties on abusive plans.[43] Finally, whenever the IRS has acted aggressively to combat perceived abuses, Congress has often imposed audit moratoriums or even repealed the implementing statute. Design and enactment of health care reform will be only one step toward expanding coverage for the currently uninsured. Implementation and enforcement of the new rules, given the challenges of the current tax laws, will be the even larger hurdle.

Notes

1. To spare the reader the need to keep track of specific statutory references, we refrain in our text from referring to specific provisions of the Internal Revenue Code (the Code). But as a service to those technophiles who are interested in such matters, our notes provide specific references to relevant provisions of the Code, Treasury regulations and related IRS guidance.

2. Even accidental death and dismemberment policies and business travel accident insurance are treated as "health insurance" excludable under Code §106 under the current tax rules, even though some benefits under these AD&D (accidental death and dismemberment) policies have elements of life insurance as well. This treatment was first proposed under the 1988 cafeteria plan regulations. It has been followed in various IRS private letter rulings (PLRs) (for example, PLRs 8939050, 8949030, 199921036, and 200002030) and is also included in the 2007 reproposed cafeteria plan regulations. See Prop. Treas. Reg. (proposed Treasury regulation) §1.125-2(a)(3)(D), which lists among "qualified benefits" under a cafeteria plan "an accidental death and dismemberment insurance policy (section 106)."

3. Code §213.

4. Code §162(l). This deduction is not available for SECA tax purposes; Code §162(l)(4).

5. Code §132(a)(3) and §132(d). The tax benefit for self-employed individuals of having this coverage provided as a working condition fringe is that the benefit is completely excluded from income, and thus it is effectively excluded for SECA tax purposes as well. Further, working condition fringes are not subject to any discrimination tests. Accordingly, many corporate directors and other high-paid corporate consultants have arranged to receive health insurance from the companies they serve to obtain health insurance that is in most instances less costly than individually purchased policies and that provides the additional benefit of avoiding any SECA taxes on the coverage. (Notably, even though the Code refers to "employees" as the potential recipients of any "working condition fringe," the term "employee" is defined to include both directors and independent contractors in Treas. Reg. §1.132-1(b)(2)(iii) and (iv).)

6. Code §105(b).

7. See Rev. Rul. (revenue ruling) 69-154, 1969-1 C.B. 46.

8. Note that these nondiscrimination rules do not apply to fully insured accident or health plans; see Code §105(h). And these nondiscrimination rules also do not apply to physicals and other medical diagnostic procedures for an employee (but not the employee's spouse and dependents); see Treas. Reg. §1.105-11(g). The Code section 105(h) on nondiscrimination rules also does not apply to retired employees, provided that "the type, and the dollar limita-

tions, of benefits provided to retired employees who were highly compensated individuals are the same for all other retired participants"; Treas. Reg. §1.105-11(c)(3)(iii). Because this limitation technically does not refer to the length of coverage, some practitioners believe that highly compensated individuals can receive employer health benefits indefinitely after termination of service (typically subject to taxation in an amount equal to relatively low workforce-average insurance rates), so long as the "type and dollar limitations" of such benefits are the same as for other employees.

9. Code §104(a)(3).

10. The only litigated case challenging the tax exemption under Code section 125 of a plan that offered discretionary choices between taxable compensation and tax-exempt benefits was lost by the IRS. *See Express Oil Change* v. *U.S.*, 25 F. Supp. 1313 (N.D. Ala. 1996), *aff'd*, 162 F.3d 1290 (11th Cir. 1998), involving a choice between current salary and health insurance under an unwritten plan.

11. Final regulations describing the nondiscrimination rules for self-insured health plans were published in 1981, but the nondiscrimination rules for cafeteria plans are vague and remain only proposed.

12. Although the FSA-enabling statute, Code section 125, was enacted in 1978, the majority of the applicable regulations are still only proposed. However, the IRS reproposed these regulations in August 2007 and has indicated that it does intend to finalize the regulations during 2008 (thirty years after enactment of section 125). See Prop. Treas. Reg. §1.125-1, §1.125-2, §1.125-4, §1.125-5, §1.125-6, and §1.125-7.

13. Code §223.

14. Code §35.

15. Code §4980B. COBRA stands for the Consolidated Omnibus Reconciliation Act of 1985, the legislation that added the continuation coverage provisions to the Code.

16. If a qualified beneficiary is determined to be disabled, the eighteen-month period may be extended to twenty-nine months.

17. See Section 1862(b)(1)(A)–(C) and Section 1862(b)(2) of the Social Security Act (as cross-referenced in Code section 5000(c)).

18. The IRS had proposed, in Rev. Rul. 2003-43, 2003-1 C.B. 935, that the use of debit or similar electronic payment cards in connection with expenditures under FSAs, HRAs (health reimbursement accounts), or both would trigger Form 1099 reporting requirements. The ruling was blocked by the Health Savings Account Availability Act on grounds that any such "regulatory reporting requirement discouraged the use of such cards and that such burden should be removed." See H.R. 2351, as reported by the House Committee on Ways and Means on June 25, 2003, 108 Cong. 1 sess. (H.R. Rep. No. 108-177).

19. Code §89. The nondiscrimination rules under Code §89 were repealed in 1989, and the nondiscrimination rules of Code §105(h) were reinstated.

20. *Leased employees* are defined in Code §414(n).

21. Code §414(n) regulations were revoked in 1993, per 58 Fed. Reg. 25556 (April 27, 1993). The IRS has made no commitment since that time to issue regulations or other guidance to taxpayers on employee leasing arrangements. The IRS did conduct a "market study" of 100 leasing companies in 1993 but never released the results. Also, in technical advice memorandum (TAM) 199918056 (November 112, 1998), the IRS concluded that a company that merely "paid wages" to certain common law employees was not in fact the common law employer of those employees, and thus the common law employer was required to treat these individuals as its employees. However, the employee leasing industry (including "profes-

sional employer organizations" as well as traditional leasing companies) has always asserted that this TAM did not involve any companies in their industry.

22. See, for example, *Vizcaino* v. *Microsoft*, 97 F.3d 1187 (9th Cir. 1996), 105 F.3d 1334 (9th Cir. 1997), *reh'ing en banc* 120 F.3d 1006 (9th Cir. 1997); *Microsoft Corp. v. Vizcaino*, U.S. Sup. Ct. No. 97-854 (review denied January 26, 1998, rejection of company's request that 9th Circuit's decision on the issue of workers' eligibility to participate in the employee stock purchase plan [ESPP] be reversed or remanded); 173 F.3d 713 (1999) (leased employees allowed to participate in ESPP); *Abraham* v. *Exxon Corp.*, 85 F.3d 1126 (5th Cir. 1996); *Clark* v. *E.I. DuPont De Nemours and Co., Inc.*, 105 F.3d 646, 1997 WL 6958 (4th Cir. 1997); *Bronk* v. *Mountain States Tel. & Tel. Co. Inc.*, dba U.S. West Communications, U.S. West, Inc., 98-1 U.S.T.C. ¶50,316 (10th Cir. 1998), *rev'g and remanding* 943 F. Supp. 1317 (D.Colo. 1996); *Hensley* v. *N.W. Permanente*, 1999 U.S. Dist. LEXIS B906 (remanded September 12, 1999, to require the plan administrators to apply the common law tests of employee status to determine which workers should have received plan benefits).

23. See, for example, Rev. Rul. 87-41, 1987-1 C.B. 296 (a compendium of twenty factors that the IRS takes into account in determining whether there is an employment relationship under the common law tests).

For classification of employees, see Code §3509. See *Independent Contractor or Employee? Training Materials*, Training 3320-102 (Rev. 10-96, TPDS 84238I) (Department of the Treasury, IRS); see also Internal Revenue Manual (IRM), "Technical Guidelines for Employment Tax Issues," §4.23.5.1, *et seq.* The final version of the Training Materials was never incorporated into the IRM but was published as a Special Supplement (Report No. 43) to BNA's (Bureau of National Affair's) Daily Tax Report (March 5, 1997).

24. 1998-15 IRB 14. The Classification Settlement Program (CSP) was initially intended to be a pilot program designed to offer eligible businesses under IRS examination the opportunity to settle their worker reclassification disputes at a potentially significant discount. The program was so successful that it was extended indefinitely; see Notice 98-21: "Extension of the Effective Date of the Classification Settlement Program" (IRS, March 31, 1998). The statutory rules limit the employer's federal income tax withholding (FITW) liability to 1.5 percent of the wages and limit the employer's liability for employee-share FICA to 20 percent of the full rate. Only the employer share of FICA (Federal Insurance Contributions Act) taxes is owed at the full rate, and the employer is not required to reclassify the workers as employees for any back years.

25. The Employee Retirement Income Security Act of 1974 (ERISA) is a federal law that sets minimum standards for most voluntarily established pension and health plans in private industry to provide protection for individuals in these plans.

26. The IRS guidance on the Health Coverage Tax Credit (HCTC) enrollment process is available online (www.irs.gov/individuals/article/0,,id=109960,00.html).

27. See, for example, Government Accountability Office, *Health Coverage Tax Credit: Simplified and More Timely Enrollment Process Could Increase Participation*, GAO-04-1029 (GAO, September 2004); Stan Dorn, "Health Coverage Tax Credits: A Small Program Offering Large Policy Lessons," prepared for the Urban Institute (Washington, February 2008).

28. As a result of numerous "technical corrections" to the parachute rules adopted in the Tax Reform Act of 1986 (1986 Act) and relatively pro-taxpayer generous regulations proposed in 1989 but not adopted in final form until 2004, twenty years after enactment of the statute, these rules do *not* apply to changes of control in non–publicly held corporations, to sales of minor subsidiaries of public corporations, to payments for services by employees

retained to work after a change in control, to any payments made to employees below the top echelon of workers, to accelerated payments of amounts that were already vested, or to payments under qualified retirement plans.

29. For example, William Agee's severance contract with Bendix Corporation, which attracted great scrutiny in 1983 and which was repeatedly cited during the 1984 development of these rules, was under $5 million, and the expected revenues from this provision were also under $5 million. There have been parachute contracts reported to the SEC in the past few years that exceeded $400 million for single, individual executives.

30. Because the executive's marginal rate includes the 20 percent excise tax, plus regular federal and state taxes, it typically costs $3.00 to reimburse an executive $1.00 of parachute excise taxes.

31. See Lee A. Sheppard, "18-Karat Parachute: Treasury End-Runs Congress," *Tax Notes* 43 (June 5, 1989): 198. See also Bruce A. Wolk, "The Golden Parachute Provisions: Time for Repeal?" *Virginia Tax Review* 21, no. 125 (Fall, 2001): 153–61.

32. Code §162(m). Although the statute applies these deduction limitations to the CEO and the top four other officers listed in the company's proxy in Notice 2007-49, 2007-25 IRB (Internal Revenue Bulletin), p. 1429, the IRS reduced the class of executives to the CEO, plus an additional *three* highest-compensated officers for the taxable year (*other than* the principal executive officer or the principal financial officer) to bring the IRS's guidelines into compliance with certain recent changes in the proxy reporting rules, effective for taxable years ending on or after December 15, 2006. This group, subject to Code §162(m), would be further changed under legislation introduced in January 2007 that would expand the definition of "covered employees" to include any individual who is (or ever was) either the CEO or one of the four highest-compensated officers (other than the CEO) (irrespective of whether such highly compensated officer's name was ever included in the Summary Compensation Table).

33. The legislation proposed in 2007 would also have eliminated this ability to avoid Code §162(m) by delaying the payment until after the executive's termination; it instead provides that executives are deemed to remain perpetually in the group of employees who are covered by Code §162(m), even after their termination of service or death. (It appears that Code §162(m) could continue to be avoided if the company reverts to private status.)

34. Notably, too, Code §3121(v)(2), enacted in 1983, had provided an additional effective incentive to defer compensation, by imposing FICA taxes at the point of deferral (or, under defined benefit plans, in the year of retirement). Typically the executive's compensation has exceeded the Social Security tax wage base in that year, so although Medicare taxes must be front-paid, the ultimate distributions (plus appreciation) are exempt from both Social Security and Medicare taxes.

35. Code §409A. The phrase *non-qualified deferred compensation plans* refers to deferred compensation plans that do not satisfy the IRS rules for qualified retirement plans.

36. Apart from the various implicit tax incentives to defer compensation, Congress itself was responsible for the lack of IRS guidance on audits of these plans. In February 1978, in reaction to controversial proposed IRS regulations (Prop. Treas. Reg. §1.61-16) that would have prevented taxpayers from filing any elections to defer compensation, Congress had blocked those proposed regulations from taking effect, by providing that the taxation of any deferred compensation plan must be determined in accordance with regulations, rulings, and case law in effect on February 1, 1978. See section 132 of the Revenue Act of 1978.

37. Code §274. This provision has been amended dozens of times since 1962.

38. See Code §6672.

39. See the discussion above (text accompanying footnotes 23 and 24 concerning independent contractor training materials and CSP) of the IRS's limited enforcement record in challenging misclassified workers.

40. The infamous Code §89.

41. For example, the regulations governing information reporting for educational assistance plans (under a statute enacted in 1978) were never finalized, and the regulations governing information reporting for incentive stock options (under a statute enacted in 1981) were not finalized until 2006. The regulations governing reporting of nonqualified deferred compensation plans (under a statute enacted in 2004) have not yet been proposed and likely will not be finalized for several more years.

42. See, for example, California Franchise Tax Board Notice 2007-1 announcing that the Code section 409A 20 percent tax applies at the state level in California as well.

43. Congress might attempt to mandate more rapid IRS action by requiring the IRS to draft implementing regulations, issue information-reporting requirements, and initiate an audit program within specified periods of time following date of enactment. In addition, Congress might seek to enforce such a deadline by providing that the IRS's budget will be reduced by 5 percent for each quarter the agency delays in either issuing implementing regulations and information-reporting requirements or failing to initiate an audit program. Of course, the IRS is not in a position to administratively correct poorly drafted legislation.

8

The Challenges of Implementing
Health Reform through the Tax System

JANET HOLTZBLATT

Designers of fundamental health reform proposals often use the income tax system to achieve their goals. These goals include expanding health insurance coverage while containing the growth of medical costs. Health reform proposals may use the Internal Revenue Service (IRS) to enforce mandates requiring individuals to obtain health insurance, provide new tax-based subsidies for health insurance, or cap or eliminate the current exclusion for employer-provided health insurance

Using the IRS to achieve health reform goals relies on strengths of the income tax system. First, the current income tax already provides substantial subsidies for health care through the exclusion for employer-provided health insurance, the deduction for health insurance purchased by self-employed workers, the itemized deduction for medical expenses, the tax preferences for contributions to health savings accounts, and the refundable health coverage tax credit for certain dislocated workers. Enforcing a mandate or distributing new health subsidies through the tax system may affect people who do not benefit from the current provisions, but most already file income tax returns or pay payroll taxes. Further, the tax system currently collects much information about people that could be used to identify those most in need of assistance.

Health reform objectives also complement many tax policy goals. The goal of the tax system is to raise sufficient revenue equitably, efficiently, and simply. Horizontal equity could be improved by treating people whose employers do

The author thanks Henry Aaron, Melissa Cummings-Niedzwiecki, Gillian Hunter, Tom Reeder, Ralph Smith, and Michael Udell for their helpful insights. The views expressed in this paper are those of the author and should not be interpreted as those of the Congressional Budget Office.

171

not offer health insurance the same as those with employer-provided health insurance. Limiting the tax preference for health insurance could reduce or remove an incentive to spend more than necessary on health care.

However, some goals of health reform conflict with tax policy goals. Providing new subsidies for health insurance or enforcing a mandate could add complexity to the tax system, adding new filers into the system, requiring current filers to attach new forms and schedules to their returns and insurers to report information about health plans to beneficiaries and the government, and resulting in the IRS absorbing millions of additional documents. At a time when the IRS is criticized for paying too little attention to the tax gap and when tax simplification and fundamental tax reform remain goals for many policymakers, new initiatives that would increase the complexity of the tax system are problematic.

The tax system faces several key challenges in administering either an individual mandate or new tax-based subsidies for health insurance. The first is whether the tax system can reach the targeted population without unduly burdening taxpayers or the IRS. The second is whether the IRS can enforce either a mandate or eligibility rules for a subsidy without causing noncompliance to increase or participation in subsidies—or more broadly the tax system—to fall. The third is whether the IRS can enforce mandates or pay out subsidies in a timely fashion, given the annual accounting structure of the income tax.

Administrative challenges are not unique to the tax system. Health reform will be difficult to administer, regardless of which agency tries to enforce it. For policymakers deciding which agency will assume new responsibilities for health reform, two questions must be addressed: First, which agency can assimilate new responsibilities at minimal cost? And second, which trade-offs are acceptable if all policy objectives cannot be achieved?

Profile of the IRS

The IRS currently balances many competing priorities. The IRS administers individual and corporate income taxes, the estate tax, and various excise taxes. It also oversees pensions and tax-exempt organizations and their compliance with Internal Revenue Code provisions. The IRS processes more than 140 million individual, corporate, and partnership income tax returns a year and, in total, collects more than $2 trillion dollars in taxes each year.

To achieve these goals, the IRS budget in fiscal year 2008 was just $11.3 billion, less than 1 percent of the total collected. More than 40 percent of the IRS budget ($4.8 billion) is for enforcement activities, including audits and collections. The second largest item ($3.7 billion or one-third of the total budget) goes for operations and support, including information technology systems.

Taxpayer services, including taxpayer assistance and education take up $2.2 billion, or 19 percent of the budget. With limited resources, the IRS relies on voluntary compliance, supported by targeted enforcement activities.

Perhaps the best known and most feared of the enforcement activities is the audit. Returns are selected for examination if they fit patterns associated with noncompliance. While the audit selection process relies on statistical methods that are sophisticated but inexpensive, the postselection process, with examiners reviewing returns and meeting with taxpayers, can be labor intensive and expensive. Over the past decade, innovations have allowed the IRS to conduct certain examinations inexpensively. For example, the IRS can link tax returns as they are processed to other government data records containing information on dependents' parents and custody arrangements. When discrepancies arise, the IRS can initiate relatively inexpensive *correspondence audits* asking taxpayers to mail in additional documentation to support their claims of exemptions and for the Earned Income Tax Credit (EITC). But even with these innovations, the IRS cannot afford to audit more than a small proportion of tax returns. In 2007 the IRS closed over 1.3 million individual income tax audits, yielding an audit rate of slightly higher than 1 percent. For business returns, the audit rate was 0.66 percent.[1]

Audits are supplemented by an information reporting program, which matches tax returns to two forms: W-2s submitted by employers and 1099s filed by other payers of income. The IRS receives over 1.8 billion information returns each year, most between February and March. Because the IRS is busy processing income tax returns during the first half of the year, the information returns are not edited and matched to tax returns until early autumn. Despite the late start-up, a larger number of taxpayers are affected by the automatic matching programs than by the audit process. Over 3.4 million taxpayers were contacted in 2007 because of discrepancies in income reporting, and another 1.4 million were contacted because they failed to file a return.[2] Still, small budgets prevent the IRS from following up with about two-thirds of questionable returns identified through the underreporting and nonfiler matching programs.[3]

Finally, the IRS can detect certain errors during the processing of returns and can take immediate action. In 2007 the IRS automatically denied 770,000 dependent exemption claims because the taxpayer failed to supply a valid Social Security number.[4] The IRS's ability to deny taxpayers' claims during processing is limited by the availability of reliable third-party data and the Internal Revenue Code. To protect taxpayers' rights, the code restricts the agency's ability to take expedited actions (known as *mathematical error procedures*) to a handful of specific instances where there is a high degree of certainty that the taxpayer has made an error.

Penalties for noncompliance can be substantial. Civil penalties are applied at a rate of 20 percent of the portion of the underpayment of tax resulting from certain types of misconduct (for example, negligence; substantial understatement of income).[5] Fraud (which requires evidence of willful intent) carries penalties up to 75 percent of the underpayment and, in some cases, criminal penalties. Failure to file a return is considered a misdemeanor, carrying a fine of not more than $25,000, imprisonment for not more than one year, or both.

IRS compliance data provide some insight into the effectiveness of the current system. The *gross tax gap* is the difference between the amount of tax that taxpayers should pay under the tax code and the amount they actually pay on time. In 2001 the gross tax gap was $345 billion.[6] As a percentage of tax liability for tax year 2001, the gap implies a voluntary compliance rate of 83.7 percent. If one counts taxes paid voluntarily but late and recoveries from IRS enforcement activities, the *net tax gap* was an estimated $290 billion in tax year 2001, implying a compliance rate of 86.3 percent.

Taxpayers incur costs complying with the tax code. The IRS relies on taxpayers to assess their own income tax liability, which means that taxpayers must learn about the tax law, obtain appropriate forms, keep records, determine their tax liability, and submit returns. The IRS estimates that taxpayers spent an average of 26.4 hours preparing their 2007 tax returns and $207 on out-of-pocket expenditures, such as computer software and paid preparers (see table 8-1.) In the self-assessment tax system, the most time-consuming task is record keeping, with taxpayers spending an average of 15 hours just collecting and maintaining receipts and other records. These time and monetary estimates do not include costs incurred after filing a return, such as time spent responding to an IRS audit, or intangible costs, such as the anxiety taxpayers may feel in dealing with the IRS.

The IRS Role in Administering Health Policy

The Internal Revenue Code contains several provisions governing the tax treatment of expenditures on medical care and health insurance. However, the IRS's role in administering these provisions varies in intensity (see chapter 7 by Mary Hevener and Charles Kerby), but it is worth highlighting again the two extremes in the IRS's administrative roles.

At one end of the spectrum, the Internal Revenue Code contains fairly specific requirements governing employer-provided health insurance plans. As Leonard Burman, Bowen Garrett, and Surachai Khitatrakun (in chapter 3) note, combined income and payroll tax subsidies for employer-provided health insurance exceed $200 billion. Penalties for violations of the tax laws governing

Table 8-1. *Average Taxpayer Burden for Individuals, by Activity*

Major form filed or type of taxpayer	Percentage of returns	Total time	Average time burden (hours)					Average cost (dollars)
			Record keeping	Tax planning	Form completion	Form submission	All other	
All taxpayers	100	26.4	15	4.7	3.3	0.6	2.8	207
Major forms filed								
1040	69	33.5	19.8	5.9	3.7	0.6	3.4	267
1040A and 1040EZ	31	10.4	4.2	1.8	2.5	0.5	1.4	72
Type of taxpayer								
Nonbusiness	71	14.1	5.6	3.3	3	0.5	1.6	114
Business[a]	29	56.9	38.4	8	4.2	0.7	5.7	440

Source: Internal Revenue Service, *1040 Instructions, 2007*, Publication 4655 (Department of the Treasury), p. 84.

a. Business filers include taxpayers who filed a form 1040 and one or more of the following schedules: C, C-EZ, E, or F or form 2106 or 2106-EZ.

health plans are high, ranging from loss of the tax benefits for the entire plan if it contains non-health-related benefits to imposition of an excise tax if portability requirements are not met. However, as Hevener and Kerby point out, enforcement is rare. Neither employers nor individuals are required to provide the IRS with documentation regarding the health benefit plans that generate such generous tax benefits.

At the other end of the spectrum, the IRS has responsibility for administering the relatively new Health Coverage Tax Credit (HCTC) for certain dislocated workers. While this program provides tax benefits to only 45,000 individuals, the IRS receives a $15 million appropriation for its administrative costs (or roughly 12 percent of total program costs) and has created a separate office to oversee eligibility determination and monthly payments to insurers on behalf of enrollees.

In the absence of compliance data and other performance data, it is difficult to compare the effectiveness of the two administrative models. It is likely, however, that neither model is optimal: even if the HCTC model achieved superior compliance and participation, its high administrative costs would be difficult to sustain on a larger scale. At the same time, Hevener and Kerby demonstrate that the absence of IRS guidance on employee health benefit rules creates confusion among employers that would probably be unacceptable in enforcing a large-scale mandate or distributing tax subsidies to most of the population.

Enforcing an Individual Mandate through the Income Tax

Since the state of Massachusetts enacted landmark health reform legislation in 2006, its Department of Revenue has enforced a mandate requiring people to obtain health insurance. Massachusetts residents who are eighteen years of age and older must report on their state income tax return if they are covered by health insurance. Although health reform is still evolving in Massachusetts, the Massachusetts experience provides early lessons for how the IRS might administer a similar requirement if enacted at the federal level.

Reaching Nonfilers

An advantage of using the tax system to achieve health reform goals is that most people already file individual tax returns. The Joint Committee on Taxation estimates that 136 million individual income tax returns will be filed in 2008.[7] However, 28 million potential tax units do not have any reason under current law to file income tax returns. Their incomes are not above the filing thresholds (see table 8-2), nor do they file to receive refunds of overwithheld income taxes or refundable tax credits.

Table 8-2. *Poverty, Filing, and Income Tax Thresholds in 2007*

Filing status	Number of child dependents	Poverty threshold (dollars)	Filing threshold		Income tax threshold[a]	
			Amount (dollars)	Percentage of poverty threshold	Amount (dollars)	Percentage of poverty threshold
Single	0	10,787	8,750	81	10,416	97
Head of household	1	14,291	11,250	79	29,275	205
Married, filing jointly	2	21,027	17,500	83	42,850	204

Source: Poverty thresholds are published annually by the Census Bureau (www.census.gov/hhes/www/poverty/threshld/thresh07.html).

a. The income tax thresholds are based on author computations and do not reflect the temporary stimulus payments enacted in January 2008.

For the estimated 28 million nonfilers, demonstrating compliance with a mandate would impose the costs of filing a tax return. The IRS is currently urging some nonfilers, many of whom are elderly, to file a 1040A return in 2008 to obtain a one-time stimulus payment.[8] Taxpayers are expected to spend an average of 10 hours and $72 completing the relatively simple forms 1040A and 1040EZ.[9] Adding new filers to the tax system would increase IRS administrative costs, as expenditures on taxpayer services and processing rise.

Any increase in compliance costs would be minimized if people who file solely to comply with health reform provisions did not have to complete an entire tax return. Creating a separate short form for nonfilers would require relatively simple eligibility rules. Moreover, the IRS may find it difficult to reach individuals with whom they have little, if any, contact. During the 2007 filing season, the IRS created a short form, 1040EZ-T, for nonfilers who wanted to claim a one-time rebate for telephone excise taxes paid between 2003 and 2006. The minimum value of the rebate was $30, which increased with the number of exemptions and the amount paid in excise taxes. The form 1040EZ-T required only the taxpayer's name, address, and Social Security number. No other information was necessary to claim the minimum rebate. Relative to the total number of nonfilers, use of 1040EZ-T was low. As of October 2007, fewer than 800,000 1040EZ-T forms were filed, even though most low-income households have telephone service.[10]

Instead, individuals who are not required to file a tax return could be exempted from the mandate. Recognizing that very low-income individuals do not have the means to purchase health insurance, Massachusetts exempts people with incomes below 150 percent of official government poverty guidelines from the mandate.[11] Because the threshold for filing taxes in Massachusetts, as at the federal level, is generally below 100 percent of official poverty levels, this test effectively exempts nonfilers from the mandate. The weakness in the Massachusetts approach is that the tax authorities do not know whether someone who fails to file a tax return was covered by health insurance. Indeed, operating a mandate through the tax system could add to the incentive to not file a return. As indicated below, reliable and timely reports by third parties could fill this information gap.

Enforcement of Mandates

While many people may comply with the mandate because they believe in obeying the law, behavior will also be affected by perceptions of the costs and benefits of compliance. People will comply with a mandate if the costs of noncompliance exceed the costs of compliance. The costs of noncompliance include the probability of being caught and the resulting penalties. The probability of detection depends on whether the IRS has access to accurate data regarding health insurance coverage and the tools and resources to use this information.

Third-Party Data. The accuracy of information improves if the reporting agent does not gain by misreporting. While the IRS requests much personal and financial information directly from taxpayers on their returns, the agency relies—to the extent possible—on third-party reporting to validate taxpayers' claims.

Under the current income tax system, information reporting from third parties is associated with lower noncompliance. The net misreporting rate of wage income, which is subject to withholding and information reporting requirements, is slightly above 1 percent. Wage information reports (more commonly known as W-2s) are matched to tax returns after the filing season. For other types of income that are subject to information reporting (for example, through 1099s) and automatic matching programs but not to withholding (such as interest and dividends), the net misreporting rate is 4.5 percent. Noncompliance rates are highest for income that is not subject to any third-party reporting requirements to the IRS. Nearly 54 percent of net income from proprietors (including farms), rents, and royalties is misreported.[12]

Enforcing individual health mandates would require verification of at least two items currently not reported to the IRS: whether someone actually has health insurance coverage, and whether that insurance meets certain minimum standards. That information is currently not available on a national scale.

Massachusetts has already taken the first step to obtain reliable information on coverage. Health insurance providers are required to send information reports (1099-HCs) to insured individuals and to the Massachusetts Department of Revenue by the end of January. The 1099-HC contains the name and identification number of the insurance company as well as the names, subscriber numbers, dates of birth, and the starting and ending dates of coverage for every person covered under the insurance policy. Taxpayers must then copy the subscriber numbers to the new schedule HC, which they attach to their tax return. When the filing season ends, the tax returns are matched to the 1099-HCs to validate the taxpayer's claim that he or she was covered by health insurance. Massachusetts officials report cooperation from the insurance companies in developing the new reporting requirements.[13]

Because health reform is being phased in gradually, Massachusetts has until 2009 to figure out how to verify whether insurance plans meet minimum standards. One option would require insurers to report whether an individual's plan includes the minimum set of benefits, but it would be in the insurers' self-interest to make this claim even if the insurance package fell short of requirements. An impartial third party—such as a state insurance regulator or, with the adoption of a managed competition system, purchasing pools—could provide some sort of identifier to indicate whether a plan provides the minimum required benefits. This approach passes administrative costs from the tax authorities to other agencies, but there should be offsetting efficiency gains if those responsibilities are assigned to agencies that have greater expertise than the IRS does in assessing insurance plans.

Data sharing among agencies would also facilitate enforcement, at relatively low cost to taxpayers. Massachusetts can determine whether a taxpayer is covered through a public plan, because state agencies report this information directly to the Department of Revenue. States, however, are currently not required to provide to the federal government information on enrollments in Medicaid or in a State Children's Health Insurance Program (SCHIP). If a federal mandate were enacted, the IRS could negotiate data sharing arrangements with individual states, but separate negotiations with fifty states plus the District of Columbia would be time consuming and likely would yield inconsistent data across states.

Alternatively, a federal registry could be established, building on a voluntary data system currently in place. The Public Assistance Reporting Information System (PARIS), a computer data matching and information exchange system administered by the Department of Health and Human Services (DHHS), matches enrollment data from the Temporary Assistance to Needy Families (TANF) program, the Food Stamp Program, and Medicaid from participating states.[14] Although PARIS provides a springboard for a mandatory federal registry, there are still significant obstacles to overcome before it could be used for broader enforcement. First, seven states (including California) currently choose not to participate.[15] Second, current rules allow states to report information only once a year. Third, some of the state-reported data are inaccurate, including dates for Medicaid coverage.[16]

Allowing exemptions to the mandate will ease financial burdens of people unable to afford health insurance but can also increase administrative and compliance costs. In addition to exempting the poor, Massachusetts also waives the mandate for people who hold "sincerely held" religious beliefs or who have experienced personal hardship that makes it difficult for them to purchase health insurance. Hardships include homelessness, large medical expenses, natural disaster, or unanticipated large expenses as a result of domestic violence or the sudden responsibility for the care of an elderly parent. With the possible exception of natural disasters, these criteria are invisible to the Massachusetts tax authorities who must rely on documentation supplied by taxpayers to support their claim of hardship. This type of review system could be expensive to administer and burdensome to individuals (many of whom may be deterred by the process from applying for a hardship exemption).

Unique Identifiers. Without unique and consistent identifiers, it will be difficult to use information received from insurers and others to track compliance with mandates. Unique identifiers, such as Social Security numbers and employer identification numbers, make it possible to link tax returns to other data, including information reports and other third-party data sets.

However, privacy laws limit the use of Social Security numbers. The Health Insurance Portability and Accountability Act (HIPPA) requires that a national individual identifier be established as an alternative to the Social Security number for tracking health records, although no action has yet been taken by DHHS. State privacy laws also restrict the use of the Social Security number as an identifier. California, for example, prohibits Social Security numbers from being printed on any materials that are mailed to a person unless required by California or federal law.[17]

Although federal health reform legislation likely would override state restrictions, state reform efforts may be hindered. As a result of privacy laws in California and elsewhere, the Massachusetts Department of Revenue is not requiring insurers to provide the Social Security numbers of policy holders and their dependents. Instead, insurers are asked to provide subscriber numbers. This information allows Massachusetts tax authorities to match tax returns filed by taxpayers and the information returns filed by insurers to verify a filer's claim of coverage. But without information reports from insurers that can be matched to other types of administrative records (such as W-2s), Massachusetts cannot easily detect individuals who evade the mandate by not filing a tax return.

Penalties. Verification through wide-spread audits or other similar interventions is expensive. As noted earlier, the IRS, with its $11 billion budget, currently audits roughly 1 percent of returns and reaches several million other questionable returns through data matches. An alternative approach is to combine fewer audits with larger penalties, hoping to obtain compliance indirectly through fear. Those subject to penalties will weigh the expected probability of being caught, and if the penalties are sufficiently high, they will comply with tax laws.

Michael Allingham and Agnar Sandmo first analyzed tax compliance under the assumption that taxpayers are risk averse and that the policymaker has three policy tools: the marginal tax rate, the probability of audit, and the penalty for misreporting of income.[18] Many of the early compliance models assumed that audits were expensive but that penalties could be imposed costlessly once an error had been detected. Not surprisingly, these models typically found that, subject to a fixed budget constraint, combining high penalties with low audit rates was socially optimal.[19]

However, there are constraints on how high penalties can be set. People usually prefer that penalties bear some relationship to the severity of the crime.[20] As penalties increase, tax evaders may take more aggressive action to avoid detection, while judges and juries may set higher thresholds for reasonable doubts in their deliberations.[21] Janet McCubbin noted that high penalties may be expensive to administer: the IRS may act more diligently to ensure that penalties are appropriately imposed, while taxpayers may be more willing to fight imposition of high penalties.[22] It also is difficult to collect fines from low- and moderate-income taxpayers who have little cash and cannot easily borrow.

Some have suggested that an advantage of administering health insurance mandates through the tax code would be that noncompliance could be penalized with the loss of tax benefits, such as personal exemptions or child tax credits.[23] In 2007 Massachusetts taxpayers could lose their personal exemption if they did not comply with the mandate. However, linking an individual's noncompliance with an insurance mandate to the loss of an unrelated tax benefit, such as the personal exemption, may strike many as unfair. The federal personal exemption is nonrefundable, which means that low-income filers receive little or no benefit from the exemption. Beginning in 2011, the personal exemption will phase out as income increases, meaning that high-income taxpayers will also receive little or no benefit from it.[24] As a result, the potential loss of the personal exemption could be an effective penalty for middle-income taxpayers but not for those at the bottom or top of the income distribution.

Beginning in 2008, failure to comply with the individual mandate in Massachusetts will be subject to a penalty equal to half the premium of the lowest-cost qualifying plan. Enrollees pay the full amount to obtain coverage or pay half the amount and remain uninsured. The response to the Massachusetts penalty will depend in part on the value that uninsured individuals place on health insurance. For some, the penalties may not change behavior, while the decrease in the relative cost of insurance may be sufficient to cause others to enroll. The appropriate penalty level is not obvious.

Monitoring Mandates in Real Time

The income tax uses an annual accounting system to measure income and tax liabilities. Although people and businesses may pay income and payroll taxes throughout the year, their accounts are not settled until the beginning of the following year when they file annual returns (and possibly the middle of the year, if they file for an extension to file). The implications of an annual accounting system go beyond bookkeeping conventions. Although each year the IRS processes millions of tax returns, billions of information returns, and billions of dollars in refunds, the institution is structured to accomplish each of those tasks once a year.[25] IRS resources are allocated on the basis of assumptions regarding the timing of the processing of tax returns and other documents during the year.

These constraints become apparent when expiring provisions are extended late in the calendar year or when the president and Congress try to provide rapid stimulus relief through the income tax system. The enactment of a temporary relief of the alternative minimum tax late in 2007 delayed the processing of some tax returns in early 2008, partly because the IRS computers could not be reprogrammed while the agency was preparing for the start of a new filing season. When Congress returned in 2008 and began deliberations regarding tax rebates in response to warning signs of a recession, the IRS determined that the first checks could not be mailed until months after the filing season had ended and, as it happened, months after the first signals of economic distress.

Health reform would challenge the current accounting conventions as well as the IRS operating structure every year. Beginning in 2008, Massachusetts requires that people have health insurance *every month*. In much the same way that employers report annual wages, insurers will report once a year the months that an individual was covered under a plan. The Department of Revenue will track compliance with the monthly mandate when returns are matched to the 1099-HC form.

The compliance data cited earlier suggest that the IRS's current system of matching information returns with tax returns is successful, despite the fact that matching often does not occur for months after the end of the tax year. Nonetheless, there can be advantages to accelerating data matching. Accelerating the matching of income tax returns and third-party data allows early detection of noncompliance, making it easier to locate taxpayers. For implementation of health reform, early detection would encourage noncompliant individuals to enroll in health insurance plans before penalties accumulate and before they continue for almost another year without coverage.

But there are limitations to how fast matching can be accelerated, using the conventional reporting model for information returns. The IRS, like Massachusetts, could require insurers to report insurance coverage for subscribers by the end of January—one to two months sooner than income is reported under current law. However, it is not likely that the IRS would be able to use information more rapidly if it were reported just one month earlier at the beginning of the year because computing capacity would already be constrained by the demands of the filing season.

Developing a workable solution begins with the recognition that insurance status is not like annual earnings, where employers must wait until the end of the year to compute the cumulative totals. Enrollment in an insurance plan generally occurs once a year and typically carries over to successive years unless subscribers stop paying their premiums. Insurers could be required to report changes in enrollment as they occur rather than after the end of the year. The information, then, would be available to the IRS continuously, and the agency could match the data to the returns as they are processed. As a result, the IRS could potentially withhold penalties from tax refunds before they are paid out.

This is not the way the IRS typically collects information, and it is possible that the agency lacks the capacity—at least in the short term—to process information from insurers on an ongoing basis throughout the year. However, the IRS has experience receiving similar data, collected by other agencies, and using it to identify questionable returns as they are filed. Data on a child's age, parents, and living arrangements are collected and maintained by the Social Security Administration and DHHS and then transmitted to the IRS in sufficient time to be matched to returns as they are processed, allowing the agency to take immediate action on questionable dependency and EITC claims. Similarly, if the IRS used data on insurance coverage during processing to identify people who are not complying with a mandate, it could then outsource the data collection tasks either to another agency or to private contractors.

An alternative would be to enlist employers to monitor compliance with an individual mandate. Employers could withhold penalties for months in which an individual refused coverage. The penalties would be aggregated and submitted as part of withholding payments, with individual reconciliation (on the W-2 form) occurring at the end of the year. However, employers may be reluctant to collect penalties, particularly when there is no existing mechanism for real-time validation for those who do not purchase health insurance through their employers.

Providing Health Insurance Subsidies through the Income Tax

The current tax system provides substantial income and payroll tax benefits for health insurance coverage, but people may not enjoy these benefits if neither they nor their spouses are employed by companies that offer health insurance.

Health reform proposals would typically increase the number of people who receive these tax benefits and might change the amount of the benefits. It might also provide benefits through tax credits or other means. Under the Massachusetts health reform legislation, subsidies for low-income individuals and small businesses are administered by agencies other than its Department of Revenue, but other health reform efforts would expand the role of the IRS in distributing assistance.

For example, in 2001 the Bush administration initially proposed a refundable tax credit to cover up to $1,000 of health insurance expenses for people who did not have access to an employer plan. Targeted to low- and moderate-income individuals, the credit would have begun phasing out when income exceeded $15,000 for a single, childless individual and $30,000 for other filers. Under the original proposal, the credit could be claimed on tax returns or—in a departure from current law—transferred to insurers in lieu of premium payments during the year. By 2007 the Bush administration had dropped this proposal in favor of a standard deduction that would replace most current health-related tax benefits. The health insurance standard deduction would be capped at $7,500 for individuals and $15,000 for families. However, taxpayers could receive the full deduction, even if their expenses were below the limits. Like the typical deduction, it would reduce taxable income and thus income tax liability; however, taxpayers could also use the health insurance standard deduction to reduce payroll taxes.

While a subsidy is the "carrot" in relation to the mandate's "stick," its administration raises the same concerns as those discussed in the preceding sections: Can the covered population be reached? Can eligibility be verified? Can the IRS administer the program in a timely manner?

Reaching the Targeted Population

Distributing subsidies to the targeted population through the tax system presents two challenges: providing assistance in the right amount to those with little or no income tax liability and reaching nonfilers.

Income tax thresholds have increased as Congress has expanded the standard deduction, personal exemptions, and various tax credits. As a result, a married couple with two children does not incur any income tax liability on their 2007 tax return until their income exceeds 204 percent of the poverty threshold—up from 86 percent in 1986. But these changes in tax law also make it more difficult to provide assistance through the income tax system to low-income families unless payments are made to those with too little income to have any positive tax liability.

One option is to make tax credits refundable, as the Bush administration initially proposed. Refundable tax credits are not limited by a taxpayer's income tax

Table 8-3. *Income Tax Units with No Reported Income Tax Liability, 2007*[a]
Units in millions

	Filers	Nonfilers	Total
Presence of wage income or any payroll tax liability	29.4	0.6	30.0
No wage income	8.1	28.2	36.3
Total	37.5	28.8	66.3

Source: U.S. Congress, Joint Committee on Taxation, *Overview of Past Tax Legislation Providing Fiscal Stimulus and Issues in Designing and Delivering a Cash Rebate to Individuals*, JCX-4-08 (January 21, 2008).

a. An income tax unit consists of a primary taxpayer, a spouse if married and filing (or would file) a joint return, and any dependents of the primary taxpayer or spouse. A dependent who files his or her own return is not included in these counts. Estimates exclude taxpayers who fail to file a required return.

liability, but people can receive the full benefit of the credit only if they file a tax return. As noted above, the 28 million nonfilers present a challenge to the administration of mandates—and one possible response is to exempt those not required to file from having to show compliance with the mandate.

A strategy could be designed that recognizes and accommodates the differences between the filing and nonfiling populations. More than half of potential filers who have no income tax liability and who would benefit from refundable tax credits already file a tax return—either because they are required to or because they file to obtain a refund of overwithheld tax or refundable tax credits like the EITC. They also generally have earnings and little, if any, contact with agencies providing means-tested assistance.[26] In contrast, nearly all legitimate nonfilers are low-income individuals with little or no attachment to the work force. (See table 8-3.) Many, especially the elderly and those with children, also receive Social Security benefits or means-tested assistance through agencies other than the IRS.[27]

Many health reform proposals would build on the current patchwork of tax benefits and transfer programs, targeting different subsidies or mandate requirements—each administered by a different agency—to specific populations. Recent Bush administration proposals to expand eligibility for health insurance tax subsidies would not cover people who receive other forms of government-subsidized health insurance, such as Medicare and Medicaid, while the proposed standard deduction could be used to offset payroll taxes, thus helping workers without any income tax liability. More generally, eligibility for tax subsidies could be limited to people with earnings, while assistance to low-income individuals outside the workforce would be provided through other means. This patchwork approach may effectively exempt most of the nonfilers from having to file a return to obtain subsidies, but some potential beneficiaries may be confused as they try to determine which program applies to them, while others may fall through the cracks.

A second approach would allow people to apply for the same subsidy through more than one agency. For workers, the point of contact could be the IRS, while low-income nonworkers could apply through the Social Security Administration or state welfare agencies. Coordination among agencies would require new information systems and ways of dealing with people whose status changes. Although there is little precedent in the United States for operating a single benefit program jointly through the tax and transfer systems, other countries—most notably New Zealand—have been developing coordination systems to provide the same family benefits to different populations through more than one agency.[28]

Targeting and Incentives for Evasion

Selective assistance can ensure that those with the greatest needs receive adequate assistance while holding down total program costs. However, such targeting can also encourage evasion and create confusion.

First, phasing out benefits as income rises is equivalent to increasing marginal tax rates, encouraging taxpayers to underreport income to appear eligible for larger benefits. Second, if phase-out thresholds for joint filers are not equal to twice the corresponding amounts as for unmarried filers, marriage incentives or penalties also occur. Some taxpayers may intentionally evade such penalties by misreporting their marital status.[29] Third, increasing benefits disproportionately with the number of dependents creates incentives to misreport family composition. A tax benefit limited to families with children increases the incentive to falsely claim a child who is not the taxpayer's dependent, while a cap on the number of qualifying children may encourage two spouses to wrongly file as unmarried and split their children between them to maximize their combined tax benefits.[30] Finally, confusion over targeting provisions can lead to unintentional errors (see box 8-1).

Similarly, the design of new health subsidies could give rise to evasion or confusion. A health subsidy that declines with income—such as the original Bush administration's proposal to create a refundable tax credit—would create incentives to underreport income (or, if married, to misreport filing status, thus effectively hiding the income of one of the spouses). A one-size-fits-all subsidy for family health insurance coverage could encourage misreporting of marital and other family characteristics, although requirements that taxpayers use the tax subsidies to purchase health insurance may deter abuse.[31] As under current law, confusion over conflicting definitions of health insurance and tax filing units may result in erroneous claims for subsidies.

Box 8-1. *When the Tax Filing Unit Differs from the Health Insurance Unit*

Determining who may claim a dependent for a health subsidy may create confusion, particularly when more than one person cares for a child. Consider an extended family, consisting of a young mother who lives with her infant son and her parents. The young mother works at a full-time job that does not provide her with any health insurance benefits. Based on her earnings, she is entitled to the EITC if she claims her baby as a qualifying child. But her father includes his grandson under his health insurance plan at work, and most likely he probably enrolled the child in his health plan months before his daughter filed her tax return for the year and learned of her eligibility for the EITC. Under current law, he is not entitled to tax benefits for the costs of his grandson's health insurance, unless his daughter decides to forgo claiming the child-related tax benefits. If the father and daughter do not understand the complicated interactions between the various tax rules (or communicate with one another about their actions), one or both may make an error and claim tax benefits to which they are not entitled.

Incentives for noncompliance can be minimized by reducing phase-outs and marriage penalties and by increasing benefits proportionately for each child. Unintentional errors can be avoided by simple eligibility rules. Yet such adjustments may seem unfair and boost program costs. The IRS could also take steps to verify compliance with targeting rules, but such efforts may be costly as well.

Enforcement of Subsidies

The tax and transfer systems offer different models for eligibility verification. At one extreme, there is the self-assessment model of the tax system, backed up by information reporting, occasional audits, and high penalties. At the other, there is the case worker approach of the traditional welfare program, associated with in-office visits, up-front documentation requests, and phone calls to third parties to validate statements made by the applicant.[32]

The largest refundable tax credit administered by the IRS is the EITC. Although between 75 and 86 percent of eligible taxpayers claim the credit, roughly 23 to 28 percent of EITC claims are paid in error.[33] In contrast, only about 59 percent of eligible households claim food stamps, but less than 6 percent of benefits are overpaid in error.[34]

The dissimilar verification processes contribute to the differences in participation and compliance rates. When EITC claimants whose eligibility could not be verified through third-party data were asked to show that they met the credit's child residency requirements, compliance improved but there was also a drop-off in claims by eligible taxpayers.[35] Studies of Medicaid and federal nutrition programs also find a link between the complexity of the application process and nonparticipation.[36]

Another challenge, then, is achieving compliance without causing those who are eligible to refrain from participating. The cost of subsidies increases if they are paid to people who are ineligible, but their effectiveness is hindered if those who are eligible fail to claim them. Balancing compliance and participation concerns, while keeping compliance burdens and administrative costs in check, requires ready access to reliable third-party data and less costly administrative devices than the traditional audit used by the tax system or the in-office interview used by welfare agencies.

To some extent, the targeting issues raised by a health subsidy are the same as those encountered with existing tax benefits. In the past decade, the IRS has begun using third-party data sets systemically to verify the existence, age, and, to some extent, relationship and residency of children claimed for exemptions and other child-related tax benefits. A new tax benefit for health insurance would be able to build on these earlier innovations in enforcement. Still, reliable third-party information on certain family characteristics is unavailable. In particular, data on the living arrangements of children are still not complete, and there is no national registry of marital status.[37] These data shortfalls hamper the administration of current tax benefits and would present similar hurdles for new health insurance benefits.

Verifying eligibility for a health insurance subsidy also introduces new challenges. The IRS will require information on whether people have purchased or received qualifying insurance. However, verification requires additional information if the subsidy is capped and employers contribute more than the cap toward payment of health insurance, as this excess must be included in taxable income. The cap could be a fixed dollar amount, which might vary with the type of coverage (single or family) but not with other individual characteristics. Or it could vary with income. Although relatively simple, a fixed dollar cap would not recognize such differences in individual circumstances as age, health status, or employment in a small business, each of which causes the price for the same package of health benefits to vary. Employees receiving a W-2 that shows taxable health benefits may experience sticker shock if—as Jeffrey Liebman and Richard Zeckhauser suggest in chapter 10—they are currently unaware of the amount employers contribute for their health insurance.

For the IRS, the greatest challenge may be determining compliance with limitations when an individual receives benefits through a self-insured employer. Verifying health payments made by self-insured employers would present challenges similar to those arising from verification of income received by the self-employed: in both instances, there is no obvious reliable third party to validate the reports to the IRS. Limiting the subsidy creates an incentive for self-insured employers to misrepresent benefits as company overhead or to reallocate costs among subsidiaries to reduce their employees' tax liability. For effective enforcement, the IRS would have to verify that health insurance benefits were accurately measured and allocated among subsidiaries. Such an effort would require a substantial investment in new enforcement resources.

Paying Subsidies in Real Time

The effectiveness of a tax benefit meant to encourage the purchase of health insurance is reduced if beneficiaries must wait a long time to receive the subsidy. Liquidity-constrained taxpayers will lack the resources to purchase health insurance until they receive the subsidies. Behavioral economists confirm what many of us know from our own lives: people procrastinate when choices are complicated, up-front costs are high, and benefits are deferred until an unpredictable (and likely unpleasant) event in the future—all of which are conditions associated with the decision to purchase health insurance.[38] Long lags between premium due dates and the receipt of tax subsidies may result in low take-up rates.

Taxpayers typically do not claim benefits for the tax year until they file their returns at the beginning of the next year. Adjusting withholding can accelerate the receipt of tax benefits, but fine-tuning withholding is difficult and is of no value to those who have no income tax liability. A second approach, then, is to pay a tax credit in advance, as has been done with the EITC, HCTC, and stimulus rebates in 2001, 2003, and 2008. The United Kingdom and several other countries also pay credits in advance.

Designing an advance payment mechanism for a tax credit providing health insurance presents several challenges: first, providing targeted benefits during the year when eligibility status cannot be verified until the end of the year; second, ensuring that advance payments are used to buy insurance; and third, and perhaps most difficult of all, developing an administrative mechanism to process applications for advance payments and pay out the credits during the year.

Verifying Eligibility in Advance. Providing a tax benefit in advance requires the taxpayers to guess what their annual income and family status will be at the end of the year. To begin receiving advance payments for the EITC in January 2008, low-income workers must make some assumptions regarding their incomes for the entire year, whether they will be married on December 31,

2008, and whether their children will live with them for more than half the year. If they decide to apply for advance payments, they must give their employers a short form asserting their eligibility for the EITC. Employers are then required to begin making advance payments. Employers are required neither to validate eligibility nor to notify the IRS that taxpayers are receiving advance payments until the end of the year. If workers earn more than they anticipated, lose custody of their children before the year is half over, or marry at any time during the year, all or some portion of the advance payments may have to be repaid when they file annual tax returns. Risk-averse taxpayers may decide to forgo receiving the credit in advance and wait until they file a return to claim the EITC.

One way to reduce this uncertainty is to limit the amount of the credit that can be claimed in advance. Since 1994, taxpayers cannot make advance claims for more than 60 percent of the EITC available to families with one child. However, the Government Accountability Office found recently that only 3 percent of eligible taxpayers claim the EITC in advance.[39] Among those who do claim advance payments, 40 percent did not file a tax return. About two-thirds of those who filed a tax return and had an advance payment reported on their W-2 form also underreported or failed to report the advance payments that they received on their tax returns. The IRS cannot detect these errors until the fall following the end of the tax year, and resource constraints prevent the agency from following up with more than a fraction of these cases.

A second way to reduce uncertainty and errors is to allow taxpayers to estimate their eligibility for advance credits on the basis of information known to them and the tax authorities at the time of payment and to hold taxpayers harmless for changes in circumstances. Recently, Stan Dorn has suggested using earnings records from state unemployment offices to verify income for advance credits.[40] It is also possible to use prior-year income and family characteristics as a proxy for current circumstances. For example, Congress enacted a rate reduction credit in May 2001, which applied to taxpayers' 2001 tax liabilities. Advance payments of the credit were automatically made shortly after enactment that were based on taxpayers' filing status and income reported on the 2000 tax returns. If taxpayers were, in fact, eligible for a larger credit based on their 2001 characteristics, they could receive the additional amount when they filed their 2001 tax returns. However, they were held harmless for changes in status between 2000 and 2001 that would have caused a reduction in the credit amount. Similarly, the refundable tax credit for health insurance proposed by the Bush administration would have used prior-year income to determine eligibility.[41]

Basing eligibility for advance payments on prior-year characteristics eliminates much of the uncertainty and risk of claiming the credit in advance but
may make subsidies less targeted and more costly. Changes in marital status or
in the number of children and, even more important, fluctuations in income
appear to cause low-income taxpayers to gain or lose eligibility for the EITC.[42]
Income can fluctuate significantly from year to year, particularly among younger
workers.[43] As a result, some people who no longer need subsidies because their
income has risen would receive advance payments, while others whose income
declined would have to wait as long as a year before receiving assistance.

Nor does retrospective eligibility determination resolve all timing and accuracy concerns. First, eligibility for advance payments based on prior-year tax
information cannot be determined until tax returns are filed and processed.
Efforts by taxpayers to accelerate filing of returns to speed payments could create bottlenecks in processing of returns. In addition, the IRS would still be
unable to verify income until information returns are processed and matched to
tax returns after the end of the filing season.

Basing eligibility for tax benefits on prior-year income is not unprecedented
for assistance programs outside the tax system. For example, food stamp recipients are held harmless for changes in earnings between eligibility certifications,
sometimes as long as six months later, if their total income remains below 130
percent of the poverty guideline.

Who Receives the Payments? Benefits may be provided directly to putative beneficiaries or indirectly to third parties. People receive many tax benefits directly.
Taxpayers can deduct property taxes and mortgage interest, medical expenses
above 7.5 percent of adjusted gross income, charitable contributions, and miscellaneous employment-related expenses from their income, which directly lowers their tax. Employer contributions for health insurance are excluded from
income, and employees' paychecks increase. Similarly, taxpayers who claim the
advanced EITC see an immediate increase in their paycheck. However, with
long lags between the receipt of the benefit and validation, many ineligible individuals receive the advance credit.

Another approach is to have third parties claim the tax benefit, although the
taxpayer may be the ultimate beneficiary. In the United Kingdom, people
reduce their payments to charities by the anticipated tax benefit associated with
the contribution. Charities file forms with HM Revenues and Customs to collect the tax benefit resulting from the individual's contribution to their organization. Although the charity claims the tax subsidy, the individual benefits by see-
ing his or her contribution effectively increased. Since the individual does not
receive the benefit directly, the incentive to make false claims should decline
(assuming no opportunities for collusion between the donor and recipient).

The HCTC combines both approaches. Taxpayers can claim the HCTC on their tax return and receive its benefits directly. Or they can pay their share of the premium to the IRS, who adds the subsidy before transmitting the combined amount to the insurer. Under the current system, the IRS does not know if someone qualifies for the HCTC until he or she has already enrolled in a health plan. Qualifying for the HCTC thus requires the taxpayer to have sufficient resources to pay the full premium amounts before becoming eligible for a subsidy.[44] Dorn and others have attributed low participation in the HCTC partly to this requirement.[45]

Advance payments could be made in other ways with the objective of boosting participation, although possibly at increased administrative costs. For example, taxpayers could apply for advance payments and receive the tax credit in the form of a voucher, which they could then submit to an insurer as payment for insurance. The insurer could then turn the voucher into the IRS for cash, reduce withholding payments by an offsetting amount, or use the voucher as a credit against any taxes that are due. Such a transferable tax credit was proposed as a way to provide health subsidies by President George H. W. Bush in 1992 and President George W. Bush nearly a decade later. Alternatively, taxpayers could apply for insurance and provide information regarding potential eligibility for the tax credit to the insurer. The insurer would transmit this information to the IRS or to another designated agency and receive an indicator as to whether the person was eligible for a premium subsidy.

IRS Capability. The EITC approach to making advance payments requires very little from the IRS during the year. Taxpayers determine their own eligibility, and employers pay out the advance credit by reducing payments of withholding taxes without requiring advance approval by the IRS. But with its low participation and compliance rates, the EITC may not be viewed as the best model for making advance payments.

The HCTC approach, as well as some of the alternatives described above, envisions a very different method of operations for the IRS. If adopted in health reform, eligibility determination and payments would be made on a recurring basis throughout the year. Workload would increase and could conflict with other IRS priorities, particularly during filing season when the IRS is operating at or near capacity.

After the HCTC was enacted, the IRS determined that it could not verify eligibility and make advance payments. The agency, instead, turned to an outside contractor to handle these responsibilities. Establishing the system cost $40 million; current operating costs are about $15 million a year or more than $300 for each of the 45,000 people served in 2005. Given economies of scale, the IRS estimates that tripling enrollment would increase administrative costs by 40 percent.[46] However, it is difficult to extrapolate from the HCTC to other programs with different eligibility requirements.

Another alternative is to spread responsibilities over several agencies. With the transferable health insurance credits proposed by President George H. W. Bush, taxpayers had the option to obtain vouchers during the year from the Social Security Administration or state agencies that they could then give to insurers in lieu of premiums. The Clinton administration proposed a pilot that would have allowed four states to choose an alternative agency (including state tax offices, welfare agencies, and unemployment compensation offices) to provide advance payments of the EITC. These proposals would have shifted costs from the IRS to other federal and state agencies. Neither legislative proposal was enacted, however.

Conclusions

Implementing health reform through the tax system would face three critical challenges: reaching the targeted population through the tax system, enforcing provisions effectively through the IRS, and administering these provisions throughout the year. These challenges arise whether health reform requires the IRS to enforce a mandate or distribute subsidies. Either task will require new resources for the IRS or offsetting reductions in other agency efforts.

Enforcing a mandate and distributing a subsidy differ in one key respect: the numbers of taxpayers affected. Enforcing a mandate means requiring everyone to have health insurance and would cover more people than the number of people with incomes below some threshold who would receive targeted subsidies. Thus the IRS would need a larger budget and more staff to contact noncompliant taxpayers under a mandate than under a subsidy. On the other hand, administrating a targeted subsidy requires information that enforcing a broad mandate may not. Tax administrators may require new—and potentially expensive—sources of information to verify eligibility for targeted benefits, including whether compensation received in excess of a cap is included in taxable income. One of the biggest challenges for the IRS would be verifying eligibility for subsidies throughout the year so that beneficiaries can receive assistance before their health insurance premiums are due.

In other regards, enforcing a mandate and distributing subsidies require similar investments in infrastructure. The IRS would have to absorb a similar number of information reports from insurers under either a mandate or a targeted subsidy. Developing information systems on insurance status that could be used to flag problems during returns processing would benefit the administration of a mandate or a subsidy, and the costs of designing such systems would be largely invariant to the number of returns ultimately affected.

Using the tax system to achieve health reform also challenges other goals of tax policy. With a voluntary compliance rate of 83 percent and a postenforcement compliance rate of 86 percent, the IRS compares favorably with compliance rates for other federal and state mandates. A recent survey by Sherry Glied, Jacob Hartz, and Genessa Giorgi found compliance rates ranging from 30 to 90 percent, with mandates covering child support at the low end and those for auto insurance and childhood immunizations at the higher end of this spectrum.[47] However, the overseers for the IRS have set higher goals for the agency. The IRS Oversight Board has adopted an 86 percent voluntary compliance goal by 2009, and Senate Finance Committee chair Max Baucus has asked for a 90 percent voluntary compliance goal by 2017. Similarly, tax simplification and fundamental tax reform remain goals for many policymakers. Some may be concerned that using the tax system to achieve health reform could hinder efforts to improve compliance and to simplify or overhaul the tax code. Yet challenges also create opportunities. The new information systems and technologies that could be used to implement health reforms might aid in other compliance efforts, and initiatives that truly simplify health-related tax benefits could serve the goals of tax reform as well.

While the IRS and the tax system would face challenges implementing health reform, other agencies would experience similar difficulties if tasked with enforcing a mandate or distributing subsidies. Other agencies may be more accustomed to enforcing mandates or providing subsidies in real time, but they would face other challenges, such as the lack of access to detailed income information from taxpayers and third parties. Choosing between agencies to implement comprehensive changes to the nation's health system requires thorough analysis of their relative strengths and weaknesses as administrators of fundamental reform.

Notes

1. This fraction includes Subchapter S and partnership returns. See the IRS enforcement and service statistics tables (www.irs.gov/pub/irs-news/irs_enforcement_and_service_tables_fy_2007.pdf).

2. Internal Revenue Service (IRS), *Internal Revenue Service Data Book, 2007*, Publication 55B (Department of the Treasury, March 2008).

3. Government Accountability Office (GAO), *Tax Administration: Costs and Uses of Third-Party Information Returns*, GAO-08-266 (November 2007).

4. IRS, *Internal Revenue Service Data Book, 2007*.

5. The IRS imposed (after abatement) about 24.3 million civil penalties on individuals, totaling $10.9 billion in fiscal year 2007. More than half the penalties were for failure to pay. Slightly more than 3 million civil penalties were imposed for delinquencies or fraud. See the *Internal Revenue Service Data Book, 2007*, table 17, "Civil Penalties Assessed and Abated, by Type of Tax and Type of Penalty, Fiscal Year 2007" (www.irs.gov/pub/irs-soi/07db17cp.xls).

6. The estimates of underreporting of individual income and self-employment taxes were derived from preliminary analysis of the 2001 National Research Program (NRP). Most of the other estimates are projections derived from older compliance studies.

7. U.S. Congress Joint Committee on Taxation, *Overview of Past Tax Legislation Providing Fiscal Stimulus and Issues in Designing and Delivering a Cash Rebate to Individuals*, presented before the Senate Committee on Finance, 110 Cong., 2 sess., JCX-4-08 (GPO, January 21, 2008). This estimate does not take into account additional returns that may be filed to obtain the one-time stimulus payments in 2008. The estimate includes returns with negative adjusted gross income and dependent filers.

8. As of June 2008, the IRS estimates that about 26 percent (or more than 5 million) of eligible Social Security and Veterans Affairs beneficiaries who normally are not required to file tax returns had not yet claimed the stimulus payment to which they are entitled. See www.irs.gov/irs/article/0,,id=184063,00.html.

9. See the IRS publication *1040 Instructions, 2007* (www.irs.gov/pub/irs-pdf/i1040.pdf).

10. Brian Balkovic, "Individual Income Tax Returns, Preliminary Data, 2006," *Statistics of Income Bulletin* 27, no. 4 (Spring 2008): 4–15, p. 8. In 2007, 95 percent of households had telephone service, and among those with incomes below $20,000, the telephone subscription rate was about 93 percent. See Alexander Belinfante, *Telephone Subscribership in the United States* (Federal Communications Commission, February 2008) (http://hraunfoss.fcc.gov/edocs_public/attachmatch/DOC-279997A1.pdf). Utilization of the rebate was low across the board. Through March 23, 2007, only about 69 percent of filers claimed the excise tax rebate, while utilization among nonfilers was less than 2 percent. From the preliminary data, it is not obvious whether low-income individuals filed the longer tax return to claim a larger rebate or did not claim the telephone excise rebate at all. Nor is it clear from the available data if people chose not to claim the credit because a $30 credit was not sufficient to make up for the costs of completing and submitting the form or because they were unaware of the rebate. See GAO, *Tax Administration: Telephone Excise Tax Refund Requests Are Fewer than Projected and Have Had Minimal Impact on IRS Services*, GAO-07-695 (April 2007).

11. Individuals with higher incomes may be exempted from the Massachusetts mandate if they have difficulty finding affordable health insurance. In 2007 individuals with incomes of up to $50,000 were exempted from the mandate if they could not find health insurance with premiums of less than $500 a month. For families, the corresponding income and premium amounts were, respectively, $110,000 and $720. Massachusetts also exempts individuals from the mandate for other reasons, including "sincerely held" religious beliefs and personal hardship.

12. Internal Revenue Service, *Reducing the Federal Tax Gap: A Report on Improving Voluntary Compliance* (Department of the Treasury, August 2, 2007).

13. Personal communication with Melissa Cummings-Niedzwiecki, director of strategy, Massachusetts Department of Revenue, December 2007.

14. The PARIS data files include beneficiaries' Social Security numbers, names, dates of births, addresses, case numbers, and public assistance benefits received as well as the dates of

receipt. PARIS also includes data on participation in certain federal programs, including veterans' benefits.

15. Nonparticipating states include Alabama, California, Iowa, New Hampshire, North Dakota, Texas, and Vermont.

16. Health Systems Research, *Evaluation to Determine the Effectiveness of the Public Assistance Reporting and Information System, Final Report*, report prepared for the Administration for Children and Families, Department of Health and Human Services (Washington, June 30, 2007).

17. Office of Privacy Protection, "Recommended Practices on Protecting the Confidentiality of Social Security Numbers," revised (Sacramento, Calif.: State and Consumer Services Agency, Office of Information Security and Privacy Protection, April 2007).

18. Michael G. Allingham and Agnar Sandmo, "Income Tax Evasion: A Theoretical Analysis," *Journal of Public Economics* 1 (November 1972): 323–38.

19. Janet G. McCubbin, "Optimal Tax Enforcement: A Review of the Literature and Practical Implications," OTA Working Paper 90 (Department of the Treasury, Office of Tax Analysis, December 2004).

20. Joel Slemrod and Shlomo Yitzhaki, "The Optimal Size of a Tax Collection Agency," *Scandinavian Journal of Economics* 89, no. 2 (1987): 183–92.

21. James Andreoni, "Criminal Deterrence in the Reduced Form: A New Perspective on Ehrlich's Seminal Study," *Economic Inquiry* 33 (July 1995): 476–83.

22. McCubbin, "Optimal Tax Enforcement: A Review of the Literature and Practical Implications."

23. Eugene Steuerle, "Implementing Employer and Individual Mandates," *Health Affairs* 13 (Spring 1994): 54–68.

24. In 2008 and 2009 the personal exemption is phased down but not entirely eliminated under the regular tax and in 2010 is not phased out under the regular tax. Beginning in 2011, the personal exemption will be phased out entirely at higher incomes. However, even during the 2008 through 2010 period, higher-income taxpayers may receive little or no benefit from the personal exemption as a result of the alternative minimum tax.

25. David Williams, testimony before the House Committee on Ways and Means (Internal Revenue Service, June 14, 2007).

26. Janet Holtzblatt and Janet McCubbin, "Issues Affecting Low-Income Filers," in *The Crisis in Tax Administration*, edited by Henry Aaron and Joel Slemrod (Brookings, 2004), pp. 148–200.

27. Jim Cilke, "A Profile of Non-Filers," OTA Working Paper 78 (Department of the Treasury, Office of Tax Analysis, July 1998).

28. Nick Johnson, "'Working for Families' in New Zealand: Some Early Lessons" (Fulbright New Zealand, July 2005). In 2003 roughly one-third of Family Support program recipients in New Zealand received their payments entirely through the tax system, one-third through the welfare system, and one-third through both agencies at different points during the year.

29. While the impact of marriage penalties on misreporting filing status has not been as thoroughly investigated as its impact on marital decisions, the EITC compliance data provide some evidence that evasion occurs. When the IRS determines that an individual should have filed as married, he or she is given a choice to file as married filing separately or jointly with his or her spouse. In the tax year 1999 EITC compliance study, about $600 million in overclaims was attributable to individuals who, after detection, refiled jointly with their spouses,

meaning that they could locate them and cooperate on a combined return. See Holtzblatt and McCubbin, "Issues Affecting Low-Income Filers."

30. The EITC is substantially larger if taxpayers reside with at least one qualifying child. The credit increases with the presence of a second child, although the return to the second child is not as great as it is for the first child. There is no additional benefit for the third child. The most common EITC error is misreporting of children, followed by misreporting of filing status. Studies by Jeffrey Liebman and Janet McCubbin have suggested that about one-third of erroneous claims for children are intentional. See Jeffrey Liebman, "Noncompliance and the Earned Income Tax Credit: Taxpayer Error or Taxpayer Fraud?" (Harvard University, Economics Department, December 1995); Janet McCubbin, "Noncompliance with the Earned Income Tax Credit," in *Making Work Pay*, edited by Bruce Meyer and Douglas Holtz-Eakin (New York: Russell Sage Foundation, 2001), pp. 237–73.

31. Consider, for example, the Bush administration's proposal to create a standard deduction for single and family coverages. Taxpayers could qualify under the plan for the full standard deduction even if the costs of health insurance were less than the deduction amount. Some couples might find it worthwhile under the circumstances to purchase two plans for the family—perhaps a higher cost plan to cover the members at greater risk and a lesser cost plan for the other members. If the cost of the second plan was sufficiently low, then the family could receive a tax reduction greater than the amounts spent on health insurance. Of course, planning and implementing this strategy requires some effort, and rational taxpayers may find that they value their leisure more than the monetary return to noncompliance.

32. Nearly all food stamp applicants must be interviewed in office by a caseworker. State rules vary, but applicants generally are required to bring extensive documentation in support of their claim. For example, Massachusetts requires documentation of identity, residence, utility bills, bank accounts, pay stubs, dependent care expenses, unearned income, self-employment income, rental income, medical expenses, and other items.

33. Holtzblatt and McCubbin, "Issues Affecting Low-Income Filers"; Department of the Treasury, *General Explanations of the Administration's Fiscal Year 2009 Revenue Proposals* (February 2008).

34. Kari Wolkwitz, *Trends in Food Stamp Program Participation Rates: 1999 to 2005*, report prepared for the Department of Agriculture (Washington: Mathematica Policy Research, Inc., June 2007); Dorothy Rosenbaum, "Food Stamp Error Rates Hold at Record Low Levels in 2005" (Washington: Center on Budget and Policy Priorities, July 11, 2006).

35. IRS, *IRS Earned Income Tax Credit (EITC) Initiative: Final Report to Congress* (Department of the Treasury, October 2005); IRS, *IRS Earned Income Tax Credit (EITC) Initiative: Report on Fiscal Year 2005 Tests* (January 2007).

36. Individuals who perceived Medicaid applications as long and complicated were 1.8 times less likely to participate. See Jennifer Stuber and others, "Beyond Stigma: What Barriers Actually Affect the Decisions of Low-Income Families to Enroll in Medicaid?" Issue Brief (George Washington University, Center for Health Services Research and Policy, July 2000). Extending the periods between eligibility certification periods made it easier for households to continue receiving food stamps. See Janet Currie and Jeffrey Grogger, "Explaining Recent Declines in Food Stamp Program Participation," in *Brookings-Wharton Papers on Urban Affairs*, edited by Janet Rothenberg Pack and William G. Gale (Brookings, 2001), chapter 5. Marianne Bitler, Janet Currie, and John Karl Scholz found that program rules that increase transaction costs of using the program—such as requiring more frequent visits to the Women, Infants and Children (WIC) office, more proof of income, and higher standards for

nutritional risk—reduce participation. See Marianne Bitler, Janet Currie, and John Karl Scholz, "WIC Eligibility and Participation," *Journal of Human Resources* 38 (Summer 2003): 1139–79.

37. The IRS is testing alternative means to better detect questionable claims of filing status, using a combination of statistical methods and data from either tax records or commercial sources. See IRS, *IRS Earned Income Tax Credit (EITC) Initiative: Final Report to Congress*; *IRS Earned Income Tax Credit (EITC) Initiative: Report on Fiscal Year 2005 Tests.*

38. Janet Currie, "The Take-Up of Social Benefits," paper prepared for a conference in honor of Eugene Smolensky (Berkeley, Calif., December 12–13, 2003).

39. GAO, *Advance Earned Income Tax Credit: Low Use and Small Dollars Paid Impede IRS's Efforts to Reduce High Noncompliance.*

40. Stan Dorn, "How Well Do Health Coverage Tax Credits Help Displaced Workers Obtain Health Care?" testimony before the House Committee on Education and Labor, 110 Cong. 1 sess. (Urban Institute, March 26, 2007). Writing about the HCTC, Dorn proposed that eligibility for advance credits could be based on the quarterly unemployment data contained in the National Directory of New Hires (NDNH). The IRS currently has limited access to the NDNH for EITC enforcement only. Information from the NDNH would be timelier and, with respect to wages, more reliable than using taxpayer's self-reported amounts on their tax returns. However, the NDNH does not include information on self-employment earnings or nonlabor income. There are also lags in the reporting of wage data. State agencies are required to report within four months of the end of the quarter, although some states are reporting quarterly wage data monthly or weekly. See "The Guide to the National Directory of New Hires" (Department of Health and Human Services, Federal Office of Child Support Services) (www.acf.hhs.gov/programs/cse/newhire/library/ndnh/background_guide.pdf).

41. In the United Kingdom, taxpayers are eligible for advance refundable Child and Work Tax Credits on the basis of current tax year characteristics with a built-in cushion for changes in income. Originally, taxpayers were required to repay overpayments if their income exceeded the prior-year amount by £2,500. However, many taxpayers had to repay substantial amounts, often because of programming errors by HM Revenue and Customs. A 2005 report by the Parliamentary and Health Service Ombudsman raised concerns about the hardships resulting from the technical difficulties, and Parliament increased the threshold to £25,000 in 2007.

42. Timothy Dowd, "Distinguishing between Short-Term and Long-Term Recipients of the Earned Income Tax Credit," *National Tax Journal* LVIII (December 2005): 807–28.

43. Peter Orszag, testimony on economic volatility before the House Committee on Ways and Means, 110 Cong., 1 sess. (Congressional Budget Office, January 31, 2007).

44. Some states have "gap filler" programs that use Department of Labor grants to pay 65 percent of health insurance premiums before the IRS certifies eligibility for the HCTC. In addition, the taxpayers may claim the HCTC on their tax return for insurance premiums paid before the start-up of the advance payments.

45. Dorn, "How Well Do Health Coverage Tax Credits Help Displaced Workers Obtain Health Care?"

46. Williams, testimony before the House Committee on Ways and Means.

47. Sherry Glied, Jacob Hartz, and Genessa Giorgi, "Consider It Done? The Likely Efficacy of Mandates for Health Insurance," *Health Affairs* 26 (November–December 2007): 1612–21.

Comment by Stan Dorn

The papers by Mary Hevener and Charles Kerby and by Janet Holtzblatt offer sobering reminders of the administrative problems that can result when the federal income tax system and health policy collide. Informed by these lessons, I want to suggest some ways in which the income tax system could be used to help cover the uninsured as part of broader health reform.

In 2006, 66 percent of the uninsured lived in households with incomes below 200 percent of the federal poverty level (FPL).[1] For health reform to succeed in covering most of the uninsured, administrative agencies thus need the capacity to identify the low-income uninsured, provide them with subsidies, and enroll them into coverage.

Despite the obstacles identified by Hevener and Kerby and Holtzblatt, the income tax system can contribute to covering the low-income uninsured, in two ways. First, it can help other subsidy programs, such as Medicaid and the State Children's Health Insurance Program (SCHIP), determine who qualifies for help. Second, it can provide subsidies through such devices as refundable tax credits that are advanced to insurers when monthly premiums are due.

Helping Other Programs Determine Eligibility

Some health policy analysts are interested in the income tax system because, to paraphrase Willy Sutton, that's where the income data are. Thanks in large part to the Earned Income Tax Credit (EITC), many low-income households who do not owe federal income tax nevertheless file returns. In fact, more low-income people are reached by the EITC than any other need-based benefit.[2] Equally important, nonfilers have administrative data reported by third parties each year to the Internal Revenue Service (IRS). Documentation is transmitted via W-2 forms for wages and 1099 forms for most other income.

Already, Medicaid and other public assistance programs are legally required to exchange data with the IRS to verify applicants' assertions about income.[3] Why not take this connection one step farther and use IRS data to identify income-eligible individuals, without waiting for families to estimate income on application forms for health coverage programs?

Such an approach has precedent. Medicare Part B determines eligibility for means-tested premium subsidies based on federal income tax data two years in the past. (In 2007, for example, subsidy eligibility was based on income tax data for 2005.) Subsidies do not fall for beneficiaries whose incomes rise following the base year. However, those whose incomes decline may apply to the Social Security Administration (SSA) for larger subsidies. *With federal income tax records establishing eligibility, every Medicare Part B beneficiary now receives an interim income determination each year, along with a corresponding subsidy, without filing any application forms.*

As a second precedent, the Bush administration during its first term advocated a refundable, advanceable tax credit to subsidize coverage for low-income working families without access to employer-sponsored insurance. Despite income fluctuations among working families that are much greater than those of Medicare beneficiaries, the administration proposed that the previous year's tax data would determine each family's annual income eligibility for subsidies.[4]

Clearly, if policymakers are willing to accept some imprecision in income measurement, significant gains are possible from using prior-year tax data to determine eligibility. Take-up will increase substantially if application forms can be avoided before enrollment, as behavioral economics teaches.[5] The Holtzblatt paper itself provides a striking example: among eligible nonfilers, only 2 percent claim telephone credit rebates, even though the applicable IRS form requests just name, address, and Social Security number.

Using the income tax system to establish income eligibility can yield other benefits. Operational administrative costs can decline substantially when data matches replace manual processing and verification of paper applications and supporting documents.[6] Moreover, program integrity can improve when income determination is based on third-party income data rather than fallible human memories and applicants' paper files.[7]

Three strategies can narrow the potential mismatch between prior-year tax data and families' current financial circumstances. First, income tax data can be supplemented by earnings information from the National Directory of New Hires (NDNH), which contains data about every new hire in the United States and every public and private employee's quarterly wages during recent months. NDNH data would capture many changes in household circumstances following the most recent tax year, since hours and wages of employment are by far the most significant component of income volatility for low-income families.[8] Data matches with NDNH already confirm eligibility for other benefits, including Temporary Assistance to Needy Families (TANF), housing subsidies, unemployment compensation, and EITC, so the proposed extension to health coverage would have some precedent.[9]

As a second strategy to address potential obsolescence of household tax data, income determinations could be made when tax data are still relatively fresh. By February and March for paper and electronic transmissions, respectively, the prior-year's third-party data must be reported to the IRS.[10] These data could be used promptly to determine eligibility for health coverage subsidies.

Third, officials administering Medicaid or SCHIP could use income tax and other available data to complete the portions of health coverage application forms that estimate income. These officials would then ask applicants to correct any errors, specifying that a failure to make necessary corrections could subject the applicant to sanctions. If the applicant makes no changes, the eligibility determination would be made on the bassis of the pre-populated form. A number of states already use this approach in renewing Medicaid and SCHIP eligibility.[11]

As with Medicare subsidies and SCHIP in most states, eligibility could be granted for twelve-month periods, on the basis of information at the time of eligibility determination.[12] Following the example of Medicare Part B, households that experience economic setbacks following the tax period could seek increased subsidies.

Exactly how these strategies are used would depend on the context. For example, to identify and enroll eligible, uninsured children into Medicaid and SCHIP, parents could receive an opportunity at various key junctures to check a single box that indicates three things: whether the child is uninsured; whether the parents want help obtaining health coverage; and whether the parents consent to disclosure of otherwise confidential information to help establish their child's eligibility. Parents seeking such help would need to disclose their Social Security numbers (SSNs) to facilitate data matching.

These steps could be taken when parents file income tax forms, when they begin or end employment or complete W-4 forms for income withholding, when they seek health care for their children, when children start school each year, or at other times. Matches with the previous year's tax data, supplemented by the most recent NDNH data showing parental earnings, would establish income eligibility. Other factors relevant to eligibility, such as citizenship and immigration status, would be shown by data matches with other sources of information whenever possible.[13] Only if data matches failed to establish full eligibility, or if families did not consent to data sharing, would standard application forms and procedures be needed. And once eligibility was established, it could be renewed annually each spring, as soon as the family's prior-year, third-party income data became available from the IRS.

To be sure, working out the details would be complex and require initial investments in information technology.[14] But such a data-driven approach offers great promise for reaching a large proportion of low-income uninsured while safeguarding program integrity and reducing ongoing administrative costs.

Tax Subsidies for Covering the Low-Income Uninsured

For many years, elected officials across the political spectrum have proposed refundable, advanceable tax credits to subsidize health coverage for the uninsured.[15] Since 2002 the country has been providing such subsidies through Health Coverage Tax Credits (HCTC).[16] HCTCs help a monthly average of 16,000 households headed either by (a) workers receiving Trade Adjustment Assistance (TAA) because trade liberalization displaced them from employment or (b) early retirees receiving pension payments from the Pension Benefit Guaranty Corporation (PBGC) because their former employers defaulted on promised defined benefit pensions. HCTC pays 65 percent of premiums for qualified health coverage, which generally consists of private insurance arranged by states and health plans offered by former employers under the Consolidated Omnibus Budget Reconciliation Act of 1986 (COBRA).[17]

HCTC is the only program that uses federal income tax credits to subsidize coverage of the otherwise uninsured. As such, it offers important lessons about the design of future tax credits to help make insurance affordable for large numbers of uninsured Americans.

HCTC has avoided marketing fraud by insurers, a notable administrative accomplishment. Such fraud was a serious problem with the so-called Bentsen child health tax credits in the early 1990s, the only pre-HCTC use of tax credits to cover the uninsured. Marketing fraud also marred early Medicaid managed care and more recent initiatives to provide private insurance under Medicare.[18]

This dismal history suggests that con artists seem almost irresistibly drawn to consumers who are authorized to pick the health plans on which taxpayer funds are spent. Although most insurers and their agents are ethical, public policy must guard against the few who are not. HCTC has avoided fraud because the credits could be used only to purchase state-qualified insurance and COBRA plans. As a result, enrollment has taken place in a defined and relatively controlled setting.[19] If future tax credits could be used to pay for any licensed non-group plan, marketing fraud could reemerge as a serious problem.

Another administrative accomplishment of HCTC was that many health insurers were persuaded to participate, although the number of credit recipients was small and differences between HCTC consumer protections and normal market rules discouraged plan participation. Despite these challenges, by March 2006, 40 states, with 87 percent of potentially eligible individuals, had arranged state-qualified coverage, which together included 280 plan options.[20]

Alas, solving this problem created another. To encourage health plan participation, the IRS built an advance payment system that gives each plan its full premium payment, from a single source, by the plan's normal monthly due date. Reaching this goal requires a costly federal administrative system with multiple transactions each month for each enrollee. Every month

—the IRS sends each enrollee an invoice for his or her 35 percent premium share,

—the enrollee must pay 35 percent of his or her premium share to the IRS,

—the IRS tracks the receipt of the 35 percent payment, assigns it to the correct account, and forwards the 35 percent payment to the Treasury Department's Financial Management Service (FMS),

—the FMS combines the 35 percent payment with the 65 percent HCTC payment and sends the complete premium payment to the taxpayer's health plan by the regular monthly due date, along with information identifying the taxpayer.

Largely because of these multiple individual transactions each month, the IRS and the Treasury Department spend $1 in administrative costs for each $4 in subsidies delivered by advance payment.[21] Of course, a tax credit with more enrollees could realize efficiencies of scale. Based on IRS estimates, if HCTC served three times as many taxpayers, per capita administrative costs would fall by more than 50 percent.

Administrative costs could be further lowered by reducing the number of monthly transactions per beneficiary. For example, if tax credits are usable in health insurance exchanges, the exchange could bill each beneficiary for his or her monthly premium share, pay each plan its full monthly premium, and present IRS with quarterly invoices for credits covering the remainder of premium costs, plus interest to cover the slight delay in payment. The IRS would engage in a single quarterly transaction for all tax credit beneficiaries served by the exchange, substantially reducing administrative costs.

The Centers for Medicare and Medicaid Services (CMS) take a similar approach today in delivering low-income premium subsidies to Medicare Part D prescription drug plans. Plans bill subsidy-eligible beneficiaries for their discounted premium share. At the end of the month, CMS pays each plan the remaining premium amounts for all its subsidized enrollees.

Another HCTC administrative problem is that most beneficiaries must pay several months of premiums in full before the start of advance payment. The reason is that workers cannot apply for HCTC advance payment unless they are already enrolled in qualifying coverage. This problem can be solved by letting taxpayers who have not yet enrolled apply for a determination that they have the individual characteristics needed for eligibility. After such precertification of individual eligibility, taxpayers could enroll in qualified coverage, paying the worker's share of premiums rather than the full premium amount.

Other health subsidy programs for which enrollees make partial premium payments, such as Medicare and SCHIP, work this way. Only after individual eligibility is established do applicants enroll, at which point they pay only their share of premiums.

Conclusion

Americans in the twenty-first century swim in a sea of personal data, for better and for worse. As a result, traditional application processes for health coverage and other public benefits are increasingly obsolete, since they deny assistance until families compile and present, in proper form and timely fashion, information that government officials may already have at their fingertips. Reengineering enrollment processes to take full advantage of existing data, including tax information, could substantially reduce the burdens now imposed on applicants and public agencies alike. These reforms could greatly increase enrollment by eligible but uninsured consumers, lower administrative costs, and strengthen program integrity.

On a second issue involving the interface between taxes and health coverage, no one should be surprised—particularly after the articles by Hevener and Kerby and Holtzblatt—that the nation's first attempt to provide refundable, advanceable tax credits to cover the uninsured has run into serious problems. Fortunately, those problems are solvable if policymakers decide to include such credits in national health care reform.

Notes

1. Kaiser Commission on Medicaid and the Uninsured and the Urban Institute, *Health Insurance Coverage in America: 2006 Data Update* (Menlo Park, Calif.: Kaiser Commission on Medicaid and the Uninsured; Washington: Urban Institute, October 2007). In 2008 the FPL is $17,600 a year for a family of 3, $21,200 for a family of 4, and so on.

2. S. G. Zedlewski, L. Dubay Adams, and G. Kenney, *Is There a System Supporting Low-Income Working Families?* (Urban Institute, February 2006); L. E. Burman and D.I. Kobes,

"EITC Reaches More Eligible Families than TANF, Food Stamps," *Tax Notes* (March 17, 2003): 1769.

3. Social Security Act, Section 1137(a)(2).

4. This example is unlike Medicare Part B for another reason. For Part B, income differences must be quite large before subsidy eligibility is affected; only if beneficiaries' income exceeds $80,000 for single individuals and $160,000 per couple, in 2007 dollars, do they receive anything less than a 75 percent premium subsidy. By contrast, the administration's proposed tax credit for working families would be phased out evenly as income rose, creating a much greater need for precise income measurement. See Council of Economic Advisers, *Economic Report of the President, together with the Annual Report of the Council of Economic Advisers* (Washington, February 2002).

5. Probably the best known example involves retirement savings. Participation in 401(k) plans rises from approximately 33 percent among new hires to roughly 90 percent when workers are enrolled unless they complete "opt out" forms. See D. Laibson, "Impatience and Savings," *National Bureau of Economic Research Reporter* (Fall 2005): 6–8.

6. For example, when the state of Louisiana began using income data whenever possible (supplemented in some cases by telephone calls) to renew children's Medicaid and SCHIP eligibilities, rather than asking each family to complete forms documenting income, the state achieved significant administrative savings while greatly reducing the number of eligible children who lost health coverage when their twelve-month coverage periods came to an end. See J. R. Kennedy, "LaCHIP Outreach, Enrollment, & Retention," paper prepared for the Winter Medicaid Administrative Management Conference (New Orleans, La., January 17, 2007). Along similar lines, the National School Lunch Program has achieved large administrative savings while increasing enrollment of eligible children and reducing eligibility errors by using data matches with Medicaid and TANF, rather than parental application forms, to establish income eligibility. See P. Gleason and others, *Direct Certification in the National School Lunch Program—Impacts on Program Access and Integrity*, report for the Department of Agriculture, Report E-FAN-03-009 (Princeton, N.J.: Mathematica Policy Research, Inc., 2003); N. Cole, *Data Matching in the National School Lunch Program: 2005, Volume 1: Final Report*, report for the Department of Agriculture, Report CN-06-DM (Bethesda, Md.: Abt Associates, Inc., 2007).

7. Gleason and others, *Direct Certification in the National School Lunch Program*. See also the discussion of WIC adjunctive eligibility and program integrity in Government Accountability Office, *Means-Tested Programs: Information on Program Access Can Be an Important Management Tool*, GAO-05-221 (March 2005).

8. C. Newman, "Income Volatility Complicates Food Assistance," *Amber Waves* 4, no. 4 (September 2006): 16–21 (USDA Economic Research Service). One question requiring further research involves the extent to which such changes in income involve, not wages, but contractor income or other earnings reported on 1099 forms. Only wage income is reported to NDNH.

9. Federal Office of Child Support Enforcement, *A Guide to the National Directory of New Hires*, updated (Washington: Department of Health and Human Services, Division of Federal Systems, January 23, 2007). With other programs, NDNH data are typically used to verify income. In this case, they would obviate applicants' provision of income estimates.

10. Internal Revenue Service (IRS), *Employer's Tax Guide for Use in 2008* (Circular E), Publication 15 (Department of the Treasury, 2008).

11. A. Cohen, M. Dutton, K. Griffin, and G. Woods, *Streamlining Renewal in Medicaid and SCHIP: Strategies from Other States and Lessons for New York* (New York: United Hospital Fund and Manatt Health Solutions, 2008). Along similar lines, EITC claimants can ask the IRS to calculate credit amounts. See Internal Revenue Service, *Earned Income Credit (EIC): For Use in Preparing 2007 Returns*, Publication 596 (U.S. Department of the Treasury). Even more analogous, "return-free" tax filing systems that encompass year-end reconciliation involve tax agencies that use third-party data to complete annual returns for taxpayers' inspection and correction. These systems are used in several European countries, have been pilot-tested in California, and are proposed for national implementation in the United States. See W. Gale and B. Harris. "Return-Free Filing: What Is it and How Would It Work?" in *The Tax Policy Briefing Book* (Urban Institute and Brookings Institution Tax Policy Center, last updated December 14, 2007).

12. D. Cohen Ross, A. Horn, and C. Marks, *Health Coverage for Children and Families in Medicaid and SCHIP: State Efforts Face New Hurdles* (Washington: Center on Budget and Policy Priorities; Menlo Park, Calif.: Kaiser Commission on Medicaid and the Uninsured, 2008).

13. With immigration status and citizenship, such sources of information include SSA, federal immigration agencies, and birth certificate data. For this approach to be most effective, federal policy changes may be needed, including some simplification of eligibility rules to fit the available data. See S. Dorn, *Eligible but Not Enrolled: How SCHIP Reauthorization Can Help*, report prepared for the Robert Wood Johnson Foundation (Washington: Urban Institute, 2007). In addition, to effectively serve the greatest possible number of applicants for health coverage, these data sources need improvements in comprehensiveness and general quality.

14. For example, income methodologies differ between Medicaid programs and federal income tax law. Protocols need to be devised that provide approximate "translations" of federal income tax information into Medicaid eligibility findings. At the same time, consumers need the ability to seek income determinations under standard Medicaid rules if tax-based methods do not show eligibility. And all of these innovations need to be structured carefully to preserve taxpayer privacy.

15. S. Dorn and T. Kutyla. *Health Coverage Tax Credits under the Trade Act of 2002: A Preliminary Analysis of Program Operations*, report prepared for the Commonwealth Fund (Washington: Economic and Social Research Institute, April 2004).

16. For a more detailed explanation of HCTC, see IRS, "Most Frequently Asked Questions," Publication 4252 (Rev.12-2007) (Department of the Treasury, 2007) (www.irs.gov/pub/irs-utl/2007_hctc_frequently_asked_questions.pdf).

17. Except as otherwise noted, all factual assertions contained in this section of the comment are documented in S. Dorn, "HCTC: A Small Program Offering Large Policy Lessons" (Washington: Urban Institute, February 2008) (www.urban.org/UploadedPDF/411608_health_coverage_tax.pdf). While the present comment is limited to administrative issues, the earlier analysis also discusses other topics, such as the size of tax credits needed for high take-up and the type of health benefits for which credits can be used.

18. See, for example, Senate Special Committee on Aging Hearing, "Medicare Advantage Marketing and Sales: Who Has the Advantage?" 110 Cong., 1 sess. (May 16, 2007) (http://aging.senate.gov/hearing_detail.cfm?id=295804&).

19. Other approaches are certainly possible to preventing marketing fraud. Medicaid programs, for example, often use independent enrollment brokers to help families select and

enroll in HMOs (42 CFR 438.810). Similarly, the health insurance industry supports proposed rules regulating the marketing of Medicare private plans. See America's Health Insurance Plans, "Strengthening Oversight of Medicare Advantage and Part D Marketing" (Washington, May 8, 2008) (www.ahip.org/content/fileviewer.aspx?docid=22559&linkid=194785).

20. F. Pervez and S. Dorn, *Health Plan Options under the Health Coverage Tax Credit Program*, report prepared for the Commonwealth Fund (Lansing, Mich.: Health Management Associates; Washington: Urban Institute, December 11, 2006).

21. When end-of-year HCTC payments are taken into account, the ratio of IRS administrative costs to subsidies becomes 1 to 5. However, since these administrative costs are mainly created by the advance payment process, the ratio in the text may be more salient.

Comment by Sherry Glied

The papers by Janet Holtzblatt and by Mary Hevener and Chip Kerby are extremely useful. Policymakers often take implementation issues for granted—as though a wave of the wand could change how large bureaucracies, like the Internal Revenue Service (IRS), work and how they interact with the rest of society. These papers are a critical reminder that government agencies, like the people and businesses whose behavior we wish to alter through policy, depend on resources, respond to incentives, and have goals of their own. The two chapters suggest that we should be humble not only about how such agencies implement policies but also about how much influence these policies can have, in practice, on the structure and performance of the health care system. As Holtzblatt points out, the IRS is an $11 billion agency and only a minute portion of its tasks involves manipulating the behavior of the $2 trillion health care system.

Why the IRS?

Current interest in implementing health care reform through the tax code system stems from a desire to expand and rationalize coverage while relying primarily on the private sector to provide health insurance and health care services. None of the politically tenable options for health care reform would involve building a new public program or greatly expanding an existing program.

This goal of using the tax code system for health care reform and the constraint that no new program be established nor an existing program expanded suggest two possible strategies. The first is to abandon the goal of extending private health insurance as a strategy for expanding access to care and to rely instead on a substantially enhanced health care safety net. From an administrative perspective, this approach has notable advantages. Safety net providers can treat their patients as they present themselves, without a need for any govern-

208

ment agency to keep track of who these patients are or how much they have paid. The flaws of this approach are equally apparent. A safety net system with low administrative costs cannot focus resources on those who most need it, effectively assess the quality of care provided, or reliably account for services provided and related costs. The costs of building and maintaining such a system in a way that would attract enough qualified providers would be very great.

That leaves direction two—maintain insurance, mainly private insurance, and use an existing government agency to distribute subsidies to those who need them the most. Two government agencies are in regular contact with a large proportion of Americans and collect information on income: the Social Security Administration (SSA) and the IRS.

Many countries operate universal health insurance programs through the equivalent of the SSA. The SSA has regular contact with workers through their employers. As Holtzblatt points out in studying the analogous situation at the IRS, tax compliance through employers is generally better than it is through individual filing. The SSA is in nearly continual contact with workers, and the timeliness of contact is important in the health insurance context. But the SSA is not in contact with nonworkers. It has information on wages but not on family incomes, which can be quite different, especially for two-earner families. The SSA would not be able to distribute family income–based subsidies. The SSA option would work best with a reform that had an automatic, subsidized default option, with the IRS conducting reconciliation at year-end.

Using the IRS for Health Care Reform

The flaws of the safety net and SSA approaches leave the IRS as the best option available. The IRS has some important strengths as a manager of health reform. For filers, who constitute most of those who would be required to pay for any portion of their health insurance premium, the IRS collects detailed data on family income. The IRS has experience in delivering subsidies to low-income families. Through its long history of working with employers, it potentially could develop methods to deliver subsidies in a more timely fashion than other agencies can. Nonetheless, as these chapters point out, the IRS has many deficiencies as a vehicle for health care reform.

Both the Holtzblatt and Hevener and Kerby chapters point out a host of specific problems with the IRS, but they all arise from the same basic institutional reality. The IRS is an agency designed to process large numbers of tax returns fairly and expeditiously so as to collect revenue for the federal government. That is its principal mission. Policy directives that require the agency to stray from that mission tend to be poorly implemented. The agency's internal and external incentives reward behavior that contributes to its fundamental mission. Hevener and Kerby provide a depressing litany of ambitious health-related policies for which the IRS has failed miserably in execution. In some cases, regulations have never been developed. In others, enforcement has been nonexistent or inconsistent. The IRS's only real success in health policy has been the tax treatment of employer-sponsored insurance (ESI), a policy that required the IRS to do nothing.

The IRS is not a natural place to conduct health care policy—but it is where policy likely will be conducted, because there is no appealing alternative. Under a mandate that each individual show that he or she is insured, the IRS might be used to determine if each person is insured and deliver subsidies if he or she is and to assess and collect penalties. Under a proposal to replace the tax exclusion with a tax credit, the IRS might be required to measure employer payments for health insurance, so that these can be counted as taxable income, and deliver tax credits for health insurance purchased by individuals. Whatever the reform strategy, the IRS will be working to force people and businesses to behave in ways that sometimes are against their self-interest.

As these chapters illustrate, the IRS's capacity to alter behavior related to the health care system is limited. The complexities of health care and health insurance are quite different from the problems of collecting data and enforcing payment and are outside the IRS's institutional competence in measuring income. To be effective, reform efforts, whatever direction they take, will need to account for these limitations. Successful reforms will need to recognize and make use of the existing competencies of government agencies and institutions as they assign responsibilities for reform. If legislators wish to assign agencies roles that push the boundaries of these existing competencies, they will need to explicitly set new priorities and reward structures for the agencies and provide staff and budgets sufficient to address these roles. Beyond program design, policymakers should provide the resources and direction to allow agencies to execute their roles. This requirement is particularly urgent when a new program gets under way; but it continues with every subsequent amendment. The public administrative costs of effective health care reform, whichever agency runs it and whatever direction it takes, are likely to be substantial and ongoing. Failure to acknowledge and budget for these costs is a prescription for failure of reform itself.

9

Reforming the Tax Treatment of Health Care: Right Ways and Wrong Ways

JASON FURMAN

Health care in America faces three fundamental problems. First, according to census estimates 47 million Americans are uninsured.[1] Second, America spends an enormous amount on health care for the insured while often getting little or no benefit at the margin.[2] And third, health care is the largest source of the long-run fiscal gap.[3] An ideal reform proposal would make progress on all three dimensions. A good reform proposal would make a worthwhile trade-off among the three dimensions. An unacceptable reform proposal would move in the wrong direction in some or all dimensions.

Evaluation of reform proposals is complicated by the enormous complexity and interdependence in the health care system, which leads to substantial uncertainty about the impact of reforms. To understand the impact of a health reform proposal requires predicting not only the behavior of individuals but also that of employers, insurance companies, medical providers, and state insurance regulators. The further a reform departs from historical experience, the less dependable the elasticities and other behavioral assumptions that derive from that historical experience become. As a result, it is important to evaluate any change, and especially major change, not just by the expected outcome but also by the uncertainty that surrounds that outcome. Everything else being equal, it is better to pursue a more certain course.

I use these criteria to evaluate two reform options and find each wanting. The first is the proposal by John Cogan, Glenn Hubbard, and Daniel Kessler to make all health expenses tax deductible.[4] The second is the proposal to make all individual market premiums tax deductible. Both of these proposals provide

Jason Furman was a senior fellow at the Brookings Institution at the time of this writing, April 2008.

new tax subsidies in the service of reforms that have uncertain benefits and could even be counterproductive. The shortcomings of these plans provide a cautionary note for many of the numerous other health tax reforms that have been proposed. My criticisms of these plans lead me to analyze a third alternative that would replace the existing tax exclusion to see if it could be done in a manner that would increase coverage, reduce costs, and lower (or at least not increase) the long-run fiscal gap. The most likely way to achieve these goals would be to combine progressive, refundable tax credits with three reforms to insurance markets: a mandate or other institutional mechanisms like automatic enrollment, pooling mechanisms like the Connector in Massachusetts, and reduction of adverse selection in existing pooling mechanisms through techniques like catastrophic reinsurance. Without these complementary reforms, however, merely replacing the exclusion would be counterproductive, causing large-scale dropping of people who have good employer coverage and potentially even increasing the net number of uninsured.

Tax Incentives to Encourage Less Spending on Health Care

The tax treatment of health care expenses encourages greater spending in a number of ways. The tax exclusion for employer contributions to health insurance lowers the after-tax price of the insurance and helps underpin an institutional system of employer-sponsored insurance. It increases the number of people with insurance and the comprehensiveness of insurance coverage, both of which increase health spending. In addition, the fact that insurance premiums are tax favored and out-of-pocket payments generally are not provides an incentive to purchase high premium plans with low deductibles and copayments, leading to even more spending.[5]

These considerations motivate reformers to propose tax changes that would reduce total health spending, so that people can spend less on health care and more on other goods and services that they would value more highly. The argument is simple: if consumers are rational and there are no market failures or tax distortions, people would allocate their consumption between health care and everything else so as to equate the marginal benefit of health spending and all other spending. Add in a tax subsidy, and people will consume even more health care. As a result, the marginal benefit of the additional health services will drop and be less than the marginal cost of producing them. This inefficiency could be remedied by reducing health spending and shifting it to other areas like food, clothing, and housing. This conclusion depends on the capacity of consumers or someone acting for them to curtail low-benefit, but not high-benefit, health care. Note that there is a trade-off: even marginal health spending still has a benefit, but the benefit is lower—more like $0.75—than the $1 it costs to produce that care. As a result, while the reallocation of spending makes people better off overall they get less health care and, as a result, may be in somewhat worse health.

In practice, however, there is little evidence that people are rational consumers, especially with something as complicated as health care. For example, the RAND Health Insurance Experiment (HIE), conducted in the late 1970s and early 1980s, found that when consumers are faced with more cost sharing they reduce spending on effective and ineffective treatments by similar amounts, a finding at odds with the assumption of a rational consumer.[6] As a result, the question of how reductions in health spending affect health is an empirical one. A substantial body of evidence suggests that there may not even be a trade-off: one can get the same health outcomes for less money. The classic evidence for this proposition is from the HIE: when prices rose, most people who cut back on spending (with the exception of those with low incomes and chronic conditions) were in no worse health than before. The reason is that households typically cut back on not only needed care but also unnecessary care and harmful care, leading to no net reduction in health. Evidence since the HIE supports these conclusions.[7] More evidence is provided by the large regional variation in Medicare spending without any commensurate variation in outcomes.[8]

The aggregate effect of the current tax incentives for spending is large. A theoretical article by William Jack and Louise Sheiner estimates that if agents choose the optimal coinsurance rate, then eliminating the tax subsidy for insurance premiums would raise the coinsurance rate from 20 percent to 33 percent (a 65 percent increase) and reduce health spending by 11 percent.[9] This finding is largely consistent with estimates based on an empirical study by Martin Feldstein and Bernard Friedman, which finds that eliminating the tax benefit for employer-sponsored insurance would increase the coinsurance rate by 41 percent, which using the HIE demand elasticity of 0.22 would translate into a 7 percent reduction in spending.[10]

Further, the effects on spending could even be substantially larger than suggested by these estimates. The HIE examined how individuals would alter their spending on existing medical technology in response to changed financial incentives. But if these incentives were adopted widely, then they would also lead to changes in the development and adoption of medical technologies and techniques. Evidence from the introduction of Medicare suggests that these general equilibrium effects could result in spending reductions three times or more than spending reductions based on individual behavior alone.[11] If these findings are generalized to the non-Medicare population, the impact on spending could easily be three times larger than these estimates suggest. I conclude that eliminating the tax exclusion for health insurance would unambiguously reduce health spending.

In contrast, adding new tax incentives has an ambiguous effect on spending. On the one hand, the extra tax incentives reduce the after-tax price of health care spending still further, which tends to increase spending. On the other hand, if the new tax incentives increase cost sharing—for example through tax subsidies for individuals with high-deductible plans or high out-of-pocket expenses—then they would tend to reduce health care spending. The net effect of these two factors depends on specific circumstances.

John Cogan, Glenn Hubbard, and Daniel Kessler propose making all out-of-pocket health spending tax deductible.[12] The goal of the proposal is to end the tax advantage for insurance premiums instead of for out-of-pocket expenses. As a result, insurance planners would have less of an incentive to design plans that raise premiums and lower coinsurance rates. Instead, plans would incorporate more cost sharing and be cheaper. The effect of this proposal on health spending is ambiguous and depends on three factors. First, how much does the coinsurance rate increase? If the coinsurance rate increases enough so that the net, after-tax coinsurance rate rises, then spending might fall.[13] Jack and Sheiner show that under relatively general conditions this is the theoretical outcome with rational, maximizing agents.[14] But there are few empirical estimates of the actual responsiveness of coinsurance to changes in the tax treatment. Given the plausible range of key parameters, the Cogan, Hubbard, and Kessler plan could increase spending by as much as 3.3 percent or reduce it by as much as 6.2 percent.[15] Second, the incentive to spend more happens the moment the tax changes are enacted, but increases in coinsurance rates may occur slowly. If so, spending would increase in the short run. Finally, to the degree that such a plan extends deductibility to out-of-pocket expenses that are not currently covered by insurance, like eyeglasses and over-the-counter medicine, then the net effect from this component of the plan is unambiguously an increase in spending.

The effects on coverage of such a proposal would likely be small and would largely be a function of the change in the price of health insurance, although such other factors as the impact on employer-sponsored coverage (addressed below) would also be important.

While the benefits of such a proposal are uncertain, the costs are not. If one disregards possible behavioral changes, the cost of fully leveling the playing field for both income and payroll taxes would be about $75 billion in 2008, assuming a 100 percent take-up rate.[16] To the degree that the proposal resulted in higher or lower health spending, the full, dynamic cost would be correspondingly slightly higher or lower.

The combination of certain costs with uncertain and potentially nonexistent benefits is a feature of a broader class of proposals to add new tax incentives to reduce distortions created by current tax incentives.[17] While some new tax incentives might reduce spending, it is hard to be confident that such measures will achieve this goal in practice. In fact, it is plausible that they will perversely end up increasing spending.

Tax Incentives to Encourage Purchase of Health Insurance in the Individual Market

In 2006, 88 percent of privately insured Americans received their coverage through employment-based plans.[18] Employer-sponsored insurance dominates coverage for a number of reasons, including the administrative savings from group coverage, the convenience of employees, and the institutional and cultural path dependence stemming from a series of historical events like wage and price controls in World War II. To the degree that these are the most important factors, employer-sponsored insurance is a rational choice based on cost, convenience, and cultural bias. A fourth factor is government tax policy, which by excluding the value of health insurance from a worker's taxable income provides a discount on such insurance averaging about 20 percent for the typical covered worker.

Critics of the exclusion argue that it distorts the market for health insurance and is fundamentally unfair to people who buy their insurance in the individual market.[19] One potential distortion is job lock, resulting when fear of losing health benefits causes workers to refuse to move to better jobs. The result is reduced productivity, wages, and overall economic flexibility.[20] Another potential distortion is a reduction in transparency, choice, and competition, which could result in inferior choices for workers. Finally, some argue that the lack of tax incentives for the purchase of insurance by workers who are not covered by employers could reduce total coverage relative to the current system, which only provides incentives to purchase coverage through employers.

These criticisms of employer-sponsored insurance need to be set against the serious market failures that plague individual health insurance markets as a result of adverse selection stemming from imperfect information about purchasers of health insurance. Employers create large pools of people linked for reasons that are largely unrelated to health status. This pooling mechanism provides one, albeit imperfect, way of solving the problem of adverse selection. Everything else being equal, these benefits of employer-sponsored insurance clearly outweigh any potential downsides.

Eliminating the differential cost between employer-sponsored insurance and individual market insurance, either by reducing subsidies for employer-sponsored insurance or by increasing them for individual market insurance, would lead some employers to drop coverage, especially smaller employers who are more marginal in their current offers and appear more sensitive to the price of health insurance in their offers.[21] Employers would drop coverage for a number of reasons. First, some smaller businesses may offer coverage so that their owners or senior managers can take advantage of the tax preference for employer-sponsored insurance. Under the current non-discrimination rules, these firms are compelled to offer insurance to all their workers. If the owners and senior managers had another option, then they might drop coverage altogether. Second, if the younger and healthier workers opt out of the firm's plan and buy coverage on their own, premiums for those remaining in the plan would rise, reducing the attractiveness of employer-sponsored insurance.

Workers in companies that drop coverage could buy health insurance individually. But the individual market has three limitations. The first limitation is the higher load factors on insurance premiums. The loading charge is the difference between premiums collected and benefits paid; it covers administrative costs and profits. The loading charge in the individual insurance market is comparatively high because small plans cannot take advantage of economies of scale, the larger cost of marketing to individuals, and the need for medically underwriting each customer. As a result, load factors in the individual market consume an average of 29 percent of the total premium, compared to 9 percent for firms with a hundred or more workers.[22]

The second limitation of the individual market is that it is plagued by adverse selection for new entrants. For people who were in the individual market before they developed a health condition, insurance works reasonably well. Bradley Herring and Mark Pauly show that guaranteed renewability, which requires insurance companies to renew policies at the class average rate, produce considerable risk pooling in the individual market.[23] But the relevant question when considering reforms that could cause employers to stop sponsoring health insurance plans is how the individual market would work for new entrants. In this case, guaranteed renewability is no help. In fact, it encourages insurance companies to select only healthy customers and to charge others extra premiums.

Adverse selection can lead to low-risk people purchasing less insurance than they would want because premiums are designed for higher-risk participants. This theoretical prediction has some evidence in the individual market.[24] The more troubling consequence of adverse selection is that some people are denied coverage, others can buy only very expensive coverage, and others are offered coverage that excludes their preexisting conditions.[25] The most vivid evidence for the pervasiveness of this phenomenon comes from work conducted by Karen Pollitz, Richard Sorian, and Kathy Thomas on behalf of the Kaiser Family Foundation.[26] These researchers invented seven individuals or families with preexisting conditions, ranging from having hay fever to being HIV positive, and sent insurance applications to a variety of states and insurers. Only 10 percent of the applications came back with a clean offer. The most common offer—40 percent—excluded benefits for the preexisting conditions; 35 percent of insurers rejected the application outright. These results point to the necessity of taking policy steps to make individual health insurance an option for all buyers, even those with chronic conditions—since half of uninsured adults have chronic conditions.[27]

The third limitation of the individual market is that it does not have an institutional or behavioral mechanism to encourage households to purchase insurance policies. One lesson from behavioral literature is that default mechanisms matter. Automatic enrollment in 401(k)s, for example, increases participation rates, with particularly dramatic increases for workers who are the least likely to participate.[28] In most companies health insurance is an active decision, wherein the employer essentially requires the employee to decide yes or no, a mechanism that in the savings context is closer to automatic enrollment than it is to opt-in enrollment.[29] In addition, the employer contribution dramatically lowers the marginal cost of buying insurance at work.[30] As a result, 82 percent of workers eligible for insurance buy it, and many of the remaining 18 percent are covered through a spouse.[31] The fact that the take-up rate for employer-sponsored insurance is substantially higher than for Medicaid and SCHIP, which have similar or even more generous subsidies but do not share the same semiautomatic enrollment administrative mechanism, suggests that the high enrollment in employer-sponsored plans is driven by institutional factors. In contrast, in the individual market it is much more likely that people will not take the time to identify and purchase such a complicated product. This lack of effort may be compounded by myopia, possibly because people have been shown to overvalue near-term costs and undervalue future benefits.

Taken together, these three limitations imply that not everyone dropped from employers' coverage will buy coverage in the individual market. These limitations are likely to be most serious for people with lower incomes and preexisting conditions. These effects may well go beyond these groups, which could offset some of the benefits of extending new tax incentives for coverage. In the worst case, the new tax incentives could even increase the number of people without coverage. For example, Jonathan Gruber estimates that fully leveling the playing field for high-deductible insurance through a payroll tax credit and income tax deduction for purchases in the individual market would increase the net number of uninsured by 1.5 million.[32]

Adding new tax incentives for the individual market is in many ways analogous to adding new tax incentives to encourage reduced spending. The budgetary costs are unambiguous. But the impact on coverage is uncertain. On the one hand, the subsidies encourage coverage in the individual market. On the other hand, they encourage employers to stop sponsoring health insurance plans. Well-designed policies can maximize the chances that the new tax incentives enhance coverage, but they cannot eliminate the partially offsetting effects of employer-based insurance being dropped.

Replacing the Tax Exclusion with a Tax Credit— and Other Reforms

A final possibility is to replace the existing exclusion with a tax credit. This approach is the most radical and has the greatest downside in terms of disrupting what works in the system today but also offers the possibility that if done right it would move forward in all three dimensions—coverage, cost, and the long-run fiscal situation. Different variants of the ideas have been proposed many times before.[33] Businesses would still be allowed to deduct the cost of their contributions to employee premiums, just as they can deduct wages and other expenses for the purpose of calculating taxable income. But workers would have to include employer contributions to health insurance in their taxable earnings. In exchange, workers who purchased qualifying insurance would get a refundable tax credit. Qualifying insurance would include limits on out-of-pocket payments, would cover a general range of medical care, and would guarantee renewability. These provisions are similar to those put forward by President George W. Bush in his proposal for a standard deduction for health insurance premiums.[34]

The Impact on Health Care Spending

The impact of such a proposal on health spending by the insured is largely independent of the details of how the replacement credit or deduction is structured. Requiring workers to include in their income employer contributions to premiums would reduce health spending by the insured in three ways. First, it would eliminate any subsidy at the margin to purchase more generous health insurance and would encourage people to buy more nonhealth consumer goods and spend less on health insurance. And unlike HSAs, this change would be neutral about how exactly individuals would reduce their premiums. People would be free to spend less by engaging in more cost sharing, but they would also be free to spend less by choosing health plans with features that reduce use.

Second, at the margin the plan would level the playing field between premiums and out-of-pocket expenses by eliminating the tax subsidy for both sets of purchases. This would be expected to give individuals an incentive to purchase plans with higher cost sharing. As discussed above, this would reduce aggregate health spending by at least 7 percent taking into account the partial equilibrium effects of higher coinsurance on individual spending decisions. Using the Cogan, Hubbard, and Kessler parameter assumptions, spending would be reduced by 26 percent, or four times the spending reductions they claim under their plan. The Congressional Budget Office (CBO) estimates that the president's proposal to replace the health exclusion with a flat deduction would reduce spending 15 percent in 2010.

In addition, eliminating the tax exclusion would potentially reduce spending even more. Technology, the primary driver of health spending, evolves partly in response to economic incentives. With less generous insurance, the incentive to develop expensive technologies would be reduced and the incentive to develop cost-saving technologies would be increased. A reduction in the rate of growth of health care spending could produce huge long-term savings in this area.

Note that these spending effects are for the currently insured. Spending by the newly insured would increase. The Institute of Medicine estimates that universal insurance would have increased health care spending in 2001 by between $34 billion and $69 billion.[35] The corresponding increase in 2008 would be between $60 billion and $120 billion. This increase is by design, because there is a substantial benefit from covering the currently uninsured.

Third, however, any of these cost benefits could be more than outweighed by a poorly designed proposal that shifted people into the individual market where they would face substantially higher administrative costs associated with the reduced economies of scale and greater costs of underwriting in this market. Even if underlying health spending went down, premiums themselves—which include these administrative costs—could go up. The net effect could be to increase premiums and reduce efficiency. Thus the degree to which the proposal reduces costs and increases efficiency depends on the complementary policies that affect the extent and nature of insurance coverage under the plan.

The Impact on Coverage

The current exclusion provides an incentive to go from no insurance to some insurance and from some insurance to more insurance. A reformed system would eliminate the incentive to go from some insurance to more insurance and would direct some or all of those dollars into encouraging coverage of the uninsured. The direct effects of the tax incentive would be reinforced by the indirect effects on health spending. Over time, these effects on health spending in a well-designed plan that did not lead to large increases in administrative costs could lower premiums and increase the demand for health insurance. In addition, depending on the design of tax deductions or tax credits that replace the exclusion, the incentive to go from no insurance to some form of insurance could be larger than it is under the current system.

Going in the opposite direction, however, would be two factors. First, large-scale dropping from employer-sponsored insurance could result in an increase in the number of uninsured. Or it might lead to a change in their composition, so that while some younger, healthier workers became newly insured, some older, sicker workers would lose their insurance. This direct effect of dropping could be reinforced if it led to an increase in premiums and thus reduced the demand for health insurance.

Some measures, however, could minimize the risks that such a radical change would have adverse effects and maximize the chances that it proved effective. These measures include progressive, income-related tax credits; institutional mechanisms to increase participation; new pooling mechanisms; and a reduction of adverse selection in existing pooling mechanisms. Other measures, however, would be ineffective (like high-risk pools, which have not proven workable in states) and measures that actually reduce pooling and increase adverse selection (like allowing small businesses to buy coverage across state lines).

PROGRESSIVE, INCOME-RELATED TAX CREDITS. A deduction lowers the after-tax price of health insurance more for high- than for low-income households. The result could be a price that is too high to allow low-income households to purchase health insurance but lower than it needs to be to encourage high-income households to purchase such insurance. In the absence of evidence that the elasticities are higher for high-income households, the optimal tool to promote economic behavior that produces diffused social benefits is a uniform, refundable credit.[36] In the case of health insurance, the price elasticity of demand is higher for low-income households, and thus progressive tax credits—those that decline with income—are warranted.

Note that the motivation for income-related credits is different from the motivation for the progressivity of the tax code as a whole. In fact, if desired the proposal could be implemented in a broadly distribution-neutral manner by combining it with a reduction in the top marginal tax rate and an increase in the bottom marginal tax rate. The result would be that the various income groups paid roughly the same amount of taxes as today but that the incentives provided by the tax system would be improved to provide more efficient incentives to purchase health insurance. In a distributionally neutral reform, it would be more efficient to convert the health care tax exclusion into an income-related credit combined with other tax changes to keep distribution constant.

INSTITUTIONAL MECHANISMS TO INCREASE PARTICIPATION. Insurance coverage depends on both financial incentives and institutional structures. Policies that have been considered include some combination of positive incentives to buy insurance, negative financial incentive for failure to buy coverage, and measures to create a self-reinforcing culture of compliance.[37] Negative incentives include mandates to buy coverage, backed by a fine for failure to do so. There is no historical experience to use in assessing the effect of a mandate. Furthermore, what a mandate means depends on the stringency of enforcement and the size of penalties for noncompliance. A mandate also has an important downside: to the degree it is effective, it forces some people to buy coverage who would have preferred to spend their money in other ways. Such people will feel that the mandate makes them worse off because it makes them spend a large sum—thousands of dollars annually—to buy insurance instead of something else on which they would have preferred to spend their money. As a result, although a mandate can be an economically efficient way to finance health insurance coverage, it is also regressive since it has no built-in redistributive mechanism.[38]

Alternative policies could realize much of the benefit of mandates while avoiding some of the downsides. Making enrollment in plans easier would help ensure that those who are passive in their decisionmaking were enrolled in a health insurance plan, but still let people make their own choices. Studying how to take advantage of behavioral psychology and the way people make choices has the potential to greatly increase the coverage potential—or even make it universal—for any given set of financial incentives.

NEW POOLING MECHANISMS. The biggest risk in eliminating the exclusion of employer-financed health insurance is that doing so would undermine pooling. In this sense, repealing deductibility resembles extending the deduction to individual purchase of insurance that levels the playing field. Both would encourage some firms, especially small ones, to drop insurance coverage. In both cases, relatively healthy workers would have an incentive to opt out of group coverage, causing premiums of those remaining in the group to increase.

How many people would drop coverage is uncertain because such a major reform moves into uncharted waters. It is impossible to use small variations in past premiums to estimate the social, institutional, and economic responses to a major change in the system of subsidizing health insurance. But there is a high probability that the dropping problem could be serious and last for a long time. As a result, many proposals take steps to limit this downside risk.

Limiting tax credits only to employer-provided insurance might seem to be a solution. But this approach is likely to be politically infeasible. Furthermore, it does not address some of the problems with the employer market described above. An alternative is to limit tax credits to the employer-sponsored market or new pools. These pools could be modeled on the federal employees health benefit (FEHB) or on the Massachusetts program, Connector. One option to make pooling more affordable would be to mandate that companies participating in the pool provide an income-related cost-sharing plan.[39] In addition, some of the downside risk for low-income and vulnerable families could be mitigated by expanding public programs like Medicaid.

REDUCTION OF ADVERSE SELECTION. The employer-provided system is one way of pooling people. Pooling reduces or eliminates market failure associated with adverse selection. It also serves the social goal of redistributing resources from the healthy to the chronically ill—for example, by ensuring that diabetics do not have to pay higher premiums even though they have predictably higher medical expenses.

If the individual market is to operate efficiently, some other mechanism will be needed to reduce adverse selection. Guaranteed renewability means that, once in a plan, enrollees are assured that their insurance premiums will not go up if they become chronically ill. But renewability does not ensure that initial entrants can find a plan at a reasonable price. The key is to shield insurance companies from the full brunt of the cost of the sickest enrollees, reducing incentives for insurers to avoid the biggest risks and marketing selectively to the healthiest potential customers. Such a shield would not only reduce adverse selection and improve pooling but would also reduce the administrative and social costs associated with the underwriting that excludes the sick from coverage.

How to accomplish these goals is still not fully understood. Some possibilities include catastrophic reinsurance and risk-adjusted payments to plans. Possibly these methods could be tried on a state-by-state basis to help determine the right combination of policies. High-risk pools have proven ineffective for this purpose in states where they have been tried.

The Fiscal Impact

A system of refundable, progressive tax credits could be designed to cost no more, and possibly less, than the current exclusion, in contrast to the revenue-losing plans described earlier. One aspect of the fiscal impact of such proposals that has gotten too little attention in previous proposals is the interaction with Social Security. In fiscal year 2008 the value of federal tax expenditures for health spending will total about $250 billion, including $164 billion in income tax expenditures and roughly $85 billion in payroll tax expenditures. Policymakers have three choices.

They could repeal the exclusion for income taxes only, which would boost revenues approximately $164 billion. This option is simple, but it creates an inconsistency that undermines some of what the proposal is trying to achieve.

Alternatively, they could repeal the exclusion for both income and payroll taxes but not count the additional earnings subject to payroll tax toward Social Security benefits. Such a policy would introduce an inconsistency that would be hard to justify on economic grounds. Moreover, using all $250 billion to pay for refundable credits for health insurance raises a potentially serious fiscal issue. The added Social Security and Medicare hospital insurance revenues would then be counted both toward the solvency of these programs and would also be used to pay for tax credits for health care. Such double counting would create the illusion that more fiscal improvement in Medicare and Social Security has been accomplished than would be the case. The way to avoid the problem would be to limit the new health tax credits to the $164 billion generated by repeal of the income tax exclusion and to protect the remaining revenues for deficit reduction and solvency.

Finally, policymakers could repeal the exclusion for both income and payroll taxes but count the additional payroll taxes toward Social Security benefits. This is the most logical and consistent treatment. But it raises some of the same problems as the previous option. Moreover, increased taxable earnings would boost Social Security benefits, undoing some of the long-run fiscal benefits associated with the proposal. Once again, the solution is either to limit the health-tax proposals to $164 billion or to take the politically difficult step of combining them with future changes in the Social Security benefit formula intended to leave benefits roughly unchanged.

Conclusion

The American health care system faces a variety of challenges. Tax reform cannot meet all of them. Research on comparative effectiveness, improved benefit designs, a move to electronic record keeping, and improved disease management and prevention are all important in ensuring higher-quality and lower-cost care.

But many proposals also include adding or changing tax incentives for health insurance. Adding new tax breaks would ameliorate some of the problems with the current system but would need to be combined with other measures to avoid having a budgetary cost. Such tax breaks, for example, tax deductions for the purchase of insurance in the individual market or for health expenditures, could even be counterproductive and worsen the very problems—inadequate coverage and excessive spending—that they purport to fix.

Another, more radical policy that has been proposed is to replace the income tax exclusion. By itself such a policy would disrupt employer-sponsored insurance, making some people worse off and not achieving significant gains. But replacing the exclusion with progressive, refundable tax credits, other institutional mechanisms, new pooling systems, and other techniques to reduce adverse selection would reduce these risks and offer the possibility of reducing health spending and expanding coverage to all Americans without increasing the budget deficit.

Notes

1. U.S. Bureau of the Census, *Income, Poverty, and Health Insurance Coverage in the United States: 2006* (2007).

2. Elliott S. Fisher, "Medical Care: Is More Always Better?" *New England Journal of Medicine* 349, no. 17 (2003): 1665; Joseph P. Newhouse and the Insurance Experiment Group, *Free for All? Lessons from the RAND Health Insurance Experiment* (Harvard University Press, 1993).

3. Henry Aaron, "Budget Crisis, Entitlement Crisis, Health Care Financing Problem—Which Is It?" *Health Affairs* 26, no. 6 (2007): 1622–33; Congressional Budget Office, *The Long-term Budget Outlook* (2007).

4. John F. Cogan, Glenn R. Hubbard, and Daniel P. Kessler, *Healthy, Wealthy, and Wise: Five Steps to a Better Health Care System* (Washington: American Enterprise Institute, 2005).

5. The deductibility of medical expenses in excess of 7.5 percent of adjusted gross income and flexible spending accounts are two exceptions to this general statement.

6. Newhouse and the Insurance Experiment Group, *Free for All?*

7. Jonathan Gruber, "The Role of Consumer Copayments for Health Care: Lessons from the RAND Health Insurance Experiment and Beyond" (Menlo Park, Calif.: Kaiser Family Foundation, 2006).

8. Fisher, "Medical Care."

9. William Jack and Louise Sheiner, "Welfare-Improving Health Expenditure Subsidies," *American Economic Review* 87, no. 1 (1997): 206–21.

10. Martin Feldstein and Bernard Friedman, "Tax Subsidies and the Rational Demand for Insurance and the Health Care Crisis," *Journal of Public Economics* 7, no. 2 (2007): 155–78. In approximate terms, the spending reduction is calculated by multiplying the percentage increase in coinsurance rates by the elasticity. The actual calculation is slightly more complicated: 0.22 elasticity is an arc elasticity, which is based on calculating the percentage change from the midpoint of the range.

11. Amy Finkelstein, "The Aggregate Effects of Health Insurance: Evidence from the Introduction of Medicare," *Quarterly Journal of Economics* 122, no. 1 (2007): 1–37.

12. J. Cogan, G. Hubbard, and D. Kessler, *Healthy, Wealthy, and Wise.*

13. If the initial coinsurance rate is $c0$, the new higher coinsurance rate is cf, and the tax rate is t, then this condition states that spending will fall if, and only if, $cf*(1 - t) > c0$. For example, suppose someone faces a marginal tax rate of 25 percent and an initial coinsurance rate of 20 percent. Suppose that new expenses are made tax deductible and the coinsurance rate levied by the insurance company rises to 24 percent. That person will face an effective coinsurance rate after taxes of 18 percent—more insulation from health spending than before—so his or her spending would rise. If instead the coinsurance rate rose to 28 percent, the after-tax coinsurance rate would rise to 21 percent, and the person would thus be more cost sensitive and thus reduce his or her spending.

14. Jack and Sheiner, "Welfare-Improving Health Expenditure Subsidies."

15. Jason Furman, "Two Wrongs Do Not Make a Right," *National Tax Journal* 59 (2006): 491–508.

16. The Center for Medicare and Medicaid Services, in its national health expenditure accounts, projects $281 billion in out-of-pocket expenses. Using an average marginal tax rate of 30 percent, the cost of full deductibility would be about $84 billion. Net of the cost of

existing deductions for out-of-pocket expenses, this is about $75 billion. The plan would also trigger substantial revenue loss for states that link their tax base to the federal tax base.

17. Emmett Keeler and others find that selection effects could mean that the adoption of high-deductible health plans by a subset of the population could lead to slightly higher health care spending. See Emmett B. Keeler and others, "Can Medical Savings Accounts for the Nonelderly Reduce Health Care Costs?" *Journal of the American Medical Association* 275, no. 21 (1996): 1666–71. Furman, "Two Wrongs Do Not Make a Right," discusses the president's FY 2007 budget proposal to expand health savings accounts and finds that the reduced spending by new adopters of HSAs is likely to be outweighed by the incentive the proposal would create for current HSA holders to increase spending.

18. U.S. Bureau of the Census, *Income, Poverty, and Health Insurance Coverage in the United States: 2006.*

19. To the degree that labor markets tend to adjust before-tax wages to equalize the after-tax wages and benefits in different jobs—taking into account the current tax treatment—then the fairness point is overstated or misleading. This is an example of the broader problems with horizontal equity arguments discussed more broadly in Louis Kaplow, "Horizontal Equity: Measures in Search of a Principle," *National Tax Journal* 42 (1989): 139–54.

20. Jonathan Gruber and Bridgette Madrian, "Health Insurance, Labor Supply, and Job Mobility: A Critical Review of the Literature," in *Health Policy and the Uninsured*, edited by C. McLaughlin (Washington: Urban Institute, 2004).

21. For a review of the evidence, see Congressional Budget Office, *CBO's Health Insurance Simulation Model: A Technical Description* (2007).

22. Ibid.

23. Bradley Herring and Mark Pauly, *Pooling Health Insurance Risks* (Washington: American Enterprise Institute, 1999); Bradley Herring and Mark Pauly, "The Effect of State Community Rating Regulations on Premiums and Coverage in the Individual Health Insurance Market," Working Paper 12504 (Cambridge, Mass.: National Bureau of Economic Research, 2006).

24. Michael Rothschild and Joseph Stiglitz, "Equilibrium in Competitive Insurance Markets: An Essay on the Economics of Imperfect Information," *Quarterly Journal of Economics* 90, no. 4 (1976): 630–49; Mark Browne, "Evidence of Adverse Selection in the Individual Health Insurance Market," *Journal of Risk and Insurance* 59, no. 1 (1992): 13–33.

25. Strictly speaking, if someone gets actuarially fair insurance, plus a load factor, it is not adverse selection. In the case of someone with a preexisting condition, such insurance might be very expensive. In practice, however, it is useful to consider insurance from the perspective of the person before he or she developed the condition. In this case, that person is in effect trying to insure not just against unexpected events in any given year but also against developing a chronic condition.

26. Karen Pollitz, Richard Sorian, and Kathy Thomas, "How Accessible Is Individual Health Insurance for Consumers in Less-than-Perfect Health?" (Menlo Park, Calif.: Kaiser Family Foundation, 2001).

27. Kaiser Family Foundation, *The Uninsured: A Primer* (Menlo Park, Calif.: 2007).

28. Brigitte Madrian and Dennis Shea, "The Power of Suggestion: Inertia in 401(k) Participation and Savings Behavior," *Quarterly Journal of Economics* 116, no. 4 (2001): 1149–87.

29. James Choi and others, "Optimal Defaults and Active Decisions," Working Paper 11074 (Cambridge, Mass.: National Bureau of Economic Research, 2005).

30. The total cost of purchasing insurance through the individual market, ignoring the higher load factors, is not higher. Most labor market models include the supposition that firms that drop coverage will ultimately pay their workers more. Workers can then spend this money on insurance in the individual market. Workers would be better off with the combination of a higher income and responsibility for the full marginal cost of insurance. In practice, however, substantial evidence from the savings literature casts doubt on the premise that people would make such a rational choice.

31. Kaiser Family Foundation and Health, Research, and Education Trust, *Employer Health Benefits 2007* (Menlo Park, Calif.: 2007).

32. Jonathan Gruber, "The Cost and Coverage Impacts of the President's Health Insurance Budget Proposals" (Washington: Center on Budget and Policy Priorities, 2006). In gross terms 2.4 million of the previously uninsured would use the new tax benefits to purchase insurance in the individual market, but this would be more than offset by 3.9 million people who would lose employer coverage and not purchase coverage in the individual market. If the new tax benefit were not limited to high-deductible policies, it is likely that the outcome would be even worse.

33. Stuart M. Butler, "A Tax Reform Strategy to Deal with the Uninsured," *Journal of the American Medical Association* 265, no. 19 (1991): 2541–44; Mark Pauly and John Hoff, *Responsible Tax Credits for Health Insurance* (Washington: American Enterprise Institute, 2002); Jonathan Gruber, "Covering the Uninsured in the U.S.," Working Paper 13758 (Cambridge, Mass.: National Bureau of Economic Research, 2008).

34. U.S. Treasury Department, "General Explanations of the Administration's Fiscal Year 2009 Revenue Proposals" (2008).

35. For a discussion of the evidence on the benefits of insurance, see Institute of Medicine, *Hidden Costs, Values Lost: Uninsurance in America* (Washington: National Academies Press, 2003); Levy and Meltzer are more skeptical of the strength of the evidence for the beneficial effects of health insurance, given the difficulty of establishing causation in the absence of randomized experiments. See Helen Levy and David Meltzer, "What Do We Really Know about Whether Health Insurance Affects Health?" in *Health Policy and the Uninsured,* edited by C. McLaughlin (Washington: Urban Institute, 2004).

36. Lily Batchelder, Fred Goldberg, and Peter Orszag, "Efficiency and Tax Incentives: The Case for Refundable Tax Credits," *Stanford Law Review* 59, no. 23 (2006): 23–76.

37. Sherry Glied, Jacob Hartz, and Genessa Giorgi, "Consider It Done? The Likely Efficacy of Mandates for Health Insurance," *Health Affairs* 26, no. 6 (2007): 1612–21.

38. Lawrence Summers, "Some Simple Economics of Mandated Benefits," *American Economic Review Papers and Proceedings,* May 1989, pp. 177–83.

39. Jason Furman, "The Promise of Progressive Cost Consciousness in Health-Care Reform," Hamilton Project Discussion Paper 2007-05 (Brookings, 2007).

COMMENT BY EMMETT KEELER

Furman begins by noting, as have many others, that current tax treatment of employer-sponsored insurance (ESI) encourages spending. He also notes that our tax policies are inconsistent in their treatment of premiums versus out-of-pocket spending and of employer-sponsored versus individual policies. ESI premiums are not part of taxable income, but out-of-pocket spending is, and the self-employed can deduct only their individual premiums and then only from income subject to personal income tax but not from earnings subject to the payroll tax. These features put the individual market at a relative disadvantage. He argues that leveling the playing field by giving more tax breaks will not solve the problems caused in part by the tax exemption of ESI. These problems include high medical costs, too many uninsured people, and low-value care. He then analyzes four plans to level the playing field.

First is the long-standing proposal to curtail the ESI subsidy, which would unequivocally lower spending. Several researchers calculate that optimal coinsurance rates would rise dramatically. Using elasticities of .22 from the RAND Health Insurance Experiment (HIE), they estimate that spending would fall 7–11 percent. General equilibrium estimates based on analysis by Amy Finkelstein are that the reduction in spending might be three times larger. I am skeptical of these larger estimates because I believe that historical random variation used in estimates based on her clever idea leads to an overestimate of general equilibrium effects.[1] Spending will surely fall, but it is hard to tell from theoretical pure coinsurance plans what might happen in the real world. Real-world plans now include other limits. Pure coinsurance plans are just too risky because of the financial impact of medical catastrophes.[2]

The experience of Singapore gives us a look at a world without tax subsidies and less insurance. People in Singapore pay for about 70 percent of their care out of pocket, more if one includes the mandatory medical savings accounts, funded by 6 percent of salary, that cover all workers and can be used only for

227

hospitalization of workers and their families—-and recently for some chronic disease care. Singaporeans spend about 4 percent of their substantial GDP on health care. Their life expectancy of eighty years is better than that of the United States.

The second plan would make out-of-pocket spending deductible.[3] If coinsurance increases enough—that is, if for an average marginal tax rate of t, $(1 - t)$ $C_{final} > C_{initial}$—it will more than offset the tax change and reduce medical spending. However, this reduction in waste is small and uncertain, and the new tax expenditures are certain and big, approximately t^* \$280 billion, where the \$280 billion is current out-of-pocket spending.[4] Furman points out that if some services not initially covered become tax deductible or if insurance changes are delayed (for example, because plans do not get enough advance notice), tax expenditures and waste would increase. It is not hard to see that if the new insurance features exactly offset the tax change, nothing would happen except for lower taxes. The third plan would make individual insurance premiums deductible. It is not clear that this shift in policy would increase the number of insured, since some employers would likely shed coverage. Furman notes three problems if ESI coverage falls: less pooling, more selection against sick new entrants, and higher administrative expenses. But some RAND researchers and others estimate that the effects of this plan on ESI coverage would be modest, precisely because of the advantages of ESI: comparatively low price, easy enrollment, and comparatively broad pooling.[5] Still, these modest effects would not be good, and the tax cost would be high. ESI is an example of the libertarian paternalism advocated by Richard Thaler and Cass Sunstein: people are automatically enrolled at work unless they opt out.[6] Notably, take up is lower for Medicaid, in which individuals must enroll but which is free, than it is for ESI.

Instead of these three plans, Furman recommends dropping the tax exclusion of ESI but with a fixed tax credit for those with acceptable insurance. I find it hard to criticize this proposal, because I like it. It is like the first plan with a carrot to induce people to get covered. Acceptable insurance, as in President Bush's plan, is defined by limits on out-of-pocket spending, coverage of a range of expenses, and guaranteed renewability. President Bush's tax exclusion—\$15,000 for families—is greater than the average premium in 2008 of about \$12,500, but the proposed credit is fixed over time to take more of a bite. Like President Bush's plan, Furman's would encourage people to buy insurance, but unlike the current deduction, it would not encourage them to buy more generous insurance. This shift is good, because encouraging people to buy some insurance rather than none produces larger benefits than encouraging them to buy more generous coverage, a finding demonstrated by RAND's HIE and other research. Another advantage of this plan is that it offers bigger incentives to the poor than does President Bush's plan. For the plan to work well, it would be necessary to ensure better pooling in the individual market. Mandatory coverage or automatic enrollment with opt-out features is a soft mandate, which behavioral economics shows is effective in increasing coverage. In summary, it looks better to level the field by taking away the ESI tax break than by giving new tax breaks. Currently, tax incentives include $165 billion from the federal income tax exclusion and $85 billion from the payroll tax exclusion; additional incentives come from exclusion from state taxes. The total should be treated as available for tax credits, but some federal money might also go to the threatened Social Security and Medicare trust funds.

Notes

1. Amy Finkelstein, "The Aggregate Effects of Health Insurance: Evidence from the Introduction of Medicare," *Quarterly Journal of Economics* 122, no. 1 (2007): 1–37.

2. Joan L. Buchanan, Emmett B. Keeler, John E. Rolph, and Martin R. Holmer, "Simulating Health Expenditures under Alternative Insurance Plans," *Management Science* 37 (September): 1067–90.

3. This plan is proposed in John F. Cogan, Glenn R. Hubbard, and Daniel P. Kessler, *Healthy, Wealthy, and Wise: Five Steps to a Better Health Care System* (Washington: American Enterprise Institute, 2005).

4. Here's a minor quibble: because of the loading fee L, the tax change is not exactly cost sharing $\times$ average tax rate. The premium = $(1 + L)$ payout, so suppose $t = 1/3$, and we go from 20 percent to 30 percent coinsurance. Before-tax expenditure = $(1 + L)$ .8 spending/3; after-tax expenditure = $[(1 + L)$ .7 spending + .3 spending]/3; subtracting, we get $(.2 − .1L)$ spending/3, which is slightly smaller than out-of-pocket/3.

5. M. Susan Marquis, Melinda Beeuwkes Buntin, José J. Escarce, Kanika Kapur, and Jill M. Yegian, "Subsidies and the Demand for Individual Health Insurance in California," *Health Services Research* 39, no. 5 (October 2004): 1547; K. Polzer and J. Gruber, *Assessing the Impact of State Tax Credits for Health Insurance Coverage* (Oakland: California HealthCare Foundation, 2003).

6. Richard Thaler and Cass Sunstein, *Nudge* (Yale University Press, 2008).

10

Simple Humans, Complex Insurance, Subtle Subsidies

JEFFREY LIEBMAN AND RICHARD ZECKHAUSER

The behavioral revolution in economics tells us that human beings often have difficulty making wise choices. The most widely chronicled difficulties in decisionmaking occur in conjunction with decisions made under conditions of uncertainty, decisions that involve significant elements of time, and decisions in complex environments. Unfortunately, these are precisely the factors involved when individuals choose a health insurance policy or choose whether and when to consume health care.

Historically, U.S. consumers have been shielded from many choices about their health care. For most workers under the age of sixty-five, employers have been responsible for designing health insurance plans and have provided employees with a single plan or a simple menu of options. For the elderly and the poor, the government provided a single plan. Traditional plans often provided first-dollar coverage without co-pays, so a consumer's choice about whether to consume health care involved comparing only the inconvenience and discomfort of obtaining care with the potential benefits.

Recent developments have put more choices and more quandaries before health care consumers. Motivated by concerns about rising costs and potential overconsumption by individuals who can obtain incremental health care resources at a price far below the social costs, firms have adopted various forms of managed care. Workers are often offered multiple types of health insurance plans, ranging from traditional indemnity plans to health maintenance organizations, preferred provider organizations, point-of-service plans, and high-

We are grateful to Henry Aaron, Len Burman, Jeffrey Kling, Edward McCaffery, Eve Rittenberg, and Chris Robert for helpful comments.

deductible plans coupled with savings accounts.[1] These plans usually charge different co-payments and reimburse a different share of costs for different types of service. They force consumers to weigh money alongside inconvenience and discomfort in deciding whether to obtain care.

Medicare and Medicaid have also sought to foster competition and choice by offering participants a range of plans, including managed care. In short, for consumers, purchasing health care has become more like buying an automobile, with many models, financial factors, and safety features to consider. Moreover, the trends in policy proposals from both the left and the right are toward options that would shift significant numbers of people away from employer-based coverage, in which employers make many of the tough choices for the consumers, and toward arrangements that would make individuals responsible for making additional, complex choices—first over which insurance plan to purchase and second when and how much health care to consume.

In this chapter we argue that traditional economic models of insurance are woefully insufficient for conducting policy analysis of the trade-offs involved in giving consumers increased responsibility for making health care choices. The traditional models need to be supplemented with key concepts from behavioral economics.[2] The typical analysis that views the design of an optimal health insurance program as setting the right trade-off between risk spreading and appropriate incentives captures neither current realities in the health care marketplace nor humans' abilities to make rational decisions. Indeed, we argue that behavioral economics provides much more of a normative justification for many of the features of our existing health care policy than do the models of traditional economics. If our argument is accepted, a logical implication is that because the justifications for those features are not understood, many current policies are poorly designed.

We begin broadly by discussing why behavioral economics provides a useful frame for viewing consumer decisionmaking about health care. We then argue that the policy analysis of the wide range of subsidies that permeate the health care system changes substantially when viewed from the behavioral perspective. Finally, we discuss how recent policy trends can be assessed using that perspective—and how doing so alters the interpretation of the relevant trade-offs.

The Challenge of Health Care Decisionmaking

We focus primarily on two types of health care choice. The first is the decision of whether to purchase health insurance and, if so, what type and which specific policy. The second is when and whether to obtain health care.[3] Both types of decision involve uncertainty, time, and complexity, thus bringing behavioral propensities in decisionmaking to the fore. Status quo bias also proves to be an important feature of health care decisionmaking.

Health Decisions under Uncertainty

In the textbook model, the price charged to consumers for insurance is greater than the average expected claims the consumers will make. For insurance companies to break even, they must charge a price above average expected claims to cover administrative expenses. Prices may also include a pure economic profit if markets are not sufficiently competitive. Even with prices exceeding expected claims, some consumers purchase insurance because they are willing to pay to avoid financial risk. The greater an individual's risk aversion, the greater the amount of insurance that is purchased at a given price. In addition, individuals who know that they face higher than average risks will purchase more insurance, a phenomenon known as adverse selection. In making the decision of how much insurance to buy, the textbook consumer calculates expected utility over the distribution of possible outcomes under each insurance option and then chooses the amount of insurance that maximizes expected utility.

Health insurance as commonly found in the United States presents a more complex set of decisions, though in theory the same expected-utility model would dictate choices. Thus for each insurance option a utility would be computed for the financial consequences of each possible illness the consumer could experience during the year. These utility values would be weighted by the probability that an illness occurs to produce an expected utility for each plan. The highest yielding plan would then be chosen. Matters are simplified because individuals can select only among a specified set of policies and rarely can choose more or less coverage on a particular policy. But the insurance choice decision is much more complex than with, for example, homeowners' or life insurance because there are so many possible "loss events," including many that are unfamiliar to the consumer. Each individual faces differing risks of the various possible medical conditions, risk levels that are extremely hard to assess. Beyond this, initial choices to secure care enmesh the individual in a stream of options that lead to further care and further expense for both the consumer and the health plan. To illustrate, a positive screening for prostate cancer may lead to half a dozen treatment options, each with different consequences for expenditures, both by the individual and by his insurance plan, and for his quality of life and survival. It is almost impossible for individuals to make sensible decisions when confronted with so many material secondary branches sprouting from so many main branches along the decision tree.

Even conscientious students of decision analysis would be challenged in attempting to purchase health insurance on a rational basis. To figure out which health insurance choice maximizes expected utility, one needs to know the probabilities, financial costs, and health-related utilities associated with each possible state of the world. Securing knowledge on any of these components is problematic.

Start with the probabilities. Ask yourself, what is the chance that you will have a heart attack this year? Or that you will be diagnosed with cancer? Or that you will need back surgery? Is there any chance that an ordinary person knows such probabilities within a factor of five? The challenge here is not simply lack of data. The behavioral economics literature tells us that most individuals make systematic mistakes in assessing probabilities. One type of error involves homogenizing probabilities. People do not distinguish sufficiently between a 5 percent chance and 20 percent chance or, for that matter, between a 1 percent chance and a 5 percent chance.[4] But they draw a big distinction between 1 percent and 0 percent. In addition, individuals are much too confident of their estimates; when subjects were asked to give a series of 98 percent confidence intervals around a list of unknown quantities, the true value lay outside the interval provided by the subjects a whopping 43 percent of the time.[5]

This is bad news for individuals making decisions about insurance for medical care. There are hundreds of possible events, many of which involve exactly the sort of small probabilities where judgment is the worst. If people are too confident about what they know, they will be unlikely to contemplate extreme events, such as a car accident or a cancer episode, that will cause them to be in the hospital for weeks.[6] If so, they will purchase too little insurance. On the other hand, they may give excess weight to salient low-probability events (such as dying in an airplane crash) and overinsure.[7]

The challenge of assessing probabilities is compounded by the problem of predicting the financial costs should one of these conditions arise. Given that the medical system presents different prices to different consumers—typically higher prices for those paying out of pocket—there is no convenient place where one could look up these prices. Informal surveys suggest that even individuals covered by insurance have little idea of how much it would cost them to be treated for something like lung cancer or a heart attack.

We have talked only about financial costs, but health care decisions involve far more. The payoffs in different states of the world involve not just financial amounts but also health-related utilities. Assessing utilities, for example, of coping with a deteriorated medical condition because one failed to treat it earlier presents its own challenge. How terrible would it be to live with diabetes in one's sixties? What would a person pay to avoid needing cataract surgery or to avoid one chance in a hundred of dying at age sixty?

In this analysis, we assess health-related utilities in quality-adjusted life years, which go by the acronym QALYs. Evidence of the difficulty of answering the questions just asked is seen in the disparities in the QALY literature between assessments made by doctors and other medical professionals and assessments generated by asking people with those same conditions: people living with the conditions generally find them less horrible than do medical professionals.[8] A similar disparity arises among patients judging before rather than after the fact. Evidence suggests that individuals living with an unpleasant condition, say incontinence after prostate surgery, generally rate it less unfavorably than those who are contemplating the possibility of the condition when they are deciding about treatment. More generally, individuals overestimate how strongly good or bad outcomes will affect their happiness.[9] Given that medical surprises are mostly on the downside, and much of adult life involves a downhill health slide, it is fortunate that there is a lot of inertia in our self-perceptions of well-being.

Since it is unlikely that ordinary consumers know their own probabilities, associated costs, and health utilities, how can they make informed decisions about what insurance to buy? One possibility is that consumers could ask their physicians. Health care represents a quintessential example of a principal-agent relationship, where the physician is the supposedly well-informed agent, acting faithfully on behalf of the patient principal. In practice, this is an unpromising strategy. Research indicates that physicians themselves exhibit the same sorts of cognitive biases that afflict patients. Even in the much more manageable circumstance where a patient already has a particular condition, doctors are often loath to assess probabilities, as anyone who has asked a doctor to do so knows well. Two common responses are, "It is impossible to put a probability on it," and "It all depends on the particular patient." Moreover, doctors generally are not inclined to give advice on choice of health insurance plan.

Another way to make informed decisions might be to observe the experiences of friends and co-workers who have chosen various insurance arrangements, including self-insurance. But given the large number of low-probability health events that could strike an individual, this technique would yield a poor estimate of the distribution of one's personal outcomes under such arrangements. Presumably, humans have some common heuristics for extrapolating from common occurrences to rare events. But the experience with probability assessment and with probability scaling (prospect theory) suggests that these methods are far from reliable for individuals who must cope with low-probability, high-consequence risks.[10] This lack of reliability should not be all that surprising. After all, prehistoric man did not buy health insurance. Primitive humans daily confronted high-probability, high-consequence risks; low-probability risks were a minor concern.[11]

Decisionmaking over Periods of Time

Many health care choices impose immediate costs to produce future benefits. These decisions include whether to contract for health insurance today that will generate financial protection later in the year and possibly guarantee access to coverage for future years, whether to have a painful or expensive medical procedure today that may yield health benefits in the future, and whether to invest money or effort now in preventive care.[12]

A central finding of behavioral economics is that people tend to underinvest in these sorts of activity, placing excessive weight on current-period costs and underweighting next-period benefits. Interestingly, though most individuals use a big discount factor between today and tomorrow (where tomorrow should be interpreted metaphorically), their trade-off rates between tomorrow and the next day are often consistent with what economists would prescribe. This behavior pattern is called hyperbolic discounting.[13] As should be obvious, such preferences lead to procrastination, putting something unpleasant off for another day. They also lead to dynamic inconsistency, since one's plans to take action tomorrow get postponed again when tomorrow becomes today.

Liquidity constraints (the inability to borrow against future income) provide a more conventional explanation of why people underconsume goods that involve current costs but offer more-than-compensating future payoffs. This explanation is particularly relevant among households that are younger, in the lower part of the income distribution, or locked into lumpy consumption commitments such as home mortgages for which there are high costs of revising consumption levels. But to explain phenomena we should not just take refuge in the easiest rational explanation. Procrastination must compete along with liquidity constraints as a potential explanation even for this group's underconsumption of future-oriented goods.

Psychology provides evidence of another behavioral factor that may cause people to underinvest in future health: people do not like to contemplate bad outcomes, particularly death, and therefore make decisions that ignore or underestimate the possibility of these adverse outcomes.[14] Others have applied these insights to economic decisions such as the failure to make inter vivos gifts, purchase life insurance, and draw up wills.[15] Insights about bad-outcome denial apply with particular force to health care consumption decisions and may well be the strongest explanation for why middle-aged men are notorious for not obtaining annual checkups. This mechanism may also partly explain why some patients fail to take the medicines prescribed for their chronic conditions, neglect to do the stretching exercises that would ameliorate future back pain, or refuse to get tested for HIV.

Decisionmaking in Complex Environments

Choosing a health insurance plan is more challenging and perilous than most purchasing decisions. Health plans are complex and rife with hidden subsidies, making it hard for consumers to determine what prices they will face and what value of resources they will receive.

BUNDLED ATTRIBUTES. The standard health insurance package bundles dozens of attributes, ranging from basic financial provisions such as deductibles, co-payments, and coinsurance, to separate pricing schedules for different medical conditions and different medical providers. Dilemmas abound. Should one purchase a plan with a lower premium but a higher deductible? Should one choose the policy that offers a private hospital room or the one with better mental health coverage? What about an add-on for pharmaceutical coverage?

We believe that, even ignoring the issues of time and uncertainty, consumers have trouble making wise decisions when faced with such complex consumption choices and pricing schedules. Real-world contexts provide ample evidence of decisions that are far from optimal even when information-gathering costs are low relative to the benefits of making the correct choice.[16] These findings indicate that the difficulties cannot be rationalized as simply a matter of people weighing the costs and benefits of optimizing and then deciding that the losses from suboptimal behavior are less than the costs of optimizing. Rather, evidence from laboratory experiments in psychology (on pigeons, monkeys, and humans) indicates that poor choices when facing complex schedules reflects hardwired cognitive behavior patterns.[17] Moreover, in cases of complex products with multiple attributes, competition will not, in general, prevent the exploitation of unaware consumers by optimizing firms.[18]

COMPLEX SUBSIDIES. Complicated cross-subsidies riddle the health care system. They are one of the features that make it difficult for consumers to sort out decisions about health care and health insurance. These subsidies make it hard to perceive anything approximating marginal prices and also make it difficult to learn from friends, colleagues, and neighbors because those people likely face different subsidies and therefore different prices.

Both the government and employers use a wide range of instruments that can influence an individual's choices of health plans and health care and that make it difficult to infer the price one faces as a consumer. Consider a typical worker. The worker's employer pays most of the health insurance premium, and the government ignores the employer-provided health insurance in calculating the worker's taxable income. Do workers understand what the total premium paid on their behalf is, and that it results in a lower wage? Do most workers, or even most employers, understand the nature of the tax subsidies associated with health insurance? Moreover, what is the incidence model that applies here? In other words, what truly is the trade-off one faces if one lobbies one's employer for more generous insurance? Do firms reduce all salaries by the dollar amount of health insurance premiums, or do they apply a fixed percentage to the wage bill and effectively charge higher-paid employees more? Do older workers receive lower salaries than otherwise because they are more expensive to insure? And what happens in decentralized situations where fringe benefits are paid for at the center, whereas hiring decisions are primarily the responsibility of the periphery? These questions are unresolved in the health policy literature; workers certainly do not know the answers.

Inferring the effective price of one's health insurance is further complicated because the pooling function of insurance causes people facing different risks to face the same insurance price. Within employee groups, the old are usually subsidized by the young, the high risk by the low risk, and at times, the low paid by the high paid. Who ultimately pays these subsidies is a matter of debate. A typical, but unanswered, incidence question would be: If high-paid workers are charged more for their health insurance than low-paid workers, do their salaries adjust to reflect this? Do employers differentially lower the wages of women of childbearing age because they are likely to have maternity expenses?[19] Of course, similar cross-subsidies exist in public insurance plans, such as Medicare and Medicaid, too.

It is worth noting that whereas many of the behavioral phenomena we have identified suggest that people are likely to underconsume insurance and health care, the hidden employer premium payments are likely to lead to overconsumption because workers may not realize that they are sacrificing cash compensation in exchange for employer premium payments. Instead, workers may perceive their own premium payments as their sole opportunity cost for acquiring more generous insurance coverage. In the old days this did not matter, since health insurance costs were small relative to salaries. But it is not uncommon today for workers to get more than 10 or 20 percent of their effective income in the form of subsidized health insurance.

STATUS QUO BIAS. Markets for health plans, like any markets, work best when individuals make effective choices among competing options. Unfortunately, even when faced with highly consequential choices and changed conditions, individuals have a tendency to stick with their prior choices. This tendency is called status quo bias.[20] The original article on this subject provides evidence that when Harvard employees allocated retirement savings or selected health plans, they had a strong inclination to stick with past decisions. There is the possibility, of course, that individuals stay with a health plan simply because it is optimal for them. To address this possibility, that analysis compared continuing employees and new employees of the same age. The analysis found that new employees chose plans significantly different from the plans chosen by continuing workers of the same age, implying status quo bias. (This was a time of particular turmoil in health plans, with plans both entering and leaving the system, and premiums for employees changing dramatically; this turmoil explains why new employees made choices different from the original choices of the continuing employees.) Only 3 percent of the continuing employees changed plans in a given year.

It is particularly striking that so much inertia is observed in the context of health insurance. The annual election period solicits an active decision from participants each year, giving them only a short period in which to respond. To be sure, many companies automatically reenroll the employee in the same health plan should the employee fail to respond to the open enrollment form. However, even then, the fact that employees may need to adjust other benefits, particularly flexible spending accounts, which must be specifically elected each year, should diminish the use of default options.[21] Nonetheless, there is little shifting across plans.

In recent years a literature has sprung up in behavioral economics on the importance of default options and their possible use for getting individuals afflicted with certain behavioral tendencies to make "wiser" choices, that is, choices that the experts recommend.[22] Perhaps the best known illustration is the "save more tomorrow" scheme, wherein employees agree in advance to put a portion of their future salary increases into savings.[23] With initial experiments, the savings rate went from 3.5 percent to 13.6 percent. The key elements were making a decision today that affected tomorrow not today (thereby avoiding hyperbolic discounting) and allocating only a portion of increases in earnings (thereby avoiding loss aversion).

The implicit approach of this chapter is similarly pragmatic. Our analysis proposes that the design of health plans, and the framework for choosing among them, should be based on an understanding of behavioral tendencies, with an effort to encourage individuals to make the same choices they would make if they could consult at length with expert advisers. In effect, we are subscribing to the agenda of libertarian paternalism: "Equipped with an understanding of behavioral findings of bounded rationality and bounded self-control, libertarian paternalists should attempt to steer people's choices in welfare-promoting directions without eliminating freedom of choice."[24] That statement leaves open the question as to how welfare is to be measured. As we observe below, our welfare criterion is the maximum number of quality-adjusted life years (QALYs) available for the dollars spent on health care. We recommend that predictions of outcomes be done by experts but that we distill as best we can QALY preference values from individuals.[25]

Implications for Health Care Policy

The bottom line is that we doubt whether many insureds—whether they hold individual insurance, employer-based insurance, Medicare, or any other coverage—could accurately describe the combination of costs that they pay for their health insurance and the nature of payoffs, both financial and health related, that they might receive. These complexities make it extremely difficult for individuals to purchase insurance sensibly and, particularly, to choose among a wide range of policies that differ on many dimensions. Moreover, the same factors that hinder individuals from making wise choices as consumers also are likely to hinder people from making wise choices as voters, where (except under the most self-interested model of voter behavior) there is a need to understand elements of the health care system beyond their own circumstances.

But simply knowing that people may fail to optimize does not tell us the direction of the biases that result and the most appropriate government response. In this section, we discuss how conclusions about optimal health care subsidies are altered by the realization that people are not making wise choices. This analysis involves both efficiency and distributional considerations. In the next section, we apply these considerations specifically to the types of health care reform proposals currently being discussed at think tanks and by policymakers.

Basis for Judging Outcomes

Judging welfare implications of policies can be challenging when individuals are behaving in ways that diverge from the standard model in an economics textbook. In particular, when people's preferences at different points in time are inconsistent, as in the case of hyperbolic discounting, or when people's choices suggest that they lack coherent preferences, as when complexity causes them to give up on making a selection altogether, then the social planner typically needs to make a choice of which perspective is the best one—a choice that cannot be validated using revealed preference.[26] On the other hand, when people are simply uninformed, the normative implications are generally straightforward. The social planner should set policies to try to obtain the same selections that individuals would have made had they been fully informed. Depending on the context and available technology, this might involve providing information, setting defaults that are best on average, or paternalistically compelling individuals to make the "right" choices.

Our general view is that since individuals are such poor decisionmakers in many health contexts, the traditional prescription for decentralized choices—simply charge people the marginal resource cost of providing health care and go with their decisions—will not in general result in the socially optimal outcome. Instead, it will be necessary to evaluate different policies by measuring aggregate health outcomes, such as QALYs gained per dollar spent under the different policies.[27]

Behavioral Economics as a Normative Justification for Subsidizing Insurance Purchase

Most arguments for subsidizing health insurance come from one of four notions: that it generates externalities (for example, immunizations), that it is a merit good, that it is a right, or that it helps to facilitate the creation of large risk-sharing pools. The fourth argument is essentially risk spreading after some lotteries have already been run, since subsidies will induce individuals who know they are at lower risk to join alongside those at higher risk when they are charged the same premium.[28]

We believe that behavioral considerations provide an additional reason for the subsidizing of health insurance and of health care. Begin with the standard diagram that illustrates how the moral hazard from insurance is exacerbated by the tax subsidy to employer-provided insurance. The x-axis of figure 10-1 measures the quantity of health care consumed. The line labeled RR is the demand curve for health care that would result given insurance for a rational individual who understands probabilities, is an exponential discounter, and chooses in his own self-interest. Thus, for example, he understands that if he gets thrust more deeply into the medical care system, his care will be heavily subsidized via insurance. The SS line shows the social cost of providing medical care. Thus the socially efficient level of care is Q^e. Absent a tax subsidy for health insurance, the consumer purchases a level of insurance that reduces his marginal cost per unit of health care to II, causing the consumer to overconsume at Q^i. With the tax subsidy, the fully rational consumer purchases extra insurance, reducing his marginal cost of consuming care to TT, and further exacerbating overconsumption to Q^t.

Now introduce behavioral considerations. We start with the case where the consumer underconsumes insurance and then turn to the case where the consumer under-perceives the full cost of generous employer-provided insurance. Consider now a second demand curve, labeled DD. Line DD is the demand curve of the mere mortal everyman, who does a poor job of looking down the road, procrastinates, is at best inadequate in considering probabilities, and so on. We have drawn the DD curve well below RR, after engaging in our speculation of

Figure 10-1. *Optimal Subsidies*

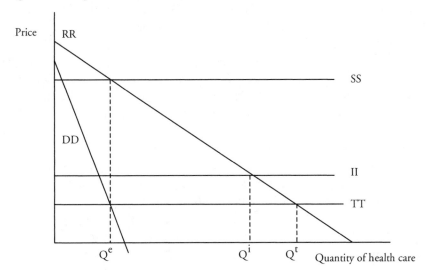

how most individuals behave.[29] In particular, we have cleverly drawn the curve so that the consumer underconsumes if he buys unsubsidized insurance but consumes exactly the social optimum Q^e with the insurance subsidy in place.

In this example, the lesson of the second best triumphs. Rather than exacerbating deadweight loss, subsidizing the purchase of health insurance moves us toward the social optimum. But is this empirically plausible? After all, the presence of generous insurance often reduces the consumer's price of obtaining care to something like 10 percent of the social cost. Could behavioral factors that encourage underconsumption be sufficiently large to offset such significant underpricing? The truth is that we have no empirical basis to judge. But it does not strike us as implausible.

In particular, there is disturbing evidence that relatively small changes in copayments can have quite large impacts on utilization.[30] This finding suggests that behavioral factors may be a big part of an underconsumption pattern. Could people mistakenly judge a 1-in-100 risk of a medical condition as a 1-in-1,000 risk? Could people myopically discount adverse health outcomes thirty years in the future at an 8 percent rate rather than at a 2 percent rate, assuming that a 2 percent rate is appropriate, thereby underweighting these payoffs by a factor of five? These orders of magnitude do not seem out of the question.

Of course, for behavioral factors to justify a health care subsidy, the factors leading to underconsumption need to be sufficiently strong not only to outweigh the moral hazard effects of insurance but also to outweigh any behavioral factors that lead to overconsumption. As we explain above, in the current U.S. system it is likely that the employer contribution to health insurance is underrecognized, causing people to negotiate excessively generous insurance packages from their employers, and thereby giving up too much in salary. If this is true, then the *TT* curve would shift down even further. A similar phenomenon among the electorate might cause older Americans to receive overly generous Medicare benefits, when they might prefer greater Social Security benefits instead.

It is worth emphasizing that there is a range of possible remedies for bad decisionmaking. Designing an optimal subsidy to offset human failures is only one such possibility. Another approach is to make the true prices and payoffs more transparent, so that even we simple humans can optimize correctly. In particular, providing information and providing it in a particularly salient way could be a much more efficient approach to achieving optimal consumption levels of health care since it would not require us to incur the deadweight loss of taxation to raise the revenue for the subsidies, including unnecessary subsidies to any sophisticated optimizers in the population. We think the transparency approach could be particularly fruitful in assisting consumers in perceiving the full cost of their health insurance. Employers could be required to either report annually to consumers the full cost of insurance or, better yet, add the employer share of premiums into gross wages on the paycheck (before subtracting it again as a pretax payroll deduction).[31] To qualify for tax deductibility, employers could also be required to provide a fixed dollar subsidy to their employee's health plans, rather than offering proportional subsidies of, for example, 70 percent of any health plan's cost. And, of course, the tax subsidy for health insurance could be capped to avoid gold-plating.[32]

Behavioral Economics as a Normative Justification for Subsidizing Small Costs

It is important to note a distinctive aspect of health insurance that is quite different from what would be proposed for ordinary insurance. Small costs are heavily subsidized, not merely large costs. For example, insurance typically pays most of the cost for routine office visits.

In part, this structure can be seen as a response to loss aversion, where small costs count heavily relative to large ones. Thus individuals tend to like insurance that protects against relatively high-frequency, low-cost events. These are precisely the costs that individuals incur most frequently with their health care. Subsidizing such costs is a further way, apart from subsidizing insurance itself, to make health care insurance attractive to the typical prospect-theoretic individual. It thus helps to build up the size of the insurance pool.

But subsidizing small costs also has a more fundamental role in our conception of health care decisionmaking. These subsidies help overcome the underconsumption of health care by people who make bad decisions, forgoing small costs today that will in expectation produce greater benefits down the road.[33] If one accepts this justification for subsidizing small health care costs, it is clear that the subsidies need to be carefully designed. A single price signal will not be enough to induce ordinary consumers to acquire the optimal amount of care. Consumers who are more likely to underconsume care will need greater subsidies, and subsidies will need to be greater for high-value consumption and for types of consumption where consumers are more likely to fail in their decisionmaking.

Given that co-payments are likely to be more of a discouragement to the health care use of low-income consumers than of higher-income consumers, it is puzzling that we do not see much variation of co-payments with income.[34] Someone earning $25,000 might well be more discouraged by a $10 co-pay than someone earning $40,000 would be by a $25 co-pay. Thus it seems clear that there should be progressivity in co-payments, not merely in premiums. Note that we are not necessarily arguing for more progressivity overall, just consistent progressivity across the plan.[35] It is also clear that there should be different co-payments for different types of visits and different subsidies for different types of care, a recommendation that others have also made.[36]

Recent evidence suggests that this sort of differential pricing can be successful. A study of a firm that decreased co-payments for five chronic medication classes finds that adherence to disease management protocols improved.[37] Another study finds that increased cost sharing for retirees in California led to decreased usage of doctor's visits and prescription drugs and to additional hospitalizations, implying that reversing this cost sharing, or at least some of it, could provide important health benefits—and perhaps yield the complementary benefit of financial savings to the system.[38] Even when preventive services and medicines treating chronic conditions are exempt from co-pays, consumers may have to pay for physician visits in order to access free services or prescriptions. However, one recent study finds that patients are not less likely to take advantage of free preventive services in these contexts.[39]

We should not exaggerate the extent to which differential pricing is likely to produce benefits. Those advancing this approach frequently propose their favorite preventive interventions as candidates for subsidy, and the best surely do extremely well. But this is argument by anecdote, illustrating the availability heuristic from behavioral decision theory: People judge the relative frequency of an event by how easily an example can be brought to mind.[40] Thus if we can readily think of some preventive measures that would gain QALYs and save dollars, or even gain QALYs at a low price, we naively conclude that such measures are widespread.

To be sure, some important preventive measures do fall in the inexpensive QALY category. Those that are most prominently mentioned are countermeasures to tobacco smoking, alcohol misuse, physical inactivity, and poor diet. It has been estimated that curing these problems could prevent 900,000 American deaths annually, nearly 40 percent of the total yearly mortality in the United States.[41] The U.S. Preventive Services Task Force identifies beneficial measures such as counseling adults to quit smoking, screening for colorectal cancer, and providing influenza vaccinations.[42] The first thing to note about these interventions is that many of them relate to actions individuals have to take for themselves, such as eating healthily and exercising. These are activities that are beyond the scope of normal medical care and might be dealt with better in a workplace program than with the annual visit to the physician, where one gets a pep talk. The other interventions are highly specific within the health care system.

Let us assume that we want to encourage individuals to get colorectal screenings and influenza vaccinations; both offer QALY gains at negative cost.[43] These services should certainly be highly subsidized. But maybe we should go further and actually pay people to get them. Should payment be implemented for all inexpensive QALY treatments? The answer is no. While there will be some services for which people should receive payment, there are other cases in which it would be a mistake. For payments to be potentially optimal, two conditions must hold. First, there must be some behavioral response to price. If the price elasticity is zero, then we are just randomly shuttling around money, which is disadvantageous. Second, there must be nonfinancial reasons (including any number of the behavioral concerns we raise above) for why people do not get the treatments. If there were no such nonfinancial reasons, we could simply offer the treatment for free and tell people to get it. Colorectal screenings, where the whole process is unpleasant, and vaccinations, which at least require a jab, both meet the test for being services where it potentially makes sense to pay people to obtain the treatment. (The unpleasant nonfinancial aspect also minimizes the chance that individuals will just collect multiple treatments to pick up the cash.) Moreover, such payments, if implemented, might provide convincing signals to individuals that experts really thought the treatment yielded substantial expected health benefits.

Critical questions then are: How widespread are such preventive interventions? And how do they compare to traditional medical treatments? Fortunately, a recent study addresses these questions.[44] It examined 1,500 cost-effectiveness ratios published in the literature from 2000 through 2005, in articles where future benefits and costs were properly discounted; 279 of these ratios applied to preventive measures and 1,221 to treatments. Surprisingly, the distribution of the ratios for prevention and treatments were much the same. Thus we conclude that prevention and treatment compete on relatively equal ground, given current practices. There are highly attractive interventions—and also poor ones—within each category.

There are other promising findings in the study. For both prevention and treatment, nearly 20 percent of procedures saved QALYs and costs simultaneously, and an additional 11 percent (prevention) and 16 percent (treatment) provided benefits for less than $10,000 per QALY. Vaccinations, colonoscopies for older men, screening for some conditions in newborns where treatment can prevent debilitation, and high-intensity smoking cessation programs fall into these categories. But the study has some extremely disturbing elements as well. At the unfavorable end, 9 percent of procedures either cost more than $1 million per QALY or actually both increase cost and worsen health. The implication of such findings is that there are significant gains to be made by promoting inexpensive QALY procedures and curtailing those that are exceedingly expensive per QALY or that actually hurt health and increase cost. A prime example of the last is surgery in seventy-year-old men with a new diagnosis of prostate cancer, as opposed to the procedure of "watchful waiting."

If we want to encourage more use of the inexpensive QALY procedures, and if we want to continue to rely on individuals to be the deciding voice in determining whether they get health care, the most immediate and promising instrument would seem to be the subsidy system, not the one administered by the IRS but the more elaborate one that is part of every health plan. Thus, for example, prostate surgery for elderly men might lose its major subsidy. By contrast, individuals might be paid to enroll in smoking cessation programs.

If health plans, or indeed employers or the government, are to use subsidies to influence health-related behaviors and medical treatment choices, they will have to attend carefully to behavioral propensities. This will require considerable amounts of experimentation to determine, for example, how much such factors as convenience, counseling from a physician, and dollar incentives matter when people are choosing their health-related activities.

Optimal Provision of Anxiety-Reducing Care

Traditional decision theory does not incorporate anxiety. All outcomes are assigned utilities at the end of the tree, with no acknowledgement of anxiety or dread along the way. But anxiety and its relief are major components of many individuals' encounters with the health care system. We argue, therefore, that anxiety should be treated as a valued component of utility and should go into life-year calculations.

Consider diagnostic testing. Some would say that it should be used only when it will affect medical treatment. But that approach ignores anxiety. Consider an individual who is suffering from persistent headaches. There are dozens of possible explanations, but one that is likely to leap to mind is a brain tumor. On a pure odds basis, this is quite unlikely, but it may be reasonable for a doctor to offer reassurance by providing a brain scan just to rule out the possibility. For some individuals, living with fear of a brain tumor may be as uncomfortable as living in constant pain. A procedure costing a few thousand dollars may relieve that concern. Anxiety, we speculate, is much less than proportional to the probability of an underlying medical condition. Thus a 1 percent risk may cause nearly as much distress as a 10 percent risk. Straightforward decision analysis will not get us to the right conclusion about medical care in such situations, if we take anxiety seriously.

Relief from anxiety does not always argue for more care or for more intensive care. It is now recognized that many women have had breast cancers that did not show up on ordinary mammograms. One possible recommendation is to proceed to MRI examinations, which are both more sensitive and more expensive, for these women. A prime argument against this approach is that MRIs produce many false positives, dangerous-looking situations that need to be biopsied. Given the availability of needle biopsies, the costs of such procedures—both in money and discomfort—are not exceedingly high. However, some doctors are hesitant to recommend turning to MRIs because they will significantly raise patients' anxiety levels when it is learned that a biopsy is required. We would argue to the contrary—that since the time from the MRI to the ultimate test results is short, the anxiety period is brief. This is different from a brain tumor scan, where anxiety is relieved for a very long period of time.

Our point is not to argue for laxity in deciding when to carry out medical procedures. There are clearly cases where procedures are high cost, low value, and anxiety producing. Instead, our point is that anxiety from health care procedures, the duration of that anxiety, and its probabilistic resolution should be taken into account when structuring subsidy systems in health care plans.

Distributional Consequences of Heterogeneity in Behavioral Propensities and Preferences

Some individuals are prey to behavioral biases. Others can mostly escape them. Unfortunately, the health care system cannot readily distinguish between these two groups of people. Thus if the lessons of this chapter are taken seriously, it will be important to determine the general distribution of different tendencies in the relevant populations. A system has to be designed to optimize health care, given the distribution of decision propensities in the population. This implies, of course, that the system will be poorly designed for some beneficiaries. If we subsidize health care to counter a general tendency toward underconsumption, those who neither have loss aversion nor are hyperbolic will end up over-consuming.

The system as a whole needs to be designed to succeed on average over the population. Nonetheless, there are opportunities for treatments to be chosen in response to the preferences of specific individuals. If you are a sixty-year-old male with prostate cancer, and your first visit is to a urologist, you will likely get a prostatectomy. A radiologist would steer you, by contrast, toward radiologic treatment. This need not be the case. One study developed a framework for eliciting patients' preferences and incorporating them into the treatment of prostate cancer.[45] If we wish to maximize QALYs for the dollars we spend, the health care system must recognize not only individuals' common behavioral proclivities but also areas where they have distinctive preferences. As behavioral economists, we are willing to question whether people make good decisions, but we do not dispute that individuals vary in their underlying preferences.

Implications for Current Policy Debates

Historically, federal tax subsidies for health insurance have been dominated by the nontaxation of employer-provided health care, a tax expenditure projected to reduce income tax revenue by $168 billion in 2009. This subsidy encourages the formation of workplace-based purchasing pools, reducing the adverse selection and high administrative costs problems of the individual market. It also encourages more people to buy health insurance and the purchasers to buy more of it, such as more comprehensive health plans. In short, this subsidy exacerbates the moral hazard problems stemming from insurance. The location of these purchasing pools at the workplace also has the potential to distort labor markets in several different ways, such as by tying workers to jobs excessively. Moreover, the particular design of the existing subsidy system tends to foster adverse distributional consequences, though this could be corrected without abandoning employment-based health insurance, for instance, by capping the subsidy or turning it into a refundable tax credit. Standard policy analysis of this tax subsidy weighs the protection benefits it affords of increased insurance versus the various distortionary costs it creates.

The trend in policy proposals from both the left and the right is to propose options that would shift people away from employer-based coverage. The most ambitious plans on the left propose to replace private employer-based insurance with publicly provided insurance, via Medicare for all. Other plans retain private insurance but abolish employer-based insurance in favor of geographically based purchasing pools.[46] More centrist plans, like the recently enacted Massachusetts plan, aim to maintain employer-provided coverage but introduce generous subsidies for those purchasing insurance through newly created purchasing pools. These pools will likely produce a modest shift away from employer-based coverage to the individual market. From the right, the most common plans attempt to "level the playing field" by providing equivalent subsidies to people purchasing insurance outside the workplace or by eliminating the employer-based subsidy altogether and providing tax credits to all who purchase insurance.

Other than the Medicare-for-all plans, each of these approaches would make individuals responsible for making additional, complex choices—both about which insurance plan to purchase and about the timing and quantity of health care consumption. Given that we believe it is unlikely that most individuals will make sensible decisions when confronted with these choices, this policy trend is troubling. Based on our analysis, we suggest four main lessons for health care reform:

—Consumers need to have their health insurance purchases mediated.

—Co-payments and subsidies should be designed using cost-effectiveness analysis.

—Efforts to cover the uninsured should reflect behavioral obstacles to coverage.

—Information gathering on the effects of behavioral interventions should be increased.

Mediating Health Insurance Purchases

Health insurance is too complicated a product for most consumers to purchase intelligently. The employer-based system works well in this regard because employers have strong incentives to act as faithful agents for their employees in selecting a very limited number of health insurance options. Effective option selection is a public good: once conducted for one, it is available for all. Moreover, employers can bargain in monopsonistic fashion with insurers; individuals cannot. This bargaining power not only reduces premiums, it also largely eliminates post-claim underwriting, a practice in the individual market whereby insurance companies attempt to retroactively deny health insurance to people who get sick based on technicalities in their original insurance application.

In theory, some entity other than employers could act as the mediator. For example, the Massachusetts Commonwealth Connector offers a menu of standardized plans to individual purchasers. While the Massachusetts experience bears watching, for several reasons we are dubious that public sector mediators will perform as well as employers currently do. First, public sector mediators will be under pressure to offer every qualified plan. Thus they will likely offer a much more extensive menu of options than most employers do. The failure to weed out the less desirable plans will lead many consumers to make poor purchases. The Massachusetts Commonwealth Choice plan brags that it offers "dozens of options." To choose among them is surely a challenge for most individuals. In contrast, the typical employer offers at most a handful of insurance options, and in many cases just a single plan. Second, public sector mediators will likely assemble plans for broader population groups and respond to consumer tastes only indirectly via the political system. Employers are likely better able to tailor plans to the needs of their workforce and to revise plans if their workers are unsatisfied with them. Third, employers, particularly large employers, may be more effective than the public sector in persuading providers to implement innovative cost-saving and quality-improving measures.

It is also possible to imagine that mediators could emerge from the private sector, quite apart from employers. If consumers value these sorts of service, they could hire health insurance "agents" to help them buy insurance packages. This possibility strikes us as a recipe for very high administrative costs, at best, and for disaster, at worst. There are many examples involving complex products for which competition fails to drive out high-cost or low-quality providers. Consumers persist in buying mutual funds with annual fees of 1.25 percentage points. Large price spreads, on the order of more than five to one, continue to exist for identical Medigap policies.[47] Many consumers fail to choose the appropriate Medicare Part D prescription plan.[48] Furthermore, evidence ranging from the U.S. subprime mortgage market to the U.K. pension mis-selling scandal shows the problems that can arise when consumers are left to rely on private sector mediators to help them buy complex products. The basic problem is that such mediators would typically represent the consumers for only one decision. Hence conflicts of interest on this purchase, such as steering customers to favored firms or shortchanging them on time, must be expected. An employer, by contrast, is engaged with employees on a continuing basis and also has a financial interest in their good health.

The current employer-based system appears to us to offer an unusual combination of aligned incentives, innovative capacity, and easy capitalization on the public goods aspects of insurance purchases. These advantages may well be enough to outweigh any labor market distortions that occur from commingling health insurance and employment. Indeed, the most serious of such distortions are being addressed through portability legislation.

Designing Co-payments and Subsidies

Many reform proposals appear to be guided by the goal of having consumers come as close as possible to facing the social price of producing care. The author of a prominent textbook concludes that the "optimal health insurance policy is one in which individuals bear a large share of medical costs within some affordable range, and are only fully insured when coverage becomes unaffordable."[49]

Our analysis suggests that this is the wrong benchmark. Most humans do not act as fully informed, rational individuals who understand probabilities, do exponential discounting, and choose in their own self-interest. This means that the traditional prescription for decentralized choices—simply charge people the marginal resource cost of providing health care and go with their decisions—will not in general result in the socially optimal outcome. Instead, insurance subsidies and co-payment rates should be set to maximize a cost-effectiveness measure of health outcomes relative to dollars spent. These subsidies and rates will need to reflect the true behavior patterns of consumers rather than the theoretical patterns of economic textbooks.

The second element of this lesson is that not all therapies, office visits, and interventions should be treated equally. The underlying goal should be to promote QALYs, and some treatments are much better at doing that than others. Subsidies should be targeted at highly cost-effective treatments. Some high-cost, low-value treatments should get no subsidy whatsoever; indeed, some should be taxed.

Understanding the Behavioral Obstacles to Coverage

The standard model of the uninsured envisions those individuals as crafty calculators who have figured out that insurance is costly to them because they are in a risk pool that charges more than their expected cost and because the benefits of insurance are truncated by the option of falling back on uncompensated care if they experience a medical emergency. This model inspires plans to assess financial penalties on those who remain uninsured as a way to change this calculus.

Our analysis of behavioral propensities suggests that underinsurance may be more a feature of inertia, complexity, and status quo bias than one of financial calculation. If we are right, efforts to expand insurance coverage should focus more on finding ways to automatically enroll people into a default health insurance plan than on punitive financial incentives. The default plan should allow an opt-out option, for example, so as not to punish those who are liquidity-constrained because they locked themselves into lumpy consumption commitments, such as home mortgages. In our conception, the threat of financial penalties for those who fail to purchase health insurance may be a useful tool not because it tilts their financial calculus but rather because loss-averse consumers hate penalties to an irrational degree. Thus the threat of penalties may be what enables them to overcome inertia and enroll in health insurance.

The Need for Additional Data

One implication of the inability of individuals to make good decisions on their own is that someone else must help make those decisions. This places an extraordinary information burden on the mediators who set up the default insurance plans and determine their subsidy and co-pay levels.

How should mediators, whether employers or the government or someone else, know what types and levels of subsidy produce what types of behavior? Fortunately, the field of behavioral decisionmaking explores a broad range of biases, such as prospect theory, hyperbolic discounting, and heuristic reasoning. The field draws on thousands of experiments and many dozens of field studies. It has now moved to actually monitoring people's brains with MRIs to assess how information is processed.

However, such understanding merely points us in profitable directions. It does not explain the relevant real-world elasticities or how people respond to monetary incentives when factors such as pain, avoided morbidity, inconvenience, and anxiety are added. Thus we need to make major new investments in statistical studies, including randomized experiments, focused on measuring how individuals respond to the wide range of tools we have for modifying their health insurance and health consumption choices. Given that we cannot rely on individuals to more than crudely approximate the maximization of their own health outcomes, these studies must focus on measuring health outcomes directly.

The ability to learn from experience is one unambiguous advantage of employer-based health insurance. Employers design offerings that differ, and in theory we can look at the data and see how individuals respond. Justice Louis Brandeis once remarked on a crucial advantage of the federal system: "A single courageous State may, if its citizens choose, serve as a laboratory" for innovative programs. When employers are the laboratories, this power of experiment is greatly magnified. We can learn about the potential for more tiers on a pharmaceutical subsidy program, how risk adjustment works in practice, or what differences emerge when employers hand out fixed versus proportional subsidies for the premiums of alternate insurers. The ability to learn from experience also provides a strong argument for standardizing information technology throughout the health insurance sector so as to enable better data collection.

Summary

The field of health insurance provides a compelling arena in which to employ behavioral economics as a policy guide. That discipline enables us to predict the biases that afflict individuals' poor decisions, to know what measures can counteract them, and thereby to produce better choices for insurance and care by individuals. QALYs are waiting to be reaped.

Notes

1. The Kaiser Family Foundation reports that, in 2007, 50 percent of workers were offered at least two types of plan and 17 percent were offered three or more types. In large firms (200 or more employees), 63 percent of workers were offered two or more types and 23 percent were offered three or more. Data are not available on how many plans of each type were offered. See Kaiser Family Foundation, *Employer Health Benefits: 2007 Annual Survey* (www.kff.org/insurance/7672).

2. Others have made similar arguments about supplementing the standard model of insurance with lessons from behavioral economics. See Joseph Newhouse, "Reconsidering the Moral Hazard: Risk Avoidance Tradeoff," *Journal of Health Economics* 25 (2006): 1005–14; Michael E. Chernow, Allison B. Rosen, and A. Mark Fendrick, "Value-Based Insurance Design," *Health Affairs* (2007): w195–w203.

3. There is a large medical literature on ways to help patients make "good" decisions about which medical treatments to undergo. For a survey, see Peter Ubel, "Beyond Knowledge: Figuring Out How to Help People Make 'Good' Decisions," University of Michigan, 2007. Our focus is not on helping people make good decisions per se but instead on how the financial incentives in health insurance plans and government policies should be designed given what is known about how people make health care decisions.

4. See Daniel Kahneman and Amos Tversky, "Prospect Theory: An Analysis of Decision under Risk," *Econometrica* 47 (1979): 263–91.

5. Marc Alpert and Howard Raiffa, "A Progress Report on the Training of Probability Assessors," in *Judgment under Uncertainty: Heuristics and Biases*, edited by Daniel Kahneman, Paul Slovic, and Amos Tversky (Cambridge University Press, 1982). This overconfidence result has been replicated hundreds of times.

6. See also Kunreuther's work showing that people do not buy insurance against floods even when they are in a flood zone. Howard Kunreuther and others, *Disaster Insurance Protection: Public Policy Lessons* (Hoboken, N.J.: Wiley Interscience, 1978).

7. A particularly bizarre type of overinsurance—the purchase of extended warranties for consumer durables—is discussed in David Cutler and Richard Zeckhauser, "Extending the Theory to Meet the Practice of Insurance," *Brookings-Wharton Papers on Financial Services* (2004): 1–53.

8. Christopher J. L. Murray, "Rethinking DALYs," in *The Global Burden of Disease: A Comprehensive Assessment,* edited by Christopher J. L. Murray and Alan D. Lopez (Harvard University Press, 1996).

9. Daniel Gilbert, *Stumbling on Happiness* (New York: Knopf, 2006).

10. Alpert and Raiffa, "A Progress Report."

11. Incidentally, if one does learn from peers, having more options for the group is likely a disadvantage, since there will not be much information on most alternatives. Concentrated choices yield more information.

12. A separate set of health decisions, mostly in the category of health behaviors, involves actions that have current benefits but generate health costs in the future. Health policy on how to reduce smoking, obesity, and sexually transmitted diseases fits in this category. Recently developed behavioral models apply to these circumstances. See Jonathan Gruber and Botond Koszegi, "Is Addiction 'Rational'? Theory and Evidence," *Quarterly Journal of Economics* 116, no. 4 (2001): 1261–303; B. Douglas Bernheim and Antonio Rangel, "Addiction and Cue-Triggered Decision Processes," *American Economic Review* (2004): 1558–90.

13. David Laibson, "Golden Eggs and Hyperbolic Discounting," *Quarterly Journal of Economics* 112, no. 2 (1997): 443–77.

14. Robert Kastenbaum, *The Psychology of Death*, 3rd ed. (New York: Springer, 2000).

15. Wojciech Kopczuk and Joel Slemrod, "Denial of Death and Economic Behavior," *Advances in Theoretical Economics* 5, no. 1 (2005): 1207.

16. John W. Pratt, David A. Wise, and Richard Zeckhauser, "Price Differences in Almost Competitive Markets," *Quarterly Journal of Economics* 93 (1979): 189–211.

17. Richard J. Herrnstein, "The Matching Law," in *Papers in Psychology and Economics*, edited by Howard Rachlin and David I. Laibson (Harvard University Press, 1997). Liebman and Zeckhauser also analyze domains in which individuals are likely to misperceive marginal prices. See Jeffrey Liebman and Richard Zeckhauser, "Schmeduling," Harvard University, 2005.

18. Xavier Gabaix and David Laibson, "Shrouded Attributes, Consumer Myopia, and Information Suppression in Competitive Markets," *Quarterly Journal of Economics* 121 (2006): 505–40.

19. The evidence suggests that the answer is, for the most part, yes. See Jonathan Gruber, "The Incidence of Mandated Maternity Benefits," *American Economic Review* 84, no. 3 (1994): 622–41.

20. William Samuelson and Richard Zeckhauser, "Status Quo Bias in Decision Making," *Journal of Risk and Uncertainty* 1 (March 1988): 7–59.

21. It is interesting that the Massachusetts health plan does not force people to elect a plan during a narrow enrollment window. Instead, people can enroll at any time, and the fine for noncompliance with the mandate is assessed continuously on a monthly basis rather than as an annual lump sum. We conjecture that a more discontinuous penalty schedule and shorter enrollment window might concentrate people's attention more and do more to overcome inertia and status quo bias.

22. For an accessible introduction to this literature, see Richard Thaler and Cass Sunstein, *Nudge* (Yale University Press, 2008).

23. Shlomo Benartzi and Richard Thaler, "Save More Tomorrow: Using Behavioral Economics to Increase Employee Saving," *Journal of Political Economy* 112, no. 1 (2004): S164–S187.

24. Richard H. Thaler and Cass R. Sunstein, "Libertarian Paternalism," *American Economic Review* 93, no. 175 (2003): 6.

25. We acknowledge that many of the same behavioral biases discussed here in the context of health insurance also arise in the contexts used to estimate QALY preferences, raising challenging questions about how one interprets existing estimates of willingness to pay for QALYs.

26. B. D. Bernheim and A. Rangel, "Behavioral Public Economics: Welfare and Policy Analysis with Non-Standard Decision Makers," Working Paper 11518 (Cambridge, Mass.: National Bureau of Economic Research, 2005).

27. See Chernow, Rosen, and Fendrick, "Value-Based Insurance Design."

28. Subsidies for health care at point of delivery—such as low co-pays relative to marginal cost—simply represent the essence of insurance, since those who are sick are likely to lose income and have other financial costs.

29. We have drawn the *DD* curve to intersect the *x*-axis at a different point than the *RR* curve. This implicitly assumes that the individual is not even good at determining when care would be good for him if the monetary cost is zero. That is not unreasonable, since there are the inconvenience and anxiety costs of going to the doctor.

30. See Amitabh Chandra, Jonathan Gruber, and Robin McKnight, "Patient Cost-Sharing, Hospitalization Offsets, and the Design of Optimal Health Insurance for the Elderly," Working Paper 12972 (Cambridge, Mass.: National Bureau of Economic Research, 2007). To the extent that adherence to cost-reducing therapies is lowered by cost sharing, the standard argument that consumers should be made more price sensitive in their health care consumption decisions is further weakened.

31. Note that if the size of the underconsumption from behavioral factors exceeds the overconsumption from insurance but not the further overconsumption caused by the tax subsidy, it could be optimal to eliminate the tax subsidy but permit the misperception of the employer cost to persist.

32. A particular challenge for firms is risk adjustment. Ideally, differences in prices across health insurance plans would not account for the differences in risk levels of employees enrolling in different plan options. Though this concept is well understood in theory, it is rarely implemented. It seems to be just too hard for employers to get the prices right.

33. Lest we be misunderstood, we are not concluding that insuring for small costs is desirable in health insurance. We are just pointing out that there are arguments in its favor. Structuring desirable subsidies should be a heavily empirical exercise.

34. In contrast, some large employers (including ours) charge different premiums for the same health insurance based on salary.

35. The Massachusetts Commonwealth Care plan is an example of a plan that gets this right. Co-payments for primary care office visits are free for families with income below the poverty line, $5 for families between one and two times the poverty line, and $10 for families between two and three times the poverty line.

36. Chernow, Rosen, and Fendrick, "Value-Based Insurance Design."

37. Michael E. Chernow and others, "Impact of Decreasing Co-payments on Medication Adherence within a Disease Management Environment," *Health Affairs* (Jan./Feb. 2008): 103–12.

38. Amitabh Chandra, Jonathan Gruber, and Robin McKnight, "Patient Cost-Sharing, Hospitalization Offsets, and the Design of Optimal Health Insurance for the Elderly," Working Paper 12972 (Cambridge, Mass.: National Bureau of Economic Research, 2007).

39. John W. Rowe and others, "The Effect of Consumer-Directed Health Plans on the Use of Preventive and Chronic Illness Services," *Health Affairs* (Jan./Feb. 2008): 113–20.

40. Daniel Kahneman and Amos Tversky, "On the Psychology of Prediction," *Psychological Review* 80 (1973): 237–51.

41. Ali H. Mokdad and others, "Actual Causes of Death in the United States," *Journal of the American Medical Association* 291 (2004): 1238–45. Also see Joshua T. Cohen, Peter J. Neumann, and Milton C. Weinstein, "Does Preventive Care Save Money? Health Economics and the Presidential Candidates," *New England Journal of Medicine* 7 (February 14, 2008): 661–63.

42. Cohen, Neumann, and Weinstein, "Does Preventive Care Save Money?"

43. Ibid.

44. Ibid.

45. Benjamin D. Sommers and others, "A Decision Analysis Using Individual Patient Preferences to Determine Optimal Treatment for Localized Prostate Cancer," *Cancer* 110, no. 10 (2007): 2210–17.

46. Peter Diamond, "Organizing the Health Insurance Market," *Econometrica* 60 (1992): 1233–54.

47. See http://findarticles.com/p/articles/mi_m0EIN/is_2004_August_16/ai_n6162126.

48. Jeffrey R. Kling and others, "Misperception in Choosing Medicare Drug Plans," Brookings Institution, 2008.

49. Jonathan Gruber, *Public Finance and Public Policy* (New York: Worth, 2005), p. 409.

COMMENT BY EDWARD J. McCAFFERY

I t is almost an embarrassment for me to comment on work by Richard Zeck-hauser and Jeffrey Liebman. The field of behavioral economics and public policy, in which I have been dabbling for a few years, may be seen as a mere footnote to Zeckhauser.[1] Liebman has been a major contributor to an impressive array of public policy domains, including such important matters as the earned income tax credit, Social Security, and housing policy. Together and apart, Zeckhauser and Liebman have set the standard to which other scholars should aspire. Their chapter in this volume characteristically contributes timely insights into the current debate over health insurance and the tax system.

If writing this commentary is an embarrassment, it is also one of riches. First, I get to point out some of the joys of Zeckhauser and Liebman's important chapter. Second, because their writing scarcely needs any critical help, I am free to offer some of my own thoughts on what behavioral economics and psychology can add to the question at the core of this volume: the nexus—if any there should be—between taxes and health insurance policy in the twenty-first century.

* * * * *

In their characteristically interesting paper, "Schmeduling," Liebman and Zeckhauser show, among other things, that it is hard to figure out how much it costs to run a dishwasher.[2] In their chapter in this volume, Liebman and Zeckhauser show that it is really, *really* hard to figure out how to buy health insurance.

This conclusion should not surprise any of us. Life today is complex in many dimensions. Ordinary people have little time or inclination to make optimal choices in a wide range of contexts. Impersonal mechanisms such as markets play a crucial role in ameliorating the attendant problems. Such institutions as markets help our limited cognitive facilities to gather and process information. They are necessary for consumers' ideal, or even adequate, functioning in modern times. But no market mechanism tells consumers how frequently they should run their dishwasher or which among a dizzying menu of health insurance policies they should choose. So problems persist. As always in public policy context, the operative question is, what can be done?

In the case of choosing health insurance, numerous factors work to impede optimal (or even acceptable?) decisionmaking. These elements include limited cognitive capacities or so-called bounded rationality, which means in part that added choices can reduce the capacity for rational choice and lower welfare.[3] Liebman and Zeckhauser cite other factors as well that hinder rational choice. And we should not forget our own common sense and experience. One need only recall recent experiences with the Medicare prescription drug plans, or the subprime mortgage crisis, or—fill in your choice of human error leading to public policy crisis. It is abundantly clear that when confronted with many complex options people often make poor choices, judged by their own later lights.

Yet policymakers persist in promulgating complex plans that force people to make decisions. Skepticism about such an approach can easily lead to an attack on the whole idea of this volume: addressing health care needs through the income tax system. The tax system is perhaps the only aspect of public policy more difficult to understand than health insurance. Running a dishwasher is bad enough; deciding on how these two problems—tax laws and health insurance—should be jointly solved is infinitely harder. Indeed, most of the chapters in this volume can be read as casting doubt on the linkage of tax and health care. Does anyone think that flexible spending accounts (FSAs) will make the task of choosing health insurance *easier*?

Liebman and Zeckhauser do an excellent job at describing the decisions faced by people looking to provide for their own or their household's health care. The authors helpfully break matters into two stages: choosing insurance and deciding on care. (As a small point, rules regarding preexisting condition require people to make insurance decisions spanning more than one year. Given that deciding on insurance even for one year—the period Liebman and Zeckhauser treat—is sufficient to overwhelm our cognitive capacities, the longer horizon certainly does.) The authors note the various aspects of these decisions that challenge cognitive capacities: uncertainty and risk, the long time horizon, and the inherent complexity of tasks and calculations chief among them.

A Few Questions and Possible Answers

Given the difficulty of these problems, I pose two questions: What does behavioral economics add to what I take to be the overdetermined case against simply dumping excessively complex choices in every citizen's lap? And can behavioral economics help frame the questions so that people can answer them?

As Liebman and Zeckhauser describe behavioral economics, it is largely a catalog of heuristics and biases, including
—Status quo bias, loss aversion, and endowment effects;
—Myopic and time-inconsistent preferences;
—Self-serving biases;
—Subadditivity and other probabilistic errors; and
—Bad-outcome myopia (the idea that people are especially ostrich-like when it comes to decisions involving potential bad outcomes, like death or disease).

The problem is that this or similar lists can often seem like just that: lists in search of a theme. As Colin Camerer observes, with reference to a then leading candidate for a general field theory of behavioral economics, "Prospect theory is a skeleton of empirical observations around which a theory is draped."[4] There is an ad hoc feel to the enterprise, a nagging suspicion that one bias can be set off against another in an endless loop of indeterminacy. Real problems require real solutions, however, and real politicians will sooner or later venture forth and offer some, whether they are informed by the wisdom of behavioral economics or not.

I believe that there are two ways out of the illusion of ad hockery. One way is to choose a bias and present an axiomatic model, as has been done on particular topics such as cigarette smoking and savings behavior.[5] Another way is to group and summarize the biases into coherent policy recommendations. Otherwise, the catalog approach itself generates cognitive confusion and a sense that the biases are ad hoc and, perhaps, cancel each other out.

One could begin fashioning some specific policy-centered advice by drawing a distinction between, on the one hand, individual heuristics and biases—or suboptimal decisionmaking procedures and protocols—and, on the other hand, the institutional settings in which choices are made.[6] In the case of publicly provided, subsidized, or mandated health insurance, in which individual choice is all but certain to retain a considerable role, attention to the individual makes the case for simplifying strong. Behavioral economics teaches that individuals usually make complex decisions in isolation, that they focus on salient clues without integrating the whole, and that they are easily misled. These general tendencies have been grouped together by various scholars under the generally helpful labels of choice bracketing, isolation effects, and focusing effects.[7] There are subtle differences among these ideas and even among different descriptions of the same term, but they all lead to the conclusion that people will make poor decisions, even by their own standards, and typically in predictable ways, because they will pay too much attention to the most salient and immediate decision to be made. This is a certain enough fact by now that it should be used in recommending policy.

It is vis à vis the other shoe, the institutional "arbitrage" mechanisms that help ameliorate cognitive error in private markets but can be missing altogether in public settings, that Liebman and Zeckhauser's chapter is most powerful. The authors begin by pointing out that "competition will not, in general, prevent the exploitation of unaware consumers by optimizing firms."[8] It is not only the catalog of heuristics and biases but also the absence of any plausible way of counterbalancing them that complicates the analysis of effective public health care and insurance policies, a point to which I return. The combination of complex choices and the lack of ways to make them more manageable leads to a strong suggestion to standardize features of health insurance options—especially their financial features—in order to allow competition based on more relevant health-related factors such as location, facilities, and quality of care. We should give people limited menus, in which the differences among options entail the variables that matter. In this case, less—that is, fewer choices—can be more, the independence axiom be damned.

Perhaps the most important contribution of Liebman and Zeckhauser's important chapter is its focus on the structure of the choice process, and not on the substantive options (or pure quantity) of choice alone. That most people decide on health insurance at the workplace is a virtue of the current, tax-influence system, according to the authors. This virtue follows from the fact that employers have a strong incentive to give employees limited but generally beneficial choices, as is usually also the case with 401(k) plans (putting aside the perverse incentive to invest in own-company stock, a problem of Enron-era notoriety). The logic calls to mind the argument for strict liability being superior to a negligence standard in products liability. This choice rests on the empirical judgment that manufacturers are better than buyers at being cost avoiders and also as loss spreaders (insurers). Consequently, manufacturers should bear the risk of nonnegligent harm, and should insure against all risks. There is an analogous case here for someone else—a managed care group, employers, the government—bearing the residual risks. We can add, as Liebman and Zeckhauser suggest, that someone other than the insured is likely to be the best decisionmaker—or, better put, decision framer. There is nothing in behavioral economics per se that suggests that employers are better than bureaucrats on this score, although common sense and experience might suggest that they are, and there may be yet other third parties who could helpfully provide this service. But the insight that someone, somehow, should narrow the range of choices that individual insurance buyers should make is a characteristically brilliant Liebman-Zeckhauser point. Note finally that the argument in torts for strict liability overcomes the objection on paternalistic terms to compulsory insurance being bundled into the cost of a good: strict liability *is* mandatory universal insurance in the consumer products context. This observation suggests that paternalism worries are contextual, a matter of perceived social defaults.

One question for behavioral economists to consider is how systematic government commitment to subsidizing health care changes the problem. In other insurance markets such as those for automobiles and houses, those insured so oppose high deductibles that this contractual option does not even exist.[9] This pattern suggests that we see high-deductible health insurance because complete coverage is too expensive. We can assume that the high price that insurers would have to charge for low- or no-deductible individual policies reflects a cognitive compromise between what people want and what they can afford. One wonders how best to strike that compromise under a system of mandates or universal care.

In short, we can move beyond behavioral economics as a seemingly endless list of mistakes and start making specific recommendations for public policy. Liebman and Zeckhauser edge toward such recommendations, but disciplinary norms deter them from being explicit. I am less bashful and so make two strong recommendations about publicly provided or regulated health care. First, policymakers should shape the choices people will face under any new health care system because people cannot choose optimally from an overly lengthy and complicated menu. Second, policymakers should pay attention to the institutional setting in which such choices are made, and in particular to who sets the choices.

A Modest Proposal

I now take two paragraphs to add my own two cents about what a behaviorally informed, government-mandated health insurance system might look like. I begin with the observation that common sense and research both suggest that underconsumption is a more serious problem than overconsumption of preventive health care. Behavioral economics certainly supports this insight: inertia, myopia, self-serving optimism, and related traits and tendencies are common and keep people from seeking enough ounces of prevention. Indeed, I wonder about the extent to which *overconsumption* of preventive care is a systematic problem at all worth addressing. If it is, it would be a problem of a few, which recalls the basic but often forgotten point that people are not all the same—cognitively or economically. Nor are people the same behaviorally, and some of this difference almost certainly depends on wealth, I believe. Although the following generalization is admittedly an oversimplification, I would stipulate that the poor are more likely to engage in risky behaviors—smoking, gambling, and not saving—than the rich, and that the rich not only are less likely to take imprudent risks but also are in a better position to cope with the consequences of doing so. Government policy, with or (probably better) without the tax code, should therefore provide coverage of high-probability conditions that can be treated at modest cost through mandated or universal coverage, with no deductibles, no copayments, and, perhaps, even bonuses for certain treatments. This would be the first and most widely provided level of care. A second level of care would cover high-probability conditions that are costly to treat and also low-probability conditions that are inexpensive to treat, for which modest deductibles and copayments could be imposed, as needed, to hold down costs and influence patients' care decisions. A third level of coverage would then cover low-probability conditions that are costly to treat, and for these there would be high deductibles and copayments—a level of care for the relatively wealthy.

This proposal is crude and simple, but it reflects market and psychological realities. In that regard, at least, it compares favorably with such policy misadventures as the Medicare prescription drug plan and the subprime mortgage crisis, which ignored both (and all other?) realities.

Last Thoughts

My suggestion, then, to Liebman and Zeckhauser and their fellow behavioral economists is to be bolder and more systematic in recommending cognitively sensitive policies. Behavioral economics has much to offer the public sphere. It is time to start offering policy proposals that are clear and forceful, if open to revision as our knowledge expands. Such behaviorally informed proposals ought to be folded into the reform options under public discussion, such as universal coverage, single-payer plans, and mandates. We know enough now to urge strongly that options should be limited and standardized and that competition should be confined to a few but important (real, nonfinancial) features. Mandates (with the choice to opt out if need be) are likely better than universal access to opt in. Highly cost-effective treatments should be free at point of care or subsidized, especially for lower-income citizens. Sensible decision framers (employers) would mediate policy choices for workers—as employers seem generally better able to do so than government bureaucrats.

My suggestion to the rest of my readers is to read as much as you can of Liebman and Zeckhauser's work, wherever and whenever it appears, and to run the dishwasher.

Notes

1. E. J. McCaffery and J. Slemrod, "Toward an Agenda for Behavioral Public Finance," in *Behavioral Public Finance*, edited by E. J. McCaffery and J. Slemrod (New York: Russell Sage,

2006); E. J. McCaffery and J. Baron, "Thinking about Tax," *Psychology, Public Policy, and Law* 12 (2006): 106–35.

2. Richard Zeckhauser and Jeffrey Liebman, "Schmeduling," unpublished paper (Harvard University, 2004).

3. H. A. Simon, "A Behavioral Model of Rational Choice," *Quarterly Journal of Economics* 69 (1955): 99–118. This important conclusion contradicts a key axiom of the model of rational decisionmaking—the independence axiom, which holds that adding a new option to a menu of available choices must not decrease welfare.

4. Colin F. Camerer, comment on Roger G. Noll and James E. Krier, "Some Implications of Cognitive Psychology for Risk Regulation," *Journal of Legal Studies* 19 (1990): 791.

5. See, for example, B. Douglas Bernheim and Antonio Rangel, "Behavioral Public Economics: Welfare and Public Policy Analysis with Nonstandard Decisionmakers," Working Paper 11518 (Cambridge, Mass.: National Bureau of Economic Research, 2005); Jonathan Gruber and Botan Koszegi, "Is Addiction Rational? Theory and Evidence," *Quarterly Journal of Economics* 116 (2001): 1261–303.

6. See Nicholas Barberis and Richard Thaler, "A Survey of Behavioral Finance," in *Handbook of the Economics of Finance,* edited by G. Constantinides, M. Harris, and R. Stultz (North Holland: Elsevier Science, 2003).

7. For choice bracketing, see D. Read, G. Loewenstein, and M. Rabin, "Choice Bracketing," *Journal of Risk and Uncertainty* 19 (1999): 171–97; and M. Rabin and G. Weizsacker, "Narrow Bracketing and Dominated Choices," 2007, unpublished mansucript on file with author. For isolation effects, see McCaffery and Baron, "Thinking about Tax." For focusing effects, see L. C. Idson and others, "Overcoming Focusing Failures in Competitive Environments," *Journal of Behavioral Decision Making* 17 (2004): 159–72; and P. Legrenzi, G. Girotto, and P. N. Johnson-Laird, "Focusing in Reasoning and Decisionmaking," *Cognition* 49 (1993): 36–66.

8. The authors here cite Xavier Gabaix and David Laibson, "Shrouded Attributes, Consumer Myopia, and Information Suppression in Competitive Markets," *Quarterly Journal of Economics* 121 (2006): 505–40.

9. David Cutler and Richard Zeckhauser, "The Anatomy of Health Insurance," in *The Handbook of Health Economics,* edited by J. P. Newhouse and A. J. Cuyler (Amsterdam: Elsevier Science, 2000).

11

Taxes and Health Insurance

PETER ORSZAG

The single most important factor influencing the federal government's long-term fiscal balance is the rate of growth in health care costs. Without any changes in federal law, the Congressional Budget Office projects that total spending on health care will rise from 16 percent of the GDP in 2007 to 25 percent in 2025 and 49 percent in 2082 and that net federal spending on Medicare and Medicaid will rise from 4.5 percent of GDP to almost 20 percent of GDP over the same period.[1] Many of the other issues central to the debate on future fiscal conditions, from the actuarial deficit in Social Security to whether the 2001 and 2003 tax legislation is continued past its scheduled expiration in 2010, pale by comparison to growth in the cost of federal health insurance programs.

There is lingering debate on whether demographic changes or rising health care costs per beneficiary will be the key fiscal driver, but it seems fairly clear that the latter is relatively more important, especially the further out in time projections are extended. To be sure, among adults health care spending generally increases with age. As the number of elderly people increases over time, health spending naturally will grow. Yet the dominance of the growth of health care costs versus demographic change can be seen by comparing the trajectory of cost growth for Social Security to that for Medicare/Medicaid over time (figure 11-1). Given the nature of these programs, a demographic shift will have similar effects on costs for both Social Security and Medicare/Medicaid. In the next ten to twenty years, the growth of spending on these programs will differ but perhaps not all that dramatically, which points to demographics as having the larger share. As one extends the time frame beyond twenty years, however, Social Security spending will level out somewhat as a share of GDP, while Medicare and Medicaid will grow even more rapidly. Some observers interpret this dominance

Figure 11-1. *Federal Spending under CBO's Alternative Fiscal Scenario, Actual and Projected, by Decade 1962–2082*

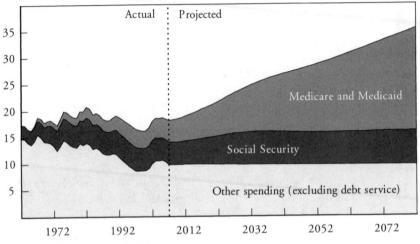

Source: Congressional Budget Office

of cost growth per beneficiary in influencing the fiscal future as an excuse for not addressing the higher costs associated with an aging population. That conclusion makes little sense to me: to say that problem A is bigger than problem B is not to say that problem B does not exist or should not be addressed.

Growth in the Cost of Health Care

Embedded in the nation's long-term fiscal challenge is a substantial opportunity for reducing health costs without adversely affecting health outcomes. Perhaps the most compelling evidence for this is that per capita health care spending varies widely across the United States (figure 11-2), and yet the very substantial variation in cost per beneficiary is not correlated with health outcomes. For example, a comparison of the Centers for Medicare and Medicaid Services' (CMS) composite quality scores versus average spending per beneficiary shows a lack of clustering around an upward slope, which suggests that higher costs do not produce better health outcomes (figure 11-3); if anything, it would appear that the clustering implies a slope in the wrong direction.[2]

Geographic variation in health care is often most dramatic when there is uncertainty about what kind of treatment to administer.[3] For example, best practice includes providing an aspirin to a patient admitted to the hospital for a

Figure 11-2. *Medicare Spending per Beneficiary, by Hospital Referral Region,* 2005ᵃ

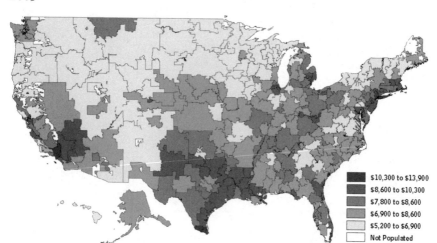

$10,300 to $13,900
$8,600 to $10,300
$7,800 to $8,600
$6,900 to $8,600
$5,200 to $6,900
Not Populated

Source: Congressional Budget Office, based on data from the Centers for Medicare and Medicaid Services.

a. The data are for Medicare spending per beneficiary in the fee-for-service program, adjusted for age, sex, and race. The geographic unit is the hospital referral region, as defined by the Dartmouth Atlas of Health Care. Areas labeled "Not populated" include places such as national parks, forests, lakes, and islands.

heart attack, and there is very little geographic variation in that practice. However, there is significant geographic variation in the use of imaging and diagnostic tests, and there is often ambiguity about which specific settings produce the best health outcomes when using these interventions. Norms among local physicians seem to drive regional custom with regard to the overuse of such interventions. Although some regions appear to commonly use low-cost though effective modalities, other regions appear to commonly use high-cost but ineffective (even harmful) modalities.

How much does this disparity cost? One estimate is that nearly 30 percent of health costs could be saved without negatively affecting health outcomes if high- and medium-cost regions reduced their spending to the levels of low-cost regions.[4] With health care spending currently representing 16 percent of GDP, this estimate suggests that nearly 5 percent of GDP goes to health care spending that cannot be shown to improve health outcomes. Of course, figuring out how to reduce spending only for inappropriate and unnecessary care is a nontrivial exercise. Nevertheless, there do not appear to be other examples in which credible academics can identify an efficiency gain of this magnitude for the economy.

Figure 11-3. *Quality of Care, by Medicare Spending in State, 2004*

Composite measure of quality of care, 100 = maximum

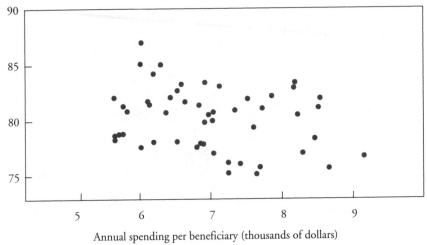

Annual spending per beneficiary (thousands of dollars)

Source: Congressional Budget Office, based on data from Department of Health and Human Services, Agency for Healthcare Research and Quality, *National Healthcare Quality Report, 2005* (December 2005); data tables appendix (www.ahrq.gov/qual/nhqr05/ index.html); and Centers for Medicare and Medicaid Services' *Continuous Medicare History Sample.*

That there is such a potentially large inefficiency in the health care system is striking. Also striking is the relatively small investment in research focused on the mechanics of restructuring health care delivery and payment so as to reduce this inefficiency.

One might note that the highest-cost regions are those served by the top medical centers, so it could be assumed that these centers drive the cost differentials. However, even among elite medical centers there is significant variation in cost. Even though the CMS composite quality scores for the UCLA Medical Center, Massachusetts General Hospital, and the Mayo Clinic (St. Mary's Hospital), for example, are similar (81.5, 85.9, and 90.4, respectively), the Mayo Clinic's cost per beneficiary for Medicare clients in the last six months of life ($26,330) is nearly half that at the UCLA Medical Center ($50,522) and significantly lower than that at Massachusetts General Hospital ($40,181). Uwe Reinhardt, the renowned professor of economics and political economy at Princeton University, asks, "How can the best medical treatment in the world cost twice as much as the best medical treatment in the world?" We do not have an easy formula for reducing these differences. Work is needed to develop the means to ensure that low-quality but expensive care is eliminated.

Tax Treatment of Health Insurance

One factor contributing to the perpetuation of these inefficiencies is a lack of clarity in the cost and incidence of health insurance, including employer-sponsored health insurance. Employer payments for employer-sponsored health insurance and nearly all employee payments for employer-sponsored insurance are excluded from individual income and payroll taxes. Although both theory and evidence suggest that workers ultimately finance their employer-provided insurance through lower take-home pay, that cost is not salient or transparent to many workers. And it is reasonable to suspect that workers demand less efficiency from the health system than they would if they knew what they pay for their health insurance via forgone wages for coverage or if they knew the actual cost of the services being provided. An interesting question then is whether greater transparency, which could be achieved either by the provision of more information or by changes in the tax treatment of health insurance premiums, would lead to greater efficiency. (Changes in the tax treatment could also affect efficiency by directly changing the after-tax price for health insurance.)

The Congressional Budget Office has developed a microsimulation model based on the Survey of Income and Program Participation (SIPP) to project how various changes in incentives related to health insurance—such as tax treatment, changes in public insurance coverage, subsidies, and employer and individual mandates—impact coverage and other dimensions of the health system.[5] One example of recent tax proposals related to the treatment of health insurance is the Bush administration's 2007 tax proposal. This proposal would repeal the current tax exclusion for employer-sponsored insurance and treat those benefits as income for income tax and payroll tax purposes. In addition, the proposal would eliminate most health-related income tax preferences and create a new standard deduction for health insurance, valued at $7,500 per individual and $15,000 per family.[6]

The model's results regarding this proposal are intriguing. Key outcomes include migration from uninsured status and employer-sponsored coverage into nongroup coverage, a net increase in coverage in early years that grows smaller in later years, and a projected decline in the actuarial value of employer-sponsored plans versus current law.

Projections of the administration's budget proposal in 2010 indicate a net decline of 7 million in the number of uninsured. This decline is the result of two shifts: a reduction in the number of people covered by employer-sponsored insurance of 7 million and an increase in nongroup coverage of 14 million. In 2016 the net positive effect would be smaller, because the deduction is indexed to inflation, whereas the average cost of insurance premiums increases at a faster

Figure 11-4. *Proposed Family Standard Deduction for Health Care as Measured against Three Levels of Employer-Sponsored Family Insurance Premiums, 2009–18*

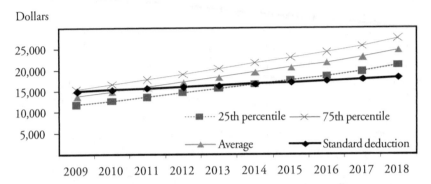

Source: Congressional Budget Office.

rate than inflation. The net reduction in uninsured would therefore diminish over time.

Under the administration's plan the proposed standard deduction for families would initially be larger than average employer-sponsored insurance premiums for family coverage, but after several years the deduction would fall below average projected premium prices (figure 11-4). In addition to affecting the net change in the number of uninsured, this differential trend over time would affect the revenue estimates generated by the Joint Committee on Taxation.[7] As the deduction became smaller than the current law's tax exclusion, the government would gain revenue.

The results of the proposal will vary significantly by type of individual, and some workers will fare better than others. For example, younger, higher-income workers in good health will have a lower premium in the nongroup market relative to the deduction compared to older, lower-income individuals in poor health. In effect, then, this proposal would shift younger, healthier, and higher-income but uninsured people toward the nongroup market. As one moves upward along the income spectrum, the share of people moving from uninsured status into nongroup coverage would increase (table 11-1). Similarly, there would be more movement from uninsured to nongroup coverage as one moved up the scale of self-reported health status (table 11-2). Both observations suggest that the healthier and the wealthier among the uninsured would initially see the most benefit. Much of the movement would be among those in the second and third income quintiles.

Table 11-1. *Projected Changes in Health Insurance Coverage in 2010,*
by Income Quintile

	Total	Income quintile (5 is highest)				
		1	2	3	4	5
Uninsured under current law[a] (millions of people)	50.9	13.4	16.0	12.4	6.7	2.4
Uninsured to nongroup (millions of people)	7.0	0.6	2.4	2.2	1.3	0.4
Uninsured moving to nongroup coverage (%)	14	5	15	18	20	17

a. Figure has since been revised downward to reflect underreporting of Medicaid in survey data.

Table 11-2. *Projected Changes in Health Insurance Coverage in 2010,*
by Health Status

	Total	Self-reported health status				
		Poor	Fair	Good	Very good	Excellent
Uninsured under current law (millions of people)	50.9	1.3	3.7	13.3	16.2	16.4
Uninsured to nongroup (millions of people)	7.0	0.02	0.3	1.5	2.5	2.7
Uninsured moving to nongroup coverage (%)	14	2	7	11	16	16

Contrary to speculation that moving from a tax exclusion for the value of insurance premiums to a standard deduction for health insurance would entirely dismantle the employer-sponsored insurance market, the Congressional Budget Office projects a reduction of about 7 million at first. This number would grow over time as the value of the deduction declined relative to premium costs. This shift away from employer-sponsored insurance and toward nongroup coverage is a point of contention with this proposal, but under these projections most workers would still receive coverage through the employer-provided market, because employers would still be more efficient in managing costs and pooling risks (and also because inertia is a significant driver of behavior). Small firms would be expected to drop insurance coverage more readily than large firms because small firms have less of an efficiency advantage over nongroup insurance.

A separate but significant outcome of the proposal is that it would reduce demand for the most generous plans. The Congressional Budget Office estimates that the proposal would bring a 12 percent reduction in the actuarial value of employer-sponsored insurance plans as well as a shift toward more tightly managed plans. In addition, as noted above, the proposal would make the underlying costs associated with employer-provided insurance more transparent. This effect may also lead to containing health care costs. As transparency increases and workers see how much their income is being reduced for employer contributions, and what those contributions are paying for, there may be a broader change in cost consciousness, which would shift demand. Note, though, the possibility that some measure of cost consciousness could be achieved without changing the tax treatment of health care—simply by providing more transparency about cost.

Notes

1. Congressional Budget Office, *The Long-Term Outlook for Health Spending* (November 2007).

2. The Medicare Payment Advisory Commission (2003) calculated an adjusted state-level measure of Medicare expenditures per beneficiary in the fee-for-service sector that controlled for input prices, beneficiaries' health status, and other factors. States were then ranked according to adjusted spending per beneficiary, and that placement was compared with states' rankings on a composite measure of quality of care. The composite measure was calculated on the basis of the percentage of patients in specific clinical situations who received appropriate treatment as defined by MedPAC.

3. The Congressional Budget Office finds that regional variation in health care costs has remained roughly stable over the last several decades and that variation in Medicare-specific health spending has decreased. Regional variation in Medicare is now about equal to the variation in health spending by the Department of Veterans Affairs, though it used to be greater. See Congressional Budget Office, *Geographic Variation in Health Care Spending* (February 2008).

4. John E. Wennberg and others, "Geography and the Debate over Medicare Reform," *Health Affairs* web exclusives (February 13, 2002): W96–W114.

5. For more background information on the model, see Congressional Budget Office, *CBO's Health Insurance Simulation Model: A Technical Description* (October 2007).

6. Note that a 2008 revision of this proposal includes some variations from the 2007 proposal discussed here.

7. Joint Committee on Taxation, *Description of Revenue Provisions Contained in the President's Fiscal Year 2008 Budget Proposal* (March 2007).

Contributors

Henry J. Aaron
Brookings Institution

Leonard E. Burman
Urban Institute

Lisa Clemans-Cope
Urban Institute

Stan Dorn
Urban Institute

Jason Furman
Brookings Institution (on leave)

Bowen Garrett
Urban Institute

Sherry Glied
Columbia University

Jonathan Gruber
Massachusetts Institute of Technology

Daniel Halperin
Harvard University Law School

Patrick Healy
Brookings Institution

Robert B. Helms
American Enterprise Institute

Mary B. H. Hevener
Baker & McKenzie

Janet Holtzblatt
Congressional Budget Office

William Jack
Georgetown University

Emmett Keeler
RAND Corporation

Charles K. "Chip" Kerby III
Liberté Group

Surachai Khitatrakun
Urban Institute

Arik Levinson
Georgetown University

Jeffrey Liebman
Harvard University

Anup Malani
University of Chicago

Edward J. McCaffery
University of Southern California

Peter Orszag
Congressional Budget Office

Douglas P. Stives
Monmouth University

Jessica Vistnes
Agency for Healthcare Research and Quality

Richard Zeckhauser
Harvard University

Index

Mandates, enforcing through income tax. *See* Individual mandates

Marginal tax rates (MTRs), 23, 24

Marketing fraud, 202

Massachusetts General Hospital, 266

Massachusetts mandatory health insurance, 10, 176–84, 221, 247–49

Maximum annual contribution to HSA, 84–85

Mayo Clinic, 266

McCaffery, Edward J., 256

McCain, John, 5–6

McCubbin, Janet, 181

Meals, entertainment, travel, gifts deduction limit, 160

Mediating health insurance purchases, 248–49

Medicaid: and altruism, 62; and cross-subsidies, 237; and data sharing, 179, 200–01; and effects of regressivity of EIS, 64; fee-for-service payment method, 20–21; growth of costs for, 263–64; and HCTC, 152; historical background of, 20–21; and managed care, 231; and marketing fraud, 202; projections on spending on, 263; spending increases since 2000, 26; take-up rate of, 217

Medical advances, 15–16

Medical Expenditure Panel Survey–Insurance Component (MEPS–IC), 122, 125–41, 144–45

Medical practice, geographical variations in, 28

Medical Savings Accounts (MSAs), 22–23, 68, 120, 123, 139

Medicare: administrative issues, 204; adverse selection in prescription drug plans, 83; and altruism, 62; and cross-subsidies, 237; fee-for-service payment method, 20–21; growth of costs for, 263–64; and HCTC, 152; historical background of, 20–21; and managed care, 231; and marketing fraud, 202; and out-of-pocket medical expenses, 146; as primary payer, 148; projections on spending on, 263;

spending increases since 2000, 26; and tax credits, 223; and variation in outcomes, 213

Medicare-for-all plans, 247, 248

Medicare Modernization Act, 67

Medicare Part B, 200–01

Medicare Part D prescription plans, 83, 249

Medicare Prescription Drug, Improvement, and Modernization Act (MMA), 67

Medicare Secondary Payer (MSP) rules, 148, 153

Medicare tax. *See* Payroll taxes

Medigap policies, 249

MEPS–IC. *See* Medical Expenditure Panel Survey–Insurance Component

Monopoly profits, 63

Moral hazard, 61–62; defined, 36; and ESI tax exclusion, 240; and government intervention in health insurance markets, 40–41; and managed care, 40; and risk exposure, 123; and tax subsidies, 37

Morrisey, Michael A., 25

MSAs. *See* Medical savings accounts

MSP (Medicare Secondary Payer) rules, 148, 153

MTRs (Marginal tax rates), 23, 24

Myopic preferences, 217, 258

National Directory of New Hires (NDNH), 200–01

National health care spending. *See* Total health care spending

National individual identifiers, 180

National Labor Relations Board, 20

National Opinion Research Center, 25

National War Labor Board, 16–18, 19–20

New employees and insurance choices, 238

Nondiscrimination rules: administrative issues, 150; compliance, auditing for, 163–65; and high-income workers, 57; history of, 157–58; purpose of, 38; reform proposals, 164; for self-insured medical plans, 57; vague and minimally enforced, 154–55. *See also* Low-income workers

IRS information reporting requirements, 164; mediating insurance purchases, 248–49; necessity for, 29–30; and nondiscrimination rules, 164; of presidential candidates, 1, 5–6; and tax credit to replace exclusion, 163, 218–23; and tax exclusions, 163; and tax penalties, 164–65
Refundable tax credits, 184
Regressivity of EIS deduction, 63–66
Reinhardt, Uwe, 266
Reinsurance, 222
Renewability, 42
Richardson, David, 78
Risk exposure and moral hazard, 123
Risk pooling, 6–7, 9, 40, 163, 237. *See also* Pooling, workplace
Risk qualifications and HSAs, 102
Robert Wood Johnson Employer Health Insurance Survey (EHIS), 121, 122
Roth IRAs, 108
Rowe, John, 79
Royalty, Anne, 49

Salary reduction rules, 38, 58
Sandmo, Agnar, 181
SCHIP (State Children's Health Insurance Program), 152, 179
Section 125 plans, 38, 120, 145
Self-employed persons: and deduction of health insurance premiums, 37; tax treatment of, 149
Self-insurance: administration of, 22, 38; and nondiscrimination rules, 57, 154–55; and tax treatment of health insurance, 29
Seligman, Jason, 78
Separate plans, rules on testing of, 154–55
Sheiner, Louise, 213, 214
Singapore, health care coverage in, 227–28
Small businesses: and Bush proposals, 269; and nondiscrimination rules, 57. *See also* large vs. small firms
Small costs, subsidizing, 11, 242–45
Social Security: growth of costs for, 263–64; and HDHPs, 108; and tax credits, 222–23

Social Security Act, 20
Social Security Administration (SSA), 200, 209
Social Security numbers, 180
Social Security tax: and exclusion of ESI, 45. *See also* Payroll taxes
Sorian, Richard, 216–17
Stabile, Mark, 49
Stano, Miron, 25
State Children's Health Insurance Program (SCHIP): administrative issues, 201, 204; and data sharing, 179; and HCTC, 152; take-up rate of, 217
Status quo bias, 237–39, 258
Stives, Douglas P., 115
Strict liability theory, 259–60
Subadditivity, 258
Subsidies. *See* Out-of-pocket health care costs; Tax subsidies
Sunstein, Cass, 228
Super-retirement savings accounts, 92
Supreme Court, U.S., rulings on union health benefits, 20
Survey of Income and Program Participation (SIPP), 267
Sutton, Willy, 199

TAA (Trade Adjustment Assistance), 202
TANF (Temporary Assistance to Needy Families), 179, 201
Tax credits: advance payment of, 189–93; in Bush proposal, 184, 189–93, 200; fiscal impact of, 222–23; impact on coverage, 219–22; impact on health care spending, 218–19; as incentives, 108; McCain proposal, 5–6; progressive, income-related, 220; refundable, 184; to replace exclusion, 163, 218–23; and Social Security, 222–23. *See also specific types*
Tax deductions: in Bush proposal, 5, 7, 184, 218–19, 228–29, 267–70; executive compensation, limits on, 159; impact of regressivity of, 63–66; meals, entertainment, travel, gifts, limits on, 160; medical expenses, 24; for self-employed persons, 37